The
LIBERAL ARTS
COLLEGE
and the
IDEAL of LIBERAL
EDUCATION

The Case for Radical Reform

Henry H. Crimmel

**UNIVERSITY
PRESS OF
AMERICA**

Lanham • New York • London

Copyright © 1993 by
University Press of America®, Inc.
4720 Boston Way
Lanham, Maryland 20706

3 Henrietta Street
London WC2E 8LU England

Library of Congress Cataloging-in-Publication Data
Crimmel, Henry H.
The liberal arts college and the ideal of liberal education : the case for
radical reform / Henry H. Crimmel.
p.   cm.
Includes index.
1. Education, Humanistic—United States.   2. Education,
Humanistic—United States—Case studies.   3. Education, Higher—
United States—Aims and objectives.   4. Educational change—United
States.   I. Title.
LC1011.C77   1993   370.11'2—dc20   93–11066 CIP

ISBN 0–8191–9173–6 (cloth : alk. paper)
ISBN 0–8191–9174–4 (pbk. : alk. paper)

The paper used in this publication meets the minimum requirements of
American National Standard for Information Sciences—Permanence
of Paper for Printed Library Materials, ANSI Z39.48–1984.

CONTENTS

PREFACE

I have written this book in the hope that it will contribute to the realization of an ideal. That we should seek to transform reality in the light of rationally defensible ideals is an assumption that cannot be proven, but, fortunately, does not need to be proven because it is already assumed in all action that is voluntary and purposive.

The reality that concerns me is the liberal arts college. Today there is overwhelming evidence that this institution has failed its institutional purpose. It continues to promise its students a liberal education, but it does not deliver on this promise.

The ideal that inspires me is one to which I was introduced many years ago by a few exemplary teachers. It is what I call the ideal of liberal education. It is what today might be called a grand narrative, but what should be called a transcendental principle.

Thus, my purpose in writing this book is to contribute to the reform of the liberal arts college in the light of the ideal of liberal education. The success of this project depends upon the truth of the criticism that I have brought against the college, and on the truth of the claims that I have made on behalf of the ideal of liberal education. Consequently, my book focuses on these two issues. It describes the liberal arts college's loss of institutional integrity, and it prescribes some of the radical reforms that are necessary if the college is to regain its integrity.

My argument is addressed to all those who share some concern for the future of the liberal arts college--teachers, scholars, administrators, trustees, donors, legislators, parents, and students. It is also addressed to a larger audience of those who may be less aware of the present crisis of the college, but who nonetheless have much to lose if this unique institution is lost. But in the end, my argument is of necessity directed to my own colleagues--the teachers of the liberal arts college. It is these *philosophiae doctores* who, organized as a *collegium*, are the proper guardians of the institution which is itself the guardian of our most fundamental values.

I want to thank the editors of *Liberal Education* and *Perspectives* for their permission to adapt portions of three of my previously published essays: "The

Myth of the Teacher-Scholar," *Liberal Education*, Volume 70, Number 3 (Fall 1984), 183-198; "Logic as a Liberal Art," *Liberal Education*, Volume 66, Number 4 (Winter, 1980), 377-381; and "The Aim of Liberal Education," *Perspectives*, Volume 2, Number 1 (May 1970), 9-19.

I am indebted to Lilly Endowment for a generous grant that supported my initial research.

I want to thank Jean Deese, René Murphy, Carolyn Filippi, Laurie Olmstead, and Hal Crimmel for their considerable help in the preparation of the manuscript.

This book owes much to a number of my colleagues, partly because they are responsible for some of the thoughts expressed here, but mostly because they have helped to create the conditions that make thought possible. This they have done by their collegiality and their criticality--that is, by their courage in resisting bureaucratic and doctrinal authority. For this I owe thanks to Guy Berard, Tom Berger, Denny Brandt, Gudrun Brokoph, Wendy Brown, Tom Budd, Doug Carmichael, Bruce Conn, Paul Connett, Bill Cropper, Tom Cunningham, Mark Erickson, Peter FitzRandolph, Clarke Gage, Dante Giarrusso, John Hall, Stuart Hills, Dick Holladay, Liam Hunt, John Jaunzems, J. J. Jockel, Cal Keene, Phil Larson, George McFarland, Karl McKnight, Dick Perry, Ali Pomponio, Jon Rossie, Bob Simpson, Chanchal Singh, and Jim Street.

This book owes most to Bernie Lammers. In his steadfast efforts to liberate and empower the college faculty so that it can recover the ideal of liberal education and reclaim the liberal arts college, he has shown that the ideal of liberal education is not beyond human aspiration.

PART ONE

THE LOSS OF

INSTITUTIONAL INTEGRITY

INTRODUCTION TO PART ONE

It is becoming all too evident that liberal education--which is what the small band of prestigious institutions are supposed to provide, in contrast to the big state schools, which are thought simply to prepare specialists to meet the practical demands of a complex society--has no content, that a certain kind of fraud is being perpetrated.

                        Allan Bloom, *The Closing of the American Mind*

Those of us who teach in a liberal arts college are by profession critics of ignorance and immorality. Our criticism is not always appreciated, but it is nonetheless understandable and commendable. After all, ignorance and immorality contravene the ideals traditionally celebrated by liberal education.

At the same time it is understandable, though hardly commendable, that, like most people, we tend to be more zealous in our criticism of others and of institutions with which we have little personal identification than we are of ourselves and of institutions with which we have a more personal identification. For instance, while we are likely to condemn what we see as the evident evils in Western culture, American society, and Washington, we often condone or even excuse what we see as the superficial imperfections of ourselves, our friends, and our own projects. At least since the time of Socrates self-criticism has rarely been widely esteemed. Yet this all too human aversion to self-criticism is the original sin that leads to deficient self-knowledge, and that allows personal and institutional failure to go unrecognized and unremedied.

Today this aversion to self-criticism is the principal obstacle to the recognition of a disturbing truth about an institution that has been of profound importance in the development of American culture. The truth is that the liberal arts college no longer delivers on its promise of a liberal education. For many years we have heard respected and impassioned voices warning us that the college is in a crisis.[1]   Today some no longer speak of the college as being in a crisis; instead they speak of it as "a disaster area"[2] and they diagnose its "moral collapse."[3]   In *The Closing of the American Mind* Allan Bloom charges that the liberal arts college's failure to deliver on its institutional promise is nothing less than "a certain kind of fraud."[4]

Of course, some will discount this criticism as mere academic carping. Others will dismiss it as perverse or absurd or traitorous. After all, they will say, liberal arts colleges continue to be popular and reputable; they are staffed by talented teachers and administrators; and they have attractive campuses and bright graduates and loyal alumni.

These responses may divert us unless we remember that the real measure of a college's success is not its popularity, talent, physical plant, or endowment, but the degree to which it fulfills its institutional promise.

To give specificity to this criticism I can cite the college in which I have taught for almost my entire professional life. St. Lawrence University's failure to deliver on its promise of a liberal education is a matter of deep personal disappointment.   That this college does in fact promise its students a liberal education cannot be doubted.   This promise is made unequivocally in the college's official statement of "Aims and Objectives." The college also promises its students that they will "enlarge [their] knowledge of [their] obligations and [their] capacity to perform," develop "the liberal arts," that is, the "means by which knowledge and judgment are acquired," achieve "breadth of learning" through an understanding of the "different ways of pursuing and organizing knowledge," and obtain "integration in learning." But the college does not deliver on these promises. Year after year it credentializes students who have no claim to have developed these capacities. Much less do they have any claim to have achieved a liberal education.

Sometimes the college seems to be at least subconsciously aware of its

---

[1]In 1906 President Schurman of Cornell charged that "the college is without clear-cut notions of what a liberal education is and how it is to be secured. And the pity of it," he added, "is that this is not a local or special disability, but a paralysis affecting every college of arts in America." Abraham Flexner, *The American College: A Criticism* (New York: The Century Co., 1908), 7. In 1931 S. E. Mezes warned in "The Passing of the Liberal College" that "forces at work for half a century and more have gradually, unconsciously, weaned the college away from . . . liberal training . . . , substituting a professional course and a professional spirit . . . . Many faculties know that there is something radically wrong with the present day 'college,' but are puzzled to know what to do about it." *School and Society* 33 (1931): 577-581.

[2]Carnegie Foundation for the Advancement of Teaching, *Missions of the College Curriculum* (San Francisco: Jossey-Bass, 1977), 11.

[3]Bruce Wilshire, *The Moral Collapse of the University* (Albany, N.Y.: State University of New York, Albany, 1990). Also see "The Decline and Devaluation of the Undergraduate Degree" in *Integrity in the College Curriculum: A Report to the Academic Community* (Washington, D. C.: Association of American Colleges, 1985), 1-7.

[4]Alan Bloom, *The Closing of the Amercian Mind* (New York: Simon and Schuster, 1987), 341.

institutional failure. With every change of administration it undertakes a review of its institutional purpose and its curriculum. Alterations are always produced, but, unfortunately, these are rarely substantive. Attempts to define the institutional purpose never seem to get beyond advertising fluff, and attempts to improve the curriculum are typically limited to the juggling of the calendar, the reshuffling of the distribution requirements, and the addition of innovative, trendy, media-oriented "programs." What is adopted one year with praise under one administration is abandoned a few years later with scorn under another.

But most of the time the college seems oblivious of its institutional failure. Incredibly, it does not possess a definition of the ideal of liberal education. No less incredibly, it does not make a serious effort to go beyond anecdotal evidence to monitor its educational outcomes. It is, therefore, without a genuine knowledge of its institutional purpose or the impact of its educational program. Its teachers go complacently about their assigned tasks, merchandising and teaching their various course offerings, advancing their professional careers through scholarly productivity, and dutifully performing their "university service." Both the academic community and the larger community seem to be unaware of the fact that in all of this busyness there is something outrageously wrong. They seem to be unaware that the college does not deliver on its promise.

Unfortunately, the perpetration of this fraud is not limited to a single college. The failure of my own college is only one example of the general failure of the liberal arts college in our time.

Certainly many of us who teach in a liberal arts college are anguished by our continuing complicity in this fraud. Today, with the very survival of the college in doubt, our obligations are evident and urgent. First, we need to confront the truth. In spite of our aversion to self-criticism, it is imperative that we understand that we have in fact failed to deliver on our institutional promise, and that our failure is indeed "a certain kind of fraud." Secondly, before it is too late, we need to reclaim the college. If we are ashamed and angered by the ignorance and immorality of others, as we should be, then we should be even more ashamed and angered by our own failure to protect the institution for which we as college teachers properly bear the ultimate responsibility. We can hope that our shame and anger will provide us with the resolve necessary to recover the ideal of liberal education and to reclaim the institution essential to its realization. If this hope should prove to be futile, then the liberal arts college will continue to fail. And as it continues to fail, more and more of our students will live lives impoverished by being denied the benefits of that form of education for which this college historically has been the primary instrument--a form of education that is in fact the institutional guardian of our most fundamental values.

This book is organized by these two obligations. Part One is a story of some of the ways that a typical liberal arts college has failed to deliver on its promise of a liberal education, and by so doing, has lost its institutional integrity. Part Two specifies the principles that must be adopted if this college--or any liberal arts college--is to provide a liberal education, and is to recover its institutional integrity. Part One is thus a critical description of a specific reality that needs to be radically reformed, and Part Two is a prescription of the principles that should guide any such reform.

1

THE RUBE GOLDBERG MACHINE

At the center of a shopping mall in Watertown, New York, there is a spectacular Rube Goldberg machine. Like all such machines, this machine exhibits ingenious means which are not informed by any commensurably intelligible end. We are diminished by its complex technology, but we are amplified by its utter inanity.

The time is much too late for polite, entertaining, tranquilizing similes. After a generation of worrying about whether people feel comfortable, we need to worry about some things that are certain to make many people feel uncomfortable. We need to know the truth. In particular we need to know the truth about an educational institution called St. Lawrence University. As teachers, students, parents, or members of a wider community this institution affects our lives in profound ways. The discomforting truth is that this college displays ingenious means, but these means are not informed by any consistent, coherent, rationally-defensible educational end. It displays constant activity, sanctified by tradition and ceremony; it commands extensive power and enjoys even more respect; and it consumes vast quantities of human energy. But to those of us who know it well, its real purpose is obscure. We officially identify the college as a liberal arts college--as an institution of liberal education--but in our candid moments we know that there is no shared and articulate understanding of the ideal of liberal education. And without this understanding of institutional purpose, all of the achievements of the college are problematic.

The evidence of the college's confusion about its institutional purpose is substantial and pervasive. This evidence can be found in the college's statements of its institutional purposes and in its institutional practices:

1.

St. Lawrence's statement of "Aims and Objectives" promises its students a liberal education. Moreover, it promises them specific outcomes, such as moral development, the skills of the liberal arts, "breadth of learning," and "integration in learning."   But these outcomes are seldom assessed or measured. Consequently, the college's impact on its students is judged only in impressionistic and apocryphal ways.   No one truly knows what kind of an education the students actually receive.

It has been said that the outcomes of a liberal education cannot be assessed because they are "too difficult to measure." This excuse is not only demonstrably false, but it is disingenuous. If outcomes cannot in some way be measured, then surely they should not in any way be promised.

Moreover, the college's official statement of its "Aims and Objectives" provides a description of the ideal of liberal education that is ambiguous, inconsistent, and operationally useless. This charge is confirmed by the following facts:

1. The statement gives the impression that the college's identification as an institution of liberal education carries with it a specific institutional obligation (as when it states that the college "is dedicated to providing a liberal education for its students"), but it also gives the impression that the college is without any specific institutional obligation (as when it states that the college is "free to pursue its own destiny in the light of its own vision").

2. The statement speaks of "liberal education" as if it requires the development of a specific capacity (as when it states that the "primary commitment" of the college is to "the intellectual development of the student"), but it also speaks as if no specific capacity needs to be developed (as when it states that the college is "dedicated to the individual" and to the "development of his or her own potentialities").

3. The statement gives the impression that the highest priority of "liberal education" is the discovery of truth (as when it states that the "enduring task" of the college is "to provide the opportunity for students and teachers to join together in the search for truth"), but it also gives the impression that the highest priority is the development in students of the methods required for the search for truth (when it states without qualification that it is "concerned with skills which serve intellectual ends").

4. The statement speaks of "liberal education" as if it has practical value (as when it states that it is "relevant to the world in which students must live"), but it also speaks as if it does not have practical value (as when it states that it "attempts to maintain a certain detachment from that world").

5. The statement gives the impression that "liberal education" is vocational (as when it states that it "provides for a large number of options in the choice of a career"), but it also gives the impression that it is not vocational (as when it states that the development of "abilities in the pursuit of specific occupations" are "the consequences, not the purposes, of a liberal education").

In addition, the college's statement of its institutional purpose in its publications and promotional literature is packed with the grossest and the most embarrassing kind of advertising fluff and empty sloganeering. The public is typically told that the college is dedicated to "the pursuit of excellence," to "quality education," to "the individual," to "flexibility," to "a well-balanced education," to "the heart of the American ideal," etc. It is inexplicable how this kind of double-talk can be condoned by faculties that otherwise are exacting in their criticism of sloppy research, political propaganda, governmental misinformation, media hype, and Madison Avenue commercialism.

2.

Evidence of St. Lawrence's disorientation with respect to its institutional purpose is also evidenced by the incoherence of its institutional practices. The college currently expends its energies in a multitude of different, academically unrelated ways. In various programs the college teaches (or recently has taught) chemists, premed students, army officers, secondary school teachers, physicists, coaches, 3-2 engineers, geologists, social workers, psychologists, elderhostelers, geographers, historians, school administrators, cheerleaders, and sports campers-- among others. The college runs (directly or indirectly, currently or recently) classrooms, restaurants, summer resorts, stables, a gift shop, a golf course, libraries, a bookstore, theaters, foreign tours, a radio station, a motel, a ski slope, fraternity houses, and spectator sporting events. It provides services for students, teachers, parents, employees, trustees, alumni, the village, the local schools, the North Country, the Mohawk reservation, the Army, the state, and the federal government. As a result, the college is less an institution for a unique kind of education than a private social services conglomerate, less a university unified by a common educational mission than a kind of academic shopping mall that provides hundreds of different goods and services to satisfy hundreds of different and constantly changing academic consumer interests.

When Robert Hutchins once defined a university as "a collection of academic departments held together by a central heating system," or when Clark Kerr defined it as "a series of individual faculty entrepreneurs held together by a common grievance over parking," they could have been thinking of St. Lawrence. With the exception of the heating system and common grievances--and perhaps the business affairs office--it would be difficult to find anything beyond the nebulous and malapropos category of "higher education" that gives unity to the bewildering mélange of activities that consume the time, energy, and resources of the college. Today what is called a university is only a sad parody of the etymological meaning of the word, "university." In no way is it an institution that seeks the universal, that converts plurality into unity.

Nowhere is the college's confusion about its educational purpose more apparent than in the comic tragedy of its periodic attempts at curriculum reform. The following may be hyperbole, but it captures the folly and frustration of these familiar rituals:

Like wars, curriculum reviews recur. Once the administrative trumpets sound, the hearts of deans-in-waiting beat faster, young professors croak, old professors posture or scurry for shelter, departmental empire builders twitch with excitement, and hobby horses are armored and mounted. There follows a paroxysm of words. Vast impactions of libidinous energy are dissipated in the conceptual joustings of ponderous egos in endless controversies in aimless committee meetings. Eventually there is exhaustion, and by the terms of the ensuing armistice, the calendar may be juggled, "distribution requirements" may be reshuffled, and some "innovative" public relations-oriented programs may be created. But substantive curricular reform is never a consequence. Soon the seasonal procession of students and the pulse of careerist ambition return the college to its familiar, ante-bellum ways. In these bizarre rituals so many learned people, heads smoking, mouths moving in pantomime, talk so much and accomplish so little.[1]

In these periodic attempts at curriculum review good intentions and ambition are hardly lacking. But what is always lacking is a shared conception of the ideal of liberal education. And without any consensus about this ideal, it is little wonder that the recurrent curriculum wars are almost always tragedies of waste and futility.

Whenever the college attempts to improve its educational program, the agents in this project invariably argue at cross-purposes. Perhaps once in a generation there will be a genuine effort to develop dialogue on institutional purposes. Such was the case for a period during the nineteen eighties when a number of faculty members known as the "Faculty Liberal Arts Group" ("FLAG") met weekly at the home of Professor Bernie Lammers to talk about the problems of liberal education. But for the most part faculty members ignore questions of institutional purpose and argue instead on the basis of departmental, program, or individual "needs." During the college's most recent curriculum review the attempt to clarify institutional purposes prior to a discussion of the curriculum proposals was blocked by faculty parliamentary maneuvers which were rationalized on the ground that any discussion of purpose would only lead to controversy and thus delay "needed" reform. (What was never explained was how it would be possible to determine what reforms are "needed" when there is no understood institutional purpose.) Today the college seems to have lost all appreciation of the truth that disputes about institutional means require an institutional end. Too many faculty members seem to have willingly and unwarily accepted the idea that academic disputes are properly resolved by what amounts to a "democratic" dictatorship by a parliamentary majority. The unfortunate effects of this assumption can be seen in the familiar Babel and incivility of most faculty meetings. These meetings are seldom occasions for academic dialogue. They are more likely to be stages for clever parliamentary machinations and sophistical arguments, for soliloquizing

---

[1]Henry H. Crimmel, "Our Recurrent Curricular Wars," *The Laurentian Faculty Bulletin* 35 (February 1985).

speeches and incessant demands for the closure of debate, for departmental and program turf battles and hardball coalition politics. With no shared understanding of the ideal of liberal education, and with little familiarity with its history or *loci classici*, the faculty's most widely held commitments seem to be to the advancement of personal careers, to departmental or academic program empire building, to a set of unexamined beliefs in the latest, fashionable social and political ideals (e.g., the need to demolish the alleged "cultural chauvinism" of students), and in the legitimacy of an educational program whose purpose by default seems to be the propagation of specialized information and gratuitous moralizing to those educational consumers who just happen to be "interested."

In the academic world, where clarity of purpose, consistency, and rational justification are especially prized, it is shocking that St. Lawrence's uncertainty of purpose should be tolerated. In the business world, uncertainty of purpose has a short life span. If General Motors, for instance, built a production line without having a precise understanding of the product to be produced, it would be laughed into bankruptcy. And if it tried to sell a product that was less than what it promised, it would be charged with fraud and vilified in every academy for greed and social irresponsibility.

But this is exactly the situation of the college today. Since this institution lacks a shared, articulate institutional purpose, it has an educational program that has not been forged out of fidelity to this purpose. Its program has simply evolved over the years largely in response to the constantly changing interests of educational consumers and to the vicissitudes of personal ambition, academic politics, and pedagogical fashion. At the same time, in the college's official publications promises are made to students which the college makes no genuine effort to deliver. The obvious glossy and saccharine vagueness of these promises betrays the suspicion that they are conceptually empty marketing mannequins.

* * * *

St. Lawrence University claims to be a liberal arts college, and to provide a liberal education for its students. At the same time, however, the college is uncertain of its institutional purpose. This is evidenced by the fact that it lacks an articulate and critically tested definition of the ideal of liberal education, and by the fact that its diverse activities are without coherence and consistency. The college displays ingenious means, but these means are not informed by any commensurably intelligible end. The college is in fact a Rube Goldberg machine.

2

THE DESECRATED TEMPLE

And he went into the temple, and began to cast out them that sold therein, and them that bought; Saying unto them, It is written, My house is the house of prayer: but ye have made it a den of thieves.

Luke 19:45-46

The college's uncertainty about its institutional purpose has momentous consequences for its relationship to society, for its educational program, and for its teachers. In this and the following two chapters we will examine these consequences.

If we were to judge St. Lawrence today solely on the basis of its proclaimed purposes or ideals, we would have good reason to regard it as a sacred institution in our secular age. The ideals of liberal education are often held to be the highest ideals of human life. But if we were to judge the college on the basis of what actually takes place today on its campus, we would have to admit that the college has patently failed. The college is no longer a place where the highest ideals of human life are the center of concern. Having forgotten its institutional purpose, the college is now without a principle of relevance. And without a principle of relevance, it is unable to distinguish between activities that are essential, peripheral, irrelevant, or even subversive to liberal education. The result is the college as we now know it--an institution that is without enduring educational priorities. In this state of disorientation it is vulnerable to appropriation by those who wish to use its power and prestige as a means for the realization of their own purposes. Having forgotten its own intrinsic purpose, it now serves a variety of extrinsic purposes.

Predictably, the college's inability to articulate its institutional purpose in an operationally meaningful way leads to widespread confusion both in and outside the academic community about the college's proper role in society. A few argue that it should be independent of society, and that this independence is sustained if it is physically isolated and insulated from the business and busyness of the larger community. Others argue that the desire for such detachment is an anachronism, a reactionary attitude characteristic of civilizations in which intellectuals evade their social responsibilities by retreating into scholarly obsessions and other-worldly myths.   In the latter and more currently-accepted view, the college is understood to be an inescapably social institution, one whose primary responsibility is to serve the interests of the society of which it is "but a part."

St. Lawrence's uncertainty about its proper role in society can be seen in its public statements and practices.   In its promotional literature there are occasionally romantic allusions to the advantages of a quasi-monastic environment.   The college promises its students and their parents an academic community that is an extended family, that is located away from the "distractions of city living," and that is devoted to lofty ideals and to "a certain detachment from the world." But today these allusions are almost certainly overwhelmed by the claim that the college's educational program is "relevant to the world," informed by the most pressing current issues, and on the frontiers of knowledge and educational technology. The college is likely to advertise that its program will benefit a spectrum of student career and leisure interests. At the same time it is likely to claim that its program serves the needs of the nation and the local community by developing responsible and economically productive citizens and by advancing compelling political ideals such as "social justice," "the protection of the environment," "affirmative action," "multiculturalism," and "positive coeducation."

Institutional uncertainty on this issue is also evident in controversies arising from recurrent efforts by factions both within and outside the college to enlist the college in support of a variety of social and political causes. For instance, in the nineteen eighties St. Lawrence, like many American colleges, used the device of divestiture in an attempt to bring political pressure on the government of South Africa to end *apartheid*. In the nineteen seventies, after the American incursion into Cambodia, the college took a public stand in protest against the Viet Nam war. This was consistent with a tradition in which American colleges had taken stands in support of the government's policy in the Second World War, in opposition to fascism and communism, and in support of the loyalty oath.[1] Thus, at many times throughout its history St. Lawrence has entered the political arena as an advocate, and has acted on the basis of institutional "partisanship," while at other times it has remained aloof from political activity, and has acted on the basis of institutional "neutrality."[2] The college, without any clear and consistent sense of its institutional mission, seems to have taken or avoided these actions not on the basis of any principle, but mostly in response to the passions, pressures, and

---

[1]During the nineteen fifties as many as forty-two states required loyalty oaths of teachers. During this period "professors and administrators ignored the stated ideals of their calling and overrode the civil liberties of their colleagues and employees in the service of such supposedly higher values as institutional loyalty and national security." Ellen W. Schrecker, *No Ivory Tower: McCarthyism and the Universities* (New York: Oxford University Press, 1986), 340.

[2]Richard Hofstadter and W. P. Metzger, *The Development of Academic Freedom in the United States* (New York : Columbia University Press, 1955).

personalities in particular situations.

The following illustrate some of the specific ways that St. Lawrence has been appropriated for purposes that are extrinsic to its stated purpose. These include institutional political actions, politicized programs, and vocational programs.

INSTITUTIONAL POLITICAL ACTIONS

In the past St. Lawrence has taken public, institutional actions on politically-sensitive issues in the form of pronouncements made by an administrative officer (such as the one made by the college president at the time of the bombing of Cambodia during the Viet Nam War), or in the form of a resolution of the faculty (such as the one made by the faculty calling for the college to divest its endowment portfolio of the stocks of companies doing business in South Africa), or in the form of the cancellation of classes as was done for the "Sexual Ethics Teach-in" in 1989.

What is at issue in these actions is not the intentions of their sponsors. These intentions were unquestionably honorable. Rather what is at issue is whether these actions appropriated the college for purposes that are extrinsic to its announced purposes or to the purposes of a liberal education.

THE VIET NAM MORATORIUM

On October 9, 1969, soon after the United States incursion into Cambodia during the Vietnam War, a group of students announced in the student newspaper that a "Viet Nam Moratorium" would be held on Wednesday, October 15. This moratorium was to be part of a nationwide protest of the Viet Nam War. The moratorium was to include a campus "Learn-in" on October 14 and a memorial chapel service and a faculty and student parade and rally in the village park on October 15. Students were urged by the sponsors to "boycott" their classes on October 15.

Today it is difficult to recapture the radicalized environment of that time. Revulsion against the war, particularly among the young men who were faced with the draft, knew few bounds. Each day new battlefield horrors were graphically recounted in the media. Demonstrations were occurring everywhere. Thousands of young men had burned their draft cards or fled to Canada. In these circumstances and for these young people the need to end the war took priority over all other needs--or at least all educational needs. In an editorial in the student newspaper on October 9 the editors deplored the "business as usual" attitude on the campus and argued that

> concluding the war should be the highest priority of the academic community. The war so totally negates the ideals of liberal education that the termination of the conflict is inextricable from the preservation

of the learning process. The prime aim of the university is to teach. Yet, how can the university effectively educate when handicapped morally, philosophically and economically by such a war?

Given the emotionally charged environment, the putative needs of the college had little status. Consequently, when the students and their faculty sympathizers announced the moratorium, President Frank Piskor was under considerable pressure to at least authorize the cancellation of classes on the day of the moratorium. In a statement issued on October 9 he acknowledged the passions generated by the war, but he nonetheless refused to authorize the cancellation of classes. This was a prudent and courageous act. Not surprisingly, though, in view of the radicalized environment of the time, he evidently felt that some kind of compromise was called for. Consequently, at the end of his official statement he wrote: "I shall respect, and expect others to respect, the decision of anyone who absents himself from class because of convictions of personal conscience."

Since "the convictions of personal conscience" could not in any way be challenged or verified, this statement in effect gave the students permission to cut classes without impunity on the day of the moratorium. The wider implications of this statement were lost in the passions of the moment. If "the convictions of personal conscience" were sufficient to justify the cutting of classes with impunity on the day of the moratorium, then there would appear to be no reason why these "convictions" could not also justify the cutting of classes with impunity on any (or even every) day.

Obviously the college cannot deliver on its educational responsibilities if students are allowed to cut classes with impunity. Consequently, while the president's statement was a compromise with the students, it was also a compromise of the interests of the college. Wisely enough, the president avoided putting the college in the position of endorsing the political position of the moratorium organizers. This would have prejudiced any critique of the war within the college's educational program, and put at risk those faculty members who were in support of the government's policy. At the same time the president's compromise put the college in the position of appearing to be at least tacitly in sympathy with the anti-war activists. Since the anti-war activists were in reality the representatives of an anti-government political position, the president's compromise indicated that the college was to some extent in sympathy with the anti-government position. To this extent the college was compromised by a political purpose.

It is interesting to note that President Piskor's statement of the college's policy on the Viet Nam Moratorium was criticized by the editors of the student newspaper because in their view he wanted the college to conduct "business as usual." This editorial response suggested that at least for some the high purpose of liberal education had been forgotten. If a college is effectively providing a liberal education, then its "business" can never be justifiably berated as "business as usual." This is true because no institution can be given priority over the institution that enables people to understand and to act on the basis of moral obligations without making a dogmatic assumption about moral obligations. If the college's educational program is truly concerned with enabling students to "enlarge their knowledge of obligations and their capacity to perform them," then it can never be treated as ordinary and dispensable. On the contrary, this institution would be privileged over all other enterprises. The morality or immorality of a war itself can only be properly determined by people who are liberally educated.

THE FACULTY DIVESTITURE RESOLUTION

On college campuses, passions, like the runoff from the winter snows, always crest in the spring. The spring of 1985 at St. Lawrence was no exception. On May 9 Dean Gibson was dismissed by President Gulick, and at a special faculty meeting on May 13 the faculty voted "a lack of confidence" in the president. Six days earlier, in a heated debate fueled by several months of racial violence in South Africa, the faculty voted to register its "rejection and condemnation of the repressive system" of *apartheid*, and to bring pressure on the government of South Africa to abandon this system. By a vote of 62-2-2, the faculty adopted a resolution to "deplore and condemn the system of *apartheid* in South Africa," and by a vote of 62-14-14 it adopted a resolution recommending to the Board of Trustees "that the University gradually divest its endowment portfolio of, and avoid future investment in, all United States corporations having direct investments in South Africa."

Throughout the spring the media reported daily on the violence in South Africa and on the efforts made by Americans and American institutions to aid those who were fighting against the policies of the South African government. Corrugated metal shacks sprung up on college quads across the country. In this environment great pressure was generated for the college to quickly "take a moral stand" and to "use its moral authority" and economic power to aid in this struggle for "social justice." In this atmosphere mere adherence to the Sullivan principles became reactionary. Divestiture became an urgent and unconditional moral imperative. Anyone who was so imprudent as to oppose this action was sure to be condemned as a bigot, and anyone who even questioned the propriety of the action risked being treated as a pariah.

Even so, the faculty's proposal for divestiture raised a number of questions that were not easily answered:

1. If the faculty has a moral obligation to make a judgment on an issue of the complexity of the divestiture proposal, does it not also have an obligation to consider the issue with care, and to avoid a rush to judgment? Shouldn't the faculty encourage thorough debate, and practice the ideals of scholarly research, careful analysis, respect for the opinions of others, and responsible action that it advocates in its educational program? For instance, in the interests of fairness doesn't the faculty have the obligation to invite a spokesperson for the

government's policy before it passes judgment on this policy?

2. What--precisely--is the purpose of divestiture? Is the purpose to bring about racial equality? Is it to bring about economic equality? Is it merely to make a "statement of conscience"? Is it to topple the government of South Africa? Is it to change U. S. policy toward South Africa? Is it to benefit domestic politics?

3. Is the faculty's purpose justifiable? And is there reasonable evidence that the proposed action will benefit this purpose?

4. On the reasonable assumption that divestiture would be possible only at some (market and commission) loss to the college, who is expected to bear the burden of this loss? Would this loss increase student fees? Would it decrease faculty salaries?

5. Would such politically-motivated action violate the New York State Education Law or the Internal Revenue Code as they apply to tax-exempt institutions?

6. Since the college's endowment portfolio doesn't belong to the faculty, what right does the faculty have to use funds contributed by others for purposes that they may not have intended?

7. If the college has a moral obligation to divest its endowment portfolio of stocks of companies doing business with South Africa, doesn't it have the same obligation to divest from its endowment portfolio stocks of companies doing business with (for example) China, or with other nations that frequently violate human rights?

8. If the college is justified in using divestment as a weapon against those who violate human rights, isn't it also justified in using divestment as a weapon against those who manufacture weapons? Or cigarettes? Or water beds?

9. If the college has the right to use its endowment for partisan political purposes, doesn't it also have the right to use student fees for these same purposes?

10. If the college has the right to pursue partisan political purposes, doesn't it also have the right to use its salary, promotion, tenure, and hiring powers to promote these purposes?

11. If the college has the right to adopt partisan political purposes, doesn't it also have the right to indoctrinate its students in the official morality?

12. If the college has the right to adopt partisan political purposes, doesn't it also have the right to use departmental budgets to further these purposes, e.g., to research political issues, to develop and distribute campaign literature, to invite orthodox speakers to campus? Shouldn't the library be purged of titles and periodicals that oppose the official morality?

13. If the college has the right to engage in partisan politics, doesn't it have the right to campaign against U. S. policy in the Middle East? Or to support prayer in the public schools? Or to fight dairy price supports? Or to endorse a candidate for Congress?

14. If the college has the right to engage in partisan politics, and since the

Board of Trustees has the legal right to act for the college, doesn't it follow that the Board has the right to commit the college to whatever partisan political position it wishes?

15. Above all, why is it not possible for faculty members to pursue their political purposes in the way that other citizens do? What gives a majority of the faculty the right to appropriate the college for its own purposes? Why cannot faculty members do politics downtown, and do education on the Hill?

Unquestionably, as these questions imply, divestiture was an act that politicized the college. Once politicized, the college was not free to pursue its announced purposes of providing "the opportunity for students and teachers to join together in the search for truth." The college was announcing that, thanks to a majority vote of the faculty, it had discovered the truth. It could now proceed to indoctrinate its students in this new truth.

Unfortunately, in the divestiture debate a statement from the college's "Aims and Objectives" was quoted out of context and was used to help justify politicalization. This statement was that "higher education carries with it an obligation to contribute to the betterment of man and society." Taken out of context this statement seems to imply that the college is itself responsible for social reform. In context, however, this statement has a different meaning. The more complete statement is that

> St. Lawrence University is dedicated to providing a liberal education for its students . . . . To these ends, St. Lawrence seeks . . . to make students aware that higher education carries with it an obligation to contribute to the betterment of man and society, to be discharged by the future exercise of leadership, constructive innovation, and the pursuit of excellence.

This statement makes it clear that the college does not have a responsibility for institutional political action, but does have a responsibility to educate its students in such a way that *they* have a responsibility for political action.

THE SEXUAL ETHICS TEACH-IN

At a faculty meeting on January 24, 1989, the following two resolutions were adopted:

> *Resolved*, That a teach-in on sexual harassment and assault be held on March 1, 1989, and that this teach-in will replace morning classes for a designated number of periods on March 1st, and that all students will be required to attend at least one of the relevant programs presented on campus that day; and be it further
> *Resolved*, That the Faculty Council is directed to consider future such programs to include racism and other issues.

Predictably, the attempt to require student attendance at the teach-in ran into stiff student opposition. Faced with this opposition, and not being able (or willing) to enforce the requirement, the college's administration backed off requiring the attendance of all students. Nonetheless, ingenious ways were found to require the attendance of all resident assistants, all fraternity and sorority members, and all students in the Freshman Program. On March 1, as planned, all classes were canceled, and the Sexual Ethics Teach-in was held.

Even without mandatory attendance, the Sexual Ethics Teach-in was an objectionable interference with the educational program of the college. There are three reasons for this:

1. If the faculty's purpose in sponsoring the Sexual Ethics Teach-in was to enforce the laws of New York State, the college's Code of Social Responsibility, and the Sexual Harassment Policy, then the faculty usurped the responsibility of the police and the Dean of Student's office. If the faculty had reason to believe that the laws, the Code, or the Policy were not being properly enforced, then it should have requested proper enforcement. In the accepted division of labor in the college it is not the responsibility of the faculty to enforce student discipline. If the faculty is to be responsible for the enforcement of student discipline, then it may have to stage Teach-ins every week throughout the year. Violations of the laws, the Code, and college policies include much more than sexual abuse and sexual assault. They include physical abuse or threats of physical abuse, racism, alcohol abuse, theft, hazing, property damage, motor vehicle infractions, drug abuse, cheating, plagiarism, possession of firearms, and so on.

2. On the other hand, if the faculty's purpose in staging the Sexual Ethics Teach-in was to change the students' sexual mores or to inform the students about their moral obligations, then such normative dogmatism is inappropriate in the liberal arts college. The promulgation of an official code of sexual ethics is an act in furtherance of a particular moral or political agenda. While it is likely to be the consequence of honorable intentions, it is no less objectionable than the promulgation of an official religious dogma. That the faculty's purpose in this instance was moral or political and not legal is suggested by the accompanying "Acquaintance Rape" campaign. In the familiar poster of this campaign, "No Means No," male students were scolded for observing the conventional meaning of the word, "no," and told that "no means no" regardless of the circumstances in which the word is uttered (as if "no means no" if one is simultaneously winking or removing one's panties). By permitting the college to be appropriated for a particular political purpose, the faculty allowed the ideal of liberal education to be compromised.

3. Regardless of the faculty's purpose in staging the Sexual Ethics Teach-in, the Teach-in itself had a subversive effect on the educational program. Once again, the argument was made that a normative concern should take priority over "business as usual." And once again, what was forgotten was that, if "the enduring task" of the college is "to provide the opportunity for students and teachers to join together in the search for truth," then this project should never be

described pejoratively as "business as usual." The proposal for the campus to give up a day of classes--rather than a Saturday morning or a party night or a hockey game--could not help but to generate cynicism and to suggest that the project was less a contribution to education than a contribution to some group's political agenda or, perhaps, just a gambit to have a good time.

POLITICIZED PROGRAMS

It is not common for a college to take public, institutional actions to advance a partisan political cause. This is in part true because such actions are likely to be recognized as partisan actions, and are likely to provoke reprisals among those who oppose the particular action taken. Not surprisingly, therefore, the college is more frequently politicized in a less conspicuous way through changes in the college's educational program. Courses may be altered, added, or deleted, curricular requirements may be changed, the extracurriculum may be restructured, or new institutional policies or practices may be adopted. At St. Lawrence this kind of politicalization has been taken or contemplated through actions such as the recent proposal for a required course in feminist theory, through the addition of the "Non-Western and Third World" graduation requirement, and through the on-going "diversity" campaign. These illustrate what are now sometimes called "politically correct" actions.

THE FEMINIST THEORY REQUIREMENT

A recent controversy concerning the St. Lawrence "Gender Studies" minor program provides a disturbing illustration of how easily a college can be politicized by an idea that happens to be riding the crest of a wave of political emotion. The St. Lawrence "Gender Studies" minor program was established during the 1986-87 academic year. In the spring of 1988 the Advisory Board responsible for the administration of this program appealed to the Academic Affairs Committee for the approval of a new course devoted to "feminist theory." Two facts about this proposed course caught the attention of the Committee, and provoked heated debate. First, from the course description, from the reading lists submitted, and from a letter which accompanied the course proposal, it seemed clear to almost everyone on the Committee that the course was designed to serve a particular political purpose. In the letter which accompanied the course proposal, for instance, it was stated that one of the benefits of the "Gender Studies program" was that it might "assist in the creation of a truly egalitarian academic community." In the proposed course feminist theories of several varieties were to be studied, e.g., the liberal theory of Mill, the Marxist theory of Lenin, and the radical theory of Firestone. But non-feminist theories of gender and criticisms of feminist theories, such as those of Gilder, Golberg, and Levin, were omitted.[3]

---

[3]George Gilder, *Sexual Suicide* (New York: Quadrangle/New York Times Book Company,

Second, the proposed course was to be a "capstone" course, and, as such, was to be required of all Gender Studies minors. Considered separately, each of these facts posed no special problem for the Committee. Many established courses have an identifiable ideological point of view or "bias," and this is commonly justified on the grounds that value-neutrality--at least in the social sciences--is impossible and, in reality, a dishonest pretense, and that professors, after all, are expected to "profess." In addition, there are a number of required courses already in the curriculum. The recent proposal for "capstone seminars" was in fact an effort to include in every major program a course that would be required of all seniors in that program. But while each of these facts, considered separately, presented no problem, taken together they were seen as presenting at least two serious problems. In the first place, the proposed course seemed to be at odds with the stated catalogue objectives of the program of which it was a part. While the catalogue description of the Gender Studies program disavowed any attempt to "form conclusions about all men or all women," and seemed to promise only an objective, non-ideological "analysis of gender," the proposed course in "feminist theory" was clearly committed to a particular "political perspective," and consisted in a non-critical study of "feminist political philosophy." In the second place, the proposed course, being both ideologically committed and required of all students in the Gender Studies program, seemed to be in violation of the generally accepted principle that a program of indoctrination is incompatible with liberal education. In the past this principle has been interpreted to require that students should always be presented with ideological diversity to facilitate individual, independent theory choice. While this principle has not been interpreted to mean that every *course* must be ideologically uncommitted, it has been interpreted to mean that the liberal arts curriculum itself and every *program* within the curriculum must be ideologically uncommitted.

The Academic Affairs Committee's reluctance to approve the required course in "feminist theory" was the occasion for a series of angry letters to the Faculty Council, the Dean, and the Committee from one of the Co-coordinators of the Gender Studies program. In these letters the Co-coordinator accused the Committee of arbitrarily "trying to block" approval of the course, and requested a Faculty Council "investigation" of the Committee. In addition, she defended the "advocacy" position of Gender Studies courses, and challenged the right of the Academic Affairs Committee to "require the addition or deletion of a political perspective within a course" on the ground that to do so would "undermine the integrity of the course."

The Faculty Council responded to this request for an investigation of the Academic Affairs Committee by publishing in its minutes the charge against the Committee, and by airing an additional charge of its own that the Committee was "philosophically unbalanced." When asked what was meant by the charge that

1973); Stephen Golberg, *The Inevitability of Partiarchy* (London: Temple-Smith, 1977); Michael Levin, *Feminism and Freedom* (New Brunswick, N. J.: Transaction Books, 1987).

the Committee was "philosophically unbalanced," a member of the Council explained that the Committee "had too many people of like minds--people who represent Western culture." The Council immediately appointed a committee to look into the need for an investigation. It also added additional members to the Committee to try to correct its "philosophical unbalance."

After the publication of the various charges against the Committee, and after a spirited speech by Professor Phil Larson, the Academic Affairs Committee itself petitioned the Faculty Council for a "full and open investigation" of the charges against it. Dean Andrew Rembert and the Faculty Council, now concerned about adverse campus publicity on a sensitive issue, looked for ways to "contain" the dispute. It therefore denied the request for a full and open investigation, and instead conducted a closed, off-the-record investigation. Although this investigation was conducted without allowing the Committee any opportunity to respond to the charges against it, it resulted in a letter from the Faculty Council charging that the Committee created a "chilly climate" for the Gender Studies proposal, and that it "should have been more encouraging" towards the proposal. Denied the right to appeal this issue, the Committee issued a letter which protested the Council's "cover-up" of the truth of this matter, and deplored its "abuse of faculty governmental power."

This essentially political controversy occupied countless hours of three important faculty committees during the spring semester of 1988. Still, since reputations had been impugned and strong political sympathies had been aroused, and since vital educational and moral issues were at stake, there was no way that the issue could be "contained" without a betrayal of some of the highest academic ideals. As a result, it is an illustration of the unfortunate effects of the politicalization of the college.

THE NON-WESTERN AND THIRD WORLD REQUIREMENT

At a faculty meeting on November 3, 1987, the faculty adopted a resolution calling for the establishment of a new graduation requirement in "Non-Western and Third World Studies." Consequently, beginning with the fall semester of 1989-90 all students were required to complete at least one course "dealing with non-Western or Third World topics."

The meaning of this requirement was never given precision in the resolution that enacted it. Embarrassingly, even the terms "Non-Western" and "Third World" were never defined. Moreover, it was never explained what would be included as "dealing with" non-Western or Third World "topics." For instance, would courses that studied the geography of China be included? Would courses which presented, say, German criticism of the culture of ancient Egypt be included? Would courses "dealing with" Arab criticism of Jewish culture be included? Would courses "dealing with" Neo-Fascist studies of the Indian caste system be included?

The purpose of the requirement was also never made clear. In the debate which led up to the faculty's adoption of the requirement, those who were in favor of it argued variously that it would be an "antidote" to student ignorance and "cultural chauvinism."   Two facts throw at least some suspicion on the genuineness of these arguments. First, no compelling case was made that this requirement met the aims of a liberal education. And no proof was offered that students were in fact cultural chauvinists. To many, today's students are more likely to be cultural relativists than cultural chauvinists. Second, St. Lawrence's action was not isolated. At Stanford the "Ho, ho, Western culture's got to go" campaign had already attracted media attention and led to Stanford's abolition of its Western culture requirement. At other colleges across the country groups were working to "de-center" Western culture and to facilitate what their critics called "ethnic cheerleading." These two facts suggest that the local effort to install a "Non-Western and Third World" graduation requirement was a distinctly political action--that is, an action that was motivated not by the needs of liberal education but by what was assumed to be a preemptive, "politically correct" need.

THE "DIVERSITY" CAMPAIGN

The issue of campus "diversity" was formally introduced at St. Lawrence by a memorandum written by President Lawry Gulick to the faculty on June 22, 1987. In this memorandum President Gulick invited the Faculty Council to form a group to "examine the meaning of diversity," and to establish specific goals for its achievement. Later, in a letter to the Chair of the Faculty Council dated September 1, 1987, President Patti Peterson requested that the Committee on Admissions and Financial Aid "address the issue of diversity of the student body." This committee issued a report and made recommendations which were approved by the faculty on February 28, 1989, and which were accepted with only a few emendations by the President the following September. The year before, on October 6, 1988, the Faculty Council voted to appoint an ad hoc committee to "investigate methods of actively recruiting minority faculty for St. Lawrence." The report of this committee, subsequently revised by the Faculty Council, and entitled, "Faculty Council Report on the Diversification of Faculty," was presented to the faculty on January 22, 1990.

The Admissions Committee report argued from the premise that "students profit educationally and socially if they are exposed to others with different talents, interests, perspectives and values." This "exposure," the report reasoned, broadens their "knowledge base" and increases "the level of awareness of similarities and differences among people," which in turn, leads to more "self-confidence" and promotes "respect for individual differences." On the basis of this reasoning the report recommended short range percentage goals for increasing the number of minority students to 6%, Jewish students to 4%, and Asian-American and Hispanic students to 1.8%. It also recommended the continuation of the present equal sex ratio and the practice of admitting students with a wide range of interests and achievements in extracurricular activities. And finally, the report made a series of recommendations for strategies to achieve these "diversity" goals.

The Faculty Council report, on the other hand, argued from the premise that the faculty should be "diversified." It recommended that the college should "actively recruit scholars in minority studies." The report also recommended the establishment of a "Distinguished Scholar's Chair" in "the area of Black Studies," five tenure track positions to "increase the number of faculty of ethnic minority groups traditionally underrepresented in the ranks of tenured faculty," four teaching fellowships for minority group faculty, and a faculty exchange program with a "historically Black college or university." These recommendations were quickly approved by the faculty at its January 22 meeting.

It is important to note that the Admissions Committee report and the Faculty Council report understood "diversity" in different ways. The Admissions Committee report defined "diversity" as "differences among individuals in terms of abilities or talents, experiences, values and attitudes." In contrast, the Faculty Council report understood "diversity" as differences in "gender, ethnicity, and race." It also limited half of its recommendations to "ethnic minority groups traditionally underrepresented in college faculty," and further limited the other half of its recommendations to "blacks." Thus, in the Admissions Committee report "diversity" was understood very broadly to include a variety of physical and mental differences, while in the Faculty Council report "diversity" was understood to be a matter of a physical difference, specifically, race. These disparate uses of the word "diversity" suggest that these two reports had very different goals in mind when they advocated "diversity" for the college. The Admissions report sought to increase ideological differences in the student body, and to further this goal by increasing the differences in such factors as "minority status, country of citizenship, religious affiliation, academic achievement and interests, socioeconomic status, gender, extracurricular achievement and interests, geographical area of residence, age, and secondary schooling". In contrast, the Faculty Council report sought primarily to increase the number of black faculty members.[4]

The Admissions Committee report justified its conclusions on the basis of the premise that "students profit educationally and socially if they are exposed to others with different talents, interests, perspectives and values."

This premise deserves close examination. The claim that the "education" of students will be advanced if they are "exposed" to certain peer group differences may be admitted to be true in some uses of the word "education." But this admission does not thereby establish that this exposure will advance a specific

---

[4]While the Faculty Council recommendations sometimes spoke of "ethnic minority groups," discussion in the faculty meeting in which these recommendations were approved brought out the fact that the recommendations were intended to increase the number of black faculty members-- "our area of most egregious underrepresentation." Evidently the provisions of Section 7 of the Civil Rights Act of 1964 discouraged such specificity in the actual recommendations.

form of education, such as liberal education. To "expose" students to certain peer group differences may provide them with certain information, and it may conceivably develop a certain tolerance toward value differences. But if a liberal education is more concerned with developing understanding than with amassing information, or if it is more concerned with developing a discriminating attitude toward value differences than with developing a tolerant attitude toward these differences, then an increased exposure to peer group differences will not necessarily advance liberal education. Similarly, the claim that students will "profit socially" if they are exposed to peer group differences may be admitted to be true in some familiar uses of the expression, "profit socially." But, once again, this admission is not an argument in favor of the proposed "exposure." For this "exposure" to be justified we would need to know that the college is responsible for a specific kind of socialization, and that this kind of socialization is obtained by student "exposure" to peer group differences. Since the Admissions Committee report did not specify the nature of the required socialization, and since it provided no proof that the required socialization is obtained by "exposure" to peer group differences, we have insufficient evidence to accept this premise as true.

The Faculty Council report justified its conclusions on the basis of a premise which contained at least three important assumptions. It assumed (1) that certain groups are, but should not be, "underrepresented" in the college's faculty, (2) that an increase in the number of black faculty members would "honor the heritage of our black students and provide them with academic role models," and (3) that this increase would provide white students with a "corrective for their ethnocentrism and culturally-generated racial stereotypes."

Each of these assumptions deserve unprejudiced examination:

1. The report assumes that the faculty should "represent" the diversity of some other social group. Although we are told that the diversity that should be represented is racial diversity, we do not know why this particular kind of diversity, rather than some other kinds of diversity, should be represented. Diversity of religious belief, politics, ideology, sexual preference, age, socioeconomic status, geographical area of residence, graduate school, personality type, hobbies, character, intelligence and an infinite number of other kinds of differences, or combinations of differences, might have been selected. The selection of some of these--for instance, sexual preference, hobbies, and intelligence--would be obviously absurd. But the principle of this selection remains obscure in the report. Moreover, we do not know what the social entity is that has the diversity that is to be represented. For instance, if the faculty is to represent racial diversity, we do not know whether the racial diversity to be represented is that of the North Country, New York State, the United States, the Western Hemisphere, the world, or some other social group. Obviously different social groups will require very different kinds of racial representation. Finally, we do not know why it is necessary for the faculty to represent the diversity of

some social group. Thus, what the report does not make clear is the ground of the faculty's putative obligation to represent some paradigm of diversity. Is it that a certain kind of diversity will improve liberal education? Is it that a certain kind of diversity will contribute to the creation of a better society? Or, is there some other ground?

The assumption that all colleges should "represent" the various kinds of diversity of some paradigm has a paradoxical implication: It means that when colleges become more internally diverse as a result of their becoming more representative of the paradigm, they ipso facto become less institutionally diverse. Thus, for instance, when colleges gain more diversity by conforming to some paradigm for representation in race, gender, ethnicity, religion, etc., they become more like each other, and thus less institutionally diverse. This makes it clear that in a "diversity" campaign, one kind of diversity is obtained only by the surrender of another kind of diversity. Obviously the Faculty Council report valued some form of racial diversity more than other forms of racial diversity, it valued racial diversity more than non-racial forms of diversity, and it valued a number of forms of internal diversity more than institutional diversity. But the principle or justification for these preferences remained obscure.

The paradox of the "diversity" campaign was compounded by the fact that its local sponsors were the board, the administrators, the faculty, and the students of a private liberal arts college. These are people who presumably believe in the importance of the private liberal arts college. Because of this belief they are at least implicitly committed to the desirability of a special set of educational objectives, a special kind of educational program, a special kind of faculty, a special kind of student body, and thus, a special kind of college. St. Lawrence, like other private liberal arts colleges, was originally founded because a sufficient number of people believed that there were in fact significant "differences among individuals in terms of abilities or talents, experiences, values and attitudes," and that a unique form of education was appropriate for those who shared a common faith, a common set of values, or a common set of educational objectives. And yet, as we have seen, the logic of the diversity campaign leads to the reduction of institutional diversity. It is especially paradoxical that those who should be expected to believe in the importance of the private liberal arts college would champion a campaign which seems to threaten the very existence of this institution.

2. The Faculty Council report also assumes that an increase in the number of black faculty members (presumably obtained by adding courses in Afro-American studies) will "honor the heritage of our black students and provide them with academic role models." This assumption itself appears to be grounded in the belief that black students will benefit educationally if their racial "heritage" is honored, and if they have "black academic role models." What is not clear in this belief is what is meant by "the black heritage," why a liberal arts college has any obligation to "honor" a racial "heritage," and what benefits result from "honoring"

a particular "heritage."   What is also not clear is why the college should encourage the idea that members of any race require role models from the same race.   This belief is prima facie racist.   It seems to be grounded in a deeper assumption that race is really important, and especially important in education. If this deeper assumption is true, it would seem to imply that white students require white role models, that Asian students require Asian role models, and perhaps that every ethnic group requires its own role models. If this implication is true, then the campaign for "diversity" would seem to be truly self-defeating.

3. The Faculty Council report makes a third assumption that an increase in the number of black faculty members will provide white students with a "corrective for their ethnocentrism and culturally-generated racial stereotypes." It cannot be questioned that ethnocentrism and stereotyping are undesirable. But what can be questioned is whether St. Lawrence students are justifiably charged with ethnocentrism. No empirical evidence was introduced to substantiate this charge. Currently, most students seem far from convinced that their own culture is superior to other cultures; on the contrary, most of them have relatively little comprehensive knowledge of their own culture, and the prevailing contemporary assumption is that all cultures, like all values and life-styles, are subjective, relative, and incommensurable.[5] Thus, the argument that today's college students need to have some corrective to ethnocentrism may have been persuasive for the generation of their parents; but today it is less than convincing. As for racial stereotyping, this error is made by many students--not just by white ones--and it calls for remedy. Hopefully a genuine program of liberal education will attenuate all forms of stereotyping and other forms of fallacious reasoning. The danger of the Faculty Council report's recommendation is that racial stereotyping will actually be encouraged by a proposal that justifies the recruitment of black faculty members on the ground of some paradigm of racial "representation," and on the ground that black faculty members are needed to honor a racial "heritage" and to act as role models for black students.

In view of the imprecisions, unsubstantiated premises, and inconsistencies of the Admissions and Faculty Council reports, it seems unlikely that the "diversity" campaign was designed to benefit liberal education.   The goals of liberal education were never specified in these reports, and were never used as premises to justify conclusions or recommendations. Together with the obvious fact that these reports were the product of considerable moral passion, the conclusion seems irresistible that this campaign was motivated by political purposes. The development of a certain kind of human being and a particular kind of society seem to be the most pressing concerns. Educational institutions--including the liberal arts college--are viewed as instruments for the achievement of these purposes. This interpretation seems clear not only from the fact that the goals of liberal education play no essential role in the campaign, but also from the fact that

---

[5]This is a point that Allan Bloom has pressed repeatedly in *The Closing of the American Mind* (New York: Simon and Schuster, 1987).

certain forms of diversity are preferred to other forms, and by the inclusion of some gratuitous and obviously partisan political comments. In the Faculty Council report, for instance, readers are told that the Reagan administration had a "questionable commitment to affirmative action," and that faculty diversity will not be achieved if colleges continue to use "white-male dominated recruitment networks."

The charge that the "diversity" campaign was motivated by political ideals is not to denigrate these ideals. On the contrary, these ideals may be admitted to be noble and commendable. The problem is that these political ideals were given priority over the ideals of liberal education. As such, they politicized the college by subordinating it to extrinsic and political purposes.

Of course for many the fact that the campaign for "diversity" politicized the college is a matter for commendation, not criticism. For these people it is the "social responsibility" of the college to use its power and influence to further certain political causes, such as the cause of "social justice," and to reconstitute the social order.

The problem with this politicalization of the college is that if the college puts itself at the service of a particular political ideal, then its faculty and students are not free to examine this ideal and its assumptions in an unbiased way. It becomes very difficult, for instance, to critically examine the morality of a de facto racial preference policy if the college is already committed to it, and it becomes difficult to defend the ideal of moral behavior if one has already been officially stereotyped as a member of a "white-dominated recruitment network."

THE PROPOSED "COMMUNITY SERVICE" REQUIREMENT

On October 23, 1990, the faculty approved a "Community Service Program." When funded, this program would include the appointment of a faculty member as director, and the offering of a course or courses which would give students academic credit for various kinds of service to the local community.

Quite clearly this program was intended to benefit both the community and the students. This goal may appear beyond reproach. However, in spite of this appearance, there are serious objections to this program. First, it was not at all clear who would decide what would count as "community service." For some, "community service" would include "helping the poor" or "working for peace." But for others, community service would include working for the chamber of commerce or for the Communist party or for the Ku Klux Klan. If the faculty were to be allowed (or denied) the power to influence such decisions, there would be relentless and merciless controversy. Every university decision would be politicized by this decision. Second, it is also not at all clear what students would be expected to gain from this program. If they are expected to develop the moral virtues, such as generosity, then it would seem inappropriate to award academic credit for generosity. But even more important, it is not at all clear who would decide what would count as the desirable virtues. For some, generosity is one of the highest human virtues; but for others, it is only a device which serves to advance "slave morality." Once again, if the faculty were to be allowed (or denied) the power to influence such decisions, all education would cease, and the campus would erupt in endless civil war.

Thus, the community service proposal was flawed in two ways. It put the college in the untenable position of providing ex cathedra answers to two questions that traditionally only each student was supposed to answer--the question of what constitutes a good community, and the question of what constitutes a good individual. If a college decides these questions in advance, then there cannot be any open criticism of the official answers. The resulting education is not a liberal education, but only an indoctrination into "politically correct" political and ethical dogmas.

VOCATIONAL PROGRAMS

THE RESERVE OFFICERS TRAINING CORPS PROGRAM

St. Lawrence's official statement of "Aims and Objectives" declares that the college is dedicated to providing a liberal education for its students, and that its "enduring task" is to provide the opportunity for students and teachers "to join together in the search for truth." In contrast, the stated purpose of the Army Reserve Officers Training Corps Program (ROTC) is "to attract, motivate, and prepare qualified students to serve as officers" in the U.S. Army. It is clear that the purpose of this program is not identical with the purpose of the college. It is also clear that a program for the training of Army officers is neither a prerequisite to, nor an essential part of, a program whose "enduring task" is to provide the opportunity for students and teachers "to join together in the search for truth." Thus, the use of the college for the training of Army officers is the use of the college for a purpose that is extrinsic to the college's announced purpose.

All of this is obvious. What is not obvious is why the college in the past has sponsored, and continues to be willing to sponsor, a program which is not authorized by its institutional aim. For the college to publicly identify itself as an institution of liberal education, and for it to accept the special status and privileges of this identification, and then for it to sponsor a program that is at variance with the aim of liberal education, is disingenuous and, at bottom, a betrayal of public trust and its own educational ideals.

During the last faculty debate on the ROTC program it was argued that the liberal arts college should include an ROTC program because our nation needs liberally educated military officers. The fallacy in this argument is exposed by the realization that our nation needs all kinds of liberally educated public administrative officers. Thus, on the same ground it could be argued that the college should include programs for the training of police officers, prison guards, firemen, and secret service agents. And since it is clear that our nation also needs liberally educated doctors, lawyers, engineers, and business executives, it could just as well be argued that the college should include programs for the training of doctors, lawyers, engineers, and business executives. But surely these national needs do not call for the liberal arts college to be converted into a "multiversity" which would include police and secret service academies, as well as schools of penology, medicine, law, engineering, and business. If our nation needs more liberally educated professionals, then more people who are, or who plan to be, professionals should be persuaded to get a liberal education. The apparent assumption that people can be liberally educated by a professional program sprinkled by a few "distribution requirements" or "liberal arts electives" is either demonstrably false or a damning indictment of the superficiality of the standard four year program of liberal education.

It was also argued that the college should include an ROTC program because this program provides financial benefits to both students and the college. The fallacy in this argument is apparent once it is realized that the contents of the college's educational program are properly determined by the college's purpose, not by the desires or needs or financial power of other institutions or individuals. If the Army is to be allowed to have or purchase instructional rights within the college's educational program, then there is no good reason why other equally qualified agents or agencies with equally attractive financial benefits should not also be allowed to have or purchase these rights. The obvious consequence of the college's auctioning off instructional rights to external agencies is the compromising of the college's ability to achieve its own, intrinsic purpose.

That professional programs, such as the ROTC program, do in fact compromise the college's program of liberal education can hardly be doubted. At a minimum, these programs appropriate student time and energies which might otherwise be devoted to liberal education. But professional programs also actively subvert the announced aims of the college. This is true because a program for the training of professionals, such as military officers, is primarily concerned with developing students' capacities to employ the *means* to achieve certain practical ends. In contrast, the college's program of liberal education is advertised as being primarily concerned with developing students' understanding of the *ends* of human life. The former enterprise is properly identified as "training," while the latter is properly identified as "education" in its most privileged sense. Professional training is successful if the students can efficiently fulfill a set of prescribed professional obligations, while the college's educational program is evidently successful only if the students have "enlarged their knowledge of obligations and their capacity to perform them." Military officers must carry out their official duties, but these duties do not include the critical or moral evaluation of these duties. In contrast, the college promises its students the development of "a system of values against which to judge their knowledge and skills." Thus, these two programs clearly have radically different ends and means, and require the cultivation of radically different and conflicting virtues.

The attempt to combine programs with such radically different ends, means, and virtues does not serve the interests of either. The interest of the nation in having trained professionals is not necessarily consistent with the rational obligation and human need for the discovery of a "system of values." Hence, the government's right to train military and other public administrative officers may be acknowledged, but this right does not carry with it the right to interfere with, or subvert, the unique interests of the liberal arts college.

The faculty's failure to recognize the incompatibility of liberal education and professional training can only be explained by its abject failure to meaningfully define the ideal of liberal education. No other explanation is sufficient to explain why the faculty can be as passionately committed as it is to the principles of the disinterested pursuit of truth, justice, faculty governance, peer review, tenure, and academic freedom, and yet include as members of the faculty people who are not professionally committed to the disinterested pursuit of truth, who are not subject to the jurisdiction of faculty governance, who are appointed by the Department of the Army without faculty peer review, who are without the protection of tenure, and who are without academic freedom.

This argument against the training of Army officers within a program of liberal education has nothing to do with ethical or political considerations about the putative evils of war or military service. We can be pacifists or jingoists, and we can have contempt or the highest respect for those who serve in the defense of our nation, but regardless of our ethics or politics we can consistently argue for the independence and inviolability of the liberal arts college.

TEACHER EDUCATION PROGRAMS

St. Lawrence's teacher certification program and other undergraduate and graduate professional programs offered by the Department of Education have aims that are determined by the needs of the public school system, and are subject to the laws of New York State and the authority of the New York State Education Department. These programs are designed to develop skills which serve various vocational ends. In contrast, as we have noted, the college's statement of "Aims and Objectives" asserts that "St. Lawrence University is dedicated to providing a liberal education for its students," and it describes a liberal education as one which "is concerned with skills which serve intellectual ends." This statement further asserts that most liberally educated people will possess "considerable ability in the pursuit of specific occupations," but it specifically points out that such vocational skills are the "consequences, not the purposes, of a liberal education." Thus, the aims of the professional programs in education are not identical with the aim of liberal education. In addition, the aims of these programs are neither essential to, nor part of, the aim of a program of liberal education. Thus, the use of the college for the training of teachers and other educational professionals is the use of the college for a purpose that is extrinsic to the college's official purpose.

Once again, for the college to publicly identify itself as an institution of liberal education, and for it to accept the rights and privileges of this identification, and then for it to sponsor a program that is not consistent with the purpose of liberal education, is disingenuous and, at bottom, a betrayal of public trust and the very ideals for which it claims to stand.

It is sometimes argued that the college is justified in providing vocational programs in education because the training of teachers and other educational professionals provides a valued service to the local community. Unquestionably these programs do benefit the local community. However, if the college's sponsorship of these programs is to be justified on the basis of their value to the local community, then the addition of a vast number of other programs would be equally justified. For instance, the college would be equally justified in providing training for medical doctors, lawyers, miners, dairy farmers, masons, and retail merchants. But, as was previously argued, once the college becomes the servant of the diverse interests of the local community, then it is no longer free or able to carry out its own unique responsibilities.

It is sometimes argued that the college is justified in providing vocational training for teachers because it is important that all public school teachers have a liberal education. But, to repeat the point that was made in the criticism of the ROTC program, it is probably equally true that all public servants should have a liberal education. We not only need liberally educated public school teachers, but we also need liberally educated lawyers, ministers, doctors, policemen, politicians, engineers, and business executives. Consequently, if the liberal arts college has the obligation to provide vocational training for teachers, then it is not clear why it does not also have the obligation to provide vocational training for other professions and vocations. But if this is the case, then the liberal arts college has limitless responsibilities. It then can no longer be a liberal arts college, responsible for liberal education, but must be a "university" or "multiversity," responsible for all forms of "higher education."

What needs to be recognized here is that it is possible to admit that public school teachers--and others--should have a liberal education, but deny that this requires the liberal arts college to provide vocational training. The ground for this opposition to any attempt to fuse these two forms of education is that there are good reasons to believe that this attempt compromises the interests of both. It would follow, then, that just as medical doctors should have a liberal education provided by a liberal arts college and a medical education provided by a medical school, so should public school teachers have a liberal education provided by a liberal arts college and professional training provided by a professional school.

There is convincing evidence that programs for the training of public school teachers that are grafted onto a program of liberal education do in fact compromise liberal education. Once again, at least student and faculty time and energy are diverted from the program of liberal education. Normally only four short years are allocated for a project that is advertised as a project that will transform a life in certain fundamental ways. The addition of professional programs in education compromises this project. But professional education does more then curtail the time available for liberal education. Professional education subverts liberal education. This is true because, as we previously noted, a professional or vocational program is by nature concerned with developing in students a capacity to employ the *means* to achieve certain practical ends. In contrast, a program of liberal education is said to be primarily concerned with developing in students an understanding of the *ends* of human life. Thus, as in the case of the training of military officers, liberal education and professional education have radically different ends and means, and require the cultivation of radically different and conflicting virtues. Once again, attempts to combine programs with such radically different purposes do not serve the interests of either. Certainly the local community needs well-trained public school teachers. But the local community, society, and humanity have even more fundamental needs. The ends of education, the ideals of the society, and the moral obligations of human beings must be known if education itself is to have direction and to have genuine value. Thus the need of the local community for trained public school teachers is not identical with the human need of individuals "to enlarge their knowledge of their obligations and their capacity to perform them." If a single institution is to be forced to serve these diverse and conflicting needs, it is likely that short-term practical needs will prevail over the long-term human need for understanding and moral insight. As a result, human nature being what it is, it is predictable that in most circumstances liberal education will suffer in any competition with professional education.

Thus, if the liberal arts college is to be able to accomplish its own, intrinsic purpose, it is self-defeating for it to include activities that will compromise the realization of this purpose. If, as it is frequently said, we need liberally educated public school teachers, then public school teachers should get a liberal education. But from this it hardly follows that the liberal arts college should sponsor programs that compromise or subvert its own interests.

PRE-PROFESSIONAL PROGRAMS

St. Lawrence University offers "pre-professional programs" for students interested in medicine, dentistry, optometry, podiatry, and veterinary medicine. It also offers a "3 + 2 Basic Engineering Combined Plan Program," and a "3 + 2 Nursing Program." These pre-professional programs allow a student to receive a bachelor's degree for only three years of study at St. Lawrence, providing that the student receives a bachelor's degree from a professional school. The college also offers a "4 + 1 MBA Program" in conjunction with Clarkson University. This program admits St. Lawrence graduates to Clarkson's MBA Program providing that their St. Lawrence programs "include certain foundation courses."

Whatever else they may be, these "pre-professional programs" are quite obviously clever marketing arrangements. They offer two degrees for less than the price of two programs. The rationale for this super-saver is less than convincing. It seems reasonable to assume that a four year program in liberal education cannot be reduced to just three years without significantly compromising the purposes of the program. In view of the immense cost of education, it would be unconscionable for a college to take four years to do what can be done in three years. It seems equally reasonable to assume that a professional program cannot be similarly reduced without significantly compromising the purposes of this program. Once again, it would be unconscionable for a professional school to require more time and money than is necessary to accomplish the purposes of the program.

Another disturbing fact about the attempt to market liberal education in a cut-rate combination with professional education is that such combinations eliminate the senior year of the liberal education program. One could reasonably expect that this senior year would be the most important of all years.

The "4 - 1" programs pose a different kind of problem than that posed by the "3 - 2" programs. The "4 - 1" programs compromise a program of liberal education by requiring courses that are not essential to it.

* * * *

The preceding examples illustrate some of the specific ways that St. Lawrence's confusion about its institutional purpose has led to its being appropriated for purposes that are inconsistent with its stated purpose and with the exalted purpose of liberal education. The college has been sequestered to advance various political agendas by institutional actions, to promulgate various ideologies through its educational program, and to provide vocational training for students. Uncertain of its own intrinsic purpose, the college has allowed itself to be pre-empted for a variety of extrinsic purposes. By these actions, it has compromised its institutional independence and, as a result, is unable to deliver on its promise of a liberal education. Today the college is a desecrated temple.

3

THE ACADEMIC THEME PARK

*What I'm trying to sell here is what everyone wants, happiness . . . .
Now, what's conducive to happiness? Simply a pleasant experience in
the company of happy, smiling, friendly people.*

Walt Disney

So far we have seen how St. Lawrence's uncertainty about its institutional
purpose has led to confusion about the college's proper relationship to society.
We will now consider how this uncertainty has affected the college's educational
program, including both the curriculum and the extracurriculum.

THE CURRICULUM

Our criticism of the curriculum will focus on its specific requirements and
options. But before beginning this criticism we will use rhetorical induction to
illustrate the curriculum's most general deficiencies. We begin by describing
some imaginary, but possible, graduates of the college:

FOUR ST. LAWRENCE GRADUATES

Mescal Ficklebucks came to St. Lawrence after attending the Summerhill
School in Ixtlan, New York. Being mainly interested in art, horses, and self-
indulgence, and being, by his own admission, a romantic and intuitive type, he
was totally uninterested (and totally inept) in logic, mathematics, and science.
The mere sight of a symbol was enough to set off an allergic reaction. His modest
analytical capacities were almost exhausted by his efforts to devise ways to avoid
any mathematical or logical course in the "Classical Liberal Arts" distribution
requirements. To satisfy the "Social Science" requirement he did some reading
on sexual exploitation, and he managed to survive the "Natural Science"
requirement by studying environmental exploitation. During his junior year he
had a mystical experience just outside a local bar. Everything after that in his

"education" was anticlimactic. He did a lot of art, riding, and partying. Except for two courses, he managed to graduate by taking all of his courses in the "humanities." He graduated without having any genuine understanding or appreciation of the natural or social sciences, without comprehensive skills in the liberal arts, and without any study of philosophy or history.

Mort Gass was second in his class at the Teller Technical High School in Genecido, New York. He was offered a Presidential Scholarship, and was given the red carpet treatment on "Scholars' Weekend." After inspecting the Chemistry Department, and after being promised a room next to the main frame, he agreed to enroll at St. Lawrence. He was pleased to discover that, as an elite "scholar" he was excused from the University's awful "distribution requirements." He felt sorry for all of those who were forced to learn things outside of their field of specialization. In order to qualify for a curriculum approved by the American Chemical Society, he took eleven Chemistry courses, plus a number of advanced courses in computer science, mathematics, physics, and German, all of which were listed as "encouraged electives." Since he believed that subjects such as history, philosophy, art, theater, and religion were schmaltzy and unscientific, he avoided all courses in these areas. He also avoided such pseudo-scientific subjects as sociology and government. When he was informed that he would have to take a year of Physical Education, he complained, but was told that "a sound mind requires a sound body," etc. When he protested that Albert Einstein couldn't even play croquet, he was advised that, if he took Military Studies (formerly known as "ROTC") he would not have to take Physical Education. This struck him as odd because Military Studies, unlike Physical Education, was said to be one of the academic departments of the college. Consequently he wondered why taking Military Studies would excuse him from taking Physical Education. He wisely decided not to be militant about the issue, and enrolled in Military Studies. He graduated in three years after having taken all of his courses, except for three courses and Military Studies, in the "hard," i.e., legitimate, sciences. He was without any interest or knowledge in ethics, government, art, music, drama, religion, or philosophy.

Golden Grunt had a hellava slap shot when he played center for the École Jacques of Barbelle, Quebec. After a helicopter visit to campus, a sweaty workout, and a juicy steak dinner, he decided to enroll at St. Lawrence. He played football in the fall, hockey in the winter, and foosball in the spring. His work, however, kept interfering with his play. After almost being forced to fumble by the "distribution requirements," he made a goal line stand, and came up with a winning curricular combination. He majored in "Fizz Ed." This made his work the same as his play. His academic program consisted of twelve required "Fizz Ed" courses. He also took Accounting (which he thought might be helpful if he eventually decided to go into business). Twenty-seven of his thirty-four courses were in his major field or in related fields. He did no work in art, music, philosophy, religion, history, government, sociology, physics, chemistry, or geology. Over half of his courses were vocationally oriented to his anticipated career in coaching.

Meri Logos' parents finally decided to mortgage their home and to send her to St. Lawrence rather than to the Berlitz School or Megalopolis Multiversity because they wanted her to have the advantages of a liberal education and a residential college. They were persuaded by what they read in the *St. Lawrence Bulletin*. "At St. Lawrence," they read, "there is a strong sense of community" and "a vital informal learning environment" because all students live on campus, and because the university has a "rural setting," a "relatively small size," and "a shared point of view towards liberal arts education." Meri had known from birth that language was her bag. After talking to several people at the Swahili table she made the interesting discovery that the old "Junior Year Abroad" programs could be taken during her sophomore year. (She was also puzzled to find out that, while St. Lawrence is famous for its International Programs, it doesn't have any foreign language requirement.) Consequently, during her sophomore year she lived off-campus and attended a foreign multiversity with English-speaking teachers in an urban setting, with a relatively large size, and with no shared point of view toward liberal arts education. After eight units of "experiential learning" and "cultural immersion," she returned to campus for her junior year and completed the required units for her "Multi-Language Major." One day while talking to several people at a departmental rush party for prospective majors she discovered that it was possible to take an Abroad Program during her senior year. At first she thought that this violated the University's "basic requirement" that at least one semester of the senior year be taken "in residence at St. Lawrence," but later, after it was explained to her, she realized that since the Abroad Programs are sponsored by St. Lawrence, everyone who takes them is ipso facto "in residence at St. Lawrence" regardless of their geographical location. Consequently, during her senior year she lived off-campus and attended a multiversity with an urban setting, a relatively large size, and no shared point of view towards liberal arts education. After more "experiential learning" and "cultural immersion," she returned for Commencement, graduating with only four units of credit outside of the humanities.

These four hypothetical *but possible* graduates should never have been awarded degrees by St. Lawrence. Even though the college proclaims that it is "dedicated to providing a liberal education for its students," these students did not receive anything that has any justifiable claim to be called a liberal education.

Some students (like Mescal Ficklebucks) are allowed to graduate in ignorance of the principles and methods of science, mathematics, and logic. Yet the college's statement of "Aims and Objectives" promises "to develop within each student the healthy and sophisticated kind of questioning that will give him the ability to use information logically and provide continuing protection against dogmatism and demagoguery."

Other students (like Mort Gass) are granted a degree without an understanding of the humanities, and without an appreciation of moral, political, or aesthetic values. And yet the statement of "Aims and Objectives" promises "to encourage each student to develop a system of values, [and] to nurture in each student his aesthetic sensibilities and capacities." The college's statement of "Character" proclaims that students "are expected, throughout their college careers and afterwards, to confront the question . . . : 'Have you enlarged your knowledge of obligations and your capacity to perform them?'"

Still other students (like Golden Grunt) are permitted to pursue an essentially vocational program, one in which the end is to earn a living, not to discover the truth, and one in which the requisite skills are technical, not intellectual. Yet the college's statement of "Aims and Objectives" proclaims that "the enduring task of the University is to provide the opportunity for students and teachers to join together in the search for truth," and states that "a liberal education . . . is concerned with skills which serve intellectual ends."

Finally, still other students, (like Meri Logos) are allowed to pursue a narrow specialization with little generalization and less integration, and are allowed to isolate themselves from the college community and its learning environment. Yet the statement of "Aims and Objectives" explains that "a liberal education requires breadth, depth, and integration in learning," and speaks in glowing terms of the educational importance of the small, private, residential college with its "sense of community" and unique environment.

Needless to say, these students cannot be blamed. In each case they met the requirements of the college's curriculum. They can hardly he reproached for failing to exercise the kind of judgment that should only be expected of those who have a liberal education.

THE REQUIREMENTS OF THE CURRICULUM

The following table summarizes St. Lawrence's curricular requirements:

"The Major Requirement"	8-12 courses
"The Distribution Requirements":	
"Natural Sciences"	1 course
"Social Sciences"	1 course
"Humanities"	1 course
"The Graduation Requirements":	
"Non--Western and Third World Studies"	1 course
"The Classical Liberal Arts"	2 courses
(One unit from two of the following areas: mathematics or symbolic logic, "arts or forms of expression," and foreign languages.)	
"The First Year Program"	3 courses
"The Physical Education Requirement"	(noncredit)
"Electives"	13-17 courses
Total	34 courses

These requirements show that the college's formal educational program is a curriculum consisting of thirty-four courses. This curriculum includes eight to twelve courses in a "major field," nine courses of "distribution" and "graduation requirements" (including the "First Year Program"), and physical education. The balance of the courses are "electives," courses chosen at the discretion of each student.

This curriculum is typical for the contemporary liberal arts college. It embodies current educational assumptions. For instance, it assumes that every student in a program of liberal education should have a "major" or "concentration," should fulfill certain "distribution" or "graduation requirements," should have a generous selection of "electives," and should normally complete the program in four years.

The typicality and familiarity of this curriculum, and the widespread acceptance of the assumptions which justify it, camouflage its substantial deficiencies. These deficiencies are of two kinds. In some ways the curriculum fails to require what it arguably should require, and in other ways it requires what it arguably should not require. These deficiencies may be identified as curricular "Errors of Omission" and "Errors of Commission":

"Errors of Omission"

First, the college promises its students "breadth" of knowledge. While this promise is far from clear, it is generally assumed to mean that the college will provide its students with an introduction to the major fields of knowledge. However, to fulfill this promise the curriculum provides only a set of permissive "distribution requirements" that seem designed more to introduce students to possible "majors" than to introduce them to the major fields of knowledge.

Second, in spite of the fact that the college claims to be a liberal arts college, and in spite of the fact that it takes the position that "a liberal education is concerned less with knowledge as information than with the means by which knowledge and judgment can be acquired," the curriculum does not develop the liberal arts--that is, the means by which knowledge and judgment can be acquired.

Third, while the college contends that a liberal education requires "integration in learning," the curriculum has no component to facilitate such integration. The curriculum does not provide for the discovery of principles that transcend specialized fields of knowledge.

Fourth, while the college states that its students have "an obligation to contribute to the betterment of humankind and society," the curriculum does not enable its students to understand or, much less, to act on the basis of their moral and political obligations. Similarly, although the college explicitly states that a liberal education requires "the cultivation of those habits of self-discipline, intellectual and moral, which distinguish a mature man or woman," the curriculum has no component to develop these habits.

"Errors of Commission"

Having noted what the college promises but the curriculum does not provide, we now examine what the curriculum does provide, but does so without any adequate justification on the basis of the ideal of liberal education:

1. "The Major Requirement"

The system of undergraduate "concentrations" was introduced to American colleges by David Starr Jordan of Stanford and Abbott Lawrence Lowell of Harvard near the turn of the century. Today, at St. Lawrence, the prevailing view is that what had been called the "concentration" requirement, and what is now called the "major" requirement is the most important element of a liberal education. Certainly the contrasting, so-called "general education" requirements-- "distribution requirements" and "graduation requirements"--are usually treated by students as obstacles "to get out of the way" as soon as possible so that the "major" can be pursued.

If we look to the college's *Catalogue* for a rationale for the importance of the "major" requirement, we will find only the single, unabashedly banal statement that "a liberal education requires breadth, depth, and integration in learning." Presumably a "major" provides a student with "depth of learning," and presumably a person with "depth of learning" possesses a lot of knowledge about some disciplinary or interdisciplinary "field" or "department" of knowledge. But what is not explained is why this kind of knowledge is essential to a liberal education. If our educational ideal is in fact the liberally educated person that is vaguely characterized in the college's statement of "Aims and Objectives," then a person can be liberally educated and not have a lot of knowledge about some "field" or "department" such as, for example, chemistry, Canadian studies, or sport and leisure studies. What the college's statement of "Aims and Objectives" does not explain is why a liberally educated person needs to be a disciplinary expert, or even an apprentice disciplinary expert.

It is a common assumption among students and parents that the undergraduate "major" is important in preparing students for a useful career. Even though this assumption is false, and even though the career that is eventually chosen by most students is totally unrelated to their college "major," the college and the academic departments are less than candid in acknowledging this fact. It is common for departments to try to recruit "majors" on the ground that a "major" in their department will benefit certain career goals.[1]

Sometimes the "major" requirement is justified on the ground that it is necessary "to avoid dilettantism." But what is seldom observed is the fact that being a disciplinary expert provides no protection against dilettantism. Both

---

[1] See: Naomi S. Baron, "Waiting for Napoleon: The Case of Undergraduate Majors," *Liberal Education* 69 (1983): 191-207.

experts and non-experts can pursue knowledge for amusement and in a desultory way. As the poets and psychoanalysts of the twentieth century have repeatedly demonstrated, the pursuit of specialized theory is often a neurotic obsession.

A common justification for the "major" today is the claim that the twentieth century's "information explosion" and cultural diversity have made it impossible to educate the generalist. Harold Taylor, for instance, in his book, *Students Without Teachers*, argues that today "there is no complete body of knowledge common to all educated men."[2] Those who defend the "major" requirement on this ground evidently confuse knowledge with information. We can agree with Taylor that there is no complete body of information common to all educated people, but we can still argue that there is a body of knowledge, and certain skills or arts, that are common to all those who are liberally educated. St. Lawrence's "Aims and Objectives" and "Character" statements certainly make this claim. These statements indicate that the task of the liberal arts college is to provide this general knowledge in order to develop the generalist, not the specialist. Too often, it appears, a liberal arts college is confused with a university. But these two institutions are radically different. As Edward Shils once succinctly pointed out, a university is an unspecialized institution for specialized people, while a liberal arts college is a specialized institution for unspecialized people.[3] Given this distinction, a university has about as much in common with a liberal arts college as it does with a barbers' college or the College of Cardinals.

Another common justification for the "major" is belief that the most unconditioned and valuable form of knowledge is attainable only by specialists or disciplinary experts. The trouble with this belief is that disciplinary specialization takes place only on the basis of assumptions--including normative ones--that make specialization possible. This means that as a field of knowledge becomes more specialized, its relationships to other fields and to human values becomes more tenuous. Consequently, specialized knowledge cannot be interpreted as knowledge that is less conditional or more intrinsically valuable than more comprehensive knowledge.

Some critics have suggested that one of the reasons that the "major" is held to be important has little to do with the ideal of liberal education or the needs of students. It has more to do with the needs of an academic bureaucracy and the interests of the professoriate.[4] The administrative bureaucracy and the professoriate thrive on the belief that a faculty is a collection of experts organized by academic departments. Each of these academic departments is understood to be a semi-private fief, appropriately ruled by a "head," and is a purveyor of a body of specialist knowledge. All of these departments are functionally equal: students can study anything from God to Trivia with equal justification and equal

---

[2]Harold Taylor, *Students Without Teachers* (New York: McGraw-Hill, 1969).

[3]Quoted by Robert M. Hutchins in *The University of Utopia* (Chicago: Phoenix Books, 1953): 46.

[4]See, for instance: *Integrity in the College Curriculum: A Report to the Academic Community* (Washington, D.C.: Association of American Colleges, 1985): 27.

credit.   The departments themselves are energized by the endless game of "departmental empire building":   Department members ingratiatingly recruit students, corral them into their "major" program, collect grants, amass equipment, get themselves a departmental lounge and coffee pot, have a few departmental cookouts for "their" students, complain modestly about the problems of being too popular, and con the Dean into getting an additional faculty member. Once this is done they collect their just rewards, gloat and bloat a bit, and start all over again. Open warfare between departments is partially allayed by the "distribution requirements," which are useful for protecting the departmental runts from the departmental wart hogs.   Various schemes are employed to get "the kids" to understand themselves as budding specialists. Even before they arrive on campus some of them get stroking letters from departments on the make. They are cutely reminded that "majoring is not a minor problem," and they soon learn to identify themselves as a Whateveritis "major".   In a like manner, faculty members are conditioned to cultivate their own "special fields," to stay out of other people's "areas," and even to utter the territorial call whenever their phone rings: "Whateveritis Department, Doctor Nitpicker speaking."

A final assumption that is used to justify the "major requirement" is the belief that somehow specialized knowledge is more demanding than more encompassing forms of knowledge. For instance, the Association of American Colleges' *Integrity in the College Curriculum* makes the claim that the major requirement should provide students with "a decent understanding and control of a complex structure of knowledge."[5] This is not persuasive. The report does not explain why it is important for the students to have "a decent understanding and control of a complex structure of knowledge." Moreover, even if this were a desirable goal, it would seem likely that the level of complexity encountered within a specialized academic field is far inferior to the level of complexity encountered in trying to understand more comprehensive fields of knowledge. Consequently, if it is merely a demanding or humbling experience that is desired, any attempt to achieve comprehensive knowledge will surely be more than sufficient.

2. "The Distribution Requirements"

As we have noted, St. Lawrence's official statement of "Aims and Objectives" takes the position that "a liberal education requires breadth, depth, and integration in learning."   The "distribution requirements" are commonly thought to provide the student with "breadth." Unfortunately, the term, "breadth," is nowhere explained in the official statement, and it is difficult to know what this term means. The rationale for the present set of requirements makes the claim that liberally educated people should "know a little bit about a lot of things." Yet this rationale never specifies what things the liberally educated person needs to

---

[5]Ibid., 28.

know "a little bit" about, and it remains to be explained why a liberally educated person needs to know "a little bit" about a number of unspecified things.

Judging from the fact that the current "distribution requirements" require students to elect one course from each of three "distribution areas," it might be assumed that these requirements are intended to provide students with a general understanding of the three generic "disciplines"--the natural sciences, the social sciences, and the humanities. This was certainly suggested in the college's "Guidelines for the New Requirements" when it was issued on May 4, 1988. The trouble with this assumption is that since students can use an almost limitless variety of courses to "satisfy" these requirements, and since there is no required course that considers the nature of the disciplines thematically, it seems unlikely that this requirement can provide students with a general understanding of these disciplines. Moreover, introductory courses are often used not for general education purposes, but as recruitment devices or foundation courses for majors.[6] Another possible assumption is that the "distribution requirements" are intended to provide students with an understanding of the methodologies of the three generic disciplines. This assumption would seem to be plausible in view of the statement in the "Aims and Objectives" that "a liberal education is concerned less with knowledge as information than with the means by which knowledge and judgment can be acquired," and in view of the fact that the published guidelines for the requirements insist that the "natural sciences" give attention to natural scientific methodology, and require a laboratory. But these same guidelines fail to limit the "social sciences" to conclusions that are established by social scientific methods, and they openly admit that there is no methodology common to the "humanities." Thus, as they are now defined, the "distribution requirements" do not provide an introduction to either the subject matter or the methods of the "generic disciplines."

An even more serious objection to the current "distribution requirements" is that the neat triad of "distribution areas" or "generic disciplines" is itself suspect. While the subject matter of the natural sciences may still be reasonably clear, the same cannot be said for the post-positivistic social sciences, much less for the so-called "humanities." As the humanities requirement currently stands it can be satisfied by courses in literature, fine art, history, music, religion, theater, ethics, politics, aesthetics, ontology, epistemology, and semiotics. (Inexplicably, mathematics is omitted.) But nowhere is there any indication of anything that these immensely diverse subjects have in common, except that they do not offer empirical theories of nature or society. Certainly it will not do to say that they study "the products of human culture" because this term would seem to be simply a synonym for "what is not the subject matter of the natural or social sciences." These considerations point to the conclusion that "the humanities" is a category that can only be defined by exclusion from other categories, and that it is really,

---

[6]See John S. Rigden and Sheila Tobias, "Too Often, College-Level Science is Dull as Well as Difficult," *The Chronicle of Higher Education* (27 March 1991): A52.

therefore, a catch-all, everything but the kitchen sink category. As such, it hides crucial differences in its membership. It also may reflect a bias in the organization of knowledge that gives priority to the natural sciences.

The "distribution requirements" presently serve no clearly stated liberal educational purpose. But their endurance and popularity suggests that they are more than mere vestiges of an earlier era in which students were expected to achieve specifiable forms of knowledge and to develop specifiable kinds of skills. The suspicion is irresistible that they serve some powerful interests in the academic bureaucracy. In any case, the system of "distribution requirements" seems to provide little in the way of benefit to general education, and much less to liberal education.

3. "The Graduation Requirements"

The college's "graduation requirements" are newcomers to the curriculum. Since 1989 three "graduation requirement" courses are mandatory for all students: one course to be elected from a category called "Non-Western and Third World Studies," and two courses from a category called "the Classical Liberal Arts."

"Non-Western and Third World Studies"

In order to complete this requirement students must elect at least one course that "deals with non-Western or Third World topics." Unfortunately, as was noted in our critique of this requirement in the previous chapter, the expressions "non-Western," "Third World," and "deals with" were inadequately defined, and as a consequence, there is no clarity about what should count as a course that "deals with non-Western or Third World topics." But there are more serious flaws. Prior to its adoption this requirement was given a rationale consisting of three arguments. First, it was said that the study of non-Western cultures and societies is necessary because "over the course of the past century, it has become increasingly apparent that the Western world does not have a corner on insights into the human condition . . . ." This argument apparently assumes that non-Western and Third World studies will "deal with" non-Western or Third World cultures sympathetically, and it similarly assumes that studies of "the Western world" will "deal with" Western culture sympathetically. These assumptions are presumptuous. Studies that "deal with" what is called "the Western world," for instance, are frequently critical of what is called "Western culture." These presumptions, together with the rationale's supercilious claim that "the Western world does not have a corner on insights into the human condition," suggests, in turn, the possibility that this requirement is being used for political, rather than educational, purposes. In the view of many, it is not properly the business of liberal education--as distinguished from political indoctrination--to decide whether or not "the Western world" has "a corner on insights into the human condition." This would be considered to be an issue that should be addressed in a systematic, open, and critical way within a program of liberal education, but not one that should be resolved in advance of it by faculty vote or administrative edict.

The second argument that was originally given as the rationale for the "Non-Western and Third World" graduation requirement maintains that, since one of the goals of a liberal education is "to prepare students for responsible citizenship," and since "the terms of that responsibility are now global," these students "need familiarity with the non-Western or Third Worlds." The difficulty with this argument is that the college's official statement of "Aims and Objectives" explicitly denies that one of the goals of a liberal education is to prepare students for responsible citizenship. The ability to pursue specific occupations and to understand and assume the responsibilities of citizenship, it says, "are the consequences, not the purposes, of a liberal education." Moreover, even if preparation for citizenship was one of the goals of a liberal education, it is not at all clear whether it is the right of a college to determine the students' "global responsibilities."

A third argument that was used to justify the "Non-Western and Third World" graduation requirement is the argument that students need to be subjected to "culture shock" to jar them out of their "cultural chauvinism." Twenty years ago it was frequently said that young adults from Westchester and Upper Montclair should be required to enroll in a course that was popularly known as "Faith-Breaking 101." The assumption was that a good dose of Darwin, Freud, and Marx would rattle upper middle class complacency. But times have changed. Many of the students who received this shock treatment are now teaching a new generation of young adults. And, not surprisingly, they're teaching them cultural relativism. Today most St. Lawrence students have no trouble with cultural relativism. They understand that all values, moral and aesthetic, are relative. They "know" that Einstein proved that everything is relative, that Heisenberg proved that everything is uncertain, that Kuhn showed that science is paradigm choice, that Nietzsche showed that culture is a product of cowardice, that Ayer demonstrated that all values are emotive, that Freud demonstrated that all culture is the product of sublimation, that Marx showed that culture is a function of class interests, that Derrida demonstrated that all interpretation is invention, that the feminists proved that all knowledge is a function of gender, that historicists demonstrated that truth is relative to time, and so on. The claim that these students need to be shocked out of their cultural chauvinism may have been convincing twenty years ago, but to many teachers today it is the least of their needs.

It is ironic that students at St. Lawrence currently have a required course in "Non-Western" culture, but do not have a required course in Western culture. In the current environment this is not atypical. A recent survey funded by the National Endowment for the Humanities found that in 1988 it was possible to graduate from 78% of American colleges and universities without ever taking a course in the history of Western civilization.[7] The survey also found that 38% of the nation's colleges and universities do not require any course in history; 45% do not require any course in English or American literature; 41% do not require a course in mathematics; and 33% do not require a course in a natural science. Former Education Secretary William J. Bennett cites additional figures: 75% can get a degree without a course in European history, and 86% can get a degree without a course in the civilizations of Greece or Rome.[8] These facts suggest that if today's students are Western culture chauvinists, they are not very well informed chauvinists.

"The Classical Liberal Arts"

In order to complete "the Classical Liberal Arts" graduation requirement students must elect one course from any two of the following categories: "Mathematics or Symbolic Logic," the "Arts or Forms of Expression," and "Foreign Languages." The "Arts or Forms of Expression" include speech, rhetoric, debate, oral interpretation, prose composition, poetry, fiction, playwrighting, studio art, musical composition and performance, and theatrical performance.

The category, "the Classical Liberal Arts," is contrived and misleading. It gives the impression that there is a well-established tradition, perhaps coming from Greece or Rome, that justifies including mathematics, symbolic logic, the diverse "arts or forms of expression," and foreign languages as "the liberal arts." There is no such tradition, as Bruce Kimball's research has convincingly demonstrated.[9]

In view of the heterogeneity of the courses included as "the Classical Liberal Arts" it is not surprising that the rationale that is provided for this requirement is obscure. It is not clear, for instance, whether "the Classical Liberal Arts" are sciences or *technai*; whether they are cognitive skills or skills of other kinds; whether they include or exclude the *trivium* and the *quadrivium*; whether they divide into "verbal subjects" and "mathematical subjects" or into the "arts of words" and the "arts of things." In addition, since foreign languages are counted as "classical liberal arts," it is questionable why the study of the English language should not also count as one of "the Classical Liberal Arts." Nor is it obvious why logic and dialectic, surely two of the most important of the medieval *artes liberales*, are not included.

These considerations intensify the suspicion that this strange category is less a category of liberal educational necessity than a category of academic political convenience.

---

[7]Lynne V. Cheney, *50 Hours: A Core Curriculum for College Students* (Washington, D. C.: National Endowment for the Humanities, 1989).

[8]William J. Bennett, *To Reclaim a Legacy* (Washington, D. C.: National Endowment for the Humanities, 1984).

[9]Bruce Kimball, *Orators and Philosophers: A History of the Idea of Liberal Education* (New

4. "The First Year Program"

What is now called "The First Year Program" originated as "The Freshman Program" in the fall semester of 1987. In the following year what had been a pilot program became a required program for all first year students. The *St. Lawrence University Catalogue* describes the program as "a two-semester combined academic and residential program that emphasizes critical thinking and active student participation in both the classroom and the residence." It has four components: a required, interdisciplinary, team-taught course "illustrative of some of the enduring themes of the human experience," an emphasis on writing, speaking and research, a coordinate advising system, and a college system in which students enrolled in the same section of the required course reside together in the same dormitory.

The objectives of this program have been matters of some dispute. When the program was originally proposed in the 1985 "Report of the Summer Study Group of the Academic Affairs Committee," the program was described as a year-long "core course" that provides students with "an integrated introduction to the arts, humanities and politics." Its purpose was said to be "to provide students with an introduction to liberal education." This was assumed to include the development of "writing, reasoning, and oral skills," later changed by the faculty to "writing, speaking, and research skills." Since the proposed program was intended as "an introduction to liberal education," and since the proposed core course was tentatively entitled "Introduction to Liberal Education," it was reasonable to assume that the program would be given its rationale on the basis of its contribution to liberal education. This did not happen. Apparently aware of the inconsistency and vagueness of the college's "Statement of Aims and Objectives," the committee that proposed the new program devoted an entire section of its report to the problem of the definition of liberal education. This was clearly an effort to provide a rationale for the program.

But the committee that proposed the program was afraid that any attempt to get a satisfactory definition of liberal education would "precipitate a protracted debate" which would "only delay the institution of needed curricular reforms." Consequently, it adopted a substitute strategy, arguing that its proposed program could be justified if the faculty could only "agree" with its selection of "truisms" which state some of the "desirable attributes" of the liberally educated person.

This strategy seems egregiously flawed. It seems to replicate the strategy of the proverbial hunter who becomes lost in the deep woods. Unable to orient himself, and panicked by cold and snow, he repeatedly sets out in what seems to him to be the right direction, only to eventually discover that he is as lost as before. At the point of desperation he comes upon some boot tracks, which he follows with renewed hope. Finally, with darkness falling and his energy exhausted, he is stricken by the terrible realization that he has been following his

York: Teachers College, Columbia University, 1986).

own tracks, and has returned to where he began. Presumably, only a last minute rescue saves the hunter and his confession of imprudence.

The obvious imprudence of the hunter's strategy was his failure to orient himself. He went before he knew where he was going. Not surprisingly, he went in circles and therefore failed to escape his quandary. The committee's strategy had a similar flaw. It tried to avoid orienting its proposal by a definition of liberal education. As a result, its strategy was circular and failed to provide a coherent rationale for the proposed program. This circularity is evidenced as follows:

First, the committee suggested that any attempt to get a definition of liberal education would result in a "protracted debate" which could be avoided if the faculty could simply agree on some of the "desirable attributes of a liberally educated person." But there is no reason to believe that controversies that emerge as a consequence of an attempt to get an agreement on a definition of liberal education will not also emerge as a consequence of an attempt to get an agreement about the "desirable attributes" of a person who has a liberal education. Moreover, any agreement about the "desirable attributes" of a person who has a liberal education already tacitly assumes a definition of liberal education.

Second, the committee claimed that any attempt to get a definition of liberal education would "only delay the institution of needed reforms." But this claim also tacitly assumes a definition of liberal education because without this definition it would be impossible to identify what curricular reforms are "needed."

Third, the committee argued that any attempt to get a definition of liberal education was unnecessary because, as long as the faculty could agree on *some* of the attributes of the liberally educated person, there was no need to know *all* of these attributes. This is objectionable, however, because it would be impossible to design a curriculum to develop "the liberally educated person" unless *all* of the essential attributes of the liberally educated person are known. (How could a curriculum to develop medical doctors be designed if only some of the attributes of a medical doctor, e.g., knowledge of anatomy and knowledge of chemistry, are known? Or, to use one of the committee's analogies, how would it be possible to "bake the bread of liberal education" if only some of the ingredients, e.g., salt and water, are known?)

Thus, the committee's strategy of trying to avoid a definition of liberal education was circular. The arguments used in this effort all presuppose the definition.

Having abandoned the attempt to justify its proposal by a definition of liberal education, the committee then attempted to justify it by finding faculty "agreement" on various "unobjectionable" and "uncontroversial" attributes of the liberally educated person. "We can," the committee contended, "be guided by whatever we agree upon."

This strategy is also flawed. There are three reasons for this. First, no justification was given for the assumed right of a particular faculty at a particular time to determine for all (and for all time?) both curricular means and curricular ends.

Second, if "agreement" here means a consensus (as would appear to be the case), then such agreement by the faculty about the attributes of a liberally educated person would likely require a "protracted debate." On the other hand, if "agreement" means a parliamentary majority, then such an agreement would not likely be "unobjectionable" or "uncontroversial."

Third, most importantly, even if it were possible to get a faculty consensus on "unobjectionable" and "uncontroversial" attributes of the liberally educated person, such an agreement should not be mistaken for a justification of these attributes, and therefore, should not be mistaken for a justification of the curricular proposals that are based on these attributes. After all, mere agreement, at least among a faculty of less than perfect knowledge and virtue, might yield a barbarous set of attributes. Justification calls for reasons, not mere agreement.

Consequently, the committee's strategy of trying to avoid a definition of liberal education by finding faculty agreement on various attributes of the liberally educated person failed to resolve the problem of justifying the proposed program.

The committee seemed to view the problem of defining a liberal education (or finding the attributes of the liberally educated person) on the model of an archaeologist trying to infer the attributes of a dinosaur on the basis of a couple of fossils. This is an inappropriate model. A liberal education (or a liberally educated person) surely is not something that was extant but is now extinct. This form of education (or this person) is an ideal which we create on the basis of justifying reasons. Thus, if we are in doubt about the definition of liberal education, we are simply not clear about our educational purposes. And obviously if we are not clear about our educational purposes, we are in no position to consider curricular revision.

The correct strategy, therefore, would be one that allows the curriculum to be oriented by a definition of liberal education. Obviously what is needed is not a common "dictionary" or "stipulative" definition, but rather a "theoretical" definition. This means that liberal education must be defined on the basis of a theory or philosophy of liberal education. Like any good scientific theory, such a definition requires clarity, coherence, and defensibility.

The first requisite is clarity. The definition should make possible the identification of a liberal education on the basis of precise, operationally meaningful descriptions. The committee frequently employed expressions that lack the precision required if these expressions were to be used for curriculum reform. For instance, the committee took the position that liberal education "prepares one for life" and "enriches one's personal life," but the meaning of these expressions is never clarified. The committee also maintained that "some, and perhaps many, of our students [get] a firm grounding in the liberal arts," but, inexplicably, the liberal arts are never again mentioned, much less, explained. Tautologies, such as the statement that "a liberal education involves depth, breadth and integration" are simply inadequate to serve as principles for curriculum reform.   Curiously enough, even "knowledge" itself is never explained, even though the discovery and transmission of "knowledge" is said to be the "main goal" of the college.

The second requisite of a definition is coherence. The definition should show that the attributes of a liberal education are grounded in a single principle, and are therefore, integrated and free from inconsistency. The committee's enumeration of the putative attributes of the liberally educated person for which it hoped to find faculty agreement lacked coherence because it was admittedly incomplete and did not establish any priorities or systematic relationships among the attributes.   It was not even clear whether the set of attributes might be inconsistent. The possibility of inconsistency was increased by the committee's procedure of developing a set of "truisms" as the apparent justifications for its curricular proposals, and then completely ignoring these "truisms" in favor of ad hoc reasons and "rationales" when it came time to justify specific curricular proposals.

Particularly troubling was the committee's syllogism that since "the primary mission of any university is the discovery and transmission of knowledge," and since "liberal education is a university education," the primary mission of liberal education is the discovery and transmission of knowledge. While it is obvious that some universities do have as their primary mission the "discovery of knowledge," it is not apparent why the liberal arts college should have this as its primary mission. Nor is it apparent how this mission meshes with the additional claim by the committee that liberal education should "equip and inspire students so that they may pursue knowledge independently."

Also troubling was the lack of clarity and possible inconsistency between the committee's claims that a liberal education should prepare student for "the pursuit of knowledge," for "life," and for an "enriched personal life." If "the pursuit of knowledge" and the "enrichment of the student's personal life" are contingently related, and if "the pursuit of knowledge" has priority, it is not apparent that this "pursuit" will "enrich" the student's personal life. On the other hand, if the enrichment of a student's personal life has priority, it is not apparent that the achievement of this goal will require the "pursuit of knowledge." Moreover, if one of the goals of a liberal education is to "enrich" the student's personal life, then, given the variety of activities that are commonly considered "enriching," it is difficult to see what would be *in*appropriate to a liberal education. The idea that a liberal education is a "preparation for life" also suggests that, contrary to its traditional conception, it rightfully includes (for instance) the development of vocational and homemaking skills, and the encouragement of student interest-oriented leisure time pursuits.   What is seriously lacking is a principle of curricular relevance, a principle for deciding what is essential and what is irrelevant in the educational program.

The final, but most important, requisite of a definition is defensibility. The definition should establish educational purposes that are justified on the basis of compelling educational reasons. It would not be appropriate to attempt to justify these purposes on the basis of contingent agreements. Neither would it be appropriate to attempt to justify these purposes on the basis of various "truisms" which are nothing more than provincial commonplaces. The need for a secure justification is dictated by the fact that the project at hand is the justification of curricular proposals and purposes by strategies that avoid the dogmatism that is inappropriate to any enterprise that is appropriately called liberal education.

In view of these considerations, the strategic flaw in the committee's report was its failure to provide a rationally defensible theoretical definition of liberal education--that is, a philosophy of liberal education. Because of this failure there was no set of clear, coherent, and defensible educational purposes to guide the design of the First Year Program. The committee's substitute strategy of seeking justification for its curricular proposals in a variety of often imprecise, unsystematic, and ungrounded assumptions about what the faculty might agree on is circular and failed to provide a compelling rationale for its proposal.

If any attempt to get a definition of liberal education is likely to "precipitate a protracted debate" which will "only delay the institution of curricular reforms," then the correct strategy would be to delay curricular reforms, and to begin the debate. A delay may be unfortunate, but even this cannot be decided unless a definition is available. On the other hand, any attempt to institute curricular reforms before there is an understanding of educational purposes would be to follow the flawed strategy of the lost hunter. It would be to institute reforms circularly, and thus, dogmatically.

In presenting the First Year Program to the faculty for approval, the Faculty Council made an arrogant and unconscionable move: it cut the program's rationale loose from the program, and presented only the program. This was unquestionably intended to avoid a debate on the rationale, one which the Council and the committee expected to jeopardize the expeditious approval of the program. This move guaranteed that the debate would be dominated by academic politics as usual, not by an appeal to reason. In a shameful spectacle faculty members were invited to accept or reject the proposed program for whatever reasons they might choose, not to judge the program on the basis of its contribution to liberal education. Such was the case, and the program, with a few special interest amendments, and with the help of some parliamentary shenanigans, received a majority vote on November 18, 1986.

Since the First Year Program was stripped of its original rationale, criticism of the program's purpose can only be based on the very brief and vague, catalogue-type statements of purpose that were approved by the faculty and on some general assumptions about the meaning of these statements and about the possible implicit purposes of the program.

1. One of the primary purposes of the First Year Program may be pragmatic. According to M. Lee Upcraft, John N. Gardner, and associates in *The Freshman Year Experience*, the four year college curriculum needs to be "front-loaded" by

special programs for freshmen in order to retain freshman students in the face of declining enrollments and high freshman attrition rates.[10] These programs further this purpose through special orientation programs, a freshman advising system, a mentoring program, freshman seminars, attention to character development, special living arrangements, etc. To what extent this purpose is being served by the St. Lawrence First Year Program is not yet clear. In any case, however, the achievement of this purpose might justify the program as a device to maintain freshman enrollment, but would not justify it as a contribution to liberal education.

2. The First Year Program is viewed by some as essentially a college preparatory program to develop "basic academic skills," to develop good study habits, and to provide an improved academic environment, especially in comparison to the anti-intellectual environment provided by social fraternities. Whether or not this goal is being achieved is also not yet clear. It seems conceivable that the program might well contribute to an improved academic atmosphere. But this victory, if it occurs, may not decide the war. The student peer group, with its persistent conformist and anti-intellectual interests, will not yield easily to any challenge to its hegemony. However, even if this war is eventually won, the contribution of the First Year Program will have to count as a contribution to the improvement of the academic environment, not as a contribution to the curriculum. As long as the program is essentially college preparatory or remedial, then to this extent it is not properly counted as a contribution to liberal education.

3. Another conceivable purpose of the program is to achieve the general education objectives that the present distribution requirement system obviously does not achieve. Here the program must confront the liberal arts college's most formidable internal enemy--the careeristic interests of a departmentalized faculty. A departmentalized faculty will tolerate a program of general education as long as it appears to serve the interests of special education. But if the program is perceived as having larger ambitions, it will be subverted. Currently those who favor some program of general education are locked in a bloody civil war with the departmentalists. The outcome of this war is still very much in doubt.

4. After the original rationale for the First Year Program was dropped, the program's "interdisciplinary, team-taught course" was given a new, brief set of purposes by several faculty resolutions. The course was given responsibility for "promoting a habit of active intellectual inquiry among the first year students and introducing them to significant human questions." Obviously the problem with this statement is its imprecision. It is far from clear what is to count as a "habit of intellectual inquiry." (For instance, did Alfred Rosenberg or Dr. Strangelove or Sartre's "autodidacte" have a "habit of intellectual inquiry"?) Neither is it clear on what is to count as "a significant human question"? (For instance, is the need

---

[10]M. Lee Upcraft, John N. Gardner, and associates, *The Freshman Year Experience* (San Francisco: Jossey-Bass Publishers, 1989).

for dairy price supports in the North Country or the use of the chador by Moslem women or the species endangerment of the coral snake a "significant human question"?) As a consequence of the imprecision of these terms, the content of the program's course is left without meaningful specification. This leaves the students without any protection against teachers who are dedicated to specialist obsessions, political proselytizing, or student entertainment. But even if this issue is ignored, a more fundamental issue is the question of why a three unit course is needed to "introduce" students to "significant human questions." It seems reasonable to expect that every introductory course in a curriculum for liberal education would introduce students to "significant human questions." What is needed here is what the faculty has already abandoned--a justification of the program in terms of its contribution to the aims of liberal education.

5. One of the stated purposes of the First Year Program is to "illustrate some of the enduring themes of human experience." This may seem to delimit the scope of the program, and to provide it with focus. But a "theme" is a mere topic, any subject of discourse. There is no topic that cannot be a theme. Moreover, to further require that these themes be "enduring themes of human experience" does not provide much in the way of specification. There are, so it would seem, no themes that transcend "human experience." About the only restriction, therefore, is the requirement that the themes must be "enduring." But this is hardly restrictive because any theme can easily be generalized in an infinite number of ways. For instance, if "feminism" were to be rejected as a possible theme for the program's freshman seminar on the ground that it was not an "enduring" theme, it could easily be accepted under the more comprehensive theme of "the relations between the sexes." Once the program has adopted themes such as its current one--"The Human Condition: Nature, Self, and Society"--it is hard to imagine any topic that would be excluded. This suggests that, in spite of its imposing title, the program really lacks focus.

6. The program's "communications skills component" is now limited to the development of "writing, speaking, and research" skills. If the real intent of this component is to develop the essential cognitive skills sometimes known as the liberal arts, then the component as it now stands is severely truncated and stunted. It is truncated because it omits logic and dialectic, two arts that once were considered to be the most indispensable of the liberal arts. It also omits the arts often classified as the arts of the quadrivium, except for what it calls "research." The component is stunted because it apparently understands the art of grammar as limited to "writing," the art of rhetoric as limited to "speaking," and the arts of the quadrivium as limited to "how to use the library." These slim pickings will hardly do justice to the spectrum of universal arts essential to the achievement of knowledge.

7. If the program is conceived as a contribution to the liberal arts curriculum, then there can be little doubt that it is much too ambitious for the limited means and time available to it. The development of "writing, speaking, and research

skills"--not to mention the full range of the skills of the liberal arts--is alone much too important and difficult to be the responsibility of a single three-unit course. Surely the liberal arts should occupy more than a bare nine percent of the curriculum of a liberal arts college.

8. The recent faculty review of the First Year Program has brought to light a most disturbing fact--that the Program has adopted some goals that were not authorized by the faculty legislation that established the Program. One of these self-generated goals is the inclusion in the curriculum of "significant and enduring issues usually unrepresented in the traditional canon of western thought, namely questions of race, class, gender, and the non-western experience." While the meaning of this statement is certainly far from clear, its intention seems to be to commit the program to a "politically correct" ideology, one that is sometimes referred to as "multiculturalism." If this is in fact the case, then this commitment is not only without authorization, but it would seem to legitimize political indoctrination.

5. "The Physical Education Requirement"

To qualify for graduation all students must complete a non-credit physical education course. In the nineteen sixties all male students--except veterans and ROTC cadets--were required to complete a one year physical education course, while female students were required to complete a two year course. The objective of these courses was to develop "carry-over sports skills and interests which will contribute materially to the worthy use of leisure time." The catalogues during the sixties never explained why veterans and ROTC cadets were "excused" from this requirement, nor did they explain why females had a two year requirement while males had only a one year requirement. Today the required physical education course has a different objective. It is not intended to develop sports skills, but to develop "the ability to maintain a physically active and fit lifestyle throughout the adult years." This shift in course objectives calls attention to the fact that on one occasion it was apparently assumed that a liberal education should help people make better use of their leisure time, while on another occasion it was assumed that a liberal education should help people have a more healthful lifestyle. This shift in the objectives of the required physical education course provides another illustration of the imprecision of the faculty's understanding of the purpose of liberal education.

What is never explained is why a liberal education should develop either "carry-over sports skills" or "an active and fit life-style." If every student should have "carry-over sports skills," then it seems inexplicable that veterans should be exempted from the physical education requirement. And if every student should be helped to have a "healthful lifestyle," then it seems inexplicable that the widespread campus use and abuse of alcohol and tobacco should be tolerated.

These questions have led some of those who have been uneasy with the anomalous role of physical education to ask a forbidden question: What, in fact, is the role of physical education within a program of liberal education? Is it conceivable that, just as the major and distribution requirements may really be devices to further the interests of the professoriate, the physical education requirement may serve a similar function?

OPTIONS OF THE CURRICULUM

In addition to a set of required programs and courses, the curriculum includes a set of programs and courses that may be elected at the discretion of each student:

"The Electives"

Approximately one-half of the course units required for graduation are "electives." The college provides no justification for requiring these "electives." This suggests the possibility that about one-half of the courses in the curriculum are superfluous, and that a liberal education could be achieved by a two year program and at one-half of the cost of the present program. In view of the fact that the current cost of requiring students to take almost two years of unnecessary, "elective" courses is in excess of $44,000, the college's failure to justify the elective requirement is inexplicable and inexcusable.

Some may argue to the conclusion that an important part of a liberal education is the students' pursuit of various idiosyncratic interests. But one can only wonder what assumption would justify this conclusion. How does the study of almost anything contribute to the realization of the aims of liberal education? And if we admit the legitimacy of "experiential" as well as "cognitive" education, how does the experience of almost anything contribute to the realization of the aims of liberal education?

Some hard questions need to be asked. Is it too cynical to suggest that two extra years are necessary to allow students to mature and to sort out their lives and to make vocational and marital decisions? If these are justifiable goals, then the college should acknowledge them and should facilitate their realization in an open and rational way by providing serious personal and career counseling, and by providing courses that would aid in the making of personal and career decisions. Is it too cynical to suggest, as have some, that college is at least partly a parental device to get teenagers out of the home and into a youth ghetto where hired hands can cope with their rebelliousness? Is it really just sarcastic hyperbole to suggest that the liberal arts college is primarily an institution for adolescent sitting?[11]

If the college does have a covert purpose for requiring four years to do what could be done in two years, then it should acknowledge this purpose. To conceal this purpose is hypocritical, and criminally so for an institution that is officially

---

[11]Robert M. Hutchins originally made this charge in *The University of Utopia* (Chicago: The University of Chicago Press, 1953), 86.

committed to the search for truth. On the other hand, to preempt four years of human life and untold financial resources for what could be done in less time and for fewer dollars is surely thievery.

Vocational Programs and Courses

As we have repeatedly noted, St. Lawrence's statement of "Aims and Objectives" explicitly commits the college to providing a liberal education for its students. "A liberal education," the statement explains, "is concerned with skills which serve intellectual ends." Assuming that the word, "intellectual," is used here in the ordinary, dictionary sense to distinguish ends that are objects of knowing from those that are objects of feeling or willing, the college's statement makes an important declaration. It declares that the college seeks to develop the skills of knowing things, not the skills of making things or doing things. We thus have reason to believe that the college is committed to a form of education that is not to be confused with vocational or professional education.

This commitment to a non-vocational or non-professional education is confirmed by the additional statement in the "Aims and Objectives" that "ability in the pursuit of specific occupations" and the ability to "understand and assume the responsibilities of citizenship" are "not the purposes of a liberal education."

In view of this commitment to non-vocational or non-professional education, it is puzzling, as we noted in the previous chapter, that the college continues to provide programs that are obviously designed to develop vocational or professional skills. The two most obvious examples of such programs are the ROTC and teacher education programs.

The college's sponsorship of these two programs is even more puzzling when viewed in the context of the college's official statement of its "Character." In this statement, published in the *Catalogue*, it is said that St. Lawrence is "independent of both church and state," and "is, and intends to remain, free to pursue its own destiny in the light of its own vision." However, such independence is hardly possible for programs in teacher education and ROTC. These programs are under external curricular and credentializing authorities. Because of this, the college is hardly "free to pursue its own destiny in the light of its own vision."

The ROTC and teacher education programs are not the only examples of vocational or professional programs to be offered by the college. "Pre-Professional Programs" are offered in medicine, dentistry, veterinary medicine, law, engineering, nursing, business administration, and applied statistics. In addition to these programs the curriculum also contains numerous vocational and professional courses. There are, for example, courses in accounting, computer programming, and coaching and teaching of physical education in New York State K-12.

There is a fiction among the professoriate that the preparation of undergraduate students for entry into a graduate school is not a vocational or professional pursuit. This is hardly the case. "Closet vocationalists" are no different than other vocationalists in subordinating their teaching to vocational or professional ends.

The problem with all forms of vocationalism and professionalism is that they are not consistent with the college's aims, and they ignore the most fundamental questions of liberal education. These programs and courses provide students with the knowledge and skills essential to a vocation or profession, but they do not provide them with the knowledge and skills essential to a liberal education. They develop the knowledge and skills essential to certain actions, but they do not develop the knowledge and skills necessary for judging the value of these actions.

"Sports Science"

There is a long tradition that supports the notion that sports build character. In classical Greece it was assumed that athletic training developed courage; in nineteenth century England it was assumed that the wars of the British Empire were won on the playing fields of Eton. In our own century, too, many have assumed that athletic training is an aid in the development of good citizens and good soldiers. But in the post Viet Nam era this traditional view met with challenge. Typical of this challenge was a much discussed article by Bruce C. Ogilvie and Thomas A. Tutko in the October 1971 issue of *Psychology Today*. In this article the authors argued that there is "no empirical support for the tradition that sport builds character." The authors clearly had one very special character trait in mind--competitiveness. For a decade that had become disillusioned with the competitive, aggressive, acquisitive aspect of American character, their argument was encouraging news.

But Ogilvie and Tutko's argument did pose a problem for college departments of physical education and recreation. It seemed to divest these departments of significant purpose. After all, if sports did not build character, then varsity sports programs might have to be justified only as entertainment, and this in turn might leave departments of physical education and recreation with little to do except to provide health and recreational programs for the campus.

At this juncture came a bold, ingenious proposal: reconstitute "health, physical education and recreation" as a new subfield of the social sciences. Departments of Health, Physical Education and Recreation would become Departments of Sports Science. This would provide full academic legitimacy for these departments. Moreover, it was seriously argued that varsity sports programs could be retained intact because these programs could be treated as "laboratories" for this new social science.[12]

In the years since this proposal was originally made, the St. Lawrence Department of Health, Physical Education and Recreation has been successfully

---

[12]A straight-faced proposal for a Department of Sports Science--with appropriate "laboratories"--was presented to a Physical Education Colloqium in the Noble Center at St. Lawrence on May 17, 1972.

transformed into the Department of Sport and Leisure Studies. Not surprisingly, however, the proposal for justifying varsity sports programs as social scientific laboratories has been quietly dropped. Still, no one seems to have noticed that varsity athletics are now without an official rationale.

These changes call for comment. First, at least since the Reagan era and the decline of world communism, competition has lost many of its hard line critics, and new studies suggest that sports do contribute to the development of liberal arts competencies.[13] Second, even if Ogilvie and Tutko should happen to be right, and if it should be conclusively demonstrated that physical training--not necessarily sports--does not develop (good) character, this in itself does not constitute an argument for "sports science." Third, while no one would challenge the right of "sports science" to be a bona fide social science, many would question whether the scientific study of sports belongs in the liberal arts curriculum. Some of the advocates of "sports science" have advanced the claim that this science should be included as an independent social science because a lot of people enjoy sports, and because sports constitute a large percentage of the Gross National Product.   However, if popularity or expenditure is to be a criterion for determining the sciences to be included in the liberal arts curriculum, then many traditional sciences will have to be dropped, and a vast number of new sciences will have to added. Not only will there have to be departments of sports science, but there will also have to be new independent social science departments devoted to drug and alcohol consumption, gambling, automobiles, tourism, entertainment, and so on.

"The International Education Program"

On April 10, 1990, the St. Lawrence faculty approved provisions of the "International Education Report" which called for "an international perspective" to be "part of the liberal arts education of all students." The rationale for this proposal was contained in a white paper issued by a faculty committee in May of 1989. Without any reference to the official aims of the college, the committee announced ex cathedra that a liberal education is "the celebration of the life of the intellect." This fact, the committee reasoned, provides the college with two specific obligations. First, the college should "induce in students a sense of cultural identity." This meant that students should have an understanding of their own culture--"the culture of Western Europe and the United States." Second, the college should "induce" in students "cross-cultural sensitivity." This meant that students should not be "cultural chauvinists." A "cultural chauvinist," according to the committee, is anyone who views other cultures as "flawed imitations of a grander tradition." To facilitate the fulfillment of these obligations the committee made a number of proposals including "adding to the diversity of the faculty,"

---

[13]David G. Winter, David C. McClelland, and Abigail J. Stewart, *A New Case for the Liberal Arts* (San Francisco: Jossey-Bass Publishers, 1981).

giving further support to study abroad programs, and "creating an international milieu on campus."

This new "International Education Program" is billed as innovative, and yet it is curiously trendy. One can only marvel at the pre-established harmony that causes all of the colleges in America to be so often simultaneously and identically innovative. The program also seems open-minded as well as high-minded, and yet it has an aura that is suspiciously both coercive and commercial. Consider the following:

1. The program is designed to meet aims which are not in fact the official aims of the college. For instance, the official aims do not call for students to be "induced" into regarding their own culture (however it is defined) as less than superior to other cultures. The college's statement of "Aims and Objectives" does call for students to be tolerant and to respect differing opinions, but it does not call for them to infinitely postpone critical judgment on these opinions, and it does not require them to eventually come to the conclusion that their own culture is less than "grand."

2. The program is supposed to provide an "antidote" to "cultural chauvinism." As we have already observed, this assumes that students, by and large, are in fact "cultural chauvinists." However, no evidence has been produced to justify this assumption, and in fact some respected social critics have argued the very contrary of this. They have argued that today's students are more likely to be cultural relativists than cultural chauvinists.[14]

3. The committee that proposed the program made the assumption that those who believe that "other cultural traditions are at best flawed imitations of a grander tradition" are "cultural chauvinists." This is a misuse of the word "chauvinists." People who believe, for instance, that a democratic culture is superior to a non-democratic culture are not ipso facto cultural chauvinists in the dictionary sense that they have "zealous and belligerent patriotism or blind enthusiasm." There may be perfectly good reasons for believing that one culture is superior to another culture. Even cultural relativists do not appear to be entirely indifferent about the culture within which they live and profess their cultural relativism.

4. The committee that proposed the program attempted to justify its belief that what it calls "cultural chauvinism" is wrong on the ground that it "brings the effort of understanding to a halt." But surely the effort of understanding "comes to a halt," at least temporarily, and properly so, when any inquiry comes to a conclusion. But more importantly, St. Lawrence's educational aims go beyond the need to obtain "understanding." According to the college's statement of "Aims and Objectives," students also need "to develop a system of values against which to judge the use of their knowledge and skills." Students who are liberally educated *should* come to some conclusions about such matters.

---

[14]For instance, see: Allan Bloom, *The Closing of the American Mind* (New York: Simon and Schuster, 1987).

5. What the committee did in its efforts to provide a rationale for the program was to invent its own statement of the aims of the college. But even if this new statement were acceptable, it would not justify the program. For instance, even if one of the aims of the college was to "induce in students cross-cultural sensitivity," and if this is interpreted to mean that students should never view other cultures as "flawed imitations of a grander tradition," there is no proof that the International Education Program would further this purpose. Some students return from abroad programs as converts to cultural chauvinism, not cultural relativism. The committee's rationale assumed that what it called "cultural immersion" will inevitably produce cultural relativists. No proof is given for this assumption. At the same time, many students are now allowed to participate in abroad programs who have little or no interest in foreign cultures or foreign languages, and some of these students return from these programs with little more than tourist interests in foreign cultures and languages.[15] An illustration of this point is provided by Professor Henry Garrity. One day as he was taking some photographs of the Roman Forum he was accosted by a student who, pointing toward the Forum, asked, "Hey, what's all that rubble over there?" and, after suffering uncomfortably through a short but erudite answer, followed it up with the question, "You seem to know your way around here. What's there to do in this town?" Such events are discomforting reminders that many of our students are woefully ignorant of their own culture, and in this respect not superior to those untutored people during the Dark Ages who used the Forum as a place to graze their cattle, evidently unaware of the cultural treasures that surrounded them.

6. The committee also assumed that today "Western culture" is being pushed on students. At St. Lawrence, at least, this is simply not true. The college abolished its required general education course in the "Western Heritage of Faith and Reason" in 1970. Since that time the only required course in the study of culture has been the "Non-Western and Third World Studies" course, initiated in 1989.

7. The weakness of the rationale for the International Education Program raises the suspicion that the program may serve unstated purposes. Seemingly implicit in the rationale is a particular political ideal. This is the "politically correct" ideal of the universal egalitarian society. And the assumed enemy of this ideal is "cultural chauvinism," the belief that some cultures are superior to other cultures. The hero of this global utopia is the "multiculturalist"--the person who "understands" that all values are relative. The advancement of this ideal is thought to require a form of education that will "induce" in students a value system that relativizes all other value systems. The "multiculturalist" feels "empathy" or "solidarity" with other "human beings." This interpretation of the program's rationale is given probability by the argument that today "we live in an age in which effective interaction with other nations is essential not only for

---

[15]See William E. Carroll, "The Experience of Ulysses and the 'Mad Flight' to Study Abroad," *Liberal Education* 69 (1983): 269-272.

economic prosperity but for mutual survival." This statement suggests that the program may subordinate liberal education to a partisan political agenda that will assure "economic prosperity" and "mutual survival." At this point we may have some ground for the suspicion that the International Education Program has been created not so much because it serves the purposes of liberal education but because it serves the purposes of liberal educators.

8. Even if the International Education Program serves educational, not political purposes, there are reasons to question the educational legitimacy of this program. The program cannot be justified on the ground that it develops foreign language proficiency because most of the current abroad programs do not require this proficiency. As we have noted, it is ironic that a college that boasts of an International Education Program does not have a foreign language requirement. The program also cannot be justified on the ground that it is essential to provide students with the alleged benefits of "culture shock." "Culture shock" has not been demonstrated to be essential to liberal education. And even if it could be shown that "culture shock" is essential to liberal education, it would remain to be demonstrated that an International Education Program is the most efficient way to achieve this goal. This program is costly, and is beyond the means of many students. Moreover, curiously enough, those who do participate in this program are ipso facto denied the well-advertised benefits of the college's on-campus curriculum and unique campus environment.

It is difficult to avoid the suspicion that the International Education Program serves the publicity interests of the college more than the purpose of liberal education. After all rationalizations have been heard, the impression remains that this program is one that allows students to enjoy an exotic variety of travel "experiences," but is not really essential to liberal education. Certainly the program takes students to the four corners of the world, but it also takes their parents to the cleaners. Young people, who could just as easily experience the "high" of "culture shock" if they hiked to one of the impoverished hamlets near the college and tried living in a poorly heated shack during January, are flown halfway around the world to experience the same shock by living for a couple of days in a mud hut in Kenya. Young people who don't really know how to read or write are given academic credit for going on expensive guided tours and "experiencing" cultural artifacts that they have never even read about. Of course some educators fervently defend the claim that students cannot be educated unless they experience far off places and peoples, but these educators seem to forget that books can provide good and cheap transportation, and that the greatest philosopher of modern times never left his hometown.[16]

THE CAFETERIA CURRICULUM AND THE ELECTIVE PRINCIPLE

Having critically examined the requirements and the options of the St.

---

[16]Immanuel Kant is said never to have left the vicinity of Königsberg.

Lawrence curriculum, we can attempt a summary generalization: Getting an education is sometimes thought to be like eating a meal. This simile provides a graphic way of envisaging the most general and lamentable defect of the St. Lawrence curriculum. This curriculum is a "cafeteria curriculum." For the most part, students are allowed to choose whatever courses they want to "take" from a sumptuous variety of programs and "course offerings." To amplify the cafeteria analogy, the curriculum has something to satisfy everybody's taste. It has tough and tasteless proteins for scientists; gourmet dishes for aesthetes and litterateurs; raw meat for jocks; exotic foreign dishes for those who tire of the regular domestic fare; and lots of creamed corn and applesauce for the intellectually toothless. There are special lunches for businessmen, engineers, teachers, and army officers; assorted International Education "cultural immersion" junkets; and the latest yeasty desserts hot out of the "innovation" ovens. Everything, of course, is a la carte. It's not cheap, but it's better than most other cafeterias because of the pleasant ambience and friendly employees.

St. Lawrence's "cafeteria curriculum" places only minimal constraints on the students' "freedom" to choose what courses they want to "take." There is a three unit "First Year Program," a three unit set of "Distribution Requirements," and a three unit set of "Graduation Requirements." But these apparent dietary restrictions are gelatinous and produce no nutritional benefits. In the past, for instance, scholarship students who had been exempted from the distribution requirements (a policy that also demeaned the requirements), would unintentionally fulfill the requirements in the process of simply choosing courses on the basis of their individual interests. Moreover, none of the requirements is intended to develop a specific body of knowledge or a specific set of skills. Consequently, each requirement can be satisfied in a variety of ways. Finally, even these constraintless constraints total only nine courses. This means that only about twenty-five percent of the curriculum is even perfunctorily prescribed. The remaining seventy-five or so percent is elected by students on the basis of their current, idiosyncratic interests. This includes the "major" and the "electives."

The "cafeteria curriculum" is typically rationalized by the so-called "elective principle." Thus, the right of students to choose the content of their education is justified on the basis of the assumed right of every individual to pursue his or her own interests.

The "elective principle" has several interpretations. It is sometimes interpreted economically. When this is the case, a "cafeteria curriculum" is justified by the economic argument that in any free market transaction, "if you pays your money, you gets your choice." Students are held to have the rights of consumers, and to be entitled to whatever they can purchase. Needless to say, the buyer gets no caveat.

The "elective principle" may also be interpreted psychologically. When this occurs, a "cafeteria curriculum" is justified by the psychological argument that an education cannot be effective if it is "prescriptive"--that is, "imposed" on students by someone else, and consequently denies to them the right to choose and to satisfy their idiosyncratic interests. It follows that educational efficacy can only be achieved by a "student-centered" curriculum--a curriculum that accords students the right to choose what they want, and thus to "actualize their own potential" and to "do their own thing."

The "elective principle" may also be interpreted politically. When this occurs, a "cafeteria curriculum" is justified by the argument that a prescriptive curriculum is authoritarian and elitist, and thus inappropriate for a democracy.

The attempts to justify the "cafeteria curriculum" by these various interpretations of the "elective principle" are specious, and can be shown to be so as follows:

1. St. Lawrence's statement of "Aims and Objectives" certainly does not promise a curriculum in which students pay their money and take their choice. On the contrary, it promises the students specific benefits, including specific knowledge, specific skills, and specific virtues.

Such curricular promises are appropriate. After all, etymologically, a "curriculum" is a systematized or prescribed sequence or route. In this sense of the word, a "cafeteria curriculum" is a contradiction in terms. It is a course of action that is essentially without purpose or structure. Like children or players in what used to be called "free games," and who make up the rules of each game as it proceeds, a cafeteria curriculum puts those who are uneducated and who hope to be educated in the absurd position of having to prescribe the structure and content of their own education.

Consequently, the fact that students pay--often dearly--for their education no more entitles them to determine the structure and content of their education than the fact that people pay for professional help entitles them to determine the nature of this help. Students need not choose to pursue a liberal education, but once they choose to pursue this end, then by virtue of having made this choice, they also implicitly choose the means that is essential to it.

2. It is an illusion to think that an education cannot be effective if it is prescriptive. A "cafeteria curriculum" itself does not really allow students to escape prescriptiveness. It does allow them to escape any serious comprehensive, liberal education requirements; but it does not allow them to escape the requirements of a major program or the requirements of individual courses. Obviously it is psychologically valuable for students in a program of liberal education to have at least a vague appreciation of the importance of a liberal education. But beyond that, all education by its very nature is inescapably prescriptive.

The prescriptiveness of liberal education is a consequence of the fact that this form of education is committed to the development of people with very specific capacities. This requires that the curriculum have a principle of relevance: some things are essential to it, and other things are at least peripheral to it. Thus, students cannot be permitted to "elect" whatever they please; the curriculum cannot be "flexible" on the essential concerns of the liberally educated person.

Implicit in the psychological arguments for the "student-centered" curriculum is a defective idea of human freedom. It is often said that students are free only if they do as they please. Such "freedom," though, is better described as license. Genuine freedom is best illustrated when individuals act rationally. If this is true, then an education that makes it possible for individuals to act rationally cannot be treated as just an "elective" for those who desire to be free. It is best not to conceive of freedom as a precondition for liberal education, but to conceive of liberal education as a precondition for freedom.

3. The assumption that a "cafeteria curriculum" will protect students from reactionary ideologies is without foundation. If students are propagandized to elect reactionary courses and programs, then the "cafeteria curriculum" will probably develop reactionary students. For the same reason a "cafeteria curriculum" will not protect students from radical ideologies. By its very nature, a "cafeteria curriculum" is likely to reinforce received opinions. It thus leaves the fate of its students to earlier biases, chance, the seductive appeals of political propaganda and commercial advertising, the uncriticized homilies of tribal life, the vagaries of secondary school education, and the indulgent fantasies of teenage culture.

The unjustifiable assumptions of the "elective principle" give witness to the truth that a cafeteria curriculum in the liberal arts college is no less absurd than a cafeteria curriculum in a medical school. To promise students a liberal education, and then to allow them to study whatever they please is as ludicrous and fraudulent as promising students a medical education, and then allowing them to study whatever they please. The liberal arts are no less specifiable than the medical arts. Education, after all, is a way of leading or helping people to achieve certain purposes. If those who need to be led are abandoned to their own uneducated devices, some consequences may follow, but it is sheer fantasy to expect that these consequences would include the development of liberally educated people.

The most general and most egregious flaw in the St. Lawrence curriculum is its acceptance of "the elective principle" and its consequent sponsorship of what is essentially a "cafeteria curriculum." By these acts the college abandons its responsibility for a liberal education.

THE ACADEMIC ENVIRONMENT

During the nineteen sixties and seventies American colleges came under mounting pressure to make major changes in their educational programs. Much of this pressure was generated by the national anxiety following the launch of Sputnik in 1957 and the intensification of the Cold War, and later, by the national disillusionment that followed in the wake of the trauma of Viet Nam. Across the country people hoped for a "cultural revolution" that would usher in a new age, a new man, and a new social order. Typical of the popular and influential expressions of this hope was Charles Reich's *The Greening of America*.[17] In a book that was then required reading for every college student and teacher, Reich faulted American society for its domination by the "consciousness" of the "corporate state," and argued that "the failure of education" was at the center of this problem. He promised that a new kind of education would be the primary means for the development of a new form of consciousness that would enable us to transcend the flawed consciousness of the corporate state.

During this period at St. Lawrence, as at other colleges across the country, efforts were made to "facilitate institutional change." In 1971 a new curriculum with an "experimental" January term was introduced. Faculty members were encouraged to attend "faculty development" workshops, such as the "Humanistic Education Workshop" held at the State University of New York at Albany in 1971. (Here staid faculty members were persuaded to take off their ties, make paper airplanes, go for "blind walks," and make teary-eyed T-group confessions.) Various on-campus events, such as the "Academic Innovation Day" of Saturday, April 24, 1971, were sponsored to encourage new ideas for the curriculum. "Change agents" were imported to campus. Predictably, it was not long before institutional change became fashionable, and ultimately, compulsory.

In spite of the euphoria that accompanied many of the changes made during this period, disenchantment was not many years away. To some of the faculty it soon became disappointingly apparent that curricular changes alone would not be sufficient to bring about the desired educational outcomes.

Research on the impact of college on students confirmed these suspicions. This research produced two conclusions that were both surprising and distressing to most teachers.   The first was that the curriculum itself has a relatively *ins*ignificant educational impact.[18]   Later studies demonstrated that student academic involvement has few effects on the development of liberal arts competencies.[19] The second conclusion from this research was the finding that the academic environment of the liberal arts college does have an important impact on students. Early studies pointed to the subtle but powerful role played by environmental factors, especially social pressures for conformity brought to bear by the student peer culture.[20] Later studies confirmed this conclusion by longitudinal and cross-sectional comparisons of student involvement in various aspects of college experience in relationship to their gains in liberal arts

---

[17]Charles A. Reich, *The Greening of America* (New York: Random House, 1970).

[18]Philip E. Jacob, *Changing Values in College: An Exploratory Study of the Impact of College Teaching* (New York: Harper & Row, Publishers, 1957).

[19]Winter, McClelland, and Stewart, *A New Case for the Liberal Arts*.

[20]Jacob, *Changing Values in College: An Exploratory Study of the Impact of College Teaching*; James S. Coleman, *Equality of Educational Opportunity* (Washington, D. C.: U. S. Department of Health, Education, and Welfare, 1966); Kenneth A. Feldman and Theodore M. Newcomb, *The Impact of College on Students* (San Francisco: Jossey-Bass Publishers, 1969). For an update on this research, see: Earnest T. Pascarella and Patrick T. Terenzini, *How College Affects Students* (San Francisco: Jossey-Bass Publishers, 1991).

competencies.[21] For instance, it was found that the major obstacle to student conceptual growth was the informal student social life centered in dormitories or other housing units. It was also found that growth in leadership capacity and in the cognitive aspects of liberal arts competencies, including critical thinking and intellectuality, seemed to be an effect of the liberal arts college as a whole, and not the effect of any particular institution, least of all the curriculum.

The prescriptions that seemed to be implied by this research were disturbing. The most disturbing one was that if liberal arts colleges wanted to improve the quality of their educational programs, then they should spend less time revising their curricula and more time creating favorable academic environments. It was clear that the most sophisticated curriculum, supported by the highest quality teaching, would not be truly effective unless it had a supportive academic environment. This prescription was a difficult pill for most college teachers to swallow. For many years these teachers had been reluctant to try to structure the academic environment on the ground that such action would be an intrusion on the rights and private lives of their students, and also on the ground that few wanted to be bothered by the frustrations of having to act *in loco parentis*.

Interestingly and embarrassingly enough, many students were leaders in this effort to improve the college's academic environment. During the early seventies one St. Lawrence student, Betsy Cameron, took up the academic environment problem as a research project. In an issue of the *St. Lawrence Journal* she argued that the college's academic environment

exerts . . . a negative influence upon highly motivated students.   [It] provides little incentive to achieve academic excellence.   And this, coupled with pressures to meet social peer priorities and satisfy personal needs, has reduced achievement motivation to a minimum.

As a result, she concluded, there is a "lack of fully developed intellectual potentials among the majority of students." Another student, J. J. Jockel, then the president of student government, and currently a member of the faculty, played an active role in heightening both student and faculty awareness of this problem. He worked to energize student government and to develop better student-faculty relations. Other students, such as Sandy McNair, resisted the departmentalists long enough to establish a multifield major; David Rhodes developed a conversation-oriented coffee house to replace the teen canteen University Center snack bar; and Chris Young succeeded briefly in transforming the student newspaper from a medium for ball scores and social notes to a medium for the exchange of ideas.

Finally, after more than ten years of student and faculty effort, after increasing faculty frustration with extracurricular subversion of the curriculum, and after a few fraternity atrocities, the faculty was goaded into taking action to

---

[21] Winter, McClelland, and Stewart, *A New Case for the Liberal Arts.*

try to improve the academic environment. Eventually, a petition of the faculty led to the appointment of a "Committee on the Academic Environment." This committee presented its report to the faculty on February 9, 1984. It concluded that "dominant social conventions seem to discourage discussion, both inside and outside the classroom, of intellectual issues," and it went ahead to make recommendations for improved student advisement, for an honors program, and for freshmen residential colleges. In 1987 the Freshman Program was initiated. Earlier a new library was built, and cultural programs received increased funding. "Distribution requirements" were repeatedly revised. Meanwhile, with each fall came a freshman class that, according to Cass and Birnbaum, was "very selective," including an ever larger group of scholarship students.

From the mid-eighties on these efforts by faculty and students continued sporadically. While it may be too soon to fully assess the impact of the latest efforts, it seems safe to say that the college's deficient academic environment is still a serious detriment to the success of its educational program.

The failure of all efforts to significantly improve the academic environment invites renewed attempts to understand its causes.

THE PROBLEM OF ANTI-INTELLECTUALITY

To say that the St. Lawrence academic environment is "anti-intellectual" is not to say that St. Lawrence students do not "study hard," "get good grades," or "learn a lot." It means, rather, that most students do not have a deep respect or capacity for intellectual activity.

For many years the college has had a reputation for being "friendly" and "laid-back." It was once known affectionately by its students as "the Country Club of the North." In the 1982-83 edition of the *New York Times Selective Guide to Colleges* the college was described as a place that "is not particularly competitive," and where students "work hard, at least on the weekdays." The college was clearly understood to be a place which was hospitable to students who were "well-rounded"--a code word that meant that the college was not intellectually demanding. It was often said, pridefully, that the college "didn't overemphasize the intellect."

Any observer of student behavior, and certainly anyone who speculates on the cause of campus anti-intellectuality, cannot fail to notice the enormous influence of the student peer group culture. As any teacher knows, it is common for a student to drop out of school for no other reason than because he or she was not pledged by a particular fraternity or sorority. Herd behavior accounts for much alcohol and drug abuse. Any teacher who has taught more than a year cannot help but notice the contrast between the vitality of the student extracurricular life and the sleepy anxiety, dullness, and superficial interest exhibited by many students towards most curricular activities. Studies have confirmed this impression, showing that twenty years after graduation most students cannot recall the name of a single professor or the general content of a single course. And yet these same students will vividly remember a football victory, a fraternity prank, or a beer blast. These reflections suggest that the student peer group, operating outside the curriculum, has considerably more impact on students than the faculty operating within the curriculum. Research has shown that the curriculum, dependent upon grades and limited teacher-student relationships, is both opposed and defeated by the student peer group culture with its complex, subtle, and powerful system of social rewards and punishments.

What are the characteristics of this dominant student peer group culture? The sociologist Nevitt Sanford provides a description. "Students," he writes,

> are expected to be friendly, cooperative, and pleasant toward one another, and polite, dutiful, and impersonal toward the faculty. College is to be taken seriously, but not too seriously; frivolity is discouraged, but outstanding faculty work is only tolerated, not applauded . . . .[22]

With respect to ideas and issues, he continues, students are expected to be "open minded and noncontroversial," and, above all, "to avoid unpleasantness." In looking to the future they optimistically envision "a stable but highly complex society in which the rewards for 'fitting in' will be a happy--that is to say, a materially gratifying--life."

This prominent characteristic of the student peer group culture is what may be called the "social adjustment ethic." Students come to believe that their most important task is to learn to "fit in." They are told that they should be "well-rounded," "well-adjusted," and "well-liked." The peer group members are ever alert to what "they" say should be said and done and worn. Moderation and leveling, discrimination against deviance from accepted norms of behavior, speech, and dress, are common. Even nonconformity is transformed into a style-conscious, conformist nonconformity. (For example, blue jeans, originally adopted by the youth counter-culture out of sympathy with the working classes and in protest against the conformism of the corporate state in the 1960's, soon became completely stylized, properly bleached, worn, and provided with holes for the knees.) This obsessive, priggish attachment to propriety in the student culture fits the dictionary definition of the word, "prudery." The prudery that results from the "social adjustment ethic" obviously differs from the sexual prudery of a century ago, and so there is no call for quaint Victorian practices such as covering the legs of pianos, but contemporary prudery is no less silly. Peer group members anxiously switch from thin ties to fat ties to no ties, from flat tops to Afros to Bart Simpsons, from minis to maxis to mods, from fruit boots to mod boots to running shoes, from this idea to that idea with robot-like obedience to television advertisers and rock stars. The student peer group culture is a prudish culture, and it is patently a serious pollutant in the academic environment of the college.

---

[22]Nevitt Sanford, *Where Colleges Fail: A Study of the Student As a Person* (San Francisco: Jossey-Bass, 1967): 148.

It is also clear that a prudish student peer culture is highly resistant to remedies. This can only suggest that there are powerful needs that sustain this culture, and that overwhelm the best efforts of reformers. The students' passionate attachment to the norms of the peer group unmistakably points to their irrepressible desire for social acceptance. This desire to be "in" is especially intense among young adults who have left the familiar environment of the home and who find themselves for the first time outside the security of the family. The existential psychoanalysts have gone even further to suggest that this obsessive desire for social acceptance is itself a manifestation of a more general flight from anxiety in the face of human finitude. Unable to reconcile themselves to the unbridgeable chasm between human aspirations and an indifferent world, too many too often seek consolation in the conformity, leveling, and bigotry of a prudish culture. Prudery is thus a psychic security blanket, an antidote to anxiety. It relieves the terrible feelings of Being-lost.

However, given the high moral aims of liberal education, it is manifest that prudery is a kind of "cop-out" morality. It covers up the truth and evades moral obligation. And it is apparently because of this tendency that a prudish student peer group culture is detrimental to the academic environment of the college. Prudery provides the comfortable fiction of social acceptance in the place of a rigorous intellectual honesty. It substitutes ritual and custom for genuine moral responsibility. It thus offers the student a sanctuary from the competition of ideas and ideals, and ultimately, from the threat of failure, both as a student and as a human being. It offers us an ideal man, well-heeled, not too bright, but loyal and pubescently virile. It offers us an ideal woman, well-heeled, not too bright, but socially adept and caring. Among the graffiti carved into the desks of the Owen D. Young library is one that summarily illustrates the way that prudery de-eroticizes the intellectual life. "I'm hungry, thirsty, sleepy, and horny," writes a well-rounded male student. And below it a sympathetic female student has provided the appropriate maternal and prudish reinforcement by writing, "Poor baby!"

If there is any truth to this suggestion that the prudery of the student peer group culture is the cause of the anti-intellectuality of the college's academic environment, then the college's previous efforts to improve its academic environment have too often treated the symptoms of the disease and not its cause. The college is constantly reinfected by anti-intellectuality because the campus is dominated by a prudish student peer group culture.

A faculty is reluctant to try to structure the academic environment simply because of the frustrations and time demands of this effort, especially at a time when colleges are more likely to reward discipline-oriented scholarship than student-oriented teaching. But the truth is that, if the faculty is unwilling to structure this environment, the student peer culture will. Once this occurs, as all can plainly see, the academic environment is effectively abandoned to a subtle tyranny that subverts the curriculum and the entire enterprise of liberal education.

SPECIAL PROBLEMS OF THE ACADEMIC ENVIRONMENT

We turn now from an attempt to provide a general characterization of the college's academic environment to an examination of several of the most obdurate problems of this environment.

1. "Anti-intellectuality and Fraternity"

Teachers have often aired the charge that one of the major causes of the college's anti-intellectual environment is the social fraternity system. Over the years many teachers have reluctantly come to the conclusion that no amount of effort to design an excellent curriculum and to conduct outstanding courses can ever make much educational difference as long as these efforts take place in an environment strongly influenced by fraternity conformism, temporizing, hooliganism, alcoholism, partying, and post-party soporiferousness. But faculty criticism of the fraternity system has always been subtly repressed. Except in reference to some recent atrocity, such criticism does not seem to advance a teacher's career or social life. Among students, colleagues, and administrators, faculty criticism of social fraternities seems to ignite unknown passions, and to turn friends into enemies in the course of a single conversation. To most students such criticism is a faculty intrusion into the domain of student rights. Among many teachers this criticism is offensive as a kind of paternalistic insolence. To administrators--especially to those who note that fraternity members are typically the most loyal alumni of the college--it seems to be a personal affront and an expression of an intellectualist arrogance. Published criticism is certain to bring indignant letters from student leaders and successful alumni. Exasperated by this repression, and convinced by my own experience as a fraternity member and teacher that the social fraternities have a significant responsibility for the college's deficient academic environment, I tried to advance discussion on this problem in an article that I wrote for the student newspaper during the seventies. It describes a problem that existed then and persists now:

One day not too many years ago I was joined to a social fraternity. I served my pledgeship, I was initiated into the secrets, and I had many experiences that I am only now beginning to understand.

It was a difficult problem of adjustment for me. I was disturbed about having to conform to a system that often seemed superficial, if not immoral. Still, few on the inside really complained and few on the outside knew what was going on in the inside. I struggled to adjust myself to what I reluctantly came to assume were the facts of life.

I recall how uncomfortable I was as a pledge. The actives were so cocky. They talked a lot about clothes and about "impressing " people. After dinner they would sit around smoking cigarettes over interminable card games and argue over sports statistics. I wondered why they never talked about their studies. After all, they were going to college to get an education, weren't they? They talked a lot about girls, too. Mostly about "getting into their pants." And they drank a lot of beer.

One night there was a racket outside the pledges' room. One of the actives was smashed again. He had a bottle of beer in one hand and one of his legs was stuck in a metal wastebasket. He staggered and shuffled along the hall on one leg, banging into everything. It was funny, and reckless. At every house party Bud Rudd would get out his saxophone. There would be frenzied dancing and yelling. Some of the actives would pass out and lay half-submerged on the beer covered floor, staring at the ceiling. Later there would be some wild drag races. And still later someone who slept next to me in the dorm belched, leaned over his bed, and vomited on the floor. It was all disgusting and it was hilarious, too. I couldn't quite make up my mind.

The Mondays after were not so fun. In fact, on Monday nights we had "Vespers." The draperies were drawn and the pledges were lined up for several hours of verbal and physical abuse. We were always "on your ass" and "lower than whale shit" and "never going to be initiated." We were supposed to memorize the Pledge Manual. I could never understand what possible good could result from memorizing the location of every one of the fraternity's chapters in the United States. Still, everyone did it. And if you wanted to be a Sigma Chi badly enough, you would do it. Later in the evening we did endurance calisthenics in the dining room.

Those late night workouts didn't help my accounting class. It met every morning at 7:30. Mr. Goyert warned me about handing problems in late. But I soon learned that he was "anti-fraternity." (Was it sour grapes because he was never rushed?) The actives warned us not to trust the faculty. I kept urging myself: Stick it out a little longer; after initiation you'll be able to rescue your studies, your sleep, and your sanity. In the meantime I made good use of the fraternity files. And I didn't mind whenever they dimmed the lights in Art Appreciation.

In addition to "Vespers" the pledges were expected to stage an occasional "walkout." We were told to sneak out of the house some evening, take in a movie, and then try to get back in the house. It was clean fun. Doors and windows and heads were routinely smashed. Of course there was no way that the pledges could win. If they broke in, they would be punished for walking out; if they didn't break in, they would be punished for failing to break in. At the time I didn't realize how symbolic it was. But it certainly made European History pretty dull.

The actives frequently lectured us on our responsibilities to the fraternity. Individually we were nothing; the fraternity was everything. Each person demonstrated his love for the fraternity by serving it in some way. One was either an athlete, an "activities man," a "personality boy," or a "brain." The athletes were the most honored. They were known by everyone (especially by the university administration and the alumni) and their only local duties seemed to be to wear their varsity sweaters and to help recruit more athletes for the house. The "activities men" played no-holds-barred campus politics. They would start out by emptying wastebaskets in the University Center, work their way up to a BMOC job, pay off their coalition, shaft their opponents, and get into Blue Key. It was considered good practice for the real world. "Personality boys" were expected to be the nattiest dressers and the smoothest talkers. Their most important responsibility was to date the sharpest women in the most prestigious sororities, specifically, Theta (rich and glamorous), Kappa (rich and wholesome), and Pi Phi (rich and stacked), and to avoid involvement with independents and the lower caste sororities, such as AOPi, otherwise known as "the House of Housemothers." Naturally the "personality boys" were expected to fix up all of the "yo-yos" for the house social functions. The "brains" included anyone who studied on Thursday nights. Their responsibility was to keep the house's GPA higher than the Beta's.

And finally there was Hell Week--officially known as "Help Week." It all began one night when the pledges were awakened by a hideous scream outside of the dorm. The lights flickered violently. In rushed a mob of drunken, teenage maniacs. As the pledges stumbled out of bed we were showered with ice water. Our rooms were in an indescribable mess. Doors were off their hinges. Books and clothes were maliciously dumped on the floors and covered with shredded paper and water and broken furniture. When we assembled in the living room, the drapes were drawn, and there stood all of the actives, boards in hand.

For four days and four nights we were almost continuously awake. Every night the house was completely torn up and piled knee-deep with hundreds of pounds of shredded newspaper. Every morning between 4:00 a.m. and 8:00 a.m. it had to be cleaned up. Every night we hopped and skipped to the crack of the boards. There was "ping pong" (with the pledges being the balls) and endless "duck-walking." For "Minnesota Shift" we formed a circle and put one thumb in our mouth and the other thumb in the anus of the "pledge brother" in front of us. Then we would move around while the actives roared with laughter. At the command, "Shift!" we would reverse our direction and switch the thumbs. The actives roared again.

Every night we looked forward to our "good night kiss." We had to line up, drop our pants, hold our genitals, and let each senior hit us. The smallest always hit the hardest. One night we had to put soda crackers between our heads and the wall as we leaned over. If a cracker broke as we were being hit, we had to do it again. I remember being hit by the house president. He had told me when I pledged that the board wasn't used on our campus.

Several times during Hell Week some of us talked of depledging. But the idea that Hell Week was an ordeal for testing our manhood, or for some other mysterious and transcendent purpose, was too deeply ingrained in our minds. In addition, we knew that the secrets of initiation and the advantages of fraternity membership were but a few days away.

The initiation ceremony was as ridiculous as the "pledge training" was repulsive. But to many it generated all of the passions of a primitive religious ritual. There was the ethereal "Prelude" from Wagner's *Parsifal*. And lots of candles and middle-aged alumni adolescents and angelic-looking hypocrites standing around in sheets. There were seven founders of the fraternity and, miraculously, there were seven official ideals. Afterwards there were firm handshakes, misty eyes, a steak dinner, and lots of good fellowship.

Today I look back in anger and embarrassment on my fraternity experience. Certainly I had some good times and made some good friends. But while gaining these I forfeited a chance for an education.

Unquestionably the social fraternity changes from generation to generation. And yet its basic characteristics--those that enable it to flourish and to gain fanatical support, and those that made it persistently anti-intellectual--tend to remain the same. What is the source of its enduring attraction? And why is the fraternity house so often opposed to the House of Intellect?

An answer to both of these questions is suggested once we realize that traditionally the social fraternity has been the apotheosis of prudery. The ethic of social adjustment with its conformism, collectivism, and bigotry have been persistent throughout the history of the institution. All members of the fraternity are bothers--that is, they are accepted solely on the basis of a quasi-blood, family relationship. The secure environment of the fraternity with its lifetime guarantee of social acceptance stands in striking contrast to the competitive environment of education where there is always the problem of making the grade, of possible non-acceptance. Thus the source of the continuing attraction of the fraternity and the source of its anti-intellectuality are the same. The human desire for social acceptance--to be "in"--is the unseen energy that has sustained the fraternity and nourished its anti-intellectuality. In this respect the social fraternity is a religion of Bad Faith: As a pledge one suffers the hell of social exclusion. Upon initiation one is humiliated, confesses his humility, and receives the grace of social inclusion. Like the guileless fool in *Parsifal*, the initiate is awarded the Holy Grail on the basis of his sociability, not on the basis of his intellectuality. People who are not yet adults barter a difficult but courageous independence for the prudish, comfortable fiction that all men in the bonds are brothers irrespective of their thoughts and their actions. One can only wonder how this self-abasement and anti-intellectuality can be tolerated by educational institutions. And one cannot help but wonder how much of the anti-intellectuality of our campus is due to fraternity prudery.

2. "Anti-intellectuality and Athletics"

For some faculty members another of the seemingly intractable causes of the anti-intellectual academic environment of the college is varsity athletics. But even more than the fraternity problem, this problem is almost impossible to confront in a critical way. There are simply too many people who are firmly committed to the status quo in college athletics. Worst of all, the people who conduct these programs are fellow teachers and friends. Not only this, but the Sports and Leisure Studies Department is superbly staffed with outstanding coaches and teachers. This means that any criticism of college athletics runs the strong risk of being interpreted as the betrayal of a friendship or as an attack on a colleague's right to exist. A few faculty members have made courageous efforts to confront this issue. During the nineteen seventies I tried to contribute to this effort in another article which I wrote for the student newspaper. While some of the details in this article are dated, the problem that it addresses is, in my mind, still acute:

Many people have charged that much of the blame for our prudery and anti-intellectuality should be placed on our intercollegiate athletics program. It has never been easy to judge the merits of this charge. Tempers have been short. And personalities have intruded upon the issues. Minds have been made up before questions were asked. The Sports and Leisure Studies Department has vast and varied facilities, a large and talented staff, and numerous responsibilities. The latter include an intercollegiate athletics program, a Sports and Leisure Studies "majors" program, a "service" program (because of the "Physical Education" requirement), an intramural sports program, and a recreational program. In the past it has been exceedingly difficult for the faculty and students to get information--especially budgetary information--on these diverse activities.

Fortunately we now have the report of the Athletics Commission. The members of the Commission--Professor R. Lufburrow (chairman), D. Hall, D. Johnston, E. Russell, J. Street, and R. N. Wells--deserve credit for producing a 121 page document that appears to be a model of objectivity and thoroughness. The report provides substantiation for the charge that the intercollegiate athletics program does in fact adversely affect our academic environment. The report also helps us to understand how this situation occurs.

1. At the root of the problem is a 14 sport intercollegiate program

that receives massive financial support. Since the Commission's repeated requests to the administration for information about specific items of the university budget were not acknowledged, the Commission had to rely on information contained in the famous "purloined budget" of 1971. On the basis of that budget the Commission estimates that the total funds assigned to the Sport and Leisure Studies Department "probably exceeds $690,000 which is more than 10 percent of the funds devoted to the part of the budget called Education and General Student Aid . . . ." This is a sum equal to one eighth of all student tuition. The great bulk of these funds is used in direct or indirect support of the intercollegiate athletics program. Since the college's financial resources are limited, the strong support given to this program inevitably means that the academic program must receive less support. For instance, while we annually spend almost three quarters of a million dollars on extracurricular athletics activities, we have less than $15,000 to spend on extracurricular cultural activities.

2. The intercollegiate program is given such priority that the "service" program and the recreational and intramural programs suffer neglect. The Commission reports that instruction in the men's "service" program is done by only one full time equivalent faculty member and four graduate students. The intramural program is supervised by only one faculty member who also carries one of the heaviest teaching loads and coaches three teams. The recreational program receives the lowest priority of all. Facilities that are not preempted by other programs are usually opened for recreational use. Meanwhile the full time effort of the equivalent of ten faculty members is devoted to the intercollegiate program. For many it seems incongruous that programs in which all students can participate are so slighted while the intercollegiate athletics program, in which only 20 percent of the students (mostly men) can participate, is so generously favored.

3. The intercollegiate program is supported by a Sports and Leisure Studies "major" program whose aim is at variance with the aims of the college. The Commission found that about 40 percent of the Sports and Leisure Studies majors are on athletic scholarships. This suggests that the major program is used at least in part to subsidize the intercollegiate program. The stated objective of the major program is "to develop a high degree of competence in those men who desire to qualify for Sports and Leisure Studies positions . . . ." The major program is thus unabashedly vocational, and obviously in conflict with our "Statement of Aims and Objectives." For many, incidentally, it seems odd that we successfully resist the temptation to offer a major in education while we somehow cannot resist the temptation to offer a major in Sports and Leisure Studies.

4. The intercollegiate program biases our admissions policy. The

Commission reports that "the admissions policy is skewed to support the athletics program by encouragement of recruiting by the coaches, by facilitation of the application of potential athletes, and . . . by the liberal scholarship support for athletes." In fact--and this is a shocking fact--the Commission estimates that "about half of the men in the freshmen class are athletes encouraged by (if not selected by) the recruiting efforts of the Sport and Leisure Studies Department. Given this situation, is it any wonder that we so often find ourselves troubled by the lack of diversity in our student body? "The diversity we presently seek," the Commission notes, "seems aimed at the goal of matching the freshman class to the diversity of our sports program." And is it now any wonder that we are so frequently distressed by the anti-intellectuality of our student body? Imagine the dramatic transformation that would take place in our academic atmosphere if, for instance, the English Department or the History Department recruited half the members of each freshman class.

5. The intercollegiate program biases the college's scholarship policy. The Commission found 73 percent of the scholarship funds available to freshman men were granted to athletes. Under the present policy, then, when financial need is equal, three out of four scholarships go to applicants who play a sport rather than to those who have other talents. In addition, the Commission estimates that 50 percent of the Sports and Leisure Studies majors are on scholarships. Not many academic departments can give such generous encouragement to their majors.

6. The intercollegiate program frequently interferes with the academic programs and the academic work of the athletes. Athletic events are often in conflict with scheduled classes and cultural events. Moreover, the Commission studied the work loads of the athletes and concluded that in terms of their overall commitment athletes carry the equivalent of at least six units of work, while the normal work load is four units. This suggests that it is not unusual for the athlete's academic program to be considerably compromised by the demands his sport makes upon him.

In these various ways, and in spite of its many valuable contributions, our intercollegiate athletics program aggravates the anti-intellectuality of our campus. With a staff of 16 faculty members, 16 full or part-time aids, a full-time member of the Public Relations staff, generous financial support, an astonishing influence on admissions and scholarship practices, and attractive and varies facilities--including one (the Riding Arena) with a budget that exceeds the instructional budgets of 9 of the 20 academic departments--the Sports and Leisure Studies Department has been able to maintain a large intercollegiate athletics program and to nourish a student culture strongly oriented to sports and saturated with sports values. The meager rewards for intellectual achievement--an inflated grade, a discredited Phi Beta Kappa key, a bare name buried in some Dean's List--pale by comparison to the heroic rewards for athletic achievement--varsity letters, sterling trophies, sports page headlines, cheering crowds, brass bands, beaming fathers, and smiling mothers, coaches, and cheer leaders. Only a small group of independent and inner-directed students can be expected to maintain a commitment to intellectual ideals in such a hostile academic environment.

* * * *

We can now summarize the criticism that has been brought against the college's educational program:

1. The present curriculum does not provide students with what the college has promised them. Much less does it provide them with anything that is justifiably called a liberal education.

The college promises its students "breadth" in learning, but this is interpreted to mean only that they have sampled a natural science, a social science, and something that is not a natural or a social science. It allows its students to graduate without a knowledge of their own culture or their own history. The college also promises its students that their education will help them to understand their "role in the world" and to "enlarge their knowledge of their obligations," but the curriculum does not require them to make any systematic study of personal and political values and obligations. While all students are required to sample the empirical sciences (such as the natural sciences and the social sciences), they are not required to even sample the normative sciences (such as ethics, politics, and the cultural sciences). These sciences are treated as mere electives for those who just happen to be interested.

The college claims to be a liberal arts college, but it gives no systematic attention to the liberal arts. While it requires its students to have some "exposure" to the sciences that study "nature," "social interactions," and "textual, visual, and the musical relations," it does not require them to develop any of the universal intellectual skills that once justified a curriculum as being a "liberal arts" curriculum.

The college promises its students "integration" in learning, but at best encourages only integration that stops short at the level of specialized, departmentalized knowledge. Students are allowed to graduate without any study of fundamental ontological, epistemological, moral, or political principles. Even though the college clearly states in its *Catalogue* that its students are expected to enlarge their knowledge of their obligations and to improve their ability to act on the basis of them, it makes no effort to help develop this knowledge and ability.

2. The college's academic environment is not intellectually stimulating because it is dominated by a prudish, conformist student peer group culture that is

hostile to intellectual values. Duped by the social adjustment ethic and by the specious argument that what the students do "outside the classroom" is their own business, the college tolerates an environment in which the virtues in the curriculum become the vices in the extracurriculum. The classroom hero becomes the "impudent snob" or "pointy-headed intellectual" outside the classroom.   And the hung-over party boy becomes the "well-rounded" extracurricular hero. While committee after committee calls for improvements in the academic environment, the college continues to permit extracurricular conflicts with scheduled classes, a snack bar with the ambience of a country club cocktail lounge, an intercollegiate athletics program that seems to wag the dog, an astonishing sports bias in our admissions policies, empty classrooms before and after vacations, and fraternity beer blasts that convulse entire neighborhoods.

St. Lawrence's educational program often provides its students with information about subjects that interest them. And during their four years of campus life students are almost certain to have many interesting experiences. But, as we have seen, this educational program is not what the college has promised its students. Much less is it anything that has any claim to be called a liberal education.   A "cafeteria curriculum" filled with "interesting" ideas collected together as "themes," and an anti-intellectual academic environment dominated by the tyranny of the student peer group culture combine to produce an academic program that seems to be designed more for entertainment than for education. What is called a "a program of liberal education" is more honestly described as an "academic theme park."

4

THE DISPOSSESSED

*I can think of no more conspicuous failure of leadership than in the
liberal arts colleges. With a few notable exceptions, the record of the
college is one of failure, at least if judged by its own claims. Whatever
else it may be, Socratic it is not, in faculty, in style, in results. This I take
to be a matter of fact. Certainly it is hard to imagine a more damningly
documented indictment of the liberal arts college than that of the Jacob
study, with its bleak conclusion that, apart from three or four colleges,
the effect of college teaching on student values is simply nil, zero, and
that what small change occurs comes from the student subculture. The
conclusion is all the more devastating because it is precisely on the
claim to teach that the American college stakes its case. Here . . . its
failure has been spectacular.*

William Arrowsmith, "The Future of Teaching"

St. Lawrence's confusion about its institutional purpose has not only had
tragic consequences for its relationship to society and for its educational program,
but it has also had similar consequences for its teachers and teaching. To describe
these consequences we consider the present status of the college teacher. We look
first at the professional goals, character, pedagogy, and professional resources of
the teacher, and then at the major conditions for teaching--the faculty
organization, the teacher compensation system, the administrative personnel
practices, and the teaching facilities.

THE TEACHER

1. CAREERISM

"The academic life may be busy and anxious, but it is the business and
anxiety of careerist ambition that fills it, not that of dangerous venture." So wrote
Theodore Roszak in *The Dissenting Academy*.[1] No statement about the current

condition of the American professoriate could be more true, more insightful, or more disturbing.   We cannot doubt that this statement aptly applies to St. Lawrence.

Many of the college's teachers do not share a sense of transcendent purpose or even magisterial obligation. The suggestion that they collectively have a high moral purpose is most likely to be scorned as arrogant and delusory. By and large, these teachers understand themselves as they are understood by others. They are employees--persons whose duties are properly assigned to them by their employers, by those who hold legal authority and who wield economic power. Not surprisingly, therefore, the wellspring of their energy is careeristic ambition. That this is so can be seen in the their slavish participation in administrative "faculty development" programs, in their ability to be endlessly stimulated by "departmental empire building" and "program development," in their insatiable appetite for personal publicity and media "exposure," and in their willingness to be conditioned by the transparently Pavlovian devices of a so-called "merit pay system."

Social scientific studies provide confirmation of this widespread college teacher subservience to careeristic ambition. One such study is Caplow and McGee's book on the academic labor market.[2] Convincing anecdotal evidence is provided by academic novels, such as Kingsley Amis' *Lucky Jim* and David Lodge's story of Professor Morris Zapp in *Small World*. Personal confirmation is more difficult to obtain, at least during the daylight hours. But once the sun sets and happy hour arrives, off-guard or off-the-record conversations frequently leave little to doubt. At those times "everyone knows" that "advancing one's career" is "just the name of the game."

2. DISEMPOWERMENT

The Disempowered Teacher

St. Lawrence University publicly identifies itself as a teaching college. In its official "Statement of Aims and Objectives" the college commits itself to the "primacy of teaching" with the following declaration:

> Because St. Lawrence is a liberal arts college dedicated to the individual, its faculty members are committed to maintaining the primacy of teaching and to assisting one another to realize their utmost potential as teachers.

For many students and parents familiar with the rigorous labor-saving

---

[1]Theodore Roszak, *The Dissenting Academy* (New York: Pantheon Books, 1968).

[2]Theodore Caplow and Reece J. McGee, *The Academic Marketplace* (New York: Basic Books, Inc., 1958).

efficiencies of even the most prestigious colleges, this declaration must sound appealing.[3] For these students and parents one of the most desired features of an undergraduate college is a teacher-intensive educational program.

Unfortunately, at St. Lawrence, as at so many contemporary liberal arts colleges, the "priority of teaching" is a promise that is not honestly kept. Since 1977, college policy has made teacher promotion and tenure conditional on the teacher's demonstrated ability to make "important contributions to scholarship and the arts." Today at St. Lawrence no teacher can be promoted to a professorship without "substantial professional productivity."[4] Not even the most outstanding teachers are exempt from this policy.

Things were not always this way. Years ago, when I was first interviewed by the college, I inquired about the policy on publishing because I had decided that I wanted to be a college teacher, not a scholar. My interviewer gave me good news. He told me simply: "We're happy if you do, but not unhappy if you don't." I decided then that I had found the right place to commit my professional life.

Unfortunately for many who make such irreversible career decisions, the promises of one college administration are not always kept by succeeding administrations. In the late nineteen seventies administrative attitudes at St. Lawrence began to tilt towards a de facto "publish or perish" policy, seemingly occasioned by the emergence of a buyer's market for college teachers. These attitudes soon found their way into academic policies and practices.

The liberal arts colleges that adopted these policies and practices are now reaping their predictable consequences. Increasingly, students are taught by teachers who by and large try to do justice to their teaching, but who are fully aware that their professional advancement is primarily determined by their scholarly "productivity." When there is a choice between an hour spent with students and an hour spent in research, the teacher's office door will close, and the microfilm reader will go on. All the while, paradoxically, most of those who are doing research would rather be teaching. A recent study found that seventy-two percent of university and college faculty members said that their primary interest was in teaching rather then research.[5] This disparity between what the majority of college students and their parents want and what they get, together with the disparity between what the great majority of college teachers want to do and what they have to do, marks a problem of increasing consequence.

This problem is exacerbated by certain practices. First, while colleges may insist that they are only interested in teachers who "keep up with their fields," their practices reveal the truth that they are really interested in publications and publicity. Research and scholarship that do not see print count for little or nothing. Second, although colleges often state that scholarship is secondary in importance to teaching, studies have shown that as a matter of practice teaching effectiveness is often taken for granted, and "scholarly productivity" becomes the

---

[3] A Harvard freshman recently reported that his smallest class exceeded 350 students.

[4] *St. Lawrence University Faculty Handbook*, 56.

[5] Lynne V. Cheney, "The Phantom Ph. D. Gap," *New York Times* (28 September 1989), A27.

sine qua non for professional advancement. Third, a Carnegie Foundation survey found that thirty-eight percent of polled faculty members reported that their publications were only quantitatively counted, not qualitatively examined, for tenure and promotion decisions. Given these kinds of malpractices, it is little wonder that cynicism and careerism are rife among the professoriate, and that, not surprisingly, college teaching has suffered significantly.

The Disempowered Faculty

To illustrate the importance that they attach to teaching, liberal arts colleges frequently advertise their favorable student/faculty ratios. St. Lawrence, for instance, recently reported a student/faculty ratio of less than 12/1. This is a relatively good ratio, and is often taken to mean that, with an enrollment of about 2,000 and a faculty of about 170, the typical class would have about twelve students. But this assumption is certainly not true, and why it is not true is of great importance. While the number of students is easily determined, it is not so easy to determine the number of faculty members. For one thing, the college does not have a definition of faculty membership. In the past, efforts have been made to formulate such a definition, but these efforts have failed because of a lack of agreement on the defining criteria. Some have held that all those employed by the college who hold a doctoral degree should count as faculty members. But this definition is objectionable because some faculty members do not hold the doctoral degree, and many people employed by the college who do hold the doctoral degree have little or nothing to do with teaching. Others have held that all those employed by the college who conduct classroom instruction should count as faculty members. But this definition founders on the fact that librarians and artists-in-residence are presumed to be faculty members, but they may not provide classroom instruction. In addition, some administrators, and occasionally even students, may provide classroom instruction, but presumably they should not be counted as faculty members. Another possibility would be to define faculty membership on the basis of an instructional relationship with students. But then coaches and counselors would count as faculty members, and they are usually presumed not to count as faculty members. Over the past few years the St. Lawrence faculty has included various program directors, professors, associate professors, assistant professors, and instructors, some of whom are tenured and some of whom are nontenured, adjuncts and visiting teachers of all ranks, the dean of students, some coaches, librarians, ROTC instructors, the chaplain, the academic dean and the associate dean, the athletic trainer, and the president of the university. Recently there have even been suggestions that certain administrators be given "courtesy appointments" to the faculty (although to date no one has suggested that any faculty member be given a "courtesy appointment" to the administration). It is a mind-bending conundrum to imagine what all of the people who are now classified as faculty members have in common that qualifies them for faculty membership.

But even if we ignore the problem of defining faculty membership, and simply follow the current policy of shamelessly counting as faculty members all those who are appointed to be faculty members, we cannot ignore the fact that this number is in important respects a grossly inflated number. For example, while St. Lawrence now counts close to 170 faculty members, roughly forty-four percent of these are without tenure, and are thus without any institutional protection of academic freedom. Since teachers by profession are committed to the profession of their beliefs, and since the beliefs of some are often offensive to others, those who teach without any institutional protection of academic freedom do so at considerable personal risk. (It should be emphasized here that what is meant by academic freedom is not merely the teacher's freedom to speak in a classroom about a microspeciality, but the freedom to speak out on the range of issues that are germane to liberal education. This is the kind of academic freedom that is essential to the vitality of any liberal arts college.) The risk that must be borne by nontenured faculty members is intensified for roughly thirty-seven percent of them because they are only marginally connected with the college as "adjunct" or visiting teachers, typically on one year contracts. Moreover, of the remaining tenured faculty members, about fifty-six percent are probationary in the sense that they are below the rank of professor, and are thus subject to administrative review for promotion. While the members of this group cannot be fired without cause, they can be kept indefinitely on a probationary status and at low compensation levels.

These considerations lead to the conclusion that, out of a total faculty membership of approximately 170, less than twenty-five percent are nonprobationary, and thus have vested academic autonomy. But on the basis of another consideration even this reduced number is still inflated. This is because about forty percent of these nonprobationary faculty members have administrative responsibilities as program directors or department chairs. This means that in terms of their responsibilities close to one-half of the nonprobationary faculty members are more appropriately classified as administrators than as faculty members. This is true because these faculty members are required to varying extents to execute administrative policy, and the execution of administrative policy is certain to involve constraints on their autonomy. These faculty members are not likely to be able to consistently put loyalty to their beliefs over loyalty to their administrative superiors. This expectation has been repeatedly confirmed in practice.

Because so many individuals who are classified as members of the faculty are not able to act with all of the rights and obligations of faculty members, the faculty is in effect considerably smaller than it is represented to be. Presently, only about 15% of the faculty are nonprobationary and uncompromised by administrative responsibilities. Thus, if we subtract from the faculty those who are not fully empowered to act as faculty members, the college's student/faculty ratio is more on the order of 80/1, not 12/1. While these numbers hardly provide any kind of quantitative fix on this problem, they do mark one of the most pressing of all academic problems. The plain truth is that the great majority of college teachers are compromised by their probationary status or their administrative responsibilities.   Finally, when we combine those who are compromised in these ways with those whose teaching is compromised by publication requirements, we have what is perhaps the most intractable and insidious of all academic problems: teacher disempowerment. The great majority of college teachers are not genuinely empowered to act as faculty members, and they are not genuinely empowered to teach.

3. LOGOCENTRISM

Dogmatic opinions have considerable inertia. Sometimes this is due to the fact that these opinions are heavily loaded with the hopes and egos of their sponsors. But at other times these opinions may be weighted out of honest beliefs and respect for teachers and tradition. In spite of this inertia, dogmatic opinions are sometimes discovered for what they are.   These discoveries are often traumatic, even when they occur within the liberal arts college, an institution supposedly hospitable to the criticism of ideas. People who have been awakened to the realization that their ideological investments have failed and that their cherished beliefs are built on the quicksands of illusion are not likely to be happy.

My own experience confirms these generalizations. When I first began teaching, I uncritically accepted many of the familiar educational assumptions of that time. I assumed that the gray haired scholarly experts whom I had known as teachers were models worthy of imitation.   These people were distinguished scholars responsible for the production and reproduction of specialist theory. Like many teachers, I designed my own college courses on the pattern of my graduate school courses taught by these scholarly experts. A logic course that I gave is a case in point. I ignored the fact that a liberal arts college is obviously not quite the same as a graduate school, and I naively took for granted that a logic course should be concerned with the theory of reasoning, never quite remembering that logic had once been one of the liberal arts. At that earlier time logic had been a "discipline" in the sense of an art or a skill, not a "discipline" in the sense of a science or body of knowledge. When so conceived, logic had been central to the liberal arts curriculum because it developed one of the liberal arts. The fact that many of my students were bored with my course in logic as theory was disturbing, but this was always interpreted as a call for more interesting lectures or for more serious students, never as an indictment of my assumption that logic was properly taught as theory.

After much wasted time, and with much anger at my blindness and guilt for having disserved my students, I concluded that the problem that entrapped me would not be solved by better lectures or better students. I also realized that this problem was not unique to me, but was endemic to the college. Many of my colleagues did not seem to sense the radical, qualitative difference between a graduate school, university, or university college, and the liberal arts college. They understood themselves to be agents engaged in the discovery and transfer of knowledge, where knowledge was understood as theory or, at least, information. This transfer was accomplished by lively lectures and easily-read books (written, like all college text books must be, at the ninth grade level). In hindsight it is apparent that this entire project was one that favored the methods of logic, and that disfavored the methods of rhetoric and dialectic. This paradigm preference can be referred to as the preference for a "logocentric" pedagogy.[6] This pedagogy emphasized the lecture and the axiomatic methods of the mathematical sciences as the paradigms for teaching.

In time the effects of this preference for a "logocentric" pedagogy became apparent. Because this pedagogy was beholden to the theoretical sciences and the principle of verification, the normative sciences were excluded as "sciences" because they were refractory to verification. The social sciences were tolerated as aspiring imitators of the natural sciences. But the humanities were treated as an embarrassing academic underclass, a motley collection of subjects that tender-minded people might think to be somehow edifying or humanizing, but which could not pass muster as "science." This logocentric pedagogy also depreciated the art of teaching and teachers. In fact, for a brief time during the nineteen seventies it even seemed possible that the college teacher might eventually become obsolete, and be largely replaced by teaching machines and computers. Sleep learning was studied in the hope that the transfer of knowledge could be more efficiently and painlessly accomplished. In addition to depreciating the non-theoretical sciences and the teacher, a logocentric pedagogy depreciated the student in favor of the "knowledge" being processed. Predictably, the graduate school became the model for undergraduate education.[7] Teachers came to be understood as teacher-scholars--specialists who could provide "knowledge" and expedite its transfer by interesting lectures. The appropriate model for this teacher was the "professor"--the departmentalized theoretical expert or authority. Meanwhile, ironically enough, the graduate schools routinely turned out graduates who were expected to spend their professional lives as college teachers, but who had never taught a single college course or a single college student.

4. MICROSPECIALIZATION

At St. Lawrence teachers are recruited by academic departments. This is because practically all teachers are expected to be theoretical experts or authorities on one of the accepted "fields of knowledge," and because only peer

---

[6] I am using "logocentric" to indicate a pedagogy that is limited to the logos mode of persuasion of classical rhetoric.

[7] Earl J. McGrath, *The Graduate School and the Decline of Liberal Education* (New York: Columbia University, 1959).

experts are considered capable of understanding and evaluating the qualifications of candidates. These teachers are also expected to have the Doctor of Philosophy degree, and to have a further specialization within their chosen speciality. This further specialization is certified by continuing scholarly research and publication in appropriate professional journals, and by attendance at appropriate professional meetings. These teachers are henceforth identified by their department and their subspeciality. Like books in a library, they are so classified by the college and by others, and so spend their lives as "Dr. So-and-so of the Such-and-such Department who is interested in micro-something-or-other."

This demand for microspecialized theoretical experts in an undergraduate liberal arts college is an issue of both comic and tragic proportions. A survey of Americans over eighteen reported by the *New York Times* on October 25, 1988, provides a profile of the typical undergraduate college population: 14% can read only at the fourth grade level (and 80% of college graduates can read only at the eleventh grade level); 64% did not know that lasers use light rays, not sound waves; 19% thought that sound travels faster then light; 28% did not know that the earth revolves around the sun. Another study found that most Harvard graduates thought that summer is warmer than winter because the earth is closer to the sun in the summer. A November 1991 Gallop Poll found that 47% of Americans believe that God created human beings less than 10,000 years ago. Other Gallup Polls report that 29% of American adults believe in astrology, 54% believe in angels, and 52% believe in the devil. Given this level of general ignorance, one can only gasp in incredulity at the fact that undergraduate liberal arts colleges aggressively recruit teachers whose main interests are in such subjects as "Interactions Between T Lymphocyte Subsets Supported by Interleukin 2-Rich Lymphokines Produce Acute Rejection of Vascularized Cardiac Allographs in T Cell Deprived Rats," "The Murine *Ah* Locus: Comparison of the Complete Cytochrome P_1-450 cDNA Nucleotide and Amino Acid," and "Deconstruction and Creation: An Examination of Emmanuel Levinas' "Autrement qu'etre ou au-dela de l'essence" in the light of Edmund Husserl and Jacques Derrida." The college's obsession with specialized theory is a subject for pathology or, perhaps, comedy. But while it may provoke laughter in academic novels and Woody Allen movies, it is tragic in its consequences for undergraduates who have hopes for a liberal education.

The tragic comedy of this obsession for microspecialized theory in the undergraduate liberal arts college is further illustrated by St. Lawrence's program of "Faculty Forums." These pretentious soirees are sponsored by the Dean to allow faculty members to report on their latest discoveries on the frontiers of knowledge. (These have to be attended to be appreciated!) The gravest problem facing those who participate in this recent addition to the college's "faculty development" program is the problem of finding anyone other then dutiful friends who are willing to act like "potted palms" or to impersonate intellectuals by adopting a grave mien and asking intelligible questions about the irrelevant minutia of microspecialization.

When liberal arts colleges seek teachers who are microspecialized theoretical experts, liberal education is impaired because most of its traditional concerns must be neglected. Generalization, integration, the liberal arts, the normative sciences, and moral education are all likely to suffer. In addition, teacher personality and character tend to be disregarded as unimportant, even though research has shown that personality and character are vitally important factors in effective college teaching.[8]

The demand for microspecialized theoreticians also significantly raises the cost of undergraduate education because research time, facilities, and libraries are extrordinarily costly. Today, for example, the St. Lawrence library subscribes to over two thousand three hundred periodicals. Moreover, as more and more teachers become adept at the art of becoming publishing scholars, staging conferences, and participating in colloquia, the number of periodicals will continue to increase. The number of scholarly periodicals has increased today to such an extent that any major university will subscribe to over ten thousand of them. The periodical budget of the University of Chicago, for instance, has for some time been in excess of $1,000,000 a year. At St. Lawrence most of these scholarly periodicals will go unread by all but a handful of the faculty, and probably by all of the students who are paying for them.

The products of specialized research in the undergraduate college are likely to be both exceedingly modest and provincial. Unlike the late nineteenth century, when American colleges contributed significantly to specialized research, by 1900, with the rise of the university, these colleges contributed only about 20% of all research, and by 1950, with the rise of government and industrial research institutes, this figure dropped to less than 2%. Today, less than fifty years later, almost no significant research is produced by the faculty of American liberal arts colleges. Most of what passes as research in these colleges is understood by insiders to be "potboiler research"--work that is obviously insubstantial and would not appear in print if it were not regarded as essential for career advancement.

THE TEACHING CONDITIONS

St. Lawrence's confusion about its institutional purpose has allowed its teachers to be dispossessed of their magisterial calling. Without any commitment to any higher cause, these teachers have become careeristic in their preoccupation with personal advancement. They have been led to believe that "teaching is not enough," and that teaching is inferior to scholarly and administrative activities.

---

[8]Philip E. Jacob, *Changing Values in College: An Exploratory Study of the Impact of College Teaching* (New York: Harper & Row, Publishers, 1958). Also see: David G. Winter, David C. McClelland, and Abigail J. Stewart, *A New Case for the Liberal Arts* (San Francisco; Jossey-Bass Publishers, 1981); Earl J. McGrath, "Characteristics of Outstanding Teachers," *Journal of Higher Education* 33 (1962): 148-152; and Mervyn L. Cadwallader, "A Manifesto: The Case for an Academic Counterrevolution," *Liberal Education* 68 (1982): 403-420.

They have become logocentric in their dependence on a logic-oriented pedagogy, and pedagogically narrow in having professional resources that are limited to a specialized field of knowledge. But the college's disorientation has also affected the conditions that are essential for effective college teaching. This disorientation has had consequences for the faculty organization, the teacher compensation system, the administrative personnel policies, and the teaching facilities. We now consider each of these in turn.

1. THE ACADEMIC BUREAUCRACY

At various times in the past the government of St. Lawrence was to a considerable extent in the hands of its faculty. During the administration of President Millard Jencks (1940-44), for instance, faculty committees were elective, not appointive, and faculty meetings were occasions for substantive and lively deliberations. In the opinion of some, this form of government was inefficient and ineffective. Consequently, during the administration of President Eugene Bewkes (1945-63), the faculty lost much of its earlier power. Faculty committees were administratively appointed, and faculty meetings became more ceremonial and less deliberative. These meetings were used less to debate academic issues and more by the president to brief the faculty on administrative achievements and policy decisions. "Faculty Workshops" were also held, but these were conducted by Dean Joseph Romoda largely to detail academic policies and to sound out the faculty on policy alternatives. For all practical purposes during this period the academic work of the college was administered by the Dean with the help of a small group of administratively-appointed "department heads" in the "Department Heads Council." It was not until a serendipitous Faculty Workshop of March 9, 1966, that Professor Donald Auster arose in the course of a discussion and had the temerity to offer an uninvited motion to abolish the class attendance policy. The motion was approved by a startled faculty and a new era began.

During the decade of the sixties the local chapter of the American Association of University Professors was instrumental in introducing and lobbying for major changes in the governance of the college. Largely as a result of the chapter's work dramatic changes soon took place. A tenure program and a sabbatical program were introduced, Saturday classes were abolished, the teaching load was reduced from 12 to 9 hours, and an elected "Faculty Advisory Council" was approved by President Foster Brown, and held its first meeting on May 25, 1966. Less than two years later, on January 8, 1968, a committee of the A.A.U.P. presented a full proposal for a genuine faculty deliberative assembly--a "Faculty Senate." The name, "Faculty Senate," was eventually changed to "Faculty Council" to reflect the fact that this body was approved by the president only as an advisory body, and not as a legislative body. After its approval by President Frank Piskor, the new Faculty Council held its first meeting on March 17, 1970.

During the last two decades the structure of college government has remained essentially unchanged. Early on, efforts were made to establish a tripartite "University Council," and to include faculty membership on the Board of Trustees, but these efforts failed. Throughout this period faculty participation in the government of the college has remained advisory. Resolutions of the Faculty Meetings and the Faculty Council have been treated only as recommendations to the President.

What has emerged as distinctly new during this period is the rapid growth of a large, professional administrative staff. Professor Richard Perry documented this so-called "administrative bloat" in a study which he shared with the Faculty Council on October 5, 1989. He showed that in the ten year period from 1979 to 1989, the increase in the administrative staff was 5.5 times the increase in the faculty.

This rapid expansion of the administrative staff included the frequent recruitment of administrative staff members from the faculty. Faculty efforts to have "department chairs" elected failed, and the older policy of administratively-appointed "department heads" was reinstated. (However, these department "heads" were now called "chairs.") These developments illustrate what may be called the "administrative co-optation" of the faculty. Many who were counted as members of the faculty were also members of the administrative staff and had administrative obligations. Many others were what Professor Richard Guarasci dubbed "deans-in-waiting." These people held teaching positions but secretly lusted after administrative power, privilege, and prestige. The result of this co-optive process was an increase in bureaucratic discipline and efficiency. Today senior administrative officers sometimes solicit faculty "input," but this "input" is understood to be strictly advisory, and is preferably done in privy councils or in "fora" (meetings of the faculty in which the faculty does not have the right to vote). The more important of these "inputs" are discreetly "managed" by senior administrative officers with the assistance of teacher-administrators who work within a system that is highly leveraged by power and personality.

Like all bureaucracies, the academic bureaucracy is hierarchical. The faculty is itself highly structured by rank, salary, department, and date of appointment. For instance, for convocations and commencement processions the faculty is lined up by rank and date of appointment. (This is, incidentally, a "tradition" that is not imposed on the faculty by presidential edict. I once offered a motion to abolish this line-up on the ground that it was appropriate for a military staff, but inappropriate for a guild of colleagues. But, to my surprise and embarrassment, my motion was defeated by the faculty.)

The academic bureaucracy is made even more effective, and the faculty organization is made even less effective, by the administrative organization of the college. The administratively-appointed "department chairs" and "program directors" help to maintain discipline and to execute administrative policy, and assiduously lead their departmental members and program staffs in the most grim and gripping of all academic endeavors--departmental and program empire building.

2. EXTRINSIC COMPENSATION

In contrast to a century ago, liberal arts colleges today do not have as presidents classically educated clerics who teach classes in ethics in addition to their administrative responsibilities. Today's college presidents are full-time, professional chief executive officers. To survive, they do not have to know anything about the classics, theology, or ethics; but they do have to be skilled managers.

The science of academic management has borrowed much from this century's advances in the science of industrial management. This can be seen in current practices in college finance, fund raising, public relations, and personnel management. In personnel management, in particular, the use of management science has had important consequences for the college teacher. This is especially true for the college personnel management subfield now known as "faculty development."

Academic administrators are interested in "faculty development" programs because, like their executive counterparts in industry, they want to induce their "employees" to perform in certain desired ways. However, unlike their counterparts in industry, these administrators normally have to rely less on what management scientists call "coercive" or "remunerative power," and more on "normative power." "Normative power" is exercised through the allocation of psychic or "symbolic rewards," such as esteem, prestige, and "positive acceptance" by leaders and peers.[9] This includes "persuasive, suggestive, or manipulative efforts to influence social norms."[10] This power may be achieved through "faculty development" programs, providing the programs "appear as essential" and have "credibility." These programs provide "a pattern of intrinsic and extrinsic or economic and noneconomic rewards that fulfills individual desires and promotes normative changes."[11]

St. Lawrence's "faculty development" program utilizes both noneconomic and economic rewards to induce teachers to perform in administratively desired ways:

1. Noneconomic Compensation

Richard P. Chait, an academic management consultant for St. Lawrence, has described some of the ways that noneconomic compensation is made available to a faculty:

---

[9]Richard P. Chait and James Gueths, "A Framework for Faculty Development," *Change* (May/June 1981): 31.

[10]Ibid.

[11]Ibid., 32.

Some extrinsic rewards cost a little money though the faculty member derives no personal financial gain: a research assistant, additional lab equipment, an increased library budget, a load reduction, travel funds, a sabbatical. Still other forms of recognition are free: opportunities to offer advice and influence decisions, appointment to key committees, more advanced courses, more compact schedules, exposure in university publications, a nonmonetary award for distinguished work, luncheons with the president or dean . . . .[12]

In addition to these noneconomic ways of "managing rewards and recognition," and, thus, "influencing social norms" and achieving "desired behaviors," St. Lawrence's "faculty development" program employs several other noneconomic devices.

As everyone knows, universities frequently sponsor events in which professors report back to their colleagues about their latest discoveries on the frontiers of knowledge, read technical papers for peer review, and, in general, carry on serious professional discussions. For many it is only appropriate that liberal arts colleges also display this evidence of a superb faculty and an invigorating intellectual atmosphere. At St. Lawrence, this is accomplished by such events as the previously mentioned "Faculty Fora," as well as "Book Fairs" (sponsored by the Bookstore for authors to sign and sell copies of their latest contributions to knowledge), Friday afternoon "Faculty Authors' Readings" (jointly sponsored by the Dean's Office and the Library to "celebrate" the publication of a new book), and "Piskor Lectureships" (annual convocation lectures given by a faculty member selected by the administration).

What many do not realize is that, while these events are frequently treated like ancient traditions, they are in reality of very recent origin. Most of them came into being during the late nineteen seventies as administrative devices to "develop" the faculty. Their obvious intent was to promote the administration's new interest in faculty research and publication.

As events serving the purposes of a "faculty development" program, these events are not entirely what they appear to be. They are not primarily intended to advance academic dialogue, but to shape values and to produce desired behaviors in the faculty. This strategy has been clearly and shamelessly spelled out by academic management consultants.[13]   From the standpoint of a "faculty development" program, the faculty who participate in these events are unwitting protagonists in a "faculty development" morality play.

As might be expected, those who recognize and express dissatisfaction or resentment at this form of manipulation are not well received. Such was the case several years ago when I gave a Faculty Forum entitled, "Why the Faculty Forum Should Be Abolished." My criticism of this latest attempt to manipulate the

---

[12]Ibid.

[13]For instance, see Chait and Gueths, "A Framework for Faculty Development."

faculty was politely tolerated, but not appreciated. Others have had similar experiences.

2. Economic Compensation

In addition to these varied practices which persuasively, suggestively, or manipulatively influence teacher norms, "faculty development" programs can influence teacher norms in a less subtle and more obvious, economic way. The best example of this is the college's so-called "merit pay system." This issue has been heatedly debated and deserves careful scrutiny.

The "Merit Pay System"

The present, so-called "merit pay system" was implemented by Dean George Gibson in a memo to the department chairs on March 5, 1980. This memo announced that "merit allocations" would be made by both the department chairs and the dean, and would be based on the same "criteria" used for tenure and promotion, viz., "effective teaching, scholarly activity, and community service."

Although few objections were heard when this system was first introduced, with each year teacher dissatisfaction with the system has grown. In 1986 a committee was appointed to review the system, and recently the faculty decisively defeated a proposal to include a "merit pay" increment in the faculty compensation policy.

One of the objections to this system is that it is unnecessary. The college already has a pay system that rewards faculty on the basis of performance in an enlightened and professional way. This is done by the promotion and tenure system. This traditional system has worked reasonably well in the past, and its reliance on an elected peer review committee provides the faculty with some protection against the subjectivity and manipulative temptations of autocratic administrators. The imposition of this new system on top of the traditional system creates another preening and paper shuffling ritual and diverts more faculty energy from the task of education.

More importantly, a so-called "merit pay system" is divisive and demoralizing for a faculty. Such systems are often useful for paying people who work independently of each other, such as those who sell brushes or pick tomatoes. But research has shown that these systems perennially fail in their applications to education and to other enterprises where it is necessary for people to work together to achieve a common goal.[14] Neither the faculty nor the college benefits from a crude, zero-sum competitive pay system that encourages faculty

---

[14]See Linda Ray Pratt, "Merit Pay: Reaganomics for the Faculty?" *Academe* (N/D 1988): 14-16; S. M. Johnson, "Merit Pay for Teachers: A Poor Prescription for Reform," *Harvard Educational Review* 54 (1984); and Richard J. Murnane and David K. Cohen, "Merit Pay and the Evaluation Problem: Why Most Merit Pay Plans Fail and a Few Survive," *Harvard Educational Review* 56 (1986): 1-17.

members to be economic "winners" at the expense of colleagues who must then be economic "losers."

But the most important objection to a so-called "merit pay system" for a faculty is that it is manipulative and repressive. For many, this charge will seem absurd. However, doubts on this matter can be removed by a review of the role that these pay systems are designed to play in "faculty development" programs. According to management consultants, these systems are classified as low cost reward systems that will enable academic administrators to "manage rewards and recognition" to produce "desired behaviors" in their faculties.[15] Thus, in terms of purpose, these systems are intended to facilitate administrative control of a faculty. One indication that this is understood comes from the fact that in the recent faculty debate over the system almost all of those who spoke in favor of it were department chairs or deans-in-waiting, and relatively few faculty members spoke against it, while in a secret ballot that followed the great majority of the faculty voted against it. Several faculty members privately acknowledged that they were strongly opposed to the system, but could not risk speaking against it when their department chairs and program directors favored it.

Thus, because a so-called "merit pay system" for the faculty is unnecessary and divisive, and because it facilitates the administrative manipulation of the faculty, it is repressive. In turn, and in time, this system damages academic freedom, faculty autonomy, and the quality of teaching.

The Teacher Evaluation System

A so-called "merit pay system" for a faculty requires criteria for merit that go beyond the vague criteria of "effective teaching, scholarly activity, and community service." Thus, this system requires a system for teacher evaluation. The evaluation system now in place was adopted by the faculty on March 20, 1990. It provides a number of "mechanisms" for the "measurement" of teaching effectiveness. These include "student evaluation of teaching," "peer evaluation of course content and coverage," "the instructor's statement of aims, goals, and accomplishments," and "evaluation of the views of former students." The primary purpose of the evaluation system is said to be "summative," not "formative," that is, it is intended not to improve teaching, but to improve the evaluation of teaching. It is designed to benefit promotion, tenure, post-tenure review, and merit pay decisions.

Objections to this system can be summarized in three propositions:

1. The system incorrectly assumes that the "measurement" of teaching effectiveness is *possible*. It assumes that the effectiveness of a teacher can in fact be "measured"--that is, assigned a value on the basis of standards that apply invariantly to all members of the faculty. While it assumes that this measurement cannot be achieved through any single mechanism, it assumes that it can be

---

[15]Chait and Gueths, "A Framework for Faculty Development," 32.

achieved through a combination of mechanisms.

Research supports the claim that there is no single mechanism that can measure teaching effectiveness.[16] The use of student (and alumni) evaluations for summative purposes has been thoroughly discredited.[17] Teaching effectiveness cannot be measured impressionistically. The use of peer evaluations for summative purposes has also been thoroughly discredited.[18] Aside from the fact that personality conflicts, ideological bias, and intolerance of diversity often prejudice peer evaluation, many pedagogical differences are necessary in a program of liberal education, and cannot be reduced without impairing the program.[19] Finally, the use of self-evaluations for summative purposes has also been discredited.[20] In addition, the persistent attempt to use scholarly activities as a measure of teaching effectiveness has been demonstrated to be invalid.[21]

In addition, research does not support the assumption that the teaching effectiveness of a faculty can be measured by a combination of mechanisms. No good reason has been given for believing that a credible measuring mechanism will result from the combination of a number of discredited mechanisms. But the most important argument against this assumption is that there are diverse and incommensurable models of the effective teacher. An effective teacher may be a scientist, an artist, a dispenser of information, a poet, a developer of skills, a maieutic, a facilitator, a coach, and so on. Since there are many different models of the effective teacher, since different models legitimize different standards of evaluation, and since the measurement of teaching effectiveness is always relative to some standard of evaluation, there is no way that the teaching effectiveness of the members of a faculty can be measured without relying on values that are relative to a variety of incommensurable models. Thus, while teaching

---

[16]"There is lack of agreement among authorities as to what constitutes a good teacher. A review of the literature over the past 25 years indicates no objective usable criterion for identifying effective teachers." M. Neeley, "A Teacher's View of Teacher Evaluation," in *Improving College and University Teaching* 16 (1968): 207-209.

[17]"Until the criterion-validity of student rating scales reaches correlations of .7 or .8 (instead of .37), reducing the current uncertainty, or until construct validity can be established, the results of student rating scales should not be used in making tenure decisions." Stanley N. Miller, "Student Rating Scales for Tenure and Promotion," in *Improving College and University Teaching* 32 (1984): 87-90. "In sum, the literature does not support a position that ratings are sufficiently valid for policy uses . . . ." D. A. Dowell and J. A. Neal, "A Selective Review of the Validity of Student Ratings of Teaching," in *Journal of Higher Education* 53 (1982).

[18]"A second finding showed colleague ratings to be not statistically reliable; the average correlation among ratings by different colleagues was about .26." John A. Centra, *Determining Faculty Effectiveness* (San Francisco: Jossey-Bass, 1979): 75.

[19]Theodore Caplow and R. J. McGee, *The Academic Marketplace* (New York: Basic Books, 1958).

[20]Centra, *Determining Faculty Effectiveness*.

[21]Stanley J. Michalak, Jr., and Robert J. Friedrich, "Research Productivity and Teaching Effectiveness at a Small Liberal Arts College," *Journal of Higher Education* 52 (1981): 578-597. Also see: Virginia W. Voelks, "Publications and Teaching Effectiveness," in *Journal of Higher Education* 33 (1962): 212-218.

effectiveness can be evaluated in a number of different ways, there is no way that this effectiveness can be "measured"--that is, assigned values on the basis of standards that are invariant for all members of a faculty. This shows that a so-called faculty "merit pay system" is conceptually flawed.

2. The evaluation system incorrectly assumes that the "measurement" of teaching effectiveness is *desirable*. Research shows that teaching effectiveness is dependent upon many independent variables. These include the subject matter taught, the course objectives, the required or elective nature of the course, the rank, age, and sex of the teacher, the class standing, preparation, age, character, motivation, and capabilities of the students, the size, composition, and hour of the class, and even the location, layout, furniture, lighting, and acoustics of the classroom.[22] The mechanisms of the evaluation system do not include these variables, and therefore, are far too crude to be accurate or fair. Even so, they are enormously complex and costly to use in terms of faculty, student, and administrative time.

Even more disturbing than the cost is the likely long-term damage that the system will cause to the college's educational program. The system is patently repressive. Teachers are forced to devote large amounts of time and energy to preparing their dossiers, plotting their campaigns, and working to produce the official evidence of "effective teaching." But they are also forced to devote even more time and energy to courting the approval of those who are in control of the mechanisms of evaluation. As a result, teaching itself is further neglected, collegial relationships are further damaged, and faculty morale and institutional loyalty are further eroded. The college's academic environment is not energized by teachers who exemplify the ideal of criticism, but is enervated by bureaucratic sycophants and apologists for pedagogical orthodoxies. In the end the quality of the college's educational program is assuredly diminished.

3. The evaluation system incorrectly assumes that the "measurement" of teaching effectiveness is *necessary*. But there has been no demonstration of this necessity. Fair and efficient promotion and tenure decisions have been made in the past without a set of "mechanisms" that "measure" all teachers against each other on the basis of a set of official and invariant standards.

A particularly objectionable feature of the evaluation system is its condonation of the summative evaluation of tenured faculty members. This kind of evaluation has been condemned by the A.A.U.P., and the college's continued use of it undercuts its own tenure system.[23]

One faculty member has suggested that teaching is like loving. This simile should be taken seriously. With wisdom, care, and some luck, good teachers, like good lovers, can be identified. But it is as foolish to seek a "mechanism" to "measure" good teachers as it is to seek a mechanism to measure good lovers. It

---

[22]N. L. Gage, "The Appraisal of College Teaching" in *Journal of Higher Education*, 32 (1961): 17.

[23]*Academe* (N/D 1983): 14a.

seems more reasonable to say that faculty performance should "be approached as a matter to be judged rather than measured."[24]   Moreover, whenever teaching effectiveness is to be judged, it seems only reasonable that this judgment should be based upon actual teaching outcomes, rather than the subjective opinions of various evaluators.   To judge teaching effectiveness by student evaluation, peer evaluation, and self-evaluation would seem to be like judging the effectiveness of a physician by the opinions of the patients, the physician's peers, and the physician's opinion of himself or herself.   But surely the effectiveness of a physician should be judged by the improvement that the physician brings about in the patient. Similarly, a teacher should be judged by outcomes.[25]

One way of demonstrating the absurdity of trying to "measure" the effectiveness of college teaching on the basis of criteria that apply invariantly to all members of a faculty is by an imaginary application of a typical teacher evaluation form to an acknowledged master teacher. The greatest teacher of all time would fail every question on the typical teacher evaluation form illustrated on page 99.

If we now take an overview of both the economic and the noneconomic ways in which a "faculty development" program attempts to manage teacher rewards and recognition, and thereby to produce "desired behaviors" in a faculty, it should be clear why this program is thoroughly objectionable. A "faculty development" program is an administrative attempt to impose administratively determined purposes on a faculty and a college. This attempt prohibits or prejudices any criticism of these purposes. It thus diverts teachers from the purposes of liberal education by the appeal of psychic and economic rewards that serve other purposes. In addition, these programs are insulting and patronizing to a faculty. They subvert the teachers' belief in the intrinsic value of their professional calling.

3. REPRESSIVE PRACTICES

Like love or depression, repression is a phenomenon that is not easily understood by those who have not experienced it. If someone had told me, soon after I arrived at St. Lawrence, that the college had repressive administrative practices, I would have dismissed the claim as absurd. In time I changed my mind. One day I approached a tenured colleague to sign a petition in support of a proposal for the improvement of faculty governance. He replied that he agreed with the petition, and wanted to sign it, but couldn't. He explained that since the proposal probably would not please the college's administration, and since he was married and had a family, he was not really free to act on the basis of his convictions. He had to think of the possible consequences of his actions on those

---

[24]Richard P. Chait and A. T. Ford, *Beyond Traditional Tenure* (San Francisco: Jossey-Bass, 1982).

[25]For an outcomes proposal, see: Winter, McClelland, and Stewart, *A New Case for the Liberal Arts*.

TEACHER EVALUATION FORM

Name of Teacher/Scholar/CommunityServer _Socrates_

Knowledge of the Teacher	Rating	Comment

Scholarly publications   4 3 2 1 ⓪ ZILCH! HE'S ONLY A TEACHER.

Knowledge of the subject matter   4 3 2 1 ⓪ SAYS HE DOESN'T KNOW ANYTHING.

Attends professional meetings   4 3 2 1 ⓪ SAYS HIS WIFE WON'T LET HIM GO AND HAVE ANY FUN.

Classroom Behavior

Explains material clearly   4 3 2 1 ⓪ HE DOESN'T EXPLAIN. HE MAKES US EXPLAIN.

Interesting lectures   4 3 2 1 ⓪ HE NEVER LECTURES.

Tolerance of disagreement   4 3 2 1 ⓪ HE SEEMS TO THINK HE'S RIGHT. HE DOESN'T UNDERSTAND THAT EVERYONE IS ENTITLED TO HIS/HER OWN OPINIONS.

Pedagogical Innovations

Evidence of course revisions   4 3 2 1 ⓪ SAYS REVISIONS INDICATE MISTAKES.

Use of teaching aids   4 3 2 1 ⓪ NEVER SHOWS INTERESTING FILMS.

Willingness to engage in the formative process   4 3 2 1 ⓪ I GUESS HE'S NOT WILLING.

Assignments and Grading Policy

Interesting course assignments   4 3 2 1 ⓪ HE'S INTERESTED IN MORALITY, BUT I'M NOT INTERESTED IN MORALITY.

Currency of reading assignments   4 3 2 1 ⓪ HE USES ONLY ANCIENT SOURCES.

Fairness of grading policy   4 3 2 1 ⓪ HE ALLOWS ONLY 3 CUTS, EVEN FOR ATHLETES REPRESENTING THE COLLEGE. ALSO GIVES POP QUIZZES THAT ARE NOT ANNOUNCED.

Teacher as "Human Being"

Attitude towards students   4 3 2 1 ⓪ DOESN'T MAKE ME FEEL COMFORTABLE.

Personal appearance   4 3 2 1 ⓪ TOO MUCH BODY HAIR. WEARS HIGH WATER PANTS.

Personality   4 3 2 1 ⓪ DEFINITELY NOT MY KIND OF GUY! TOO INTELLECTUAL.

who were dependent upon him. From that point on I began to see things that I had not seen before. I soon discovered that many innocent-looking practices were really efficient instruments of control. These practices--in addition to the college's administrative bureaucracy and compensation system--included various myths and rituals. The following illustrations are only modestly caricatured.

Myths

"The Collegiate Family"

On ceremonial occasions the college president, no matter whoever he or she was, often spoke of the college as a kind of family. This image seemed reassuring. It also seemed somehow appropriate. After all, at convocations faculty members sang the alma mater with gusto and without embarrassment--as if St. Lawrence was *their* alma mater--and they sometimes debated their responsibility to act *in loco parentis*. It was easy to fill in the details of this image. The students were obviously the "kids"--the little brothers and sisters. They drank too much beer and made too much noise. The teachers, coaches, and counselors were the big brothers and sisters. They adolescent-sat their little brothers and sisters, worked the fields of the plantation, and, above all, were obedient to their parents. They were assisted by their cousins--the secretaries, cooks, and custodians. At the head of the family was the big father or the big mother. He or she lived in the big house, occupied the *cella* of the Parthenon, knew all of the family secrets, and made the big decisions.

"Keep Picking the Cotton!"

As laborers on the family's plantation, the big brothers and big sisters were expected to diligently work their assigned disciplinary fields. Afterwards they were required to fill out their "Annual Faculty Activity Reports" to determine who would merit the smiles and appreciation of the big father or mother. They were expected to be trustworthy, loyal, helpful, . . . and obedient. They regularly received free copies of the *Faculty Bulletin*, the plantation's official information organ. Its main function seemed to be to remind everyone that everyone else was busy picking the cotton. Sample: Assistant Professor E. Z. Cowed of the Such-and-such Department attended the Northern New York Conference on Nit-picking and delivered a paper on "Nit-picking in the North Country."

"Be Professional!"

The big brothers and sisters were expected to understand themselves as workers in the fields of knowledge who have the obligation to endlessly and selflessly harvest data for someone else's ineffable purposes. They were expected to be "professional"--a composite of Mr. Magoo, Dr. Pangloss, and Dr. No--an individual too myopically specialized to have general understanding, too theoretical to have practical wisdom, and too ideologically warped to have moral responsibility. (Naturally such achievements would excuse them from the burdens of academic policy-making!)

"Publish or Perish!"

Faculty members were obliged to keep busy with their distinctions and their abstractions. After all, if they were busy in the fields of knowledge, they couldn't be on the barricades. They needed to recall that their only worthy audience was their professional peer group--the distant, the disinterested, and the powerless.

"Making the Times"

Faculty members who were mentioned in the *New York Times* for any reason (other than, presumably, for the commission of a capital crime) were treated by the big father or big mother as celebrities. Obviously garnering such parental favors required the big brothers and big sisters to play new games but to remain old cynics. Lost in this malarkey was the question of what "Making the Times" had to do with educating students.

"Waiting for Guggenheim"

Just in case the big brothers and big sisters might become too confident or complacent about their scholarly "productivity," there were occasionally very subtle administrative reminders that St. Lawrence did not yet have a Guggenheim winner. Or a Nobel Laureate.

"Be Flexible!"

Prudent faculty members understood that they should stay in the middle on most issues. Staying in the middle was clearly the way to make ends meet! Don't close any doors! Take a poll before you take a position! Keep an eye on the competition! Don't get caught in lock steps or sleep in Procrustean beds! And, above all, beware of those "principled" types! "Pragmatists" are the best. They understand that politics is the art of the possible!

"Never Look a Gift Horse in the Mouth!"

At one time faculty members were told that the college did not have an operating budget. Then a student ingeniously "found" a copy of the budget, and published it in the student newspaper. After that, faculty members were told that there was a budget, but that they were not really capable of understanding it. Much less were they capable of determining priorities! For example, if Mrs. Ficklebucks offered the college one million dollars for the biggest stable in the North Country, what's the big problem about priorities? After all, King Faud might drop in on the Madison Square Garden Horse Show some day and, after seeing a St. Lawrence horse, give the college two million dollars for a zoo.

"It's Not Nice to Polarize!"

Faculty members were expected to behave themselves during faculty meetings. These were not occasions to argue with colleagues, or to raise questions that might make people feel uncomfortable. Someone might get excited! Or, even--horror of horrors--polarize a group! Sophisticated, well-mannered professors should make polite talk and erudite jokes over tea and cookies. Serious faculty debate produces gas in the bowels. Consequently, all debates should have time constraints. If they threaten to encroach on the cocktail hour, it's time to "call for the question." And if curmudgeons complain about illicit process and steam rollers, it's always helpful to suggest that "it's time to get on with it." A faculty meeting is no place to just "muck around."

"Take It Out on Tricky Dick!"

Faculty members who find themselves being knee-jerk conservatives in faculty meetings and knee-jerk liberals during the cocktail hour, shouldn't be befuddled. After all, it's only natural for people to keep their noses clean when the boss is around, and it's just as natural for them to try to compensate for their compromises when they're safe at home having more than one. That's the time for them to take it out on Slick Willie or George or the Gipper or Jimmy or Tricky Dick--that Sonofabitch. After all, the big boss in Washington is too far away to hurt you, whereas the big boss in the Parthenon might growl the next time he sees you sniffing around his territory.

"Don't Overemphasize the Intellect!"

Faculty members were expected to rationalize all of those fun and games for the students. Majoring and minoring, cutting classes, getting wasted, getting the distribution requirements "out of the way," bouncing balls, hazing pledges, playing hide and seek in the library--all of these *sine qua non*s of "the College Experience" help students to be "well-rounded" and repress any residual curiosity about the meaning of life. Students were expected to be "making their grades," of course, but this was certainly not to be confused with becoming--God forbid--an "intellectual." What really matters is "making friends," "making the team," and "making out."

Rituals

In addition to repressive myths the college's structure of authority is sustained by various rituals.   The following are unfailingly effective in domesticating the faculty:

"High Masses"

Several times a year convocations were held in Gunnison Chapel.   To outsiders these were no doubt "nice," colorful ceremonies.   There were Gothic arches and stained glass windows and pageantry and trumpet voluntaries and all kinds of people with all kinds of beards dressed in black robes with mortarboards on their heads and male inflorescences in their eyes looking slightly foolish and slightly embarrassed.   For the naive, convocations were performed out of respect and reverence for mysterious, medieval traditions.   But even guileless fools could recognize some unmistakable signs of the workings of superior wills: The faculty was always meticulously lined up by one of their own in order of academic rank and date of appointment.   Meanwhile at the head of this procession was the big father or the big mother, usually accompanied by a VIP.   One faculty member voluntarily bore the awesome symbol of parental authority, the President's Spiked Mace.   On these grand occasions rewards were passed out to the big brothers and sisters for selfless labor in service to the latest parental projects.   During these ceremonies the big father or the big mother coyly kept the older siblings in breathless, clammy suspense by encouraging each of them to think, until the very last second, that maybe he or she was the big winner of a big award.

Years ago it was said that convocations were conducted for the benefit or edification of students, perhaps to remind them of the seriousness of the academic life.   But today's students have little interest in attending convocations, and since no one would dare try to require them to attend anything, not surprisingly, they don't attend convocations.   Oddly enough, though, these ceremonies continue to be held.   This may provoke the nasty little thought that these ceremonies are not really for the benefit of the little brothers and sisters, but are for the benefit of the big brothers and sisters: Is it conceivable that these ceremonies are staged by those in power to sanctify their own authority?   This possibility is mind boggling, but how else can one explain the fact that the celebrants of Academic High Mass always give their homilies in sophisticated English punctuated by Latin quotations and esoteric puns, but nonetheless always find their text in the Boy Scout Laws?

"The President's Christmas Dinner"

The collegiate family met together on a few other occasions.   Early in the fall everyone was invited to the family's "camp" in the Adirondacks to escape the heat of the plantation, to admire the family's latest tax windfalls, and to chat benignly with all of the relatives. In the winter the big father or the big mother entertained the big brothers and sisters to a night of roast beef, burgundy, and lively dancing. While it was rumored that this lavish event was really not paid for out of the president's own pocket, it was nonetheless, for some reason, called "The *President*'s Christmas Dinner."

"The Black Larry Rocking Chair Ceremony"

After twenty or thirty years of adolescent-sitting and working the plantation's fields of knowledge, the big brothers and sisters were urged to make room for "new blood." On these solemn occasions there were embarrassing little speeches culminating in an awesome ritual in which each burned-out, white haired big brother or sister dutifully genuflected to the big father or big mother, and then settled mutely into a Black Larry Rocking Chair in full view of the averted eyes of the assembled family.

"Rat Hole Committee Service"

If faculty members really insist on having a "voice" and a piece of the action, they must be prepared to serve on a committee. But they can be sure that they will first have to serve on a subcommittee which will have to run a survey and calculate the standard deviation before sending its "reactions" to the full committee, which will be dominated by Uncle Toms and administrative clones, and which must then report to the Faculty Council, which must advise Thelmo and the Department Chairs Council, which must go to the faculty meeting and the Dean, and which then must go to the President who must consult the Trustee Committee (after advice from counsel), which must be approved by the Board, provided, of course, that it doesn't violate somebody's by-laws or offend Mrs. Ficklebucks. If these teachers are inclined to be faculty "activists" who want to change things, they must remember that "St. Lawrence can't afford to experiment," and if they don't want to change things, they need to remember that "St. Lawrence can't afford not to experiment." If they believe their professional expertise isn't being appreciated, they can always volunteer for the Hospitality Committee or the High Commission on Parking Lots. They should expect a faculty meeting to be called if there is some *pro forma* nonsense, such as approving the graduation lists, but they shouldn't expect a meeting to be called to debate the aims of the college or the deficiencies of the curriculum.

"The Farm Club for Administrators"

The faculty was regularly raided by the big father or big mother for ambitious and cooperative people for appointment as department chairs, program directors, and for other administrative duties. Inevitably these positions carried with them pay, power, privileges, perks, and promises that were far superior to the rewards of teaching. One might get the impression that teaching was a kind of farm club for administrators.

"The Owen D. Young Bee Hive Under Glass"

On the biology floor of the Bewkes science complex there is a bee hive the inside of which has been exposed by being attached to a plate glass window. Visitors can thus easily and safely see the frenetic activity of the bees going about their business. Similarly, in the Owen D. Young Library there is a large, carpeted room which is designed like a bee hive. It contains two levels of faculty cell-like carrels each of which is fronted with plate glass. Visitors to the library can actually see the incredible spectacle of teacher-scholars laboring on the frontiers of knowledge. Obviously these glass-fronted studies were not constructed so much to facilitate faculty research as to show the collegiate family what a faculty should be doing.

A summary is in order. It doesn't take too much beyond a slight loss of gullibility to see that these myths and rituals are not what they appear to be. They are not really hallowed, ivy-covered, innocent traditions. Rather, they are contrived, and they are contrived to maintain the institution's structure of authority.

These parodied myths and rituals are repressive in the sense that they systematically debilitate the faculty. They inhibit the criticism of ideas. In particular, they stifle institutional self-criticism. They render the faculty ineffective as the primary agency for the maintenance of academic freedom and for the realization of a truly intellectual environment. By administrative encouragement and through their own lack of courage, faculty members thus compromise their most important professional rights and responsibilities. They surrender the ideal of a college--an association of equals united by the concern for truth--for a ridiculous attempt to act like "the collegiate family," and they become a hierarchy of inferiors divided by an obsession with status. Faculty members accept the idea that they should "keep picking the cotton" and "be professional," and in doing so they tolerate the caricature of themselves as being too specialized, too theoretical, and too biased to have the right to participate in academic decision-making. They "publish or perish," dutifully discharging their energies and talents in potboiler research. They learn that much of the pursuit of truth is really the pursuit of publicity, and so they invest their efforts in "making the Times" and "waiting for Guggenheim." They are told to "be flexible" and they end up being spineless. They are unable to judge priorities because they've been immobilized by the idea that one should "never look a gift horse in the mouth." They fudge their intellectual honesty because "it's not nice to polarize." When they get frustrated by their ineffectuality or conscience-stricken by their cowardice, they "take it out on Tricky Dick." And in the end they know that what they've failed to do isn't all that important because well-rounded people "don't overemphasize the intellect." Meanwhile they dutifully participate in the college's hallowed rituals, and they find that their critical instincts have been bought out.

The college's myths and rituals embody the categorical imperative of every repressive institution: "Loyalty Before Intellect!" Once the Chairman of the Board of Trustees actually let the cat out of the bag: "You can buy brains," he said, "but you can't buy loyalty!" This is the principle that obligations are determined by the personality of an authority and not through the criticism of ideas. In ordinary times this imperative is the "Loyalty Ethic"; in extraordinary times it becomes the *Führerprinzip*.

It may be argued that the "Loyalty Ethic" is justifiable in most forms of human organization such as the family, the army, or business. But a liberal arts college is not a family, an army, or a business. Its concern should be the development of intellectuality through the criticism of ideas. And "The Loyalty Ethic" defeats intellectuality and silences the criticism of ideas by the covert devices of repression. The end result of this repression is that both the institution and the individuals involved become (in Marcuse's words) "one-dimensional, incapable of self-transcendence." By almost any definition, liberal education then becomes an impossible project.

4. DISPIRITING FACILITIES

No college teacher who has fought in the endless struggles against student apathy can avoid being confounded and demoralized by the striking contrast between student interest in what takes place in the classroom and student interest in what takes place on the athletic field. Sometimes this contrast is captured in an unforgettable instant: The dull, droning monotones and sleepy, glazed eyes of a class discussing the supreme principle of morality or the ideal state may be momentarily interrupted by the spectator cheers from a nearby athletic field where an intramural football team has just made a two yard gain.

Of course we all realize that this is a complex matter. Classrooms are gray and filled with theory, while playing fields are green and filled with life. The thoughts in a classroom are cerebral and convoluted, while the actions on the playing field are visceral and primal. We teachers understand that our task is not easy. Work is always more difficult than play.

At the same time we cannot help but note that the contrast between the classroom and the playing field is striking. The classroom is not only gray, but unattractive, uncomfortable, uninviting, and certainly uninspiring. It too often looks like a sweatshop, and has the blandness of a shower or public toilet. It is either too small or too large, and often crowded with cramped, uncomfortable, metal and plastic chairs arranged in ways that are appropriate for elementary schools or military briefings. If the walls are not gray, they are greenish yellow or yellowish green, and bare (except for a bulletin board stapled with posters displaying bikini-clad women advertising spring break in Daytona Beach). The room is stuffy, poorly heated and ventilated, with impulsive thermostats, and poorly lighted with flickering fluorescent lights, noisy with squeaky chairs and screechy blackboards, buzzing flies and coughing students. Stacked in the back are broken chairs, while somewhere in the front is a giant wall clock, inevitably out of time, but nonetheless a constant reminder to all students of the lethargy of time. The classroom is obviously not a place where something of significance might take place. But contrast the playing field. Here important things can happen. There are expensive facilities, seats for spectators, boxes for the media, electronic scoreboards, fluttering flags, loudspeakers, and martial music. And in support of all of this there are budgets and facilities that dwarf the budgets and facilities of academic departments. There are colorful uniforms, sophisticated training equipment, popular coaches, photographers, sports writers and publicists, and halls lined with glass cases containing sterling trophies and the smiling, glamorous pictures of emeriti heroes. At this point classroom teachers may well fantasize about how their struggles just might be aided if their classrooms and departments received comparable lavish aid--attractive, functional classrooms, halls lined with glass cases containing the pictures of former majors and their prize essays, attention by academic writers and publicists, and so on.

The functional and aesthetic neglect of classrooms and support facilities advertises to everyone that what happens in a classroom is of no profound significance. Unlike athletic fields and sports facilities, classrooms are not objects of interest for donors or college media or campus tours for prospective students and their parents. If a class gets media attention at all, it is one held outside in the grass, where teachers can drone on and students can simultaneously relax and get a suntan. In any case, classrooms are obviously not places where important things take place, much less, places where lives are changed.

Sometimes it doesn't take much to transform a classroom from an item of the "physical plant" into a place for inspiration. Years ago an enterprising purchasing agent of the college, Bill Beckman, found a way to purchase a reproduction of David's painting, "The Death of Socrates" to hang on the bare, gray walls of a seminar room in Piskor Hall. Since that time, countless discussions of ethics and aesthetics have been occasioned by that single painting.

Above all others, academicians should not have to be reminded of the educational value of art and architecture--of the way that the artifacts of a culture can be used to inspire and instruct.

* * * *

Our review of the status of the teacher and the conditions of teaching at St. Lawrence has revealed a situation in which the ideal of liberal education has been forgotten.   As a consequence, the teacher has become disoriented and disempowered. The force that now drives the college faculty is not the inspiration of a unique and compelling educational ideal, but the energy of personal, careerist ambition.   Teachers are now compromised by scholarly and/or administrative responsibilities. These teachers have allowed themselves to be isolated from each other and from the traditional concerns of liberal education by agreeing to play the role of academic bureaucrats or logocentric pedagogues who are responsible for the discovery and transmission of microspecialized theory.   The conditions under which these disciplinary experts work are those of an academic bureaucracy that is hierarchical and departmentalized. Teachers, as scholarly "workers" in the education "industry," are managed by professional administrators, sustained by bureaucratic values, and disciplined by extrinsic compensation. Administrative decisions are imposed by subtly repressive myths and rituals that are orchestrated by "senior management" with the cooperation of a co-opted faculty. Teaching facilities, reflecting the dispirited state of the profession of college teaching, are themselves dispiriting. All together, this review of the status of the teacher and the conditions of college teaching is an unhappy story of how college teachers have allowed themselves to be suborned by others. These teachers have allowed themselves to be dispossessed of their magisterial rights and responsibilities.

PART TWO

THE RECOVERY OF

INSTITUTIONAL INTEGRITY

INTRODUCTION TO PART TWO

All inquiry and all learning is but recollection.

Plato, *Meno*

To this point we have conducted a critical examination of a particular liberal arts college's institutional aims, its relationship to society, its educational program, and the status of its teachers. We have taken this college to be typical of the contemporary liberal arts college.

Our examination substantiates the charge that the contemporary liberal arts college is in fact guilty of "a certain kind of fraud." Specifically:

1. In spite of its impressive reputation, wealth, and sophisticated technology, the college is an institution without a clear and coherent purpose. It lacks an articulate definition of the ideal of liberal education. Its official statement of its aims and objectives lacks precision and coherence. The college is in fact a Rube Goldberg machine.

2. Without an articulate definition of the ideal of liberal education, the college has allowed itself to be appropriated for purposes that are extrinsic to this ideal. It has been used to advance various political agendas by institutional actions, to promulgate various ideologies through its educational program, and to service the varying and disparate interests of its students. As a result of these acts it has compromised its institutional independence. The liberal arts college is the desecrated temple of our society.

3. Because it lacks an understanding of the ideal of liberal education, the college has been unable to provide a coherent program for the realization of this ideal. Instead, it provides a "cafeteria" curriculum that is given pseudo-legitimacy by the so-called "elective principle," and it tolerates an anti-intellectual academic environment. These two combine to create an educational program whose effective and sustaining purpose is entertainment. The curriculum is filled with

"interesting," trendy themes constantly varied in response to administration and faculty orchestrated "student demands." In this program nothing is truly essential, and almost nothing is truly irrelevant. Meanwhile, the extracurriculum provides endless and mindless distractions for a youth ghetto. Whereas the college once prided itself for having a pastoral location that enabled its students to escape the distractions of the hurried life, it now spends large sums of money to bring the distractions of the hurried life to its campus to satisfy the constantly changing interests of its adolescent academic consumers. Its greatest fear is that its students will complain that "there's nothing to do." Consequently, every hour of every day is filled with divertissements. Like geese in flight, today's college students tranquilize themselves by constant social "honking" with their peers. Every threatening silence is cashiered. But this frenetic activity is spiritually vacuous. It is busyness--activity that is not disciplined by nobility of purpose. By tolerating these conditions the college defaults on its profound educational and moral responsibility. The college's educational program is accurately described as an academic theme park.

4. Finally, college teachers, having forgotten the ideal of liberal education, have forgotten their professional calling. Driven by their own careeristic ambitions, and herded like sheep by manipulative "faculty development" programs, they willingly become disenfranchised departmentalized micro-specialists or co-opted middle-management academic bureaucrats. Today the college is staffed by teachers who have been dispossessed of their magisterial rights and responsibilities.

To charge the contemporary liberal arts college with fraud does not imply that today's college students don't get what is popularly known as "a good education," or don't get "to know a lot about some things and a little bit about a lot of things," or don't make some friends, or don't have a lot of "interesting experiences." But what they do not receive is what they have been solemnly promised--something that is justifiably called a liberal education.

The main stages--if not the causes--of the decline of the liberal arts college during the last century are reasonably clear. In the beginning, with the rise of microspecialization there was a breakdown in the unity of knowledge.[1] The college was then predictably Balkanized by "the academic revolution"--the professionalization and departmentalization of the faculty. The "elective principle" abetted these developments, and it did so under a mantle of democratic freedom and with the imprimatur of economic success. The departmental "major" then became the centerpiece of the college curriculum. But since the "major" left the student with little more than a body of specialist information that was totally isolated from more fundamental theoretical and normative concerns, "distribution requirements" were introduced to remedy some of its obvious defects. Debates

---

[1]See Edward J. Shoben, Jr., "Departments vs. Education," in Oakley Gordon, ed., *Profess or Perish: Proceedings of the Thirteenth Annual Pacific Northwest Conference on Higher Education* (Corvallis, Oreg.:Oregon State University Press, 1968), 17.

over these "distribution requirements" soon developed into a hundred years war between the proliferating academic departments. In time the "distribution requirements" became the vassal of departmentalism. The core and survey courses initiated by the "General Education" movement of the nineteen thirties and forties soon met this same fate. And more recently, the "Freshman Year Experience" movement has tried to maintain enrollments, revive general education, and improve the academic environment. But, because it is a direct challenge to departmental hegemony, and because it has been unable to resist politicalization, it seems destined to suffer the same fate as its predecessors. Without a clear vision of the ideal of liberal education, and without the courage and the will to regain this vision, the college has evolved and rationalized an educational program that for the most part is determined not by a high moral purpose, but by the confluence of the vacillating personal, political, career, and commercial interests of students, faculty, administrators, and the larger society.

It seems almost inexplicable that contemporary educators can so easily ignore or dismiss the criticism that has been directed against the liberal arts college over the last century. Surely the sheer volume of this criticism is enough to suggest that it cannot all be the neurotic carping of chronic malcontents. We may be able to explain the college's failure by noting that most people in our society do not understand the ideal and unconditional importance of liberal education, and that most of those who do understand this ideal and its importance have been cowed by administrative repression, paralyzed by value relativism, exhausted by careerism and academic politics, and disenfranchised by departmentalism and microspecialization. But while we may be able to explain this failure, we can hardly excuse it. The failure of the liberal arts college in our time is truly an astonishing and shameful spectacle.

How could it happen that those who were privileged to understand what many have considered to be the most valued of all educational ideals would allow it to fall into oblivion? How could the priests of the temple of our culture allow this temple to be desecrated? How could "doctors of philosophy" allow an educational program to be transformed into an academic theme park? How could these teachers betray their magisterial calling? How could the liberal arts college become guilty of "a certain kind of fraud"? In cultures that believe in cargo cults or burning witches, the failure of the college to deliver on its promise of a liberal education is comprehensible; but in a culture that can send men to the moon and develop democratic constitutions, this failure is almost beyond belief!

It seems likely that many people will hold that the preceding criticism of the liberal arts college is too cynical, harsh, radical, reactionary, utopian, or naive. Others, according to the current fashion, will "accept" the criticism, but will discount it as the expression of merely one more "point of view," one which simply provides additional confirmation for the skeptical opinion that these matters can never be rationally resolved. In any case, the enterprise of criticism is almost certain to be deprecated. Criticism, it will be said, is "negative" and "not constructive," etc. It does not "reveal the truth" or "build bridges" or "bring people together" or "contribute to the conversation of humanity."

But before becoming critics of criticism, it is important to remember that the critics of criticism are themselves critics. And it is important to remember that all criticism presupposes rational principles. Consequently, criticism is not inevitably "negative" or "destructive." It will, of course, appear "negative" or "destructive" to those who represent entrenched, dogmatic interests. But all genuine criticism is positive and constructive and life-affirming. It is in fact the life-giving effluence of an ideal onto the desert of received opinion.

This insight opens up the possibility of using the criticism that has been directed against one liberal arts college, and by generalization, against the contemporary liberal arts college, to develop a set of principles for liberal education. This would be done by recollecting the assumptions implicit in the foregoing criticism. These would constitute the principles that are essential if the liberal arts college is to recover its institutional integrity. Part Two of this book is devoted to this constructive project.

5

THE PRINCIPLE OF LIBERAL EDUCATION

Any theory and set of practices is dogmatic which is not based upon critical examination of its own underlying principles.

John Dewey, *Experience and Education*

THE PROBLEM OF DEFINING THE IDEAL

That the origin of the continuing crisis of the liberal arts college may be attributed to the college's failure to articulate a rationally defensible ideal of liberal education seems hardly to be doubted. Recently, in *College: The Undergraduate Experience in America*, Ernest L. Boyer reported that

> we found at most colleges in our study great difficulty, sometimes to the point of paralysis, in defining essential purposes and goals . . . . A prestigious eastern college we visited . . . has no statement of objectives . . . . A faculty member [at another institution] said the university's goals are meaningless to faculty and students: "I'll bet you a thousand dollars if you asked students, 'Do you know what the University's goals are for you?' they would give you blank looks." We asked and they did. Even the student body president, who might be expected to have a better idea of such things, said: "If there are any goals around here, they haven't been expressed to me."[1]

If there is to be any hope that in the future the liberal arts college will be able to recapture its institutional integrity and deliver on its promise of a liberal education, then the college's most urgent need is for a definition of the ideal of liberal education. Above all, the faculty--and, if possible, the board and administration--must understand that the realization of this ideal is the institutional purpose of the liberal arts college. This purpose must be embodied in

---

[1]Ernest L. Boyer, *College: The Undergraduate Experience in America* (New York: Harper & Row, 1987), 59.

the college's constitution, curriculum, traditions, iconography, and vocabulary in such a way that the college will have some protection from the subversive efforts of its natural enemies and from the infidelity and forgetfulness of those who should be responsible for maintaining the light of the college's ideals.

There are some who oppose any attempt to define the ideal of liberal education on the ground that any such attempt will "get in the way of progress." One writer advises ambitious college administrators not to "force specification of goals" on the ground that "'principled' values and goals" then "become protective armor for the selfish interests of intellectual gladiators."[2]   For this writer, the successful college administrator is a "pragmatist"--one who keeps all options open. The trouble with this advice is that it is both cynical and disingenuous. The advice is cynical because it assumes that all goals are merely the selfish interests of individuals. The advice is disingenuous because it is not really opposed to all goals; it is only opposed to goals that might get in the way of the administrator's own goals.

A definition of the ideal of liberal education is necessary because, like all forms of intentional action, liberal education requires an understood institutional ideal--a purpose, mission, end, aim, or goal. Without such an ideal an educational institution is incapable of educating--incapable of "e-ducing" or "leading" people from an undesirable, real state to a desirable, ideal state. Moreover, an ideal must be defined if it is to be articulate and operationally useful. To the extent that an ideal is undefined, then to that extent it cannot be an ideal, and cannot be a guide for action.[3]

The need for a definition of the ideal of liberal education may be understood in a number of different ways. It may be taken as a call for an ordinary dictionary definition of the term "liberal education."   Unfortunately a good dictionary provides not one, but a number of accepted definitions of this term.   In one, a liberal education is defined narrowly as one that is "based on the liberal arts," and the liberal arts are in turn defined as "the trivium and quadrivium of the middle ages," and, alternately, as "subject matters" such as "language, philosophy, history, literature, and abstract science."[4]   But a liberal education is also defined as a form of education that develops "general knowledge and general intellectual capabilities, as opposed to professional, vocational, or technical studies."   The term "liberal education" is also correctly used in a very loose sense to mean something like "a wide experience."   In addition, the literature of education is filled with a bewildering variety of other uses of this term.   This variety may be

---

[2]Mary Regan, "Political Fragmentation in Institutions," *Liberal Education* 58 (1972): 237.

[3]"To ask questions about the aims of education is . . . a way of getting people to get clear about and focus their attention on what is worth while achieving." Richard S. Peters, *Authority, Responsibility and Education* (London: George Allen & Unwin Ltd., 1959), 88.

[4]For an analysis of the ways that post-Renaissance education transformed the liberal "arts" into "subject matters" see: Richard P. McKeon, "The Liberating and Humanizing Arts in Education," in Arthur A. Cohen, ed., *Humanistic Education and Western Civilization* (New York: Holt, Rinehart and Winston, 1964).

illustrated by the fact that for some a liberal education is the name of an institution that is in conspiracy with "liberal" politicians to brainwash the young with radical and un-American ideas. At the other extreme, and no less prevalent, is the view that a liberal education is the name of a reactionary institution that reinforces aristocratic privilege by promoting high culture. The fact that the dictionary and the literature of education provide us with not one, but with many accepted definitions of the term, "liberal education," reminds us that our interest here is not a mere interest in the conventions of linguistic practice.

The need for a definition may also be understood as a request for "the historical meaning" of the term "liberal education" (or its foreign language cognates). The difficulty with this strategy has been demonstrated recently in considerable scholarly detail by Bruce A. Kimball in *Orators and Philosophers: A History of the Idea of Liberal Education.*[5] Kimball makes a convincing case that the term "liberal education" is not the possession of any single historical tradition.

The need for a definition may also be interpreted as a request for a "stipulative definition." For instance, the ideal of liberal education may be said to be to develop people with a certain religious faith or political persuasion, or to provide students with a knowledge of "Western culture" or "the Great Books," or to satisfy student career or personal interests. Unfortunately, this kind of strategy is defeated by the charge that any resulting definition is inevitably *dogmatic*.

The charge that the ideal defined by a stipulative definition is inevitably dogmatic would be justified on the ground that any stipulative definition is necessarily relative to a particular set of contingent assumptions. As a consequence, a great variety of stipulative definitions would be possible, and this variety could even include definitions that would be incompatible with each other.

The charge that the ideal is inevitably dogmatic would justify the additional charge that the ideal lacks *intrinsic value.*[6] In other words, the ideal would be seen as having only conditional importance, or as having only instrumental or extrinsic value, since it would be important or valuable only to those who shared the particular assumptions and purposes used to justify the definition. This charge would contradict the opinion often expressed in classical arguments for liberal education that a liberal education is the best form of education because it is the only form that is independent or free of dogmatic assumptions and purposes.[7]

We might attempt to avoid these charges by providing extended arguments for a particular stipulative definition. We would then have what is sometimes

---

[5]Bruce A. Kimball, *Orators and Philosophers: A History of the Idea of Liberal Education* (New York: Teachers College, Columbia University, 1986).

[6]"Over the years liberal education has been thought of as having great value, indeed as an education having greater value than any other." Jane R. Martin, "Needed: A Paradigm for Liberal Education," in Jonas F. Soltis, ed., *Philosophy and Education: Eighth Yearbook of the National Society for the Study of Education* (Chicago: University of Chicago Press, 1981), 43.

[7]For a recent and influential example of a stipulative definition of liberal education see Paul H. Hirst, *Knowledge and the Curriculum* (London: Routledge and Kegan Paul, 1968). For a criticism of this definition, see: Martin, "Needed: A Paradigm for Liberal Education."

called a "theoretical definition." But the arguments used to justify a theoretical definition would seem once again to be dependent upon a variety of contingent assumptions or purposes, and if these assumptions or purposes were not accepted, then the definition that was based on them would remain dogmatic and lacking in intrinsic value.

This kind of reasoning seems to lead us to the skeptical conclusion that any definition of the ideal of liberal education is inevitably dogmatic and only contingently or extrinsically valuable. In any case, the ideal could in no way be said to be the best or most important of all educational ideals. We are thus left with a conclusion that apparently denies us the possibility of defining a form of education that is undogmatic and intrinsically valuable. In making this inference we merely echo the pervasive educational skepticism of our time.

In the face of this skepticism the assumptions and aspirations of many of the traditional models of the liberal arts college do indeed seem presumptuous. To the modern skeptic the ideals of these traditional models seem to be ancient monuments which attest to the nobility of human aspirations, but which also provide evidence that human aspirations often far exceed their critical warrant. From the standpoint of those who have great nostalgia for these lost ideals, many of the contemporary liberal arts colleges are certain to appear like slums built in the shadow of a great cathedral. But for modernity it is preferable to have slums than a cathedral built on illusion and sustained by dogma. The continuing existence of these educational slums attests to the continuing crisis of liberal education in our time. From Robert Hutchins' passionate defense of liberal education during the nineteen thirties in books like *The Higher Learning in America*, to Earl McGrath's diagnosis in the nineteen fifties of the "crisis of liberal education" in such books as *The Graduate School and the Decline of Liberal Education*, to the Carnegie Foundation for the Advancement of Teaching's claim that general education is today "a disaster area," and Bruce Wilshire's recent criticism in *The Moral Collapse of the University*, we have been warned repeatedly of the precarious condition of this institution.[8] During our own century the skepticism that has undermined any hope for a revitalization of liberal education has not ameliorated, but, on the contrary, has intensified.

In the midst of this skepticism most contemporary liberal arts colleges seem to have given up on any conscientious effort to define the ideal of liberal education. Typically these colleges insert a line or two dealing with their institutional purpose in the bulletins distributed to prospective students and their parents, and they usually include at least a paragraph, enhanced by literary embellishments, in the promotional and accreditational literature. Frequently,

---

[8]Robert M. Hutchins, *The Higher Learning in America* (New Haven: Yale University Press, 1936); Earl J. McGrath, *The Graduate School and the Decline of Liberal Education* (New York: Bureau of Publications, Teachers College, Columbia University, 1959); Carnegie Foundation for the Advancement of Teaching, *Missions of the College Curriculum: A Contemporary Review with Suggestions* (San Francisco: Jossey-Bass, 1977); Bruce Wilshire, *The Moral Collapse of the University* (Albany, N. Y.: State University of New York, Albany, 1990).

however, these statements are unabashed window dressing. They give the impression of lofty purposes, thereby appealing to idealistic students, parents, and potential donors. But their disingenuousness is betrayed by their glossy vagueness, by their lack of internal consistency, and above all, by the fact that they are largely ignored in educational decision-making.

Among the colleges which claim to provide a liberal education today and which make a conscientious effort to define their institutional ideal, the result is generally limited to two equally sterile alternatives. In some cases a definite but dogmatic formula is devised. Typically this is an attempt to define the ideal by listing a number of character traits which supposedly identify the liberally educated person. While the precision of this procedure is commendable, it is nonetheless open to criticism as being dogmatic and as having only extrinsic value inasmuch as the traits enumerated are dependent upon the prejudices and preferences of the individual or group making the selection. In other cases a less dogmatic but less precise formula is furnished. Usually but unfortunately this attempt avoids criticism only by retreating to vague generalities. While the undogmatic intent of this procedure is commendable, it nonetheless fails as a definition because of its operational uselessness. These two alternatives have familiar illustrations:

Sometimes the ideal adopted gives priority to theory. In this case the college seeks to develop people who hold a set of important truths. These truths typically constitute a "religious faith" or a body of "common knowledge." Though currently out of favor, the ideal of "religious faith" was frequently held in high esteem in the past, as is evidenced by the original close relationship in this country between the liberal arts college and denominational religion. During the twentieth century the ideal of "common knowledge" was adopted by many colleges partly in response to criticism that the ideal of "religious faith" was dogmatic. Subsequently, this ideal has itself been criticized on the ground that there is no agreement on the content of this body of knowledge.

At other times the ideal adopted gives priority to practice. When this is the case, the college tries to develop people who act on the basis of certain norms. For instance, it is sometimes held that the college is responsible for developing people who have "good citizenship." However, since the definition of "good citizenship" depends upon the definition of the good society and the good person, and since there is scarcely unanimity on these fundamentals, the adoption of this ideal often results in charges that this ideal leads to the production of apologists for the reigning ideology.

When each of the above ideals is criticized, dogmatism is avoided by sacrificing precision. For instance, the ideal of "morale" has recently been proposed as a replacement for the ideal of a denominational religious faith.[9] As a

---

[9]In "The Need for Normative Unity in Higher Education" Mordecai M. Kaplan argues that "morale," the specific concern of all religions, is essential to genuine education. In Lyman Bryson, Louis Finkelstein, and R. M. MacIver, eds., *Goals for American Education* (New York: Harper, 1950).

result, a declaration of belief in any particular religious creed is avoided. But if the term "morale" is to descend from an ecumenical abstraction into the world of concrete discourse, it must be given precision. Yet it seems likely that any improvement in precision will increase the grounds for the charge of bias. Sometimes it has been argued that the ideal of liberal education is "the development of the intellect."[10] This ideal seems less constraining than the ideal of "common knowledge" because it does not make any judgment about what every liberally educated person should know. But the price of this license is that what once was a definite formula tends now to become an empty slogan. Attempts to specify the character of the "developed intellect" seem only to reinstate the original dogmatism.

The ideal of "excellence" seems for some to escape the objectionable bias of the ideal of "good citizenship."[11] With this modification it no longer appears mandatory to describe the character of the good citizen or to accept a particular set of normative judgments as inviolate. Again, however, the avoidance of dogmatism is purchased by a retreat from specificity. Hopefully "excellence" will characterize *any* enterprise; consequently, without further specification it is a bare superlative, unable to designate a form of education that is in any way distinctive.

During the twentieth century many liberal arts colleges have tried to avoid charges of dogmatism by disavowing any responsibility for a serious institutional definition of the ideal of liberal education. These colleges then license their students to determine their own educational goals. The inappropriateness of this tactic has been concealed by the college's canonization of the so-called "elective principle," and its rationalization of this principle in the name of "democratic values" and the putative "right of individual choice." As a result, the college avoids institutional dogmatism, but it does so only by subordinating its educational program to the uneducated interests of individual students, who thus by default largely determine both the end and the means of their own education. Since these students lack a liberal education, their choices must be based on their uncriticized assumptions and purposes, and are, therefore, dogmatic. As a consequence, the contemporary liberal arts college is typically driven by manipulated, constantly changing, and uncriticized student interests, and the college shamelessly rationalizes its very existence on the basis of its ability to satisfy these interests. The dogmatism that results from this timorous pandering to "the market" is more pernicious than any institutional dogmatism because it reinforces dogmatic assumptions and purposes and conceals this fact from students and the public.

---

[10]An attempt to specify this kind of ideal is made by Paul L. Dressel and Lewis B. Mayhew in *General Education, Explorations in Evaluation: The Final Report of the Cooperative Study of Evaluation in General Education of the American Council on Education* (Washington, D. C.: American Council on Education, 1954).

[11]This ideal is proposed by John Gardner in *Excellence* (New York: Harper, 1961) and by the "Rockefeller Report," *The Pursuit of Excellence: Education and the Future of America* (New York: Doubleday, 1958).

Clearly, the task of devising a definition of the ideal of liberal education that is specific and yet both undogmatic and intrinsically valuable is as difficult as it is desirable. Unless the ideal is specific, no articulate or operationally meaningful definition has been achieved. And, unless the ideal is undogmatic, the form of education defined will not, strictly speaking, be education in its best sense at all, but mere training, propagandizing, indoctrination, or entertainment. And, finally, unless the ideal is intrinsically valuable, the form of education defined will have value only to those who just happen to share certain contingent assumptions and purposes, and will lack the kind of universal value that would make it a rationally and morally compelling ideal.

THE DIALECTICAL DEDUCTION OF THE IDEAL

We must now wonder whether it is at all possible to define an ideal of liberal education that is undogmatic and intrinsically valuable. Skeptics claim that any definition will reflect some idiosyncratic set of assumptions and values. Moreover, these skeptics argue that today there is no single set of assumptions or values to which all people can, or should, subscribe. It is in fact characteristic of contemporary thought to admit that all theoretical judgments are relative to different points of view, conceptual frameworks, or speech communities, just as all normative or "value" judgments are relative to particular cultures or personal preferences. Consequently, in our pluralistic, skeptical age it may seem anachronistic and naive to seek an educational ideal that is meaningful and not the expression or the instrument of a particular interest or ideology.

It is appropriate at this crucial point to consider the possibility that our inquiry may be handicapped by our current neglect of the liberal arts. The historical record shows that the Greek philosophers and the scholastics, among others, encountered problems of radical skepticism very similar to the kinds that trouble us today. They also cultivated an art that helped them to resolve these problems, and to protect their society and its educational institutions from the corrosive effects of radical skepticism. This art was called dialectic [*dialektike, dialectica*, and cognates], and it was valued as the supreme liberal art.[12] It was developed with astonishing genius by Plato and Aristotle during the fifth and fourth centuries B.C. and by Abelard and others in Paris during the twelfth and thirteenth centuries. Unlike logic, which has developed prodigiously in the twentieth century, and unlike rhetoric, which has been neglected during all but the latter part of this same period, dialectic is for our time and for practical purposes a lost liberal art. In view of its past value in ameliorating problems of skepticism, it seems appropriate to bring its strategies to bear on the kind of skepticism that appears today to be an insurmountable obstacle to a definition of the ideal of liberal education.

---

[12]"Then dialectic, and dialectic alone, goes directly to the first principle and is the only science which does away with hypotheses in order to make her ground secure." Plato, *Republic* 533D.

The strategy of dialectic requires the unpacking of the tacit assumptions or presuppositions of the skeptics' claims.[13] We now turn to this project.

When we consider the presuppositions of the educational skeptics' claims, we must first recognize that these skeptics always assume that their claims merit some action. Certainly these skeptics do not go to the trouble of advancing claims for the purpose of disinterested contemplation. They advance their claims because they consider them to be at least worth thinking about as justifying certain courses of action. They evidently believe that the skeptical ideal which they advocate is more rational or reasonable than the dogmatic reality which they criticize.[14] This means that skepticism must be limited in at least one way. The skeptics cannot believe that all claims are dogmatic and mere subjective preferences, and thus without any intrinsic value. They must believe that at least their own claims are not dogmatic and mere subjective preferences. If the skeptics' own claims are included within the claims that are to be regarded as dogmatic and lacking in intrinsic value, then these claims are incoherent because they are then no less dogmatic and no more valuable than any other claim. Thus, the skeptics must at least tacitly assume that the ideal of *rational action* (of some kind) is undogmatic and intrinsically valuable. The crucial question then becomes: What specifically is presupposed by the notion of rational action?

1.

The skeptics' charge against the proffered definitions of the ideal of liberal education is that they are dogmatic and lacking in intrinsic value. In making this charge the skeptics must assume more than the undogmatic character and intrinsic value of rational action. Since a charge of dogmatism is nothing else but a charge of an ungrounded truth claim, the skeptics must also assume that for any action to be rational it must be guided by knowledge, not by an ungrounded truth claim or mere opinion. Thus, skepticism must be limited in a more precise way. The skeptics cannot be skeptical about all claims to knowledge. In particular, the knowledge that is assumed to justify the skeptical action advocated by the skeptics cannot be impugned. In other words, the skeptics must be discriminating

---

[13]In the last chapter of *The Philosophy of Education* Richard S. Peters provides insight into this strategy. Richard S. Peters, *The Philosophy of Education* (London: Oxford University Press, 1973).

[14]"Rational" is not being used here in a metaphysical sense, but in the ordinary sense of being "reasonable." This seems to be an important distinction to make in the light of the current postmodernist "crisis of reason." "There is a crisis of reason," Umberto Eco writes, "if we are referring to the reason of Descartes, Hegel, and Marx. But if we accept the premise that our behavior in the world ought to be not *rational* but *reasonable*, then I will say (and with a certain satisfaction) that if there is a crisis of reason, there is not a crisis of reasonability." Stefano Rosso/Umberto Eco, "A Correspondence on Postmodernism," in Ingeborg Hoesterey, *Zeistgeist in Babel* (Bloomington, Ind.: Indiana University Press, 1991), 244. On this issue also see: Israel Scheffler, *Reason and Teaching* (Indianapolis, Ind.: Bobbs-Merrill, 1973), 62.

in the sense that the range of their skeptical claims must be restricted so as not to include their own at least implicit claims to knowledge. Otherwise the skeptical claims themselves are subverted by the fact that the skeptics' argument is inconsistent, and therefore, incapable of producing any definite conclusion. Thus, the skeptics' charge that the proffered definitions of the ideal of liberal education are dogmatic and lack intrinsic value carries a second presupposition. It assumes that knowledge, in contrast to mere opinion, is essential to rational action, and is thus also undogmatic and intrinsically valuable.

In assuming that knowledge is undogmatic and intrinsically valuable the skeptics necessarily include two kinds of knowledge. They necessarily assume knowledge of the ideal that they criticize, and they necessarily assume as well knowledge of the skeptical ideal that is at least implicit in their criticism. They thus assume knowledge of the reality that they find objectionable and knowledge of the ideality that they advocate. They cannot doubt the undogmatic character and the intrinsic value of both empirical and normative knowledge--that is, knowledge of what is, and knowledge of what ought to be.[15]

We may summarize the skeptics' two assumptions by saying that in making their criticism of the proffered definitions of the ideal of liberal education, the skeptics necessarily presuppose the ideal of rational action--action that is guided by both empirical and normative knowledge. Skepticism itself is incompatible with the assumption that there is no rational action in the sense that there is no action that is guided by empirical and normative knowledge.

This dialectical insight is of decisive importance for liberal education because it means that if liberal education has as its ideal the development of people who have the capacity and inclination for rational action, then it will have an ideal that cannot be charged with being dogmatic or lacking in intrinsic value. Unlike those ideals which merely express contingent assumptions and subjective preferences, and which can be defended only by rhetorical appeals, an ideal which is the presupposition of any skepticism would be affirmed even by all skeptical attempts to disaffirm it. It would, therefore, be undogmatic and intrinsically valuable.

Historically, the ideal of rational action--the ideal of action based on knowledge of reality and ideality--has sometimes been identified as "wisdom." Consequently, if this ambiguous word is understood in this special sense, then the ideal of liberal education can be defined in an undogmatic and intrinsically valuable way as the development of wise people.[16]

---

[15]I adopt the expression "empirical knowledge" in preference to "theoretical knowledge" because the latter expression is commonly used to mean knowledge that is purely speculative or hypothetical, rather than knowledge of reality. I adopt the expression "normative knowledge" in preference to "practical knowledge" because the latter expression is commonly employed to mean knowledge of means to ends, rather than knowledge of ends or norms.

[16]There are different ways of summarizing this ideal. For instance, for Plato it is "the love of wisdom" or "the examined life." For Aristotle it is "activity of the soul which follows or implies a rational principle . . . throughout a complete life." For Dewey it is "philosophy" or "reflection" or "criticism."

This definition can be given greater specificity by drawing out the kinds of dogmas that it opposes. These dogmas divide into two types according to whether they are empirical, and pertain to the knowledge of reality, or normative, and pertain to the knowledge of ideality. The first is an assumption which restricts knowledge to a given topic, model, or frame of reference. For instance, it has been variously assumed that the paradigm of knowledge is knowledge of a physical, spiritual, or transcendent reality. Such knowledge is achieved on the basis of numerous ontological, epistemological, and semantic assumptions, however, and is, therefore, hypothetical or specialized, not comprehensive. In contrast, knowledge in its undogmatic, paradigmatic sense is comprehensive because it admits no assumption that has not passed critical examination. This requirement of comprehensiveness provides no ground for the absurd view that people cannot know anything unless they know everything; it merely entails that, strictly speaking, people don't know anything as long as they lack the premises that ground their conclusions, and that true comprehension (as is suggested by etymology) requires such comprehensiveness.

The second type of dogma is an imposed imperative, the demand that knowledge serve some preordained purpose or ideal. For example, it has variously been held that knowledge should serve religious ends, social or political ideals, or individual interests. Such knowledge, however, has been subordinated to a specific application and consequently is technological or "applied," not independent or "pure." In contrast, knowledge in its intrinsically valuable, paradigmatic sense is "pure" or independent, and therefore "useless" because it is not sought as a means to any given end. This need for independence gives no support to the absurd view that the achievement of knowledge is possible only by an ascetic detachment from the world; it is merely the recognition that if knowledge is to be intrinsically valuable, it must be an end, not a means, that all action is "sound and fury, signifying nothing" unless it is subordinated to an ideal, and that, contrary to the propaganda of tyranny, what is best cannot be what is useful.

As has been previously noted, a liberal arts college may try to avoid an empirical or normative dogma by allowing students to determine their own educational ideals on the basis of individual interests. In this all too familiar situation this action is always patronizingly rationalized on the basis of "democratic procedures" under the supposed sanction of the so-called "elective principle." While this smoke and mirrors maneuver does succeed in avoiding institutional dogmas, in reality, as has been argued, it merely substitutes a variety of individual dogmas for an institutional dogma. In this way a few conspicuous, well-worn, old dogmas are replaced by many surreptitious, naive, new dogmas.

It follows from these considerations that, since the ideal of rational action requires action that is guided by empirical and normative knowledge, and since empirical and normative knowledge must exclude specialization and technology (in the sense of holding uncriticized assumptions and purposes), the ideal of liberal education requires knowledge that is comprehensive and pure (in the sense that it requires criticism of all assumptions and purposes). Liberal education is thus committed to the development of what might be called the *liberal empirical and normative sciences*--those bodies of knowledge about reality and ideality that are not prejudiced by uncriticized assumptions or purposes.

If the ideal of liberal education is understood as the development of wise people, liberal education is unique among all forms of education: through its agency all other forms of education are subject to criticism. Because of this fact, liberal education so conceived is correctly said to be the best, or most valuable, form of education. Strangely and ironically enough, it is this profound and counter-skeptical assumption that is the fundamental presupposition of the criticism of the skeptics.

2.

The definition of the ideal of liberal education as the development of wise people--that is, people who possess the capacity and inclination to act on the basis of knowledge of reality and ideality--is still lacking in specificity. This definition can be made more specific by unpacking still further the presuppositions of the educational skeptics.

We have seen that the skeptics presuppose that rational action, or action grounded in empirical and normative knowledge, is an intrinsically valuable ideal. Knowledge in itself carries some important assumptions. These become clear in any contrast of knowledge with mere opinion. Knowledge differs from opinion in that it consists of conclusions of arguments that are grounded, or justified, by means of certain methods.

The methods required for the justification of conclusions that qualify as knowledge vary depending on the object of knowledge. For instance, certain methods are appropriate to the empirical sciences, such as physics and biology, where knowledge of reality is the object, and other methods are appropriate to the normative sciences, such as ethics and aesthetics, where knowledge of ideality is the object. For example, certain methods are appropriate to the natural sciences such as biology and geology, which seek knowledge of physical reality, while other methods are appropriate to the social sciences such as sociology and anthropology, which seek knowledge of social reality. These different methods have sometimes been identified as the liberal arts. The systems of conclusions that have been justified by these methods constitute the various special sciences.

In presupposing that empirical and normative knowledge is an intrinsically valuable ideal the skeptics also presuppose that the various methods required for the justification of the conclusions that constitute this knowledge are also intrinsically valuable. Thus, liberal education is necessarily committed to the development of the *theoretical liberal arts*--that is, those arts or skills that are essential for the justification of the conclusions of the liberal sciences.

3.

Knowledge not only carries with it the assumption that its conclusions are the consequences of the application of certain methods, but it also carries the assumption that these conclusions and the methods themselves are justified in terms of rationally defensible principles.

Since the defense of principles and the liberal arts cannot be accomplished by means of principles that are hypothetical or dependent upon contingent assumptions, the defense must be accomplished by means of the art of dialectic. Thus, the principles of morality, the laws of logic and mathematics, the principles of the empirical sciences, the laws of induction, and the principles of dialectic itself can only be justified by dialectic.[17] Consequently, the skeptic's implicit commitment to the value of the liberal sciences and the liberal arts presupposes a commitment to *philosophy*, understood in a special sense as the art of dialectic.

4.

In their criticism of the proffered ideals of liberal education the skeptics make one final kind of assumption. This is the assumption that rational action consists not only in action that is based on empirical and normative conclusions that have been grounded by rational methods in dialectically defensible principles, but also, given the nature of human reality, in action that is achievable only because human beings can develop the prudential skills and the moral virtues (the habits of self-discipline, such as courage, justice, and temperance). Thus, the skeptics' implicit commitment to the value of rational action also carries with it an endorsement of the need for the development of the *practical liberal arts*--those practical skills and virtues without which rational action itself would be impossible.

THE RHETORICAL DEFENSE OF THE IDEAL

The preceding argument is intended as an outline of a theoretical definition of the ideal of liberal education. Beginning from the general assumption that this ideal must be undogmatic and intrinsically valuable, this argument concluded that there is in fact an ideal that meets these unique and stringent requirements. This is the ideal of the development of the wise person--that is, the person who has the capacity and inclination to act rationally. All other ideals are either dogmatic or lack intrinsic value because they are either based on assumptions that are excluded from criticism within the educational program that they justify, or because they serve purposes that are similarly excluded from criticism within the educational program that they justify.

---

[17]It is important to note that this means that the supreme principle of morality is a rational principle. The Platonic allegory of the cave embodies this idea in the metaphor that the supreme achievement of the lover of wisdom is to catch sight of that which makes sight possible--the sun, or idea of good. For a brilliant modern statement of this insight, see Alan Gewirth, *Reason and*

The preceding argument is dialectical in the sense that it imitates the method of the classical liberal art of dialectic. It does not reason forward to conclusions on the basis of premises that are hypothetically accepted, as in scientific demonstration, but instead reasons back to a principle on the basis of its being a necessary presupposition of anyone who engages in criticism--that is, reasoning or argumentation. The ideal of developing the wise person is such a presupposition. This is true because anyone who engages in criticism is necessarily committed to the ideals of criticism, and fundamental to the ideals of criticism are the ideals of the discovery of truth (and thus the avoidance of dogmatism) and the pursuit of rational action (and thus the achievement of intrinsic values). To engage in argumentation is therefore necessarily also to be committed to the ideals that are necessary for the discovery of truth and the pursuit of rational action. This in turn entails a commitment to the institution that is essential to any realization of these ideals.

While the claim that the ideal of liberal education is the development of the wise person is properly defended by dialectical methods, this claim may also be defended by rhetorical methods. In a rhetorical defense of this ideal, dialectical claims are waived and the ideal is defended only by showing that it is justified on the basis of the prevailing assumptions or rhetorical commonplaces held by the community. This kind of defense is especially important in view of current "postmodern," "poststructuralist," and "antifoundationalist" skepticism. A rhetorical defense will not only provide additional and pragmatic arguments for the claim that the proper ideal of liberal education is the development of the wise person, but it will also provide a more precise definition of this ideal. In order to advance these two goals we now turn to a rhetorical defense of the proposed ideal, and argue for the probability of the following two conclusions:

1: The ideal is superior to alternative ideals.
2: The ideal is confirmed by classical arguments.

1. THE IDEAL IS SUPERIOR TO ALTERNATIVE IDEALS

Alternative ideals of liberal education may be classified on the basis of their giving priority to theory, practice, or interests.

1. IDEALS GIVING PRIORITY TO THEORY

"To provide a religious faith"

Infrequently today the purpose of liberal education is held to be the propagation of a particular religious faith. When this ideal is adopted by an educational institution, a set of theological dogmas, general articles of faith, or a

---

Morality (Chicago: University of Chicago Press, 1978).

specific denominational creed determines the structure and content of the institution's educational program.

This ideal is objectionable because, once it is adopted by an educational institution, this institution can no longer subject this ideal to criticism within its educational program without violating its commitment to this ideal. But for an educational institution to be committed to a particular faith and thus to exclude criticism of this faith is a dogmatic act.

"To provide specialized knowledge"

Recent surveys show that most students and parents believe that the main purpose of a liberal education is fulfilled by the academic "major." By "majoring" in some "academic subject" the student is introduced to the conclusions, methods, and principles of a specialized field of knowledge. Ordinarily the choice of this specialized field of knowledge is left to the student, even though this choice is limited by the fields that are made available by the college. The fields made available are largely determined by contingent and often conflicting interests, such as a desire to include the "traditional academic subjects," a desire to be fashionable or "innovative," a desire for favorable media attention, an inability to resist the pet projects of faculty and administrative empire builders, and the need to abide by the college's budgetary constraints. The "major" programs of most colleges require at least a quarter of the students' course "load," and consist in one or more required introductory courses that provide an overview of the field, a number of required advanced courses, and perhaps a "capstone" seminar designed to provide "integration" for the "major."

To adopt the ideal of specialized knowledge as the ideal of liberal education is to adopt a dogmatic ideal. This dogmatism is a consequence of the fact that a specialized field of knowledge is dependent upon principles and methods that distinguish it from other fields of knowledge. But these principles and methods cannot themselves be subjected to criticism on the basis of the principles and methods which they make possible. Thus, a "major" in physics, for instance, does not include the study of the logical, epistemological, ontological, and normative principles that are tacitly assumed by a physical theory. Such theoretical "framework" or "external" questions cannot be grounded in the way that questions "internal" to a theory are grounded. The fact that the acquisition of a specialized theory requires the assumption of principles and methods that are not themselves subject to criticism on the basis of principles and methods internal to the theory means that any education which is limited to the ideal of providing specialized knowledge is inescapably dogmatic.

This charge of dogmatism cannot be evaded by justifying the acquisition of specialized knowledge on the ground that such knowledge is a means for the achievement of career or vocational purposes. Despite the fact that about three-fourths of college students change their career choices during their college years, and despite the fact that the great majority of students eventually pursue careers that are not even remotely related to their undergraduate "majors," most students believe, and few colleges discourage, the idea that the acquisition of specialized knowledge through a "major" is a device for career preparation.[18] However, even if the acquisition of specialist knowledge could be justified on the basis of career or vocational purposes, this acquisition would still be dogmatic. This is true because career or vocational purposes themselves are not legitimately subjected to criticism within a career or vocational program.

Sometimes the ideal of specialized knowledge is defended by the claim that all knowledge requires "depth," and by the additional claim that by obtaining such "depth" education avoids "dilettantism." The trouble with this ploy is that it is not at all clear what it means to characterize knowledge as having "depth." Presumably to know something "in depth" is to possess a relatively large number of conclusions or theorems of some scientific theory. If this is what is meant, the ideal of providing students with specialized knowledge is dogmatic because the possession of a relatively large number of conclusions or theorems of some scientific theory does not include an understanding of the principles that delimit this theory, or the principles that are otherwise assumed by this theory. A person who possesses a relatively large number of conclusions about some subject, but who does not also understand the principles that are presupposed by these conclusions is properly said to be "knowledgeable" or "well-informed," but not to be "wise." On the other hand, if knowledge "in depth" is interpreted to include information about some academic field along with an understanding of the principles grounding the field, this kind of ideal would no longer be the ideal of providing specialized knowledge.

The excuse that students need to possess "knowledge in depth" in the sense of a relatively large number of conclusions about some academic field in order to avoid dilettantism is lame. Dilettantism is the treatment of a subject desultorily or superficially, and this kind of attitude may be taken as easily by those who possess a relatively large number of conclusions about some academic field as those who possess relatively few conclusions. The desire for specialization may be compulsively neurotic, and the desire to avoid such specialization may be a consequence of the desire for wisdom.

"To provide general knowledge"

Others have held that the task of liberal education is not to develop people who know "a lot about some things," but rather to develop people who know "a little about a lot of things." Such a goal is often interpreted to mean that the student should possess some information about a number of academic fields, or

---

[18]Alexander W. Astin and Robert J. Panos, *The Educational and Vocational Development of College Students* (Washington, D. C.: American Council on Education, 1969). Also see: Alexander W. Astin, *Four Critical Years: Effects of College on Beliefs, Attitudes, and Knowledge* (San Francisco: Jossey-Bass, 1978).

perhaps some information about what a number of academic fields have in common. This goal is typically the justification for various "general education" programs, "survey courses," "core courses," and for the familiar curricular device of "distribution requirements."

Obviously any requirement that a student should possess specialist information about a number of academic fields, or information about what a number of academic fields have in common, rests on a principle that justifies this inclusiveness as well as a principle that defines what is to be included as an academic field. But these principles do not themselves belong to the fields that they make possible, and therefore cannot be subjected to criticism within an educational program committed to the development of people who have a "general" knowledge. Inasmuch as such an education assumes but does not criticize these principles, it is dogmatic.

"To provide both specialized and general knowledge"

It is a familiar assumption today that the ideal of liberal education is the development of knowledge in "depth and breadth." The fulfillment of this ideal is usually entrusted to a curriculum that combines both "major" and "distribution" requirements.

While the claim that knowledge has both "depth and breadth" has a superficial kind of plausibility, it is hard to find any insightful interpretation of this spatial metaphor. In consequence, we are left with the unattractive conclusion that the liberally educated person possesses a body of information about some (any) specialized academic field, together with some general knowledge about a number of other academic fields. Since each of these requirements is in itself dogmatic, it is not clear why the combination of them is not also dogmatic. To expect students to gain specialized knowledge without also requiring them to understand the principles that ground this specialized knowledge is dogmatic, and to expect them to gain a general knowledge about a number of academic fields, or even to be acquainted with the entire spectrum of academic fields, without also requiring them to understand the principles that ground this general knowledge is equally dogmatic.

Too often the ideal of providing students with knowledge in "depth and breadth" by means of "major" and "distribution" requirements turns out to be nothing more than a more subtle form of the ideal of providing them with specialized knowledge. This occurs when the hidden purpose of "distribution" requirements turns out to be to introduce students to possible "majors," or, as is sometimes admitted, to stabilize the curriculum in the face of the volatility of student interests.

An even more fundamental objection to the ideal of providing students with knowledge in "depth and breadth" is that this ideal assumes that liberal education is simply a matter of providing students with "knowledge." But in itself "knowledge" has no evident value: it may range from the sublime to the ridiculous, depending on its object. It may consist in the generalization and particularization of the most sublime issues of morality, or it may consist in the generalization and particularization of the most ridiculous of cognitive obsessions. The unqualified pursuit of knowledge lacks intrinsic value.

"To understand the Great Books"

The ideals surveyed so far have been criticized for inadequate conceptions of knowledge and for harboring prejudiced assumptions about the organization, methods, and principles of knowledge. One way to escape this criticism is to deny that the purpose of liberal education is to provide people with a specific body of knowledge, and to claim instead that the ideal is to acquaint students with a body of canonical texts. The best known model for this ideal is the St. Johns College "Great Books" program.

The indisputable problem with the "Great Books" solution is that some decision has to be made on what texts are to be included as "Great Books." Whether this decision is made by an individual or a group, there is evidently no way to escape the prejudices of this individual or group. This criticism of the "Great Books" ideal is illustrated and detailed by Gerald Grant and David Riesman in *The Perpetual Dream: Reform and Experiment in the American College.*[19] The authors charge that, in spite of its admirable features, the St. John's "neo-classical" model of the undergraduate college "is oppressive in its dogmatism and its contempt for the world's 'cheap and obvious standards'. . . ." Only one measure is permitted: "the platinum yardstick of the Program."[20]

"To develop cultural literacy"

One way to escape the charge of dogmatism that is commonly brought against "Great Books" programs is illustrated by E. D. Hirsch, Jr., in *Cultural Literacy: What Every American Needs to Know.*[21] Hirsch argues that functional literacy and effective national communication require "background knowledge." "Background knowledge" is that body of shared information that defines a particular language community. Hirsch bases his argument on psychological research showing that, because of the limits of short-term memory, people cannot understand written and spoken language unless they can efficiently connect this language with previous meanings. This fact about the psychology of learning points to a community's need for "cultural literacy"--a core of shared meanings.

Unlike the "Great Books" ideal, the ideal of "cultural literacy" is not

[19]Gerald Grant and David Riesman, *The Perpetual Dream: Reform and Experiment in the American College* (Chicago: University of Chicago Press, 1978).

[20]Ibid., 75.

[21]E. D. Hirsch, Jr., *Cultural Literacy: What Every American Needs to Know* (New York: Vintage Books, 1988).

dependent upon a "prescriptive list of books," but rather on a "descriptive list of the information actually possessed by literate Americans."[22]   Reviewers of *Cultural Literacy*, ignoring this caveat, and worried about the conservative implications of a canon of "what every American needs to know," have generally failed to realize that this list is not prescriptive, but simply a book of *topoi*, or rhetorical commonplaces.[23]

But the fact that Hirsch's list of "what every American needs to know" is simply a book of commonplaces makes it important as a means for liberal education, but unsuitable as the end or ideal of liberal education.   Liberal education cannot take place unless students are culturally literate, but cultural literacy is only instrumental to the critical development of a knowledge of reality and ideality.   Cultural literacy is thus unsuitable as the ideal of liberal education because it lacks intrinsic value.

"To provide an understanding of Western culture"

During the twentieth century liberal arts colleges have often taken for granted that their primary institutional mission is to develop people who have an understanding of their own culture.   For the American college this has required a curriculum that is focused on the culture of "the West," the culture otherwise identified by its historical origins as Greco-Roman and Judeo-Christian, or identified by its primary contemporary geographical locale as "North Atlantic." The most widely emulated model of this curriculum has been the Contemporary Civilization core course developed by Columbia College during the nineteen twenties, thirties, and forties.

In his 1966 review of the Columbia College general education program Daniel Bell reaffirmed Columbia's commitment to providing its students with "a common learning" and "a comprehensive understanding of the Western tradition."[24]   For Bell this ideal was justified by the need to develop the person who has "self-consciousness, historical consciousness, and methodological consciousness."[25]   This ideal seemed to incorporate the assumption that, while it might be desirable for students to understand non-Western cultures, they should first understand themselves, their own history, and their own culture.

Nonetheless, the ideal of developing an understanding of Western culture has lost favor during the later decades of the twentieth century.   The disaffection with Western values and politics that surfaced during the Viet Nam war and the civil rights struggle, together with the popular acceptance of cultural relativism and the

---

[22]Ibid., xiv.

[23]For instance, one reviewer charges that Hirsch's list is a "hodgepodge of miscellaneous, arbitrary, and often trivial information."   This criticism should be directed not to Hirsch's list, but to American culture.

[24]Daniel Bell, *The Reforming of General Education: The Columbia College Experience in Its National Setting* (New York: Columbia University Press, 1966).

[25]Ibid., 8.

academic acceptance of revisionist historiography and epistemological skepticism, has led many educators to be diffident about any educational program that gives a privileged status to Western culture. The ideal of developing people steeped in the ideas and norms of the West, but uninformed about, or unsympathetic towards, "non-Western" and "Third World" cultures, is now routinely charged with being elitist and chauvinistic.

Those who charge those who privilege Western culture with being elitist and chauvinistic typically do so on the ground that "the West has no corner on truth or morality." However, even if it were to be universally agreed that Western culture should be privileged over all other values, this would not justify its uncritical acceptance within a program of liberal education. In a program of liberal education all putative truths and values should be subjected to criticism. To proceed otherwise is to proceed dogmatically.

"To provide an understanding of world cultures"

Recently many educators seem to have been persuaded that the dogmatism of conceiving of the mission of liberal education as the study of Western culture can be avoided if this mission is expanded to the study of world cultures. This may have encouraged some colleges to add required "non-Western" and "Third World" studies to their curricula.

Unfortunately, this new ideal does not escape dogmatism. This is true because the new, more culturally inclusive ideal still employs a principle of inclusion that is not itself subject to criticism within the educational program that the principle justifies. For example, the new ideal typically requires students to gain an understanding of "important" existing "world" cultures, but not an understanding of every one of the almost infinite number of present and past cultures and subcultures. In addition, it is often the case that the principle of inclusion serves political interests. For instance, it is common to justify the need to understand world cultures on the basis of the political need to develop tolerance for cultural diversity in an increasingly interdependent world. However, when the study of world cultures is justified by some putative political need, then the ideal ceases to be intrinsically valuable, and becomes only instrumental to some putatively superior social or political purpose. This social or political purpose cannot be subject to criticism within the program that it justifies. It is, therefore, dogmatic.

"To provide an initiation into the forms of knowledge"

One of the most interesting and widely-discussed contemporary theories of liberal education is provided by Paul H. Hirst in his book *Knowledge and the*

Curriculum.[26]   Hirst conceives of a liberal education as an "initiation" into the forms of knowledge. This concept is advanced with the understanding that, while it is a reaffirmation of the classical ideal of liberal education, it is a concept that is in need of a modern justification that avoids "the assumptions of classical realism."

Hirst interprets the Greek ideal of liberal education as the pursuit of knowledge. He assumes that for the Greeks this ideal was justified on the metaphysical ground that the achievement of knowledge was the entelechy of the human mind and thus essential to human life. This ideal defined a form of education that produced truth, not dogma, and that was an intrinsic good, not a mere extrinsic good.

Unwilling to adopt the metaphysical and epistemological assumptions that he takes to be the Greek justification for this ideal, Hirst suggests that an adequate definition and justification of the ideal "can in fact be based directly on an explication of the concepts of 'mind' and 'knowledge' and their relationships."[27] In Hirst's opinion the Harvard "Redbook"[28] attempted to define and justify a general (i.e., liberal) education in this manner, but was unsuccessful because it failed to demonstrate that the logical relationship between the concepts of "mind" and "knowledge" was sufficient to guarantee that the achievement of knowledge is necessarily the development of mind.

Hirst's own analysis of these two concepts shows that "to acquire knowledge is to learn to see, to experience the world in a way otherwise unknown, and thereby come to have a mind in a fuller sense."[29]   "A liberal education," consequently, is one that is "determined in scope and content by knowledge itself," and "is thereby concerned with the development of mind."[30]

According to Hirst, this concept of liberal education cannot receive its justification from the metaphysical and epistemological assumptions of classical realism, but must receive it from a "conceptual analysis" of the concept of knowledge itself. Hirst argues that this concept has an unimpeachable status because to question the pursuit of any kind of "rational knowledge" is in the end self-defeating. The questioning itself, he says, "depends on accepting the very principles whose use is finally being called in question."[31]

Once liberal education is understood as "the comprehensive development of the mind in acquiring knowledge," and once it is understood that this requires

---

[26]Paul H. Hirst, *Knowledge and the Curriculum* (London: Routledge and Kegan Paul, 1974), chap. 3. This chapter originally appeared as "Liberal Education and the Nature of Knowledge" in Reginald D. Archambault, ed., *Philosophical Analysis and Education* (London: Routledge and Kegan Paul, 1965), 113-138.

[27]Hirst, *Knowledge and the Curriculum*, 33.

[28]*General Education in a Free Society: Report of the Harvard Committee* (Cambridge: Harvard University Press, 1945).

[29]Hirst, *Knowledge and the Curriculum*, 40.

[30]Ibid., 41.

[31]Ibid., 42.

"achieving an understanding of experience in many different ways," there remains only the task of distinguishing these different ways of "understanding experience." These "forms of knowledge" include "moral knowledge" and a number of "disciplines" which are distinguished by their dependence on some particular kind of test against experience for their distinctive expressions."[32] Hirst lists seven basic "disciplines": mathematics, physical sciences, human sciences, history, religion, literature and the fine arts, and philosophy. A liberal education will immerse students in the concepts, logic and criteria of these "disciplines" so that they can come to "use the appropriate concepts, logic, and criteria," and can appreciate the "range of understanding" in each form.

Hirst's theory has two especially praiseworthy virtues: First, it recognizes that the classical concept of liberal education is as important today as it was in antiquity, and that this importance is a consequence of the fact that this education aspires to truth uncompromised by dogma, and aspires to values that are uncompromised by extrinsic purposes. Second, it correctly sees that this ideal must not be defended by a dogmatic metaphysics or epistemology, but instead must be defended in some way that will escape dogmatism.

In spite of these virtues Hirst's theory must be faulted on two counts. First, Hirst mistakenly takes the ideal of liberal education to be a form of knowledge. This, as some critics have pointed out, is too narrow.[33] It is too narrow because an education that is limited to the achievement of knowledge cannot be one that is intrinsically valuable so long as knowledge is understood to include ideals and the means to action. And as twentieth century philosophers such as Heidegger and Dewey have argued, theorizing is but one form of activity, and it is a form that is dependent upon human purposes. In addition, the case can be made that the Greek philosophers--as least Plato and Aristotle--do not in fact subscribe to the idea that abstract knowledge is intrinsically valuable. For Plato, the highest form of knowledge is wisdom, a knowledge of the good, but the philosopher, or lover of this knowledge, is not permitted to treat this knowledge as a matter for disinterested contemplation, but is required to descend back into the cave in order apply this knowledge. For Aristotle, the highest good for man is a kind of activity, not a mere potentiality or disposition, and this activity must be in accordance with both intellectual and moral virtue, throughout a complete life. Since Plato and Aristotle did conceive of liberal education as undogmatic and intrinsically valuable, if they did in fact try to justify it on the basis of a metaphysical or epistemological theory, they would by virtue of this effort be engaged in an inconsistent project, for they would be trying to justify that which they clearly recognize to be justifiable in itself.

Second, Hirst's narrow, theoretical conception of a liberal education leads him to dogmatic conclusions about the necessary constituents of any program of liberal education. For instance, he provides various "forms of knowledge," but he

---

[32]Ibid., 45.
[33]Martin, "A Paradigm for Liberal Education," 37-59.

provides no principle that requires these specific forms. His seven "disciplines," for instance, are introduced as if they were discovered by accident. Consequently, there is no justification for the specific disciplines he regards as essential, and no proof that this particular list is complete. Moreover, Hirst tells us that students will be initiated into these "disciplines" so that they will have "a series of discrete ways of understanding experience."[34] But nowhere is there any justification for the need for students to have "a series of discrete ways of understanding experience." Finally, after arguing that a liberal education is intrinsically valuable, Hirst hedges his argument at the end and suggests that liberal education has a valuable outcome. This outcome, he says, should not be thought of as producing "ever greater disintegration of the mind" but rather should be thought of as producing "the growth of ever clearer and finer distinctions in our experience."[35] As a metaphor for this he suggests that the "forms of knowledge" are like "voices in a conversation, a conversation to which they each contribute in a distinctive way."[36] The trouble with these suggestions is that there is no demonstrated value in "understanding experience" in these discrete ways, and no demonstrated value in contributing to a "conversation" that has not been distinguished from prattle. More important is the fact that if liberal education is indeed intrinsically valuable, then, barring some rhetorical purpose, it would be inconsistent to seek an extrinsic justification.

"To develop the critical thinker"

The current "critical thinking movement" has provided sponsorship for the ideal of "critical thinking." While this ideal is not specifically recognized as the ideal of liberal education, it is identified as an ideal that is of "the first importance in the conception and organization of educational activities."[37] This ideal has evolved in the writings of Robert Ennis, Richard Paul, John McPeck, Harvey Siegel, and others.[38]

The latest defense of this ideal is given by Harvey Siegel in *Educating Reason*.[39] Siegel identifies the critical thinker as the person who is able to properly assess reasons and their ability to warrant beliefs, claims and actions. This person has a good understanding of, and an ability to use, both scientific and logical methods. In addition, the critical thinker has an understanding of "the nature of reasons, warrant and justification generally, as these notions function across fields."[40] But Siegel argues that this person cannot be identified as one

---

[34]Ibid., 52.

[35]Ibid.

[36]Ibid.

[37]Israel Scheffler, *Reason and Teaching*, 1.

[38]For a survey and critique of this movement, see: Harvey Siegel, *Educating Reason: Rationality, Critical Thinking, and Education* (New York: Routledge, 1988).

[39]Ibid.

[40]Ibid., 38.

who merely has the ability to assess reasons. This person must also have "the critical spirit," and thus be properly disposed to assess reasons. This means that the critical thinker must have "certain attitudes, dispositions, habits of mind, and character traits."[41] The critical thinker is thus a "certain sort of person," a "rational actor," not merely a thinker.

Siegel's description of this ideal as a person, and his addition of what he calls a "critical spirit component" to the "reason assessment component" provides an educational ideal that goes beyond the more narrowly theoretical scope of some of the earlier formulations of the ideal of "critical thinking."[42] With this emendation the ideal of the "critical thinker" (understood also as the "critical actor") would seem to approximate the ideal of the wise person--the person who has the capacity and inclination for rational action. The wise person has been identified as the person who acts on the basis of knowledge of reality and ideality, who possesses the skills necessary to gain knowledge, who grounds this knowledge in rationally defensible principles, and who possesses the practical and moral virtues that are essential to rational action. Siegel's account of the critical thinker would seem to include these specifications.

If this conclusion is justified, criticism of Siegel's conception of the ideal of critical thinking must be limited to relatively minor issues: (1) Terminologically, the expression, "critical thinking"--and even the expression, "the critical thinker"--still carry the connotations of earlier exclusively theoretical interpretations. The history of the critical thinking movement provides evidence that this terminology is apt to be misleading. (2) Siegel explains why a critical thinker is inclined to think critically (because he or she values critical thinking), but he does not explain why the critical thinker is necessarily a critical actor. The ideal of the wise person makes this necessity clear on the ground that critical thinking is one of the necessary qualities of the wise person. (3) While it is clear that Siegel believes that the critical thinker possesses certain "epistemological" principles, in addition to his or her possession of "subject-specific" and "subject-neutral" principles, it is not clear that this person must understand the principles of morality. The wise person must understand these principles because any knowledge that lacks this knowledge is less than unconditionally rational.

2. IDEALS GIVING PRIORITY TO PRACTICE

"To provide vocational training"

Studies have shown that the vast majority of students and their parents believe that among the main purposes of going to college is "to prepare for a

---

[41]Ibid., 39.

[42]See, for instance: Robert H. Ennis, "A Concept of Critical Thinking," *Harvard Educational Review* 32 (1962): 81-111.

specific occupation" and "to have a more satisfying career."[43]   If the ideal of liberal education is to prepare people for a career or vocation, then this ideal justifies any of a variety of vocational, professional, or pre-professional programs.

While the ideal of preparing people for a career or vocation will justify educational programs that develop vocational knowledge and skills, it will not justify programs that develop the knowledge and skills necessary to judge the value of vocational knowledge and skills. For instance, a vocational program might develop the knowledge and skills essential to being a lawyer or a business executive, but it cannot justifiably develop the knowledge or skills necessary to judge the morality of the law or the ethics of business. This is true because the knowledge and skills required to judge the morality of these vocations are not justified by vocational ideals. As a consequence, an educational program designed to achieve a vocational purpose must exclude fundamental questions of morality, and as a consequence, must rest on a dogmatic purpose and have value only to those who share such a purpose. In contrast, a liberal education must avoid dogma, and be intrinsically valuable. It therefore cannot be subordinated to a vocational purpose.

In spite of the fact that educators never seem to tire of trying to ignore the difference, the difference between liberal education and vocational training is still marked in our language by contrasting expressions such as "education" and "training," "knowledge" and "technology," and "the liberal arts" and "the technological arts." The difference that is marked by these expressions is a profound one: it is the difference between vocational training's concern with the means to achieve given ends, and liberal education's concern with the ends that justify means.

The difference between liberal education and vocational training is sometimes muddled by the argument that "liberal arts education" is not "incompatible with preprofessional, careerist aspirations" because both vocational training and liberal arts "studies" are valuable for professional and career purposes.[44]   The error in this argument is the assumption that the crucial difference between vocational training and a liberal education is that the former is useful while the latter is useless. But a liberal education differs from vocational training not because of differences in their respective utility when viewed as means to ends, but in the fact that these two forms of education have radically different ends.

The difference between liberal education and vocational training is also often confused by the assumption that a "liberal education" is simply a form of education that possesses the quality of being "liberal." Since the word "liberal" is used in many different ways, an education that is "liberal" may mean one that is

---

[43]Ernest L. Boyer, *College: The Undergraduate Experience in America* (New York: Harper & Row, Publishers), 11.

[44]Paul J. Zingg, "The Three Myths of Preprofessionalism," *Liberal Education* 69 (1983): 209-244.

"not narrow-minded," "not prescriptive," or "not politically conservative." Once "liberal education" is understood to be "liberal" in one of these ways, then it is easy to argue that vocational training can also be "liberal" in one of these ways.[45] What needs to be kept in mind is that the difference between "liberal education" and vocational training is not the difference between "liberal" education and vocational training.

Those who wish to erase the distinction between liberal education and vocational training frequently cite the fact that for Cicero and the oratorical tradition a liberal education was used to prepare citizens for their civic duties.[46] What is forgotten in this claim is that in the oratorical tradition the ideal orator was not a bureaucratic functionary, but a person who had the capacity and inclination for rational action. The orator of Cicero's *De Oratore* united wisdom and eloquence, and was the philosopher in practical action. The education of the orator was not one that emphasized the training of people for work in a civic bureaucracy, but one that enabled civic leaders to think and act in rational ways.

"To prepare students for graduate school"

Some college teachers are strongly opposed to the inclusion of vocational programs, such as business, nursing, computer programming, or military training, in the liberal arts college. At the same time, however, these teachers may accept without question the assumption that one of their primary professional responsibilities is to prepare students for graduate school. In preparing students for graduate school these "closet vocationalists" fail to see that graduate school preparation does not differ in principle from any of the standard examples of vocational programs that they object to.[47] Like other vocational programs, an academic preprofessional program has a career or professional purpose and makes certain theoretical assumptions concerning the nature and value of an academic field that are not properly questioned within the preprofessional program itself. Consequently, those who assume that one of their primary professional responsibilities is to prepare "their students" or "their majors" to "go into their fields" are privileging certain purposes and assumptions, and thereby treating liberal education in ways that make it dogmatic and lacking in intrinsic value.

---

[45]For instance, Bruce Kimball makes the claim that those who argue that "useful" studies are liberal often have appealed to Franklin, while those who oppose this usually have appealed to Aristotle. Both of these historical appeals are flawed, Kimball argues, because "neither Plato nor Aristotle was committed to the exclusionary rationale that studies useful in one's work, career or profession are ipso facto illiberal." Bruce A. Kimball, "Liberal vs. Useful Education: Reevaluating the Historical Appeals to Benjamin Franklin and Aristotle," *Liberal Education* 67 (1981): 286-292.

[46]For instance, Maxwell H. Goldberg cites this fact in his advocacy of "career-oriented liberal education." Maxwell H. Goldberg, "Vocational Training, Career Orientation, and Liberal Education," *Liberal Education* 61 (1975): 309ff.

[47]David French, "Closet Vocationalists among Proponents of the Liberal Arts," *Liberal Education* 65 (1979): 470-477.

"To prepare for a mature, effective, adult life"

Sometimes education is taken to be a means to promote psychological growth, "ideal adult functioning," or "maturity." This is the ideal, for instance, of "psychological education" as described by Alfred S. Alschuler, J. McIntyre, and D. Tabor in *How to Develop Achievement Motivation: A Manual for Teachers.*[48] In this book the authors argue that the "process as well as the content of formal education should be designed to prepare students to live mature, effective, adult lives."[49] This view is illustrated by the familiar, general claim that the goal of liberal education is to prepare students to live a "full" or "rich" life.

There are a number of obvious objections to this position. (1) Among different "psychological educators" there is no consensus on what is meant by a life that is "mature," "effective," "full," or "rich." While it seems difficult to object to these goals, this difficulty may well be due to the fact that words like "mature," "effective," "full," or "rich" may be used as mere superlatives, and in this case would be empty of descriptive content. (2) To the extent that these words are given descriptive content, then to that extent important disagreements on the acceptability of this ideal are likely to surface. Psychologists as well as non-psychologists disagree on what counts as a "full" or "rich" human life. (3) Psychological norms tend to reflect the values of a particular culture. This conservative tendency is evident in "psychological education's" position that "whatever motives are taught in school should be consistent with cultural values and societal demands."[50]   (4) Even if there were general or even universal agreement on the psychological ideal of the human being, this agreement would not be sufficient to justify this ideal as the ideal of liberal education. A society could have at least general agreement on what should be called a "full" or "rich" human life, and this life could nonetheless be immoral. The twentieth century alone provides us with ample illustrations of this possibility.

These objections highlight the fact that the ideal of human reality is itself problematic. This problem is not one that should be decided in advance of a liberal education, but is one that should be addressed by a liberal education. For the college to resolve this problem in advance would remand it to moral indoctrination.

---

[48]Alfred S. Alschuler, J. McIntyre, and D. Tabor, *How to Develop Achievement Motivation: A Manual for Teachers* (Middletown, Connecticut: Educational Ventures, Inc., 1969). Other sources for "psychological education" recommended by the authors are: Gordon W. Allport, *Pattern and Growth in Personality* (New York: Holt, Rinehart and Winston, 1961); Abraham H. Maslow, *Toward A Psychology of Being* (Princeton, N. J.: Van Nostrand, 1968); and Erik Erikson, "Identity and the Life Cycle," in *Psychological Issues* I, 1 (1959). For a comprehensive bibliography on humanistic education, psychological education, the eupsychian network, affective education, curriculury of concerns, the human potential movement, personological education, sunectics, personal learning, intrinsic education, etc., see *Educational Opportunity Forum* 1 (Fall, 1969): 184-203.

[49]Alschuler, McIntyre, and Tabor, ob. cit., 110.

[50]Ibid.

"To provide political liberation"

Today a number of educational theorists hold that the fundamental responsibility of all education is the political "liberation" of all human beings. This view is shared by a variety of people who may otherwise be identified as "humanists," "critical theorists," "socialists," "Neo-Marxists," "radicals," or "liberation theologists." One of the most influential of these theorists, Paulo Freire, argues that education is one of the main instruments for the resolution of "man's central problem"--the problem of "the emancipation of mankind," the revolutionary project of "human liberation."[51]

Friere believes that this revolutionary project is imperative because of the historical truth that everywhere man is endemically oppressed by social and political structures which interfere with his "ontological and historical vocation to be more fully human."[52] Moreover, these structures are resistant to change because they are sustained by the "dominate classes" to repress or "domesticate" the "subordinate classes." For this reason, Friere maintains, it is "extremely naive to expect the dominant classes to develop a type of education that would enable subordinate classes to perceive social injustice critically."[53] Thus, a "pedagogy of the oppressed" is needed to overcome the "false consciousness" brought about by the "hidden curriculum" of education that functions as "cultural action for domination." Only a revolutionary "cultural action for freedom" can "orient the people to the unveiling of reality" and "empower" them to achieve their own liberation.[54]

For Freire this historical reality means that there can be "no neutral education." Consequently, the ideal of education as a "temple of pure knowledge" that should "soar above earthly preoccupations" is a myth contrived by the dominant classes.[55] Education is correctly understood as a "springboard for changing reality," and for the "emancipation of mankind."[56] It is therefore "partisan to its core."[57]

Freire's ideal of "political liberation" identifies a particular ideal human type and a range of oppressive structures that must be removed if this ideal is to be realized. We may respect this ideal and accept Freire's analysis of the socio-economic obstacles to its realization. We may even agree with the charge that much of "*status quo* education" is repressive and "domesticating," and therefore,

---

[51]Paulo Freire, *Pedagogy of the Oppressed* (New York: The Seabury Press, 1974). See also: Paulo Freire, *The Politics of Education* (South Hadley, Mass.: Bergin & Garvey, 1985), and Samuel Bowles and Herbert Gintis, *Schooling in Capitalist America: Educational Reform and the Contradictions of Economic Life* (New York: Basic Books, 1976).

[52]Freire, *Pedagogy of the Oppressed*, 40.

[53]Freire, *The Politics of Education*, 152.

[54]Ibid., 86.

[55]Ibid., 118.

[56]Ibid., 170.

[57]Henry A. Giroux, "Introduction" to Freire, *The Politics of Education*, xxiv.

dogmatic. But if "political liberation" is then adopted as the ideal of liberal education, education will remain dogmatic. This is true because once the ideal of "political liberation" is adopted as the ideal of an educational program, then this ideal cannot be subjected to criticism within this same program (since this action would not further "political liberation"). This is to say that Freire's ideal of "liberated" humanity cannot itself be problematic within an education for the "liberation" of humanity. In contrast, only the ideal of wisdom--that is, the ideal of subjecting all ideals to criticism--can avoid dogmatism because as the ideal of an educational program it can, and must, be subjected to criticism within the program that it justifies. Unlike the ideal of "political liberation," the ideal of wisdom is a necessary presupposition of any criticism of educational ideals, and therefore, is the only undogmatic ideal, and, in consequence, the only intrinsically valuable educational ideal.

The dogmatism of the ideal of "political liberation" may be illustrated in three ways:

1. Freire argues that the ideal of all education is the development of a specific type of human being. This human type is said to have an "ontological and historical vocation to be more fully human." This means that a human being must be in "the pursuit of self-affirmation," must be "animated by authentic (not humanitarian) generosity,"[58] must be "guided by strong feelings of love," etc.[59] While this human type may be universally admired today, it is not the only conceivable ideal human type. We can imagine that at least some kind of a case might be made on behalf of alternative types, ranging all the way from the other-worldly ascetic to the *Übermensch*. Consequently, any education that prejudges this ideal is itself prejudiced.

2. Freire assumes that the relationship between the "dominant classes" and the "subordinate classes" is one of exploitation, and thus a relationship that should be replaced. Once again, while today there may be universal agreement that this interpretation is accurate, it is not the only conceivable interpretation of this relationship. Some would claim that it is not always so easy to distinguish the exploiter from the exploited. For instance, although it will seem wretched and far-fetched to the citizens of a liberal democracy, it is not inconsistent to Social Darwinists or to those who accept Nietzsche's analysis of "the ethics of pity" to argue that the relationship between the "dominant classes" and the "subordinate classes" is no more exploitative that the relationship between predator and prey in the animal world. Since this alternative interpretation is at least conceivable, it would be dogmatic for an educational program to prejudge this issue.

3. Freire assumes that the capitalist economic system is opposed to the ideal of "human liberation." But once again, while we may consider this assumption to be plausible, it is nonetheless arguable. Conceivably, in a world of limited economic options some form of capitalism might be more humanizing or less dehumanizing than all other available options. In any case, the morality of

---

[58]Freire, *Pedagogy of the Oppressed*, 39-40.
[59]Ibid., 78n.

alternative economic systems is an important and difficult issue and merits consideration within a program of liberal education. It is not an issue to be resolved institutionally prior to such a program, thus resulting in a theory to be dogmatically promulgated.

Consequently, while we may grant that Freire makes persuasive arguments for his educational ideal, we must still insist that his ideal rests on assumptions that are at least conceivably false. Because of this, the adoption of his ideal as the ideal of liberal education, and therefore, as an ideal that is exempted from criticism within a program of liberal education, is to prejudge an important issue. For this reason Freire's ideal of "political action" must be regarded as dogmatic. Its adoption turns liberal education into political indoctrination.[60]

"To develop solidarity"

After his celebrated polemic against the correspondence theory of truth and his petition for the pragmatic theory of truth in *Philosophy and the Mirror of Nature* and *The Consequences of Pragmatism*, Richard Rorty has expanded on the moral and political implications of these arguments in *Contingency, Irony, and Solidarity*.[61] In this book he argues that moral progress is "in the direction of greater human solidarity." "Solidarity" he understands as "the ability to see more and more traditional differences (of tribe, religion, race, customs, and the like) as unimportant when compared with similarities with respect to pain and humiliation . . . ."[62] "Solidarity" is both a moral and a political ideal. As a moral ideal it describes the "liberal ironist," the person who "faces up to the contingency of his or her most central beliefs and desires," and who includes among his or her "ungroundable desires" the hope "that suffering will be diminished, that the humiliation of human beings by other human beings may cease."[63] As a political ideal "solidarity" describes an "equally desirable" "postmetaphysical" utopia, a "liberal democracy"--a polity designed "to diminish cruelty," to "make possible government by the consent of the governed," and to "permit as much domination-free communication as possible . . . ."[64] Such a polity will allow its citizens to be "self-creative": They "will be able to be as privatistic, 'irrationalist,' and aestheticist as they please so long as they do it on their own time--causing no harm to others and using no resources needed by those less advantaged."[65]

---

[60]For an analysis of the kind of political indoctrination now called "political correctness" see: Dinesh D'Souza, "Illiberal Education," *The Atlantic Monthly* (March 1991): 51-58. See also: John Searle, "The Storm Over the University," *The New York Review of Books* (6 December 1990): 34-42.

[61]Richard Rorty, *Contingency, Irony, and Solidarity* (Cambridge: Cambridge University Press, 1989).

[62]Ibid., 192.

[63]Ibid., xv.

[64]Ibid., 68.

[65]Ibid., xiv.

In *Contingency, Irony, and Solidarity* Rorty explains that the ideal of "solidarity" has been "created" in response to the contingencies of language, selfhood, and community.   The contingency of language is summarized by reference to Wittgenstein, Kuhn, and Davidson's insight that "there is no way to step outside the various vocabularies we have employed and find a metavocabulary . . . ."[66] The contingency of selfhood is summarized by reference to Freud, Nietzsche, and Harold Bloom's demonstration that conscience, like language, is also the product of time and chance. And finally, the contingency of community is summarized by reference to Dewey, Michael Oakeshott, and John Rawls' rejection of "the idea of a transhistorical 'absolutely valid' set of concepts which would serve as 'philosophical foundations' of liberalism."[67]

These inescapable contingencies discredit the efforts of philosophers to find ahistorical foundations for knowledge. As a consequence of this historicism, the traditional philosophical search for foundations or theoretical justifications of ideas and ideals--including the ideal of "solidarity" itself--must be abandoned. Rorty argues that "there is no answer to the question 'Why not be cruel?'--no noncircular theoretical backup for the belief that cruelty is horrible."[68] He holds that any effort to find philosophical first principles is "reasonable if it means merely that we should seek common ground in the hope of attaining agreement"; but it is "misleading if it is taken as the claim that there is a natural order of premises from which moral and political conclusions are to be inferred . . . ."[69] In these circumstances our only recourse is to recognize that certain practical and moral purposes must be given precedence over our theoretical compulsions. We need to recognize that "the goal of thinking and social progress is 'Freedom,' not 'Truth.'"[70] This means that "democratic politics" should take priority over the interests of philosophy.[71] Such "light-mindedness" toward philosophy, Rorty says, "helps make the world's inhabitants more pragmatic, more tolerant, more liberal, more receptive to the appeal of instrumental rationality."[72]

Although Rorty does not address the problems of liberal education in *Contingency, Irony, and Solidarity*, he does address the related issue of "general studies" in a lecture which he gave to a seminar at George Mason University in April, 1981,[73] and the problem of "nonvocational higher education" in a keynote address which he gave to the American Association of Colleges' Annual Meeting

---

[66]Ibid., xvi.

[67]Ibid., 57.

[68]Ibid., xv.

[69]Ibid., 268.

[70]Ibid., xiii.

[71]Richard Rorty, "The Priority of Democracy to Philosophy," in M. D. Peterson and R. C. Vaughn, eds., *The Virginia Statute for Religious Freedom* (Cambridge: Cambridge University Press, 1988).

[72]Ibid., 271.

[73]Richard Rorty, "Hermeneutics, General Studies, and Teaching," in *Selected Papers from the Synergos Seminars*, vol. 2 (Fairfax, Virginia: George Mason University, 1982).

in January, 1989.[74] In the seminar contribution Rorty takes the position that "there is nothing much to be said about general studies or the teaching of such studies," except that they should not be understood as the pursuit of truth but as "an invitation to join a community, a community of problem-solvers, united by the romantic sense that solving these problems is the point of living."[75] In the A.A.C. address Rorty states that "the point of nonvocational higher education . . . is to help students realize that they can reshape themselves . . . into a new self-image, one which they themselves have helped to create."[76] While Rorty sometimes speaks of this self-creation as a "growth" whose "direction" is "unpredictable," there seems little doubt that for him self-creation is always at least assumed to be subordinate to the needs of "liberal democracy."[77] This interpretation seems fully justified by the following passage:

> With a bit of help, students [in "nonvocational higher education"] will start noticing everything that is paltry and mean and unfree in their surroundings. With luck, the best of them succeed in altering the conventional wisdom, so that the next generation is socialized in a somewhat different way than they themselves were socialized. To hope that this way will only be *somewhat* different is to hope that the society will remain reformist and democratic rather then be convulsed by revolution. To hope that it nevertheless will be *perceptibly* different is to remind oneself that growth is indeed the only end which democratic higher education can serve . . . .[78]

Thus, though Rorty speaks of "nonvocational higher education" as having no end beyond "growth," he is here explicitly speaking about "*democratic* higher education*." In this address and in the earlier seminar contribution Rorty provides confirmation for the view that the ideal of liberal education--understood as "general studies" or "nonvocational higher education--is in fact the ideal that he has recently described as "solidarity." According to this view liberal education is responsible for the promotion of "liberal democracy" and, in consequence, for the development of "liberal ironists"--people who are "self-creative" but who "avoid cruelty" and "face up to contingency."

The ideal of "solidarity" may be thought to avoid dogmatism because it gives priority to "Freedom" over "Truth," and is considered to be supremely valuable because it provides a normative principle that is not subordinated to any other theoretical or normative principle.

In an age characterized by deep skepticism and cultural diversity, and

---

[74]Richard Rorty, "Education, Socialization, and Individuation," *Liberal Education* 75 (1989): 2-9.

[75]Rorty, "Hermeneutics, General Studies, and Teaching," 13.

[76]Rorty, "Education, Socialization, and Individuation," 5.

[77]Ibid., 9.

[78]Ibid., 8.

threatened by the ever-present possibility of political repression and global disaster, any ideal which promotes "liberal democracy" is likely to appear attractive to most people. Nonetheless, there are two important objections to the adoption of "solidarity" as the ideal of liberal education:

1. Appearances to the contrary, the proposal that "solidarity" should be the proper ideal of liberal education is in fact dogmatic. It is dogmatic because, if this ideal is adopted by an educational institution, then this institution cannot permit, much less require, criticism of this ideal within its educational program. This is to say that if an institution commits itself to the promotion of "liberal democracy" and to the development of "liberal ironists," it cannot condone activities that question or otherwise disserve these ideals. For instance, since for Rorty the promotion of "liberal democracy" requires that students discover "everything that is paltry and mean and unfree in their surroundings," and that the society "remain reformist and democratic rather then be convulsed by revolution," the adoption of an ideal for the promotion of "liberal democracy" already assumes the need for certain political reforms and already assumes the means by which these reforms should be achieved. Thus, by virtue of its commitment to the ideal of "solidarity" an institution already commits itself to a specific political end and to a specific political means. As a consequence, this institution has no justification for the unprejudiced consideration of alternative moral or political ends and means. For instance, the claim that "cruelty is the worst thing that we do" cannot be challenged unless the ideal of "solidarity" is itself to be abandoned as a consequence of our making the at least tacit assumption that cruelty may not be the worst thing that we can do.

At this point defenders of the ideal of "solidarity" may respond to the charge of dogmatism by arguing that this charge begs the question because it tacitly assumes that all theoretical and normative claims require justification. There are two problems of inconsistency in this response. First, since "solidarity" has been seriously proposed as the ideal of liberal education, it is only reasonable to assume that this proposal has some justification. Second, any charge that the demand for justification begs the question of the necessity for justification already at least tacitly assumes that at least one kind of justification--a *petitio principii*--cannot count as a justification.

2. The second objection to the proposal that "solidarity" is the proper ideal of liberal education is that "solidarity" is in fact subordinate to superior ideals. It therefore cannot be the ideal of the most valuable form of education. The subordinate status of "solidarity" is apparent from the fact that insofar as "solidarity" is proposed as the proper ideal of liberal education, this proposal must already presuppose a set of procedures for making and adjudicating such proposals. Any claims about moral and political ideals already assume a practical situation in which there are at least implicit principles and procedures for their adjudication.

"To actualize human potential"

The ideal of liberal education may be held to be "personal growth," or the development of people who "actualize their human potential." This ideal has been championed in the pedagogy of "humanistic education." While this pedagogy had its greatest impact in the United States during the nineteen seventies, its influence continues to be felt at every level of education. Humanistic educators continue to defend the merits of "open" and "affective" education, and "student-centered" and "experiential" learning.

The pedagogy of "humanistic education" owes much to the pragmatism of John Dewey, to the "existential" philosophers like Kierkegaard and Heidegger, to the educational psychologies of Piaget, McClelland, and Erikson, and probably most importantly, to the client-centered clinical psychology of Carl Rogers and the "Third Force" psychology of Abraham Maslow.[79]

In general the humanistic educators emphasize the immense creative possibilities of human beings, and deplore the numerous ways that these possibilities are repressed by institutions and individuals. One of the ways that this repression of "human potentiality" is said to occur is through traditional education. Carl Rogers has provided an influential statement of this position in a paper entitled "Personal Thoughts on Teaching and Learning."[80] Rogers' statement can be summarized in order to give some content to the ideal of "actualizing human potential."

In his paper Rogers reports on a "demonstration" of "student-centered teaching" which he gave in the form of a talk at Harvard in 1952. Toward the end of this talk Rogers listed some important "conclusions" or "consequences." For him, and for those who agree with him, he said, "We would do away with teaching. People would get together if they wished to learn. We would do away with examinations, . . . grades and credits, . . . degrees, . . . [and] the exposition of conclusions . . . ."

These "conclusions" are indeed perplexing. They are presented almost prophetically, as if they are revealed truths, not subject to the possibility of disconfirmation. And they are, he says paradoxically, "in no way intended as conclusions for someone else, or a guide to what others should do or be."

Fortunately, Rogers later provided some commentary on his 1952 statement in which he explains that his intention in the demonstration was to express "some

---

[79]On this issue see the following: Alfred S. Alschuler, J. McIntyre, and D. Tabor, *How to Develop Achievement Motivation: A Manual for Teachers* (Middletown, Conn.: Educational Ventures, Inc., 1969); Abraham Maslow, *Toward a Psychology of Being* (Princeton: Van Norstrand, 1968); Abraham Maslow, "Some Educational Implications of the Humanistic Psychologies," *Harvard Educational Review* 38 (1968): 685-696; Erik H. Erikson, "Identity and the Life Cycle," in *Psychological Issues* I, no. 1 (1959); Neil Postman and Charles Weingartner *Teaching as a Subversive Activity* (New York: Delacorte Press, 1969). For an overview, see: Marie Jahoda, *Current Concepts of Positive Mental Health: A Report to the Staff Director, Jack R. Ewalt, 1958* (New York: Basic Books, 1958).

[80]Carl R. Rogers, *On Becoming a Person* (Boston: Houghton Mifflin Co., 1961).

highly personal opinion of [his] own," and then to endeavor "to understand and accept the often very divergent reactions and feelings of the students." Hopefully, he thought, this would result in a "meaningful class discussion." In the light of this statement we have no reason to doubt that the "highly personal opinion" expressed by Rogers is anything but on-the-level. In fact, he explicitly says that he tried to write as "honestly" as he could, and that he is expressing some of his "deepest views in the field of education." He also states that he is using the word "teaching" as it is defined "in the dictionaries," and he chides his critics for suggesting that he has said things that he does not mean. These statements surely justify an ordinary, literal, on-the-level interpretation of his "conclusions."

When we interpret the conclusions in this way, we find that some of them seem clear as they stand. The conclusions that we would "do away" with examinations, grades and credits, and degrees leave little room for misunderstanding. But the conclusion that we would "do away with teaching" seems contradictory in view of the apparent fact that Rogers himself is engaged in some kind of teaching.

If we are to save Rogers from self-contradiction on this conclusion, we must make some assumptions about the meaning of the word "teaching." We must immediately exclude from this meaning what Rogers calls "non-directive" or "student-centered" teaching, the kind of teaching that Rogers himself is doing. A further limitation on the meaning of this word is necessary because Rogers repeatedly emphasizes that his conclusions are "shocking," "absurd," "ridiculous," and "fantastic." If Rogers is using "teaching" in a way that would be interpreted by his audience to be obviously pejorative, then his proscription would hardly be "shocking," etc. Consequently, he cannot be proscribing teaching that is, for instance, irredeemably dogmatic.

Between these two unacceptable interpretations of "teaching" as "non-directive" and as dogmatically "directive" would be a more limited range of meanings in which teaching is in some sense "directive," but not dogmatically so. We would seem to be left, then, with "teaching" in its more standard uses. And so it would appear that Rogers wants to proscribe teaching as it is most commonly and favorably understood, teaching in which the teacher seems "to instruct," "to guide," "to show," "to make aware." This would be teaching in which the teacher undogmatically seeks to direct or influence the beliefs or behavior of the students. Clearly this proscription *is* shocking. It would "do away" with the kind of teaching that we ordinarily commend. Moreover, if Rogers' own lectures and essays may be said to seek to direct or influence the beliefs or behavior of his students, then Rogers is in the untenable and self-defeating position of proscribing his own conclusions. In view of the constraints on the possible interpretations of Rogers' proscriptions, it is difficult to see how this predicament can be escaped.

The situation is much the same, if not worse, when we attempt to make sense of Rogers's conclusion that "we would do away with conclusions." This would appear to be itself a conclusion. If it is, any demand that we "do away with conclusions" would be self-defeating. At this point we are apt to agree that this conclusion is indeed shocking.

We must now wonder why Rogers would want to "do away" with degrees, grades and credits, examinations, and the exposition of conclusions. The answer is given in the 1952 statement: he wants to do away with teaching, and these are the instruments of teaching. But why does he want to do away with teaching--that is, with teaching in which the teacher undogmatically seeks to direct or influence the beliefs or behavior of the students? The only apparent answer to this question in the 1952 statement is the following:

> When I try to teach, as I do sometimes, I am appalled by the results, which seem a little more than inconsequential, because sometimes the teaching appears to succeed. When this happens I find that the results are damaging. It seems to cause the individual to distrust his own experience, and to stifle significant learning.

Thus teaching and the instruments of teaching must be proscribed because they "seem to cause the individual to distrust his own experience . . . ." The meaning of this claim is not clear from the 1952 statement. But in an essay written in 1961 Rogers provides a likely explanation for his earlier claim:

> Let me turn now to some . . . learnings which [have to] do with my own actions and values. The first of these is very brief. *I can trust my experience.* One of the basic things which I was long time in realizing, is that when an activity *feels* as though it is valuable or worth doing, it *is* worth doing.[81]

Thus, to "trust one's own experience" is to trust one's feelings, one's "inner non-intellectual sensing." But *why* should one trust one's own experience, and *why* should one oppose whatever leads one to distrust his own experience? Rogers leaves little room for doubt here: "Experience," he says, "is for me, the highest authority. The touchstone of validity is my own experience."[82] This is confirmed in *On Becoming a Person* by the following two statements:

> Neither the Bible nor the prophets--neither Freud nor research--neither the revelations of God nor man--can take precedence over my own direct experience.[83]
> I have come to feel that only one person (at least in my lifetime, and perhaps ever) can know whether what I am doing is honest, thorough,

---

[81]Ibid., 22.
[82]Ibid., 23.
[83]Ibid., 24.

open, and sound, or false and defensive and unsound, and I am that person.[84]

This surprising claim demands at least one final question: Why should one recognize his own experience as the highest authority? The answer to this question makes it clear that the bedrock assumption grounding Rogers' pedagogy is a value-premise concerning the good life. In his essay, "A Therapist's View of the Good Life," he writes:

Yet as I observe the clients whose experiences in living have taught me so much, I find that increasingly such individuals are able to trust their total organismic reaction to a new situation because they discover to an ever-increasing degree that if they are open to their experience, doing what "feels right" proves to be a competent and trustworthy guide to behavior which is truly satisfying.[85]

The decisive claim here is that if one trusts his own experience, then he will act in such a way "as to provide the maximum satisfaction of his greatest needs."[86]

We may now summarize Rogers' argument: We would (i.e., should) do away with teaching (and the instruments of teaching--examinations, grades and credits, degrees, and the exposition of conclusions) because (1) teaching causes the individual to abstain from doing what "feels right," and (2) to abstain from doing what "feels right" causes the individual not to satisfy his "greatest needs."

In assessing the soundness of Rogers' argument there is obviously no need to question the premise that teaching causes the individual to abstain from doing what "feels right." Most people would agree that the primary purpose of education is to persuade people that often what "feels right" (even in a "total, organismic" sense) is not what *is* right. Illusion, deception, and prejudice enter too easily into human thought and action. By education we learn how subjectivity can be minimized, and how objectivity can be maximized by the application of rational and scientific methods and instruments, by the use of logical, linguistic, mathematical, and rhetorical skills, by the study of history, by an awareness of our psychological idiosyncrasies and disabilities, by the development of good character, and by an abiding commitment to criticism and to the life of reason.

Rogers' second premise that to abstain from doing what "feels right" causes the individual not to satisfy his "greatest needs" is surely no truism. In point of fact the very contradictory of this premise is an assumption of every educational institution. Since humankind's earliest discovery that decisions based on what "feels right" are often disasters, and result in the frustration of our "greatest needs," people have established, and have depended upon, educational

---

[84]Ibid., 23.
[85]Ibid., 189.
[86]Ibid., 194.

institutions. These institutions have made it possible for people to better realize their "greatest needs" by relying less on the subjectivity of what each "feels right" than on reasoning and the collective experiences of all people.

Since Rogers' second premise is so patently in conflict with this basic principle of education, since counterexamples to his premise are so easily cited, and since the falsity of the premise is otherwise so easily demonstrated, we can only be astonished by Rogers' acceptance of it. It is no wonder that he (and his audience) finds his conclusions "shocking," "absurd," "ridiculous," and "fantastic." They are indeed. And they are so because they are conclusions of an unsound argument--an argument which rests on a premise that may be romantically appealing, but which is nonetheless false.[87]

We are now in a position to answer the question, "Should the ideal of liberal education be to actualize human potential?" At least in Rogers' theory the actualization of human potential evidently includes whatever causes satisfaction to the individual. But what causes such satisfaction is subjective, and thus dogmatic because the legitimacy of these subjective satisfactions is not open to question. In fact these subjective satisfactions may well be irrational and immoral. Because of this possibility we cannot provide a rational justification for the ideal of "actualizing human potential." Any education worthy of the name of liberal education has an obligation to actualize some, but not all, human possibilities. For liberal education the human potential that needs to be actualized is the potential to act rationally or wisely.

It is a paradox that an ideal that is championed by so many for being undogmatic should be charged with being dogmatic. But many critics have noted that when the "human potential" or "human development" or "open education" ideal is institutionalized it inevitably becomes a new educational dogma.[88]

The appeal of this dogma is easy to understand. It appeals to our romantic inclinations. It promises us relief from the anxiety of moral obligation. It tells us that human beings are "basically" good but corrupted by society. It promises us relief from the strictures of the intellect. It tells us that intellectuality is not as important as having strong feelings. It tells us that the path to salvation is not through the hard competition of ideas, of thought and study, of dialogue with

---

[87]Kenneth Strike has made a similar point in emphasizing that moral agents are made, not born: "Persons are significantly the result of initiating children into cultural resources for understanding and appreciating and acting. To the extent that the romantic tradition in education [e.g., Rogers and A. S. Neill] fails to understand this and seeks to substantiate a 'natural education' for initiation into available cultural resources, it is perverse." *Liberty and Learning* (Oxford: M. Robertson, 1982), 157.

[88]For an example of this, see the criticism of Kresge College as an exemplar of the "communal-expressive" college model by Gerald Grant and David Reisman in *The Perpetual Dream: Reform and Experiment in the American College* (Chicago: University of Chicago Press, 1978), 134: "Organic growth was for [the human potential educators] inexplicably bound up with ecstacies of the T-group and a participatory style of human encounter through which they had come to feel born again. It was difficult for them to recognize that what they experienced as dramatic renewal, others sometimes felt as constraining and, on occasion, manipulative."

others, but through the ability to "listen to the small voice within." It tells us that Platonic love is inferior to affective love.

"To cope effectively with change"

During the period of social upheaval during the late nineteen sixties and seventies Neil Postman and Charles Weingartner published *Teaching as a Subversive Activity*.[89] In this book the authors took note of the rapid changes in American society and the mounting criticism of American education. They expressed sympathy for Marshall McLuhan's charge that the schools were "irrelevant," Norbert Wiener's accusation that education "shielded children from reality," John Gardner's claim that students were being educated for "obsolescence," Jerome Bruner's criticism that the schools were not developing intelligence, John Holt's accusation that education was dependent on "fear," Carl Rogers' charge that teaching discouraged "significant learning," Paul Goodman's accusation that education induced "alienation," and Edgar Friedenberg's charge that the system punished creativity and independence. To remedy this situation Postman and Weingartner described the ideal for a "new education." "The basis function of all education," they wrote, "is to increase the survival prospects of the group."[90] From this it followed that "the essential criterion for judging the relevance of all education was to enable people to cope effectively with change."[91]

Postman and Weingartner's criticism of American education's inability to adapt to rapid change and their proposal that teaching should be understood as an activity that helps students develop "built-in, shockproof crap detectors" were persuasive in the post-Viet Nam era. But if their proposal that the ideal of education is to produce people who can cope effectively with change, and thus, who can contribute to the survival of the group, is to be understood as a proposal for the ideal of liberal education, then objections must be raised. While it seems reasonable to expect liberally educated people to be able to cope effectively with change and to be able to contribute to the survival of the group, it also seems reasonable to expect liberally educated people to do more than this. Coping with change and contributing to group survival are not unqualified goods. There are conceivable conditions in which coping with change and contributing to group survival are morally intolerable. This fact indicates that, in spite of its general reasonability, this ideal must be subordinated to a superior ideal. That this is necessary indicates further that the ideal of coping with change and contributing to group survival is dogmatic and lacking in intrinsic value. As such it cannot qualify as the ideal of liberal education.

---

[89]Neil Postman and Charles Weingartner, *Teaching as a Subversive Activity* (New York: Delacorte Press, 1969).

[90]Ibid., 207.

[91]Ibid., 154.

"To develop the citizens of a free society"

Perhaps the most influential twentieth century statement of the ideal of liberal education is presented in the so-called Harvard "Redbook."[92]   The faculty committee that wrote this report was appointed in 1943 by President James Bryant Conant, who charged it with finding a concept of general (i.e., liberal) education "that would have validity for the free society which we cherish."[93] Prefiguring the committee's eventual conclusions about the ideal of general education, President Conant stated:

> The primary concern of American education today is not the development of the appreciation of the 'good life' in young gentlemen born to the purple . . . . Our purpose is to cultivate in the largest possible number of our future citizens an appreciation of both the responsibilities and the benefits which come to them because they are Americans and are free.

Consistent with President Conant's charge, the theory of liberal education developed by the Harvard committee is one that understands the ideal of liberal education to be subordinate to the needs of American democracy. The term, "general education," the committee writes, "is used to indicate that part of a student's whole education which looks first of all to his life as a responsible human being and citizen."[94] This ideal is understood as requiring students to gain knowledge of the three "traditional areas" of natural science, social studies, and the humanities, and to develop four "traits of mind": the ability "to think effectively," "to communicate thought," "to make relevant judgments," and "to discriminate among values."[95]

While the ideal of subordinating liberal education to the needs of American democracy no doubt seemed more compelling in the nineteen forties than it does in the nineteen nineties, this ideal is still powerfully attractive to most people. Nevertheless, this ideal must be faulted because it gives value to liberal education only insofar as it serves a particular set of political purposes. As a result, liberal education has only extrinsic, not intrinsic, value. Within any educational program justified by this political ideal, it would not be possible to criticize American democracy. The ideal would thus be dogmatic. This objection would continue to hold if the ideal of developing the citizens of American democracy were to be replaced by the ideal of developing the citizens of any other "free society." Either of these ideals would fail to attain the intrinsic value and freedom from dogmatism that are essential to the ideal of liberal education.

---

[92]*General Education in a Free Society: Report of the Harvard Committee* (Cambridge: Harvard University Press, 1945).
[93]Ibid., xiii.
[94]Ibid., 51.
[95]Ibid., 65.

"To develop 'the democratic personality'"

In *The Closing of the American Mind* Allan Bloom charges that over the last fifty years American colleges have abandoned their traditional goal of trying to develop "the democratic man," and have adopted a new goal of trying to develop "the democratic personality."[96] "The democratic personality" is the person who is properly adapted to a democracy understood as a universal egalitarian society. Unlike "the democratic man," the "democratic personality" is not concerned with natural rights and the historical origin of our democracy, but with being "open to all kinds of men, all kinds of life-styles, all ideologies."[97] An egalitarian society is thought to require "openness," and "openness" is thought to require the "relativism" of truth and values, and is believed to be facilitated by a "diversity" of cultures and peoples. Consequently the sacred buzzwords on many college campuses today are those of "political correctness": "cultural relativism," "diversity," and "multiculturalism."

"Cultural relativism" is variously used, but is generally understood to be the theory that all cultures are more or less of equal merit. Sometimes this theory is presented as a conclusively verified empirical hypothesis. Authorities cited for this truth range all the way from field anthropologists and ethnologists to philosophers and scientists like Nietzsche, Freud, Marx, Einstein, Heisenberg, Ayer, Derrida, Wittgenstein, Heidegger, Sartre, and various skeptics and postmodernists. At other times "cultural relativism" is presented as an a priori truth that is not dependent upon observation. At other times it appears to be more properly identified as a passionately held article of faith.

"Diversity" is typically taken to refer to the variegation of a society. Curiously enough, the variegation that is currently desired seems to be largely limited to race, gender, and sexual preference.

"Multiculturalism" (in the words of one college's definition) "includes providing an educational and social climate that encourages an appreciation and a sensitivity for various (diverse) cultures--recognizing that each representative culture . . . has merit." Thus defined, "multiculturalism" has an undisguised political commitment. It is, after all, one thing to insist that students in a program of liberal education should have an "appreciation and sensitivity for various (diverse) cultures" and quite another to insist that they should "recognize that each representative culture has merit." Considering the fact that these diverse cultures are being judged sight unseen, it is surely dogmatic for a college to decide in advance that they all have "merit." What these colleges are in fact doing is discouraging their students from discriminating between different and sometimes antithetical cultural values. One might easily think that the development of this ability to properly discriminate among different cultural values would be one of

---

[96]Allan Bloom, *The Closing of the American Mind* (New York: Simon and Schuster, 1987), 27.

[97]Ibid.

the highest achievements of a liberal education.

Bloom's criticism of this ideal of "the democratic personality" is a corollary of his thesis that what American education now bills as a great "openness" is in reality "the closing of the American mind." Today, he charges, the social sciences in particular are concerned "not so much to teach the students about other times and places as to make them aware of the fact that their preferences are only that-- accidents of their time and place."[98]   "True openness," he argues, "is the accompaniment of the desire to know," and so when "openness" becomes an unconditional imperative it precludes the possibility of our knowing the truth and the nature of our moral obligations. In leveling out all truths and all values, just as it levels out all people, this kind of unconditional openness enables us "to avoid testing our prejudices."[99]   It thus suppresses true openness, and, as such, is a form of close-mindedness. It is a subtle form of dogmatism.

"To develop a person"

Jane Roland Martin has outlined "a new paradigm" for liberal education in the course of a criticism of Paul H. Hirst's theory of liberal education.[100] She claims that Hirst's theory that liberal education is an "initiation into the forms of knowledge" leads to conclusions that are "narrow," "intolerant," and lacking in "generosity," and that this theory is erroneously grounded. The theory is said to be "narrow" and "intolerant" because it is exclusively concerned with "the forms of knowledge," and as a consequence ignores such needs as the need to develop "noncognitive states" like feelings and emotions, and "procedural knowledge" (knowledge of how to do things).   Because of this exclusive concern with intellectual development, Hirst's curriculum for liberal education excludes "physical education and vocational training," as well as "the development of artistic performance, the acquisition of language skills including the learning of a second language, and education for effective moral action." Hirst's theory is said to be lacking in "generosity" because the kind of person it develops is "an ivory tower person," one who is not taught to care about justice and the welfare of others, nor to desire to solve "real problems in the real world." Martin charges that Hirst's theory is erroneously grounded in what she calls "the epistemological fallacy."   This fallacy consists in "arguing from a theory of knowledge to conclusions about the full range of what ought or ought not to be taught or studied."[101] For Martin this strategy is in error because it mistakenly assumes that it is possible to have a theory of knowledge which is not itself prejudiced by our aims or purposes.

Presupposed in Martin's criticism of Hirst's theory of liberal education is the general assumption that liberal education is the most valuable form of education.

---

[98]Ibid., 30.
[99]Ibid., 40.
[100]Martin, "Needed: A Paradigm for Liberal Education."
[101]Ibid., 47.

"Over the years," she writes, "liberal education has been thought of as an education having great value, indeed as an education having greater value than any other."[102] On this assumption, she reasons, an education that is limited to initiating people into the forms of knowledge cannot count as liberal education because it is concerned only with intellectual development, and an education that develops "a thinker but not a doer, an experiencer but not a maker, and a feeler but not a moral agent" cannot be the most valuable form of education.

For Martin, the most valuable form of education is one which would "free us not only from ignorance, but also from the constraints of habit, custom, and inertia."[103] It would not only free us as minds, but it would also free us as persons. In addition, it would "bind human beings to one another" and would "bind us to the natural order of which we are a part."[104] Presumably this new paradigm of liberal education would provide justification for a curriculum that would go far beyond the development of the intellect to include the development of certain feelings and emotions, the development of certain artistic, athletic, linguistic, mechanical, and vocational skills, and the development of a moral commitment to solidarity with other people and with the natural environment.

Martin's criticism of Hirst's ideal of liberal education is valuable. On the received view that the adoption of the theoretical standpoint is but one way that human beings can relate to the world, Hirst's proposal for limiting liberal education to the development of the forms of knowledge defines an ideal that is indeed "narrow"--that is to say, dogmatic.[105] On the additional received view that theorizing is not the most valuable form of human action, Hirst's proposal is unsatisfactory because it fails to define an ideal that has supreme, or intrinsic, value.

But while Martin's charge that Hirst's ideal is dogmatic and lacking in intrinsic value appears justified, her proposed "new paradigm" would appear to be also dogmatic and lacking in intrinsic value. This dogmatism is a consequence of the fact that Martin's ideal subordinates liberal education to the propagation of certain preferred moral and political values. Because of this subordination, liberal education cannot be supremely or intrinsically valuable.

This problem may be illustrated by the fact that Martin wants to substitute a "person" who can engage in both thought and action for Hirst's "mind" who can only employ the "forms of knowledge." The trouble with this proposal is that Martin evidently wants to specify the personality and moral values of this person. For instance, this person must have certain "feelings and emotions," must act "kindly" toward others, must want to solve "real problems in the real world," must be "disposed to exercise and eat wisely," must be "altruistic" and "other-directed,"

---

[102]Ibid., 43.

[103]Ibid., 54.

[104]Ibid., 56.

[105]This is the burden of Heidegger's analysis of the worldhood of the world in *Being and Time*, I, chap. 3 (London: SCM Press Ltd., 1962), and Dewey's criticism of "the spectator theory of knowledge" in *The Quest for Certainty* (New York: Minton, Balch & Co., 1929).

must be suited to "developmental democracy," must have "solidarity with other living things," must possess the "warmer virtues," etc. It is obvious that this list includes many of the feelings, dispositions, and virtues that we most admire. But it would be a mistake to forget the historical fact that these feelings, dispositions, and virtues have not always been universally admired. At other times and in other places they have been regarded as inauthentic and as expressions of the ethics of pity. But of even greater significance is the fact that they have not been demonstrated to be necessary or to have intrinsic value. Consequently, we need to realize that these feelings, dispositions, and virtues are in fact expressions of our own cultural values--those of "North Atlantic" liberal political thought in the latter part of the twentieth century. They are in fact Martin's own moral and political preferences. Without some demonstration of their necessity, they must be counted as personal and subjective, and therefore, as dogmatic and lacking in intrinsic value. To adopt them as the goals of a program of education would be to preclude the possibility of liberal education.

3. IDEALS GIVING PRIORITY TO INTERESTS

"To satisfy student interests"

It is a common practice today for liberal arts colleges to avoid any definition of the ideal of liberal education, and, either by default or intention, to allow their educational programs to be determined mainly by student interests. It is also a common practice for these colleges to try to make a virtue out of this vice. While at one time the ideal of satisfying student interests was elaborately publicized and defended by theories of "progressive" or "humanistic" education, today it is more likely to be defended by the claim that it is in harmony with the principles of a market economy or the principles of a democratic society. Or, more likely yet, it is simply assumed in practice and ignored in educational theory.[106] If a college adopts this ideal, consistency requires it to avoid "required" or "core" programs and to determine its academic "offerings" on the basis of constantly changing student interests. While this ideal may seem to lack any cogent theoretical justification, it certainly does not lack some practical benefits. It is attractive to many because of its tolerant spirit, simplicity, flexibility, compatibility with faculty professional aspirations, popularity with students, and, above all, profitability. Popularity and profitability aside, there is a formidable educational objection to basing a program of liberal education on student interests. Simply stated, students may have all kinds of uneducated, prejudiced, trivial, irrational, and immoral interests, and there is no evident reason why any institution should have any obligation to service such interests, and no evident reason why an institution that does service such interests should be privileged by any society.

---

[106]Harold Taylor, *Students Without Teachers: The Crisis in the University* (New York: McGraw-Hill, 1969).

In view of this objection it not surprising that the ideal of satisfying student interests is rarely adopted without qualification. In the great majority of cases the ideal is understood to be restricted to the satisfaction of student "academic" interests. This qualified ideal is then justified by a modified version of the "elective" principle. As a consequence, the college is not under any obligation to satisfy student interests which are at variance with the interests of society, morality, or "good taste," but is only under obligation to satisfy those student interests that are "academic," or otherwise, "reasonable."

The problem with this qualified ideal is that, as long as the content of "academic" or "reasonable" is left unspecified, the definition is at the mercy of any subjective interpretation.   It thus falls short of being articulate, and consequently is incapable of serving as the ideal of liberal education. On the other hand, once the ideal is specified, it seems likely to be one of the theoretical or practical ideals that we have previously considered and rejected as being dogmatic or lacking in intrinsic value.

"To satisfy a plurality of interests"

Today liberal arts colleges may operate on the stated or tacit assumption that their goal is to satisfy a plurality of interests--students, teachers, administrators, benefactors, business, the government, and other individuals or groups. If this assumption is tacit, these colleges may ignore, or try to excuse themselves from, any responsibility for providing a definition of the ideal of liberal education. Instead, they typically will rely on a college catalogue-type statement that merely enumerates in general terms a number of different, not necessarily related institutional goals, aims, or objectives. This preference for a plurality of ideals stated in very general terms instead of a precise and integrated definition of the ideal of liberal education is encouraged by the perceived difficulty of achieving any kind of agreement on a genuine definition. This difficulty is augmented by the colleges' increasing dependence on committee decision-making in which the coherence of committee decisions must be compromised by the need to accommodate the diverse egos and interests of the committee's representative membership. This preference is also encouraged by the desire of many colleges for "flexibility"--that is, for the same kind of freedom from commitment and responsibility that they accord to their students. Additional encouragement for this preference is provided by the current widespread skeptical contempt for educational traditions and canons.

A college catalogue-type statement enumerating in vague terms an institution's goals is an inadequate substitute for an articulate and integrated definition of the ideal of liberal education. This is not surprising in view of the fact that these college catalogue-type statements are primarily designed for marketing and promotional purposes, not for institutional guidance and decision-making. Consequently, they put less emphasis on precision, coherence, and consistency than they do on pleasing tautologies and ingratiating imagery. They find their greatest use in admissions and public relations literature where they are juxtaposed with full-color pictures of students representing all genders, races, and cultures using state-of-the-art sports and recreational facilities, experimenting with hands-on high tech hardware, enjoying safaris and exotic foreign cities, and in general having a roaring good time. The success of these statements is judged not by how effectively they discriminate between educational priorities, but by how effectively they elicit applications and acceptances from their targeted markets. In view of their purpose it is no accident that these statements seem to promise all things to all people.

The lack of precision in a college catalogue-type statement enumerating a plurality of institutional goals may permit a college to sponsor programs that satisfy all kinds of interests, but the satisfaction of these interests may provide the college with goals that are in basic conflict with each other. For instance, these amorphous statements may sanction both liberal and vocational arts, general and specialized education, and prescriptive and elective curricula.

More importantly, whenever a college subscribes to an unintegrated plurality of ideals, there is always a question as to the relationship and relative priority of these ideals, even if these ideals are consistent. For instance, for any college subscribing to an unintegrated plurality of ideals there is no basis for determining the proper level of institutional support for each of these ideals in view of the inevitability of limited resources. This means that two or more ideals will always require a third and superior ideal to establish the relationship and priority between them. In cases where this superior ideal is absent or not explicitly recognized, the stated ideals can only be dogmatic, since they cannot be subject to criticism within the educational programs that they justify. On the other hand, in cases where a superior ideal is explicitly recognized, then the inferior ideals ipso facto lack intrinsic value since they are merely means to the realization of the superior ideal. This reasoning leads to the conclusion that a catalogue-type statement listing the college's various unintegrated goals cannot suffice as a definition of the ideal of liberal education not only because the equivocality of its terms makes it inarticulate as a definition, but also because any set of ideals which fails to be integrated by a superior ideal will be either dogmatic or lack intrinsic value.

The preceding general conclusions may be illustrated by reference to Ernest L. Boyer's *College: The Undergraduate Experience in America*.[107] This report makes a strong case for the need to renew the undergraduate college, and it makes an equally convincing case for the claim that the major cause of the undergraduate college's current crisis is its confusion over its institutional goals. Nonetheless, the report fails to resolve this confusion. It does not provide an integrated ideal for liberal education. The report takes the position that the goals of "the undergraduate college in America" "flow from the needs of society and also from the needs of the persons seeking education."[108] This means that "through an

---

[107]Ernest L. Boyer, *College: The Undergraduate Experience in America* (New York: Harper & Row, 1987).

[108]Ibid., 38.

effective college education, students should become personally empowered and also committed to the common good."[109] The report frankly admits that this definition of the goal of "undergraduate education" is the product of the demands of two "powerful traditions"--one that wants the college to give priority to "individuality" and one that wants the college to emphasize "community." The problem with this position is that it identifies different goals, but it does not identify a superior goal that can integrate and justify these. The imprecision of these goals may be seen in the following statements of the goals of the "undergraduate college in America":

"[To prepare students] to be engaged in life"[110]
"[To] enrich the lives of students, broaden their perspectives, and relate learning to wider concerns."[111]
"[To provide students with] the skills and perspective they will need to live confidently in tomorrow's more interconnected world."[112]

While these statements certainly convey a sense of high purpose, it is hard to envisage what specific competencies that they entail. Meanwhile, instead of trying to discover a superior and integrative goal, the report moves to increase this plurality by enumerating additional goals, some of which seem to be in conflict with each other, and many of which seem hopelessly vague:

"[To advance] knowledge"[113]
"[To help] students better understand themselves, their society, and the world of which they are a part."[114]
"[To] act as a moral force, to discover and transmit knowledge and larger meanings . . . ."[115]

These statements give the impression that the college's primary goal is theoretical. It is concerned with knowledge. But it is not clear whether the college is an institution for the advancement of knowledge, for the transmission of knowledge to students, or for both. Consequently, it is not clear whether the college should be committed to research, to teaching, or to both research and teaching. It is therefore not obvious how the college is supposed to differ from the university or the university college.

This plurality of goals is compounded even further by additional statements that emphasize normative or practical, rather than theoretical, goals:

---

[109]Ibid., 69.
[110]Ibid., 234.
[111]Ibid., 99.
[112]Ibid., 234.
[113]Ibid., 126.
[114]Ibid., 92.
[115]Ibid., 227.

"[To] prepare the undergraduates for careers, [and] to enable them to live lives of dignity and purpose; . . . to give knowledge to the student, [and] to channel knowledge to humane ends."[116]
"To make a healthy transition to adulthood, to work out an identity."[117]
"[To develop] habits of good citizenship."[118]

These statements seem to sanction vocational training, moral instruction, psychological development, and social service. But many of these goals seem to be in inescapable conflict. Career needs may conflict with the goals of living "lives of dignity and purpose"; the desire for knowledge may conflict with the need to "channel knowledge to humane ends"; the need to live "lives of dignity and purpose" may conflict with the need to develop "habits of good citizenship," and so on. The report does not suggest how these conflicts can be resolved. Instead of an integrative ideal the report offers an even greater plurality by adding still other goals:

"The individual preferences of each student must be served."[119]
"[To help students] be truly creative and fulfilled as individuals."[120]
"[To help students be] placed [in a job]."[121]

These statements indicate that the college not only has the responsibility for the "discovery and transmission of knowledge" and for the furtherance of "humane ends," career training, human development, and "good citizenship," but also for the satisfaction of student "individual preferences," "fulfillment," and job placement interests. But once again many of these goals seem to be in inescapable conflict; and even if they are not, they require a principle that establishes their relative priority. Most obvious is the conflict between the "preferences" of those who are uneducated and the needs of the community and, above all, the imperatives of veracity and moral conduct. The report does not provide a superior ideal that can justify and integrate these diverse goals.

Since no integrative ideal is provided, the unintegrated plurality of goals listed can only be regarded as dogmatic. Some of these goals are also prejudiced in the more obvious sense that they represent a commitment to certain partisan political and moral purposes, which, by virtue of this commitment, are exempted from criticism within the educational program that they justify. For instance, the report claims that "the undergraduate college" should affirm "diversity" and prepare students "for American life."[122] This would commit the college to the

---

[116]Ibid., 219.
[117]Ibid., 217.
[118]Ibid., 246.
[119]Ibid., 68.
[120]Ibid., 277.
[121]Ibid., 270.
[122]Ibid., 82, 73.

defense of a particular social dogma ("diversity") and the defense of a particular way of life ("the American way").

In addition, as we have seen, any attempt to provide a superior, integrative ideal to escape the dogmatism of the plurality of ideals given would have the result of denying the intrinsic value of these ideals.

These considerations provide substantiation for the conclusion that an unintegrated plurality of ideals is unsatisfactory as the ideal of liberal education. Those who today defend a plurality of unintegrated ideals certainly speak in the fashionable language of the day, but they fail to provide an educational ideal that is undogmatic and intrinsically valuable.

The assumption that the purpose of liberal education is the satisfaction of whatever "academic" or "reasonable" interests students and others may happen to have is the educational scandal of our time.   It allows colleges to present themselves as educational institutions nobly serving the public interest and advancing the most exalted of human purposes, whereas in reality they are simply commercial enterprises catering to the uneducated interests of academic consumers. The cumulative consequence of this duplicity is what in general we see before us today: undergraduate "higher" education is now largely a publicly subsidized subsidiary of the entertainment industry. As I argued in Chapter 3, contemporary liberal arts colleges are best described as academic theme parks. Like Disney World or Busch Gardens, they consist of well-landscaped facilities where families pay dearly so that their children can take what is essentially a four year tram ride through a wonderland of adolescent-sitting entertainment. In pandering to the constantly changing interests of the uneducated, liberal arts colleges no longer help students cultivate the liberal arts and gain insight into the transcendentals. They no longer make it possible for students to separate cultural treasure from cultural trash. As a consequence, they cannot act as the instrument by means of which passing generations bequeath their most cherished ideals to a successor generation, and by doing so, contribute to the continuing life of the species in spite of the ephemeral life of the individual.

The idea that seems to have been so easily forgotten--but one that is still remembered in the etymology of the word, "education," is that in its most valued sense education is literally a "leading-out" from ignorance and immorality into knowledge and rational action. Such a project is an institutional enterprise, an enterprise that requires a purpose that transcends the interests of individuals, and that imposes obligations on those who elect to be led and on those who have been elected to lead.

The idea that those who have little more than an intimation of the importance of a liberal education are capable of understanding its end and means, and thus of determining the knowledge and values that are most worth having, is as absurd in conception as it is tragic in its consequences. This idea survives only because in our time those who should be defending the integrity of liberal education have failed their most sacred professional responsibility. In willingly providing whatever courses and curricula satisfy constantly changing academic consumer interests, the college exploits its students' preoccupation with personal freedom and transient distractions at a vulnerable time in their lives. This action is a disservice to students because it fails to make clear to them that freedom and intelligent choice require wisdom--a virtue that should not be a mere elective option for those who just happen to be interested, much less for those who aspire to a liberal education.

A Postscript on Postmodernism

The possible skeptical outcomes of current philosophical controversies might be seen as posing a serious threat to the proposed definition of the ideal of liberal education as the development of the wise person. The ground for this belief is the assumption that if the skeptical claims of contemporary "postmodernist" epistemological relativism and antifoundationalism are warranted, then any form of education that aspires to knowledge, truth, rational ideals, rational methods, or philosophical principles would be pointless. It might then be argued that minimally a definition of the ideal of liberal education should not be pursued until all skeptical claims have been laid to rest, and that maximally, the ideal of developing the wise person is hopelessly misguided and utopian.

One example of this contemporary skepticism is the neo-pragmatism of Richard Rorty. As has been previously noted, Rorty claims that the historicist consequences of the post-Enlightenment "contingencies of language, selfhood, and liberal democracy" discredit all attempts to discover ahistorical grounding principles. According to this view, traditional thought has been dominated by Plato's "Theory of Recollection"--the belief that "we have an innate ability to recognize the truth when we hear it."[123] Rejecting this theory as "a survival of religious beliefs," Rorty demands that philosophy give up its traditional pursuit of "objective truths." The notion that truth is to be found in a correspondence to reality, and that the mind is properly conceived as the mirror of nature, is, Rorty thinks, "what Nietzsche called 'the longest lie'--the lie that there is something beyond mankind to which it is man's duty to be faithful."[124]

Since Rorty believes that it is necessary for us to give up the traditional search for ahistorical grounding principles and "objective truths," he proposes that we replace the traditional philosophical sciences of metaphysics and epistemology with "pragmatic" or "hermeneutic" thought. Henceforth philosophy is to be understood only as an edifying "conversation" which is justified only by its service on behalf of American liberal democracy.

Any analysis of the threat posed to the proposed ideal of liberal education by the various forms of contemporary skepticism, including Rorty's, would be a

[123]Richard Rorty, "Hermeneutics, General Studies, and Teaching," in *Selected Papers from the Synergos Seminars*, vol. 2. (Fairfax, Virginia: George Mason University, 1982): 1.
[124]Ibid., 2.

major theoretical project. While the fact that this project remains incomplete is at least a reminder of the need for caution, there are nonetheless some reasons to believe that the educational ideal that we have defined is immune to skeptical criticism:

1. It is by no means clear that contemporary skeptics have as yet made a conclusive case for any kind of non-trivial relativism, let alone one that could in any way be a threat to the ideal of wisdom. Rorty's premises about the contingencies of language, selfhood, and community are in dispute, as are his conclusions that these contingencies justify the adoption of the ideals of American liberal democracy. Particularly controversial is Rorty's claim that these contingencies prohibit any noncircular theoretical preference for one set of conclusions over another. As a consequence of this, Rorty is forced to say that the ideals of American liberal democracy cannot "be discovered by reflection," but can only be "created."[125] They can only be justified, he says, "by increasing our sensitivity to the particular details of the pain and humiliation of other, unfamiliar sorts of people."[126] He defends his position from "vulgar" relativism and dogmatism by restating his historicist premises and admitting his ethnocentrism, while reminding his critics that any "vocabulary" is inevitably ethnocentric, and incapable of neutrality.[127] He summarizes this provocative conclusion in "The Priority of Democracy to Philosophy":

> We have to insist that not every argument needs to be met in the terms in which it is presented . . . . The idea that moral and political controversies should always be 'brought back to first principles' is reasonable if it means merely that we should seek common ground in the hope of attaining agreement. But it is misleading if it is taken as the claim that there is a natural order of premises from which moral and political conclusions are to be inferred . . . .[128]

This conclusion has drawn vehement criticism. Henry Veatch, for instance, alarmed by what he believes is its "total intellectual permissiveness," questions its practical consequences when he asks: "Is not this conclusion frightening in its implications?"[129] Bernard Williams answers this question with another question when he asks: "What can the pragmatist say to the secret police 'when they break down the door, smash his spectacles, take him away'?"[130] Frederick Suppe, among others, questions the coherence of Rorty's argument. He writes:

> It is clear that Rorty really believes [that any philosophical position is true so long as it is possessed by, and embodies the prejudices of, a

---

[125]Rorty, *Contingency, Irony, and Solidarity*, xvi.
[126]Ibid.
[127]Rorty, "Hermeneutics, General Studies, and Teaching," 2.
[128]Rorty, "The Priority of Democracy to Philosophy," 286.
[129]Henry Veatch, "Deconstruction in Philosophy," *Review of Metaphysics* 39 (1985): 315.
[130]Bernard Williams, *Ethics and the Limits of Philosophy* (Cambridge, Mass.: Harvard

suitable community and that other philosophical positions are wrong].
But, paradoxically, if he is correct, [then those who constitute a
community that embodies contrary prejudices] are not wrong.[131]

Christopher Norris charges that Rorty's claim that "any reasons adduced for a
given line of argument are valid only within the culture which holds them
justified" makes it impossible to criticize any system of belief.[132] Presumably this
charge would also apply to Rorty's own belief in the virtues of "American (or
'North Atlantic') bourgeois society and culture as it presently exists."[133]
Frederick Will suggests that Rorty has been so eager to discredit deductivist
foundationalism that he has failed to recognize that a non-deductivist,
"ampliative" foundationalism is legitimate and indispensable.[134]

Some have attempted to defend Rorty against the charge of incoherence on
the ground that this charge rests on the very foundationalist assumptions that are
the object of his criticism.[135] But Rorty's defenders may in turn be vulnerable to
the counter charge that their criticism of Rorty's critics is itself dependent upon
foundationalist assumptions.

Of course Rorty's neo-pragmatism represents only one variety of
contemporary skepticism. Nevertheless, similar comments may be made about
the consequences and coherence of other forms. The deconstructionists, for
instance, have also been interpreted as offering conclusions that have skeptical
and antirational implications for contemporary philosophy. But at least in the
case of Derrida and de Man, so argues Christopher Norris, "it is a flat misreading
of deconstruction that sees it as merely suspending [the issues of meaning,
reference and truth] in favor of an infinitized 'free play' of language devoid of
logical rigour or referential grasp."[136] On the contrary, Norris writes, since
deconstruction recognizes that "some kind of truth-conditional semantics is
implicit in the nature of linguistic understanding," it cannot be interpreted as part
of the neo-pragmatist, "post-philosophical" consensus view of knowledge and
truth.[137]

2. The most obvious skeptical threat to the ideal of liberal education is posed
by what is sometimes called "extreme" or "vulgar" relativism. An "extreme" or
"vulgar" relativism is one that denies the availability of criteria which permit the
adjudication of competing truth-claims and value-claims. Such a denaturalization

---

University Press, 1985), 23.

[131]Frederick Suppe, "Hermeneutics, Eros, and Education: Reply to Rorty," in *Selected
Papers from the Synergos Seminars*, vol. 2. (Fairfax, Virginia: George Mason University, 1982),
25.

[132]Christopher Norris, *The Contest of Faculties* (London: Methuen, 1985.), 153.

[133]Ibid.

[134]Frederick L. Will, *Beyong Deduction* (New York: Routledge, 1988).

[135]For example, see John Churchill, "Realism, Relativism, and the Liberal Arts," *Liberal
Education* 69 (1983): 33-43.

[136]Norris, *The Contest of Faculties*, 227.

[137]Ibid., 228.

of claims to knowledge and obligation would obviously defeat liberal education because it would make it impossible to develop people who can make rational decisions about the way things are and the way things ought to be.

"Extreme" or "vulgar" relativism is incoherent because in rejecting the possibility of rational thought and action it takes what it regards as a rational action and does so on the ground of what it assumes to be a rational thought. A skeptical conclusion is asserted, but it is asserted on the basis of methods and principles that are exempted from the skepticism that these methods and principles justify. Since "extreme" or "vulgar" relativism is incoherent, it, like all arguments with inconsistent premises, cannot be articulate, and therefore cannot advance a conclusion, let alone one that could be a threat to the ideal of liberal education.[138]

3. Any coherent skepticism cannot deny the need for the development of the wise person. This is true because a coherent skepticism presupposes the need for rational thought and action insofar as it advances conclusions and rational arguments in support of these conclusions.

The dependency of any coherent skepticism on the ideals of argumentation demonstrates the uniqueness of the proposed ideal of liberal education, and explains its immunity from skeptical criticism. This immunity is a consequence of the fact that wisdom--understood as the capacity and inclination for rational action--is a presupposition of all criticism.

4. Even if it were conceivable that some of the outcomes of current philosophical controversies might constitute a threat to the proposed ideal of liberal education, it would not make practical sense to suspend or delay liberal education pending the resolution of these controversies. This is so because, regardless of the outcomes of these controversies, there will always be a need for people who have the wisdom and rational skills to understand and to act on the basis of these outcomes.

The current controversies over antifoundationalism and relativism are certainly not the first nor are they likely to be the last philosophical controversies to promise outcomes that appear to threaten the proposed ideal of liberal education. In fact, it seems certain that if the definition of this ideal were to be postponed pending the resolution of important philosophical controversies, no definition would ever be available. This consequence is obviously unacceptable to a community that is in urgent need of people who have the capacity to resolve these and other pressing theoretical and practical problems. Moreover, this consequence will surely be unacceptable even to those neo-pragmatists who are committed only to "solidarity," and who ask only that we have a "willingness to talk, to listen to other people, to weigh the consequences of our actions upon other

---

[138]For a critique of this position, see: Harvey Siegel, *Relativism Refuted* (Dordrecht: D. Reidel, 1987).

people."[139] It would seem that any depreciation of theory in favor of practice already presupposes that practice be guided by those who have the capacity and inclination for rational action.

These reflections on the skeptical criticism of the proposed ideal of liberal education may be summed up in the paradoxical but reassuring conclusion that, at least as long as "postmodern" skeptics continue to criticize this ideal, we have some reason to have confidence in it. Only when these skeptics stop writing their scary books will we have some reason to be apprehensive.

2. THE IDEAL IS CONFIRMED BY CLASSICAL ARGUMENTS

The proposed ideal of liberal education can be rhetorically defended in a second way by the demonstration that this ideal is confirmed by the *loci classici* of liberal education. We will pursue this kind of rhetorical defense of the proposed ideal in Chapter 9 as part of a general project to confirm the four principles of liberal education that are developed in Part 2.

* * * *

If the dialectical deduction and the rhetorical defense of the ideal of liberal education are successful, we have an outline of an ideal that is undogmatic and intrinsically valuable, that is superior to all available competing ideals (including the claims of vulgar skepticism), and that is confirmed by important classical arguments for this ideal. The ideal of liberal education is the development of wise people, where wise people are understood to be those who possess the capacity and inclination for rational action. This ideal is *the principle of liberal education*.

The acceptance of this principle has important consequences for the liberal arts college's institutional relationship to society, for its educational program, and for the college teacher and the conditions of teaching. We now turn to a consideration of these three consequences.

---

[139]Richard Rorty, *Consequences of Pragmatism: Essays, 1972-1980* (Minneapolis, Minn., 1982), 172.

6

THE PRINCIPLE OF INSTITUTIONAL INDEPENDENCE

The lover of wisdom is like a plant which, having proper nurture, must necessarily grow and mature into all virtue, but, if sown and planted in an alien soil, becomes the most noxious of all weeds, unless he be preserved by some divine power.

Plato, *Republic*

THE NECESSITY OF INSTITUTIONAL INDEPENDENCE

The liberal arts college's current uncertainty about its societal role betrays its infidelity to the ideal of liberal education. If the college is genuinely committed to the ideal of developing the wise person, then its proper relationship to society and to other institutions is unequivocally determined.

Prior to the twentieth century the American liberal arts college was typically a religious institution. Like its medieval prototype, the college was understood to be responsible to a church for the propagation of a religious faith. Later, and especially during the world war years of the twentieth century, the college was often regarded as a social institution, one that was responsible to the nation for the preparation of democratic leaders and productive citizens. More recently, and especially since the Viet Nam era, the college has been considered to be an institution of a free market economy with which individuals or groups may contract for various kinds of academic services to satisfy various kinds of interests.

In spite of the historical fact that the liberal arts college has usually been subordinate to a church, to a state, or to group or individual interests, if the college is to realize the ideal of liberal education, it cannot be subordinate to any institution, polity, or interest. It cannot act as the instrument for the realization of any purpose extrinsic to its own. Thus, the ideal liberal arts college is the truly *independent* liberal arts college.

The necessity for this independence can be demonstrated by the following argument:

1.

As has been argued in the preceding chapter, a liberal education is an enterprise whose purpose or ideal is the development of the wise person. Within the liberal arts college--the institution of liberal education--policies and practices that properly serve this purpose are thereby justified, while policies and practices that do not properly serve this purpose are not justified.

2.

As has also been argued, the development of the wise person requires the development of the capacity and inclination for rational action. Rational action is action that transforms reality under the guidance of ideality. It transforms what is into what ought to be. This action requires both empirical and normative knowledge--knowledge of reality and knowledge of ideality.

3.

Since an opinion is always a claim to knowledge, knowledge is presupposed as an ideal by any opinion. Whereas an opinion is a conclusion that is justified by premises that are hypothetical, knowledge is a conclusion that is justified by premises that are demonstrable. Premises become demonstrable by the process of criticism. In the process of criticism conclusions are challenged in order to determine their justifiability. If criticism is compromised by some unjustified assumption or purpose, and is, therefore, incomplete or prejudiced, the justifying premises will not be demonstrably true, but will be only hypothetically true. In order to obtain knowledge, rather than mere opinion, criticism must be complete and unprejudiced. It must be unrestricted, and therefore, uncompromised by any dogma. Since knowledge is essential to liberal education, the process of unrestricted criticism is also essential to it.

4.

The achievement of knowledge through the process of unrestricted criticism requires ideological diversity. Unless there are contrasting and contested opinions, received opinions will not be challenged, and unless received opinions are challenged, knowledge cannot be achieved. Plato's metaphorical representation of this profound epistemological insight is embodied in the notion that Platonic love is the condition for the conception of ideas, the achievement of happiness, and the realization of immortality. The Platonic dialogues frequently provide dramatic demonstration of this insight through the persona of Socrates, the subversive whose antithetical objections to the opinions of his compatriots constitute the condition for dialectical progress toward the synthesis of knowledge. In *On Liberty* John Stuart Mill provides another description of this insight when he points out that even if an idea may be admitted to be the truth, and the whole truth, if it is not "vigorously and earnestly contested, it will, by most of those who receive it, be held in the manner of a prejudice, with little comprehension or feeling of its rational grounds."[1] Today, this identical insight is succinctly captured by Karl Jaspers' dictum that "the truth begins with two."[2]

5.

Ideological diversity and criticism can flourish best in an environment of academic freedom. This is true because ideological diversity and the unrestricted criticism of ideas will normally be repressed as a threat to the orthodoxy of established interests. Criticism is always a "dangerous venture."

6.

Academic freedom requires institutional protection. Traditionally, the most effective device for the protection of academic freedom has been the institution of professional tenure. By providing some assurance of continued employment, tenure provides college teachers with some encouragement to question the orthodox, to be ideologically subversive, and thus to engage in the "dangerous venture" of criticism. It provides teachers with some protection against the intolerance and repressiveness of entrenched power. Another device for the protection of academic freedom is the organization of teachers into a collegium--a guild or society of colleagues that enables all to share in the responsibilities, risks, and rewards of criticism. Finally, academic freedom is also enhanced by the presence of rituals and traditions that facilitate, justify, and celebrate this ideal.

7.

An educational institution cannot genuinely encourage the criticism of ideas if it is itself already beholden to some dogma or committed to some partisan purpose, and therefore subservient to some ideal other than the development of liberally educated people. Academic freedom is not possible unless there is institutional neutrality and thus, institutional independence.

The liberal arts college, like the church in a more devout era, is a sacred place that makes possible the miracle of wisdom. Through this institution people can learn about reality and ideality, and can develop those skills that will make it possible for them to realize ideals. If rational thought is to be possible, then our opinions must be free of prejudiced assumptions, and if our opinions are to be free of prejudiced assumptions, then the institution that enables us to escape

---

[1] John Stuart Mill, *On Liberty* (New York: Appleton-Century-Crofts, Inc., 1947), 52.
[2] Karl Jaspers, *Way to Wisdom* (New Haven, Connecticut: Yale University Press, 1951), 124.

prejudiced assumptions must itself refrain from prejudicing assumptions. Similarly, if rational action is to be possible, then our actions must be free of prejudiced purposes, and if our actions are to be free of prejudiced purposes, then the institution that enables us to avoid prejudiced purposes must itself refrain from prejudicing purposes. Once we realize that rational thought and action are moral obligations for all human agents, and once we realize that the development of rational thought and action requires an institution that assiduously refrains from prejudicing assumptions and purposes, then we can understand why the liberal arts college must have uncompromised independence.

If the liberal arts college is not independent of extrinsic assumptions and purposes, then these assumptions and purposes are exempted from criticism, and thereby become official dogmas. They then prejudice the process of education. Whenever this occurs, liberal education degenerates into indoctrination.

THE WAYS OF COMPROMISING INDEPENDENCE

Institutional independence is as difficult to realize as it is desirable. This difficulty may be evidenced by the many ways that the liberal arts college compromises its independence. Some of these ways are familiar and relatively easily recognized as compromises; they are overt. Others are less familiar and less easily recognized as compromises; they are covert.

THE OVERT WAYS OF COMPROMISING INDEPENDENCE

The college may compromise its institutional independence by subordinating itself to religious creeds, political ideologies, or vocational interests:

Religious Creeds

Many of the great modern universities began under the auspices of a church. Such was the case with the late medieval cathedral and monastic schools. The University of Paris, for instance, a model for Oxford and Cambridge, and thus indirectly a model for the American colonial colleges, developed in the twelfth century as an important center for Catholic theology as the result of the licensing of teachers by the chancellor scholasticus of the cathedral church of Paris. Later, universities were established by papal or imperial bulls to propagate the faith or to suppress the spread of heresies. The University of Toulouse, for example, was founded in 1229 to counter the threat of Albigensianism. During the Reformation new universities were founded to promote the new Protestant religions. Such was the case, for instance, in 1527 when the University of Marburg was established to advance the cause of Lutheranism.

The religious obligations of both Catholic and Protestant universities were not taken lightly. Teachers were often required to take loyalty oaths to the church and its dogmas. Censorship of books and lectures was common. At one time, for instance, the Spanish Inquisition prohibited the study of anatomy. And in Paris in 1624 any questioning of the Church's official interpretation of Aristotle was punishable by death.[3] In more recent times the penalties for doctrinal deviance have been less final, but no less effective in preserving the faith. At one point, for instance, even Immanuel Kant was forbidden to lecture on religion by the University of Königsberg.

In America, with the exception of Franklin's College of Philadelphia, all of the pre-Revolutionary colleges were founded to serve Protestant faiths. The first, Harvard, was founded in 1636 by Puritans to protect their church from an illiterate clergy, and to educate people "in knowledge and godlynes." Subsequently, William and Mary was established by the Anglicans, Yale and Dartmouth by the Congregationalists, Princeton by the Presbyterians, King's College (later Columbia) by the Anglicans, Brown by the Baptists, and Rutgers by the Dutch Reformed Church.[4] In these colonial colleges religious discipline was strict. Only during the last century or so has there been a significant relaxation of religious discipline in the colleges. As late as 1854 even Oxford University still required religious tests for degrees in the arts, law, and medicine.

Especially during the nineteen twenties religious dogma clashed with empirical science in American colleges when Darwinian evolutionary theory was proscribed by law in some states because of its conflict with the creationist account of the origin of man in the Book of Genesis.

Many American colleges, whether "sectarian" or "interdenominational," continue to identify themselves as "church-related liberal arts colleges." The firm religious commitment of these colleges can be illustrated by a statement of purpose of a typical "interdenominational liberal arts college":

> [The first purpose of the college is] to provide a liberal education that introduces the student to the organized fields of learning and presents the Christian theistic view of the world, of man, and of man's culture in the light of Biblical and natural revelation.[5]

The faculty members of this college are required to sign a "statement of faith" which proclaims:

> We believe in the Scriptures of the Old and New Testaments as verbally inspired by God and inerrant in the original writing, and that they are of supreme and final authority in faith and life.[6]

In recent years the rise of charismatic religions has led to the development of

---

[3]James Mulhern, *A History of Education* (New York: The Ronald Press Co., 1946), 294.
[4]Ibid., 297.
[5]Myron F. Wicke, *The Church-related College* (Washington, D.C.: The Center for Applied Research in Education, Inc., 1964), 35.
[6]Ibid., 36.

new educational institutions which are dedicated to the propagation of new religious creeds. One of the largest of these new "church-related" institutions is Oral Roberts University in Tulsa, Oklahoma. Opened in 1965, this institution identifies itself as a liberal arts college, a university, and a graduate school. It is committed to "the historic Christian faith," and seeks to "assist the student in his quest for knowledge of his relationship to God, man, and the universe." Both students and faculty are annually required to sign a Code of Honor that states that it is their aim to "follow in the footsteps" of Jesus Christ and "to develop in the same ways in which He did."[7]

Criticism of Religious Creeds

The church-related college's commitment to a particular religious creed requires that this creed be exempted from criticism within the college's educational program. In consequence, certain articles of faith must be taken as dogmas. But for a college to institutionally adopt any dogma is ipso facto to reject unrestricted criticism within the college's educational program, and therefore, to renounce knowledge in favor of dogma. By this action the college abandons the ideal of liberal education.

Political Ideologies

From the earliest times the fact that knowledge is power did not escape the notice of those seeking to establish political authority. Consequently, ever since the founding of the Academy and the Lyceum, and ever since Plato was recruited to serve as an adviser to Dionysius the Younger, and Aristotle was employed as a tutor to Alexander the Great, kings and councils have sought to appropriate the university for political purposes.

In Rome, after the informal private and domestic education of the aristocracy under the monarchy and the republic, education came increasingly under centralized governmental control during the empire. This culminated in an edict of Theodosius and Valentinian in 425 A.D., proclaiming that all schools were state institutions, and that it was a penal offense to teach without imperial authorization.[8] The state control of education continued until 529 A.D. when the emperor Justinian outlawed pagan education and closed the University of Athens.

In Medieval society the universities were predominately under ecclesiastical control, and served the interests of the church by propagating the faith and training men for the priesthood. But in the late Medieval period, as during the time of the Roman empire, some educational institutions came under the control of the state, and served its interests by training people for professions such as law and medicine. Such was the case with a few schools that continued the Roman

---

[7]G. Oral Roberts, *Oral Roberts University 1965-1983* (New York: The Newcomen Society of the United States, 1983).

[8]James Mulhern, *A History of Education*, 178.

rhetorical and secular traditions, and with the "royal schools" and the schools of chivalry.

Many of the colonial colleges in America combined service to the church and the state under the ideal of developing the "Christian gentleman."

With the post-Enlightenment decline of religion and the rise of the modern nation state, the university emerged as a more secular institution with increased political influence.

In 1808 Napoleon set a precedent for the modern state control of education when he placed the entire French educational system (with the exception of the College de France) under the authority of the Imperial University. Having no proclivity for the disinterested pursuit of truth, academic freedom, or the development of independent thought, he sought to use the universities as instruments in the exercise of political power. His hope was to use the universities to shape the mores of the citizens of the empire, and to produce the officers and administrators of the army and the government bureaucracy.

In a similar way in the nineteen thirties Hitler appropriated the entire German educational system, schools and universities alike, to serve the interests of the National Socialist state. The educational system was brought under the control of the Nazi Party so that it could develop the loyal citizens, technocrats, and soldiers of the Aryan "folkish state"--the nation envisaged as a creation of the unconscious action of the *Volkgeist*. A landmark in the history of this project was a lecture given in 1932 by Professor Adolf Rein of Hamburg University. This lecture, entitled, "The Idea of the Political University," gave currency to the idea that the "political university" was the evolutionary successor to the pre-eighteenth century "university of faith" and the eighteenth and nineteenth century "university of reason." Rein argued that the task of the "political university" was simply "to support and justify the state."[9] Subsequent arguments in support of the "political university" were accompanied by attacks on the traditional ideals of the university, including the ideal of scholarly and scientific objectivity. In a speech in 1939 Hitler's Minister of Education went even further, arguing that "a university based on purely scientific principles alone ought not to survive." Assuming historicist principles, he proclaimed that the university must be thoroughly Nazi, for otherwise "it can not keep abreast of the times." And the National *Führer* of students warned that "the university stands in constant danger of degenerating into a purely intellectual institution, whereas its true function is that of a training center."[10] The "political university" soon became an efficient

---

[9]Geoffrey J. Giles, *Students and National Socialism in Germany* (Princeton, N. J.: Princeton University Press, 1985).

[10]"The National Socialists were pledged to carry through a political revolution in the universities . . . . The rector was chosen by the Minister of Education in Berlin as 'the *Führer* of the university.' No longer was there any institutional barrier between the political sovereign and academic policies . . . . The National Socialists required the teacher to 'demonstrate his personal, moral, and especially his political, fitness . . . . Part of the *Dozentur* examination was service at a 'Community Camp' for the development of 'group-spirit,' and attendance at a 'Teachers Academy' for training in political and social attitudes. Non-Aryans were excluded. A loyalty

instrument in the service of the ideological, scientific, technological, and cultural interests of the "folkish state." In due course education became indoctrination: the humanities, the social sciences, and the natural sciences were subordinated to politics.[11] In the end even Einstein's theory of relativity was impugned as a flawed and Jewish doctrine.[12]

But the "political university" was not invented by Hitler, and it did not come to an end in 1945. In 1961 a renewed defense of the "political university" was given in *The Programme of the Communist Party of the Soviet Union*. In delineating the tasks of the party in the spheres of ideology, education, instruction, science, and culture, the responsibilities of education were described as follows:

> In the struggle for the victory of communism, ideological work becomes an increasingly powerful factor . . . . The Party considers that the paramount task in the ideological field in the present period is to educate all working people in a spirit of ideological integrity and devotion to communism, and cultivate in them a communist attitude to labour and the social economy; to eliminate completely the survivals of bourgeois views and morals; to ensure the all-round, harmonious development of the individual; to create a truly rich spiritual culture.[13]

Until recently, students in Soviet institutes of higher learning were required to take courses in Marxist political economy and philosophy and to take annual state examinations on Marxism-Leninism.

Throughout its history the "political university" has punished those who opposed its political agenda. Even in our own century many of our most celebrated academicians have been harshly punished for their political affiliations. During the First World War Bertrand Russell was dismissed from Cambridge

---

oath to Hitler was required. Travel was controlled by the Ministry. Teachers could become 'state enemies' by citing non-Ayran authorities in scholarship. Scientists had to demonstrate their usefulness to the nation. They could be assigned research projects in 'the nation's "army" of science' whether they desired it or not." E. Y. Hartshorne, "The German Universities and the Government," *Annals of the American Academy of Political Science* 200 (November 1938): 210-234.

[11]Ibid. E. Y. Hartshorne quotes from a speech given by Prof. Kahrstedt at Göttingen on Empire Day, January 18, 1934: "We renounce international science. We renounce the international republic of learning. We renounce research for its own sake. We teach and learn medicine, for example, not to increase the number of known microbes, but to keep the German people strong and healthy. We teach and learn history, not to say how things actually happened, but to instruct the German people from the past. We teach and learn the sciences, not to discover abstract laws, but to sharpen the implements of the German people in their competition with other peoples."

[12]Giles, *Students and National Socialism in Germany*, 253.

[13]*The Programme of the Communist Party of the Soviet Union* (Moskow: Foreign Languages Publishing House, 1961).

University for his pacifism. During the Second World War Karl Jaspers was forbidden to teach or to publish, and narrowly escaped extermination for his opposition to National Socialism.

Criticism of Political Ideologies

The "political university" is conceived as an institution to serve the purposes of the state. However, if the university is to serve the purposes of the state, then it must accept the purposes of the state as dogmas, and in doing so it tacitly renounces the principle of unrestricted criticism. Consequently, if the university is to serve the purposes of the state, it cannot at the same time serve the purpose of liberal education. An institution that serves as a means to advance the ends of the state cannot at the same time serve as a means that makes it possible for people to rationally determine what ends the state should serve.

Vocational Interests

The history of education is replete with examples of attempts to appropriate the liberal arts college for the propagation of a religious creed or a political ideology. Today, when these attempts are resisted by the college, they are often resisted not because they compromise institutional independence, but because those in a position of power within the college are not in sympathy with the religious creed or political ideology of those who want to appropriate the college. This is illustrated by the fact that recently many colleges have been willing to risk some loss of endowment through divestment in order to bring economic pressure on the government of South Africa to end *apartheid*, but no college could be found that would accept an eccentric Texan's offer of a million dollars to any college that would teach white supremacy.

This anomaly points to the fact that today, unlike the past, the principal threat to the institutional independence of the liberal arts college does not come from institutions external to the college, such as the church or the state, but from interests within the college. The tendency of a college's board or administration or faculty to try to impose its own religious or political ideals on the college is now unexceptional. Administrative officers may make pronouncements on pressing political issues, as was sometimes done during the Viet Nam war, and faculties may debate and promulgate resolutions on a variety of political issues, as was done recently in the campaign for divestiture. Typically, these actions are taken on the assumption that they are legitimized by "personal conscience" or by "democratic procedures." When parliamentary procedure is relied upon, a bare majority of the membership of a board or a faculty is able to impose its will on the entire college, and to constrain not only its minority opposition but also those who protest that such actions are not consistent with the institution's official purpose. Sometimes the fact that such actions are not consistent with the institution's official purpose, and are not authorized by the institution's charter, will be openly admitted, but will be arrogantly justified on the basis of a putatively pre-emptive moral principle, such as the possibility of a cataclysmic crisis or the existence of a unique opportunity. But more often than not, such decisions and actions are taken with little concern for the possibility that the college may be acting in violation of its own institutional purpose.

While the principal threat to institutional independence today is posed by those within the college, this threat is no longer limited to religious and political matters, but now includes various student interests. More often than not these interests are vocational. Since these interests come from those who are within the college community, they are less often perceived as threats to institutional independence. Instead, as a consequence of the liberal arts college's confusion about its own institutional purpose, the view that has gained supremacy is the view that the mission of all "higher education" is to serve student interests, and especially, student vocational interests. For instance, a recent survey showed that over 80% of college freshmen believe that a "very important reason" for attending college is "to be able to get a better job."[14] Confirmation of this view is also given by the fact that most people no longer recognize any difference of purpose between a liberal arts college and a university. Both the college and the university are thought to be forms of "higher education" and as such, concerned with preparing students for a vocation. The college and the university are thought to differ only superficially in that the college is assumed to be smaller in size, to provide a more intimate learning environment, and to develop only very general marketable skills, while the university is thought to be larger, to provide a less personal environment, and to develop a wider range of more specialized marketable skills. There seems to be little awareness of the possibility that the liberal arts college and the university could have radically different purposes.

Criticism of Vocational Interests

The use of the liberal arts college for the satisfaction of student vocational interests is currently rationalized in a bewildering variety of ways:[15]

1. The least compromising of these arguments holds that, while the liberal arts college originally had a religious and moral purpose, with the secularization of society it no longer has such a purpose. Consequently, so it is argued, the college should be appropriated so that it can help in the resolution of "today's most pressing needs." In order to do this, it should treat "the student as a consumer by offering him the kinds of educational experiences he demands and needs."[16]

---

[14]Alexander W. Astin, et al., *The American Freshman: National Norms for Fall 1990* (UCLA Higher Education Research Institute, 1990).

[15]Henry R. Weinstock, et al., "A Critique of Criticism of Vocationalism," *Educational Forum* 37 (1973): 427-433.

[16]Stephen J. Clarke, "Secularization and the Liberal Arts College," *Liberal Education* 57

The difficulty with this argument is that it ignores the thesis previously advanced that the liberal arts college is the appropriate institution for liberal education. If the college is merely an instrument for the satisfaction of the felt needs of educational consumers, then students must remain morally ignorant. They can be in no position to make rational judgments on what are "today's most pressing needs," on what felt needs are legitimate needs, or even on whether the college should, or should not, help in the resolution of "today's most pressing needs."

2. It is sometimes said that "liberal and practical studies should go hand in hand in the undergraduate curriculum because each can benefit the other."[17] "Liberal studies" can benefit "practical studies" by "placing them in a broad theoretical context." "Practical studies" can benefit "liberal studies" by providing them with "concrete embodiment," by providing a "medium for the exercise of the liberal arts," by providing a "test of the truth" of the concepts developed, and by providing the liberal studies student with a more "vivid" practical, and not merely "aesthetic," motivation for study.

The problem with this second argument is that it assumes that liberal education consists in the cultivation of the intellect for its own sake. The goal of this form of education is thus seen to be a pure, theoretical act of contemplation which is detached from practical or moral concerns, and which is motivated only by a disinterested, aesthetic interest. However, if liberal education is understood to be a form of education that develops people with the capacity and inclination for rational action, then liberal education can no longer be seen as lacking in practical application and motivation.

3. It is sometimes argued that the college should provide vocational training in addition to liberal education because "being trained specifically for a professional career and being educated broadly in the liberal arts" are not "mutually exclusive undertakings."[18]

The problem with this third argument is that it assumes that a liberal education is merely a form of education that provides students with some "broad" or "general" knowledge and skills, while vocational (or "professional" or "preprofessional") training is a form of education that provides students with more "specialized" knowledge and skills. There is thus no difference between liberal education and vocational training except for the level of generality of the knowledge and skills developed. What is not understood in this conception is that liberal education and vocational training differ from each other in qualitative, not quantitative, ways. The difference between them is not in the *level* of knowledge and skills developed, but in the *kind* of knowledge and skills developed. For vocational training, the knowledge and skills developed are subordinate to various

---

(1971): 385-393.

[17]John S. Brubacher, "Should Liberal Education Bake Bread?" *Liberal Education* 45 (1959): 532-547.

[18]Paul J. Zingg, "The Three Myths of Preprofessionalism," *Liberal Education* 69 (1983): 211.

vocational goals, whereas for liberal education, the knowledge and skills developed are ends in themselves. As was argued above, these two goals are in inevitable conflict. An educational institution cannot have as its goal the development of people who are committed to the disinterested pursuit of truth and intrinsically valuable action, and at the same time have as its goal the development of people who are committed to the pursuit of knowledge that is limited by vocational purposes and by the assumptions that are implicit in these purposes. The pursuit of either one of these goals interferes with the pursuit of the other. Human nature being what it is, vocational interests constitute a perennial threat to the interests of liberal education.

4. It is frequently said that a liberal education is simply any form of education that "liberates" or "frees" its students from bondage to certain undesirable ideas. If a liberal education is understood in this way, then vocational training (or any form of education) can count as liberal education if it adventitiously happens to "liberate" or "free" the student from bondage to whatever ideas are considered to be undesirable.

When liberal education is understood as it is in this argument, its content becomes irrelevant. All that matters is whether this education somehow succeeds in "liberating" the student from the undesired ideas. As a consequence, a student could be both liberally educated and woefully ignorant, having been liberated from the undesired ideas, but having learned nothing more.

In addition, if the task of the liberal arts college is to "liberate" its students from certain undesirable ideas, then it is surely obligatory for the college to precisely and publicly identify these undesirable ideas, to provide specific programs to achieve the desired liberation, and to test students to determine if the promised liberation has been achieved. But there seems little evidence that liberal arts colleges ever respect or even recognize this kind of obligation.

Moreover, it would be dishonest of an institution to claim that its purpose is to "free" its students from bondage to certain undesirable ideas, and then for it to provide a variety of what are quite obviously vocational training programs or courses. For instance, it would seem not only disingenuous, but also inane for a university to provide an expensive program in (say) physics if its real purpose is to free students from ideas such as value-free science, racial prejudice, or technocracy. It would seem equally dishonest and inane for a university to claim that its real purpose is to "liberate" its students from certain undesirable ideas, but then to grade and credentialize its students on the basis of their knowledge of subjects such as physics.

5. Often it is argued that liberal education is simply a form of education that develops in students a certain skill or "habit of mind."[19] On the basis of this assumption it may be concluded that "no particular subject matter is either intrinsically appropriate, or intrinsically inappropriate to liberal arts study," and

---

[19]Thomas B. Coburn, "Nattering Nabobs, Habits of Mind, Persons in Relation: The Future of Liberal Arts Education in a Specialized Society," *Liberal Education* 71 (1985): 1-11.

that, as a consequence, a vocational education may also be a liberal education if it happens to develop the desired "habit of mind."[20]

The assumption in this argument, as in the previous one, would deny any content to liberal education, and would thus allow ignorant people, for instance, to count as being liberally educated. Once again it would seem disingenuous, if not ridiculous, for a college to claim to provide students with certain vocational knowledge and skills, to provide courses of study in which vocational knowledge and skills are thematic, and to test and credentialize students on the basis of their mastery of vocational knowledge and skills, and yet at the same time to claim that its real, though unstated purpose is to develop a certain "habit of mind."

6. Some evidently believe that liberal and vocational education are not incompatible because the difference between liberal education and vocational training is simply the difference between an education that is concerned with "technique" and an education that is concerned with "intellectual vision":

> The antithesis between a technical and liberal education is fallacious. There can be no adequate technical education which is not liberal, and no liberal education which is not technical: That is, no education which does not impart both technique and intellectual vision.[21]

The difficulty with the view represented here is that, while it may be true that both liberal education and an "adequate" vocational education impart technique and intellectual vision, it would in any case also be true that the technique and intellectual vision provided by an "adequate" vocational education would differ radically from the technique and intellectual vision provided by liberal education. A vocational education by definition develops only the technique and intellectual vision that are essential to a specific vocation, whereas a liberal education by definition develops the technique and intellectual vision that are essential to rational action. A vocational education does not develop a comprehensive knowledge of reality and ideality; it does not develop the liberal arts; and it does not develop insight into fundamental principles. Similarly, a liberal education does not develop the knowledge or skills essential to a specific vocation.

7. It is occasionally admitted that liberal and vocational education are by nature incompatible, but it is still argued that the liberal arts college should provide vocational education because society has an overriding need for liberally educated professionals. Consequently, the liberal arts college is said to have a social responsibility to provide both liberal education *and* professional training.

While the assumption in this argument that our society needs liberally educated professionals may be granted, it does not follow from this that it is the responsibility of the liberal arts college to provide both liberal education and

---

[20]Ibid.

[21]George W. Hazzard, President, Worcester Polytechnic Institute, in a letter to *The Hill News*, St. Lawrence University, April 12, 1973.

professional training. To restate a point made in Chapter 2, if we were to argue in this way, we might just as well argue that since our society needs all kinds of liberally educated people--parents, farmers, police, business executives, etc., it is the responsibility of the liberal arts college to act as a training center for parents, an agricultural school, a police academy, and a business institute, etc. To argue in this way would be to justify abolishing all institutions of higher education except for the liberal arts college, and making this college responsible for providing all vocational training programs. The inference that, since our society needs liberally educated professionals, the liberal arts college should be responsible for professional training is no less objectionable than the inference that, since our society needs ministers who can speak grammatically, the grammar school should be responsible for training ministers.

8. Sometimes the liberal arts college is not held to have a responsibility for the training of most professionals, but it is still held to have a special responsibility for the training of teachers. This position is sometimes justified by the assumption that a college has a responsibility to provide benefits to the local community of which it is "only a part."

What must be asserted in the face of all arguments of this kind is that the liberal arts college cannot serve its own purposes if it must serve the purposes of a particular community. This is true because the invariant purposes of liberal education are often in conflict with the varying purposes of a particular community.

9. A liberal education may be understood as an institution for the enculturation of the novitiates of a leisured aristocracy. Such an education, with its disdain for manual labor and its veneration of high culture as an end in itself, is considered inappropriate for the modern classless, democratic state. In consequence, the claim is made that the proper role of the liberal arts college is not to provide a liberal education, but to prepare people for a productive role in society. In an age where practically all persons must engage in productive labor, the "unproductive separation between the liberal arts and the useful arts tends to leave the students poorly served."[22] In this view a traditional liberal education is "aristocratic," open only to the few, while vocational education is "democratic," open to all.[23]

Contrary to the assumption of this argument, the proper purpose of a liberal education is not to provide high culture for an effete leisured aristocracy, but to develop wise people. Liberal education does not prepare people to lead lives that are limited to contingent economic obligations; it prepares them to lead lives centered about categorical, moral obligations.

10. A liberal education may be admitted to be incompatible with vocational education, but in spite of this it may be held to be economically viable only if it is combined with vocational education.

---

[22]Ernest L. Boyer, *College: The Undergraduate Experience in America* (New York: Harper & Row, Publishers, 1987), 102.

[23]Benjamin Fine, *Democratic Education* (New York: Thomas Y. Crowell Company, 1945).

Given the present confusion about the purpose of liberal education, and given the current demand that all education be useful for a vocational purpose, it is likely true, as assumed by this argument, that an uncompromised liberal education will not have the appeal of vocational education. But what needs to be remembered is that a compromised liberal education is no longer a liberal education. Consequently, to require that liberal education be subordinate to vocational purposes is at once to deny it the possibility of being liberal education.

11. Often liberal education is understood as an education in the "liberal arts," where the "liberal arts" are understood to be the studies which develop "basic skills," such as those necessary for "understanding, reasoning and communicating,"[24] or alternately, fundamental "skills, methodologies, and systematic knowledge" necessary as a "foundation for a sound professional education."[25] Given this common conception of liberal education as a prerequisite for vocational education, it would follow that there would be no reason to regard liberal education as being incompatible with vocational education. On the contrary, there would be every reason to believe that these two forms of education should be integrated on the ground that liberal education provides the basic skills required by vocational education.

The flaw in this argument is the assumption that the purpose of a liberal education is the development of "basis skills." A person who possessed the "basic skills," but who lacked any unconditional knowledge of reality or ideality, could not be considered to be liberally educated. The view that a liberal education consists merely in the acquisition of the "basis skills" (or even the liberal arts) fails to realize that a liberal education is concerned with ends, not just means to ends. Once liberal education is understood to have a purpose that transcends the development of various skills, then the demand that it be segregated from vocational or professional education can be seen to be not some bit of cultural snobbery or a romantic mystique, but a reasonable effort to protect the integrity of two radically different forms of education.

12. A liberal education may be understood by an operational definition as "that kind of education which a liberal arts college program provides."[26]

Given this way of understanding a liberal education, it is emptied of any essential purpose or content. As a result, all questions about the purpose and content of liberal education are simply displaced into questions about the purpose

[24]C. E. Elebash, and B. W. Cutchen, "Liberal Education and Business Education: Are They Mutually Exclusive?" *Journal of Business Education* (January 1983): 151-153.

[25]James M. Powell, "Professionalism and the Liberal Arts in the American University," *Liberal Education* 69 (1983): 225-232.

[26]Louis T. Bénézet, *General Education in the Progressive College* (New York: Bureau of Publications, Teachers College, Columbia University, 1943), 28. Bruce Kimball notes that this kind of definition is still used today in studies such as "National Project IV: Liberal Education Varieties and Their Assessment," sponsored by the federal Fund for the Improvement of Post-secondary Education. Kimball, *Orators and Philosophers: A History of the Idea of Liberal Education*, 4.

and content of the educational program of a specific liberal arts college. This is a profitless maneuver.

We can now generalize over these diverse arguments. What needs to be emphasized is that if the liberal arts college serves student vocational interests, it allows these interests and their implied assumptions to interfere in the unrestricted criticism that is required to obtain the knowledge that is essential to liberal education. The pursuit of knowledge of reality and ideality cannot proceed without prejudice if the knowledge that is sought in the college's educational program must be subservient to vocational purposes and their covert assumptions. The requirements for becoming a soldier, a school teacher, or a business executive, for instance, are not identical with the requirements for becoming a wise person.

Thus, the various attempts to rationalize the legitimacy of vocational interests within liberal education are flawed by their failure to recognize that liberal education and vocational training have radically different purposes.

As we have noted, some educators have argued that, while liberal education and vocational training do have different purposes, these two forms of education can be combined in ways that will provide mutual enhancement.[27]   This suggestion is sometimes accompanied by the argument that the coexistence of these two forms of education is no less impossible or unreasonable than is the coexistence in human life of the search for wisdom and the need for vocational knowledge and skills. The proper counter to this argument is to note that in every human life there are many activities that are best not pursued simultaneously. Such would be the case, for instance, with working and playing, drinking and driving, and so on. The attempt to combine liberal education and vocational training in a single educational program ignores the fact that, while within the lifetime of most individuals the need for wisdom must coexist with the need for the development of vocational knowledge and skills, within an educational context there may be compelling reasons to separate these two very different endeavors.

The most compelling reason for not combining liberal education and vocational training in a single educational program is that these two activities have purposes that are in endemic conflict. It is plainly one thing to persuade people to be critical of their own assumptions, and another thing to provide them with conclusions and methods which reinforce their assumptions. Consequently, any program for the development of wise people will be disadvantaged by being placed in a competitive relationship with a program for the development of vocational knowledge and skills.[28] Moreover, in any situation in which a market economy exists, a liberal education is certain to be disadvantaged. This is true

---

[27]See, for instance, John S. Brubacher, "Should Liberal Education Bake Bread?," *Liberal Education* 45 (1959): 532-547.

[28]For an explanation of this point, see: A. Whitney Griswold, "American Education's Greatest Need," *Saturday Review* (14 March 1959): 15ff. Also see: Robert Maynard Hutchins, *The Higher Learning in America* (New Haven, Conn.: Yale University Press, 1936).

because for most people without a liberal education, a program that leads to vocational knowledge and skills is valued highly, while a program that leads to wisdom is valued poorly. This exemplification of Gresham's law means that a program to develop wise people requires substantial institutional protection, and that, consequently, liberal education and vocational training are best pursued in institutionally separate ways.

THE COVERT WAYS OF COMPROMISING INDEPENDENCE

During the twentieth century the independence of the liberal arts college has been occasionally compromised by the acceptance of religious creeds, frequently compromised by the adoption of political ideologies, and almost constantly compromised by the demand that the college serve student vocational interests. But the college's independence has also been compromised in a number of ways that are not so common or obvious. These covert compromises, no less than the more familiar, overt ones, forfeit the independence of the college, and subvert liberal education by their opposition to unrestricted criticism.

Philosophical Dogmas

Sometimes colleges and universities have been subordinated to a particular philosophical doctrine. This was the case during medieval and early modern times when universities were forbidden to question the philosophy of Aristotle. In 1600, for instance, Giordano Bruno was tried by the Inquisition and burned at the stake for anti-Aristotelian and Copernican views. After Galileo discovered the satellites of Jupiter in 1610, Cremonini, a Reader in Philosophy at Padua, refused to look through the telescope, holding that Galileo's claims were anti-Aristotelian and violated the Holy Writ that limited the number of heavenly bodies to the perfect number seven, just as the number of holy sacraments and the number of days in the week were limited to seven. In 1633, after the Inquisition had condemned his views, Galileo was forced to confess his doctrinal error and to plead for mercy to escape the fate of Bruno.

While it is unquestionably true that Aristotelianism exerted the most pervasive philosophical influence on the development of the medieval and early modern university, other philosophical doctrines had significant impacts. Neo-Platonism was periodically influential. In the seventeenth century Cartesianism arose as a threat to the reigning Aristotelianism. So serious was this threat that, for instance, in 1653 the philosophical faculty of the University of Marburg passed an official resolution banning Cartesianism from the university.[29]

In the twentieth century Soviet allegiance to Marxist philosophy singularly shaped the university in the Soviet Union. The best known example of this was the way that Marxist political dogma influenced the development of "Soviet

---

[29]E. Y. Hartshorne, "The German Universities and the Government," 210-34.

genetics." During the Stalin era the geneticist T. D. Lysenko and his followers, recognizing that the theory of the inheritance of acquired characteristics was more compatible with Marxist doctrine than the generally accepted chromosome theory, attacked the defenders of the chromosome theory as "enemies of the people," and impugned the theory as a form of "racism, cosmopolitanism, sophism, scholasticism, Machism, idealism, and Kantism."[30] With the help, and at one point, even the editorial assistance of the Soviet dictator, Stalin, Lysenko's theory was given the imprimatur of the Communist party, and Lysenko himself was installed as the doctrinal authority. Subsequently virtually all criticism of Lysenkoism was discontinued. Genetic literature was removed from libraries, and genetic research in animal husbandry was ended. Those not sympathetic to Lysenko were removed from the universities, and leading geneticists were arrested as "socially dangerous."[31]

Criticism of Philosophical Dogmas

Any college that is officially committed to a particular philosophical doctrine is, by virtue of this commitment, not free to engage in unrestricted criticism of this doctrine. This means that the college's educational program must take this doctrine as a body of unimpeachable truths. All conclusions that are inconsistent with this doctrine will be rejected on a priori grounds. As a result, the college will be unable to develop students who are free of unexamined assumptions.

Educational Dogmas: Theories of General Education

A college may structure its educational program on the basis of a particular philosophy of education. As a consequence, its program will have a particular set of educational objectives, a particular program of instruction, a prescribed body of texts, or a prescribed group of pedagogical practices. Once such commitments have been made by a college, criticism of the official principles is without institutional legitimacy. As a result, the adopted philosophy of education has the status of a dogma, a truth that is not itself subject to criticism.

Examples of this kind of educational dogma can be found in several familiar theories of "general education." Programs of "general education" were introduced in the United States in the early decades of the twentieth century in an attempt to counter the emphasis on research and disciplinary specialization that was created by the spreading influence of the German universities. The goals of this movement were clearly announced in the first issue of the *Journal of General Education* by its editor, Earl J. McGrath. Protesting the prevailing specialization and vocationalism of the university, general education was described as "that

---

[30]Zhores A. Medvedev, *The Rise and Fall of T. D. Lysenko* (New York: Columbia University Press, 1969), 121.
    [31]Ibid.

which prepares the young for the common life of their time and their kind." It was committed to a more prescribed curriculum, and to a renewed emphasis on teaching.[32] It was understood to be an attempt to revitalize liberal education.[33]

One of the best-known theories of general education is that which justifies the so-called "Great Books" program, usually associated with St. John's College in Annapolis, Maryland. This college seeks to develop "free and rational men and women committed to the pursuit of knowledge in its fundamental unity, intelligently appreciative of their common cultural heritage, and conscious of their social and moral obligations." St. John's strategy for achieving this is through the study of "the books in which the greatest minds of our civilization . . . have expressed themselves."

One of the most influential theories of general education is the body of doctrine that developed, especially during the period from 1919 to 1954, in support of the general education program of Columbia College. In reviewing the history of this program in *The Reforming of General Education* Daniel Bell takes the position that this program avoided the dogmas of the major alternative programs. Specifically, he argues that it avoided the assumption that "a common learning had to be a specific number of 'great books.'"[34] Moreover, he contends that the Columbia program, unlike its rivals at Chicago and Harvard, did not make "a doctrinal commitment" to any "single" educational philosophy.[35] Instead it accepted a "broad intellectual diversity as a . . . general principle of liberal education."[36] Bell explains the Columbia emphasis on "intellectual diversity" as the result of the belief that "the student should be the focus of the undergraduate college," the strength of the departmental organization of the college, and especially, the influence of John Dewey's idea that the most important attitude that can be formed in education is "the desire to go on learning."

The hallmark of the Columbia program was the Contemporary Civilization and Humanities courses. Beginning as a one year course required of all students, the Contemporary Civilization course evolved into a two year sequence in 1919. The first year focused on the intellectual traditions and institutional development of Western society, while the second focused on contemporary socioeconomic problems. The Humanities course, like the Contemporary Civilization course, began as a one year required course, but became a two year sequence in 1947. The first year examined masterpieces of literature and philosophy from Homer to the nineteenth century, while the second year emphasized masterpieces of music and the plastic arts.

---

[32]Daniel Bell, *The Reforming of General Education: The Columbia College Experience in Its National Setting* (New York: Columbia University Press, 1966), 180.

[33]Richard P. McKeon, "The Liberating Arts and the Humanizing Arts in Education," in Arthur A. Cohen, ed., *Humanistic Education and Western Civilization* (New York: Holt, Rinehart and Winston, 1964).

[34]Bell, *The Reforming of General Education*, 282.

[35]Ibid., 24.

[36]Ibid., 26.

Criticism of Theories of General Education

The "Great Books" program is commonly criticized on the ground that any selection of books to be regarded as "Great" inevitably involves subjective differences of criteria. These differences are usually said to reflect irresolvable differences in "personal values." Today, for instance, it is common to hear charges that specific lists of "Great Books" are biased toward "Western culture," "liberal politics," "Greek ontology," "dead white males," etc.[37] Moreover, it is evident that any decision as to which books are to be canonized as "Great Books" already assumes some at least implicit educational purpose. Consequently, a "Great Books" program can escape dogmatism only if the educational purpose of the program is articulated, and if this purpose can be demonstrated to be itself undogmatic.

Even though Daniel Bell regards the Columbia College general education program as free of dogma because of its emphasis on "intellectual diversity," he does note that one of the reasons why it was supplanted by the "major" system in 1954 was the fact that it had certain "intellectual difficulties." The content of the Contemporary Civilization course, for instance, seemed to change in ways that merely reflected the changing interests of American society. In the beginning, Bell suggests, an emphasis on economic problems and policy reflected the depression years and the New Deal. Later, interest in anthropology and sociology led to an emphasis on the study of culture. Still later, interest in existentialism and neo-orthodox theology led to an emphasis on moral attitudes. Overall, the course was fractured into a "loosely quilted patchwork" that was determined by the various past and current interests of the students and the interests of the increasingly powerful academic departments.[38]

While the Columbia Contemporary Civilization course appeared to be free of bias at its inception, and while it evidently appeared free of bias to Bell as late as 1966, the rapid changes since that time have brought to light apparent biases that were not clear to an earlier generation. Today, for instance, the use of history as an integrating device would be recognized as providing no guarantee of objectivity.[39] Also today, the traditional emphasis on Western civilization would likely be viewed as an expression of cultural chauvinism. Similarly, the Columbia Humanities course would probably be regarded now as exhibiting a bias toward "high culture" and "phallocentric narratives."

In various ways these theories of general education place restrictions on the process of criticism. To the extent that this is accomplished, then to that extent

---

[37]See Beverly Guy-Sheftall's response to Richard Rorty's keynote address to the American Association of Colleges 1989 Annual Meeting in *Liberal Education* 75 (1989): 19. Also see: Martin Heidegger, *Being and Time* (London: SCM Press Ltd., 1962), 43.

[38]Bell, *The Reforming of General Education*, 198-199.

[39]History's dependence on philosophical principles is explored by Richard P. McKeon in *Freedom and History* (New York: Noonday Press, 1952) and by Heidegger in *Being and Time*, II, chap. 5, "Temporality and Historicality."

these theories are obstacles to the process of unrestricted criticism, and therefore, to the achievement of liberal education.

Educational Dogmas: Theories of Special Education

Not long ago, and for many centuries before that, it was common for educators to give priority to the question, "What knowledge is most worth having?"[40] This question was, in fact, the question that often informed classical liberal education. It bespeaks a time when people could aspire to the learning of an Aristotle, a Leonardo, or a Goethe, and could seek that comprehensive knowledge of universals and first principles that the Greeks regarded as essential to *sophia*. Today, however, most educators would consider this question naive or presumptuous, and would regard any individual or educational institution that would attempt to answer it as arrogant and dogmatic. Harold Taylor, for instance, in his book, *Students Without Teachers*, asserts that today there simply is "no complete body of knowledge common to all educated men." Any attempt to find such a comprehensive body of knowledge is now thought to be impossible because the prevailing skepticism of the twentieth century has silenced any hope of obtaining any knowledge beyond a variety of specialized "theories," and because the "knowledge explosion" has produced far too many theories for any one person to comprehend.

Faced with these consequences of twentieth century skepticism and the "knowledge explosion," the contemporary liberal arts college has tried to escape the charge of dogmatism by abandoning the ideals of liberal education. In spite of the fact that the college's description of its program in its promotional literature continues to appropriate the language and homilies of the past, the college no longer provides anything that has any conclusive historic right to be called "liberal education" or even "general education." In place of a curriculum of liberal or general education the college now offers a variety of specialized programs tailored to constantly changing student interests. In this twentieth century metamorphosis the theoretical sciences have multiplied into countless autonomous departmental and "interdisciplinary" specialities, the normative sciences have simply disappeared and, until recently, have been replaced by value-neutral social sciences, the liberal arts have been forgotten, and the traditional integrative disciplines, such as philosophy, history, theology, rhetoric, metaphysics, epistemology, speculative grammar, and ontology, have been relegated to the status of being just additional specialized theories. As a result, since the end of the general education movement in the post World War I period, the American liberal arts college has been transformed from an institution dedicated to the development of people who possess "the knowledge most worth

---

[40]Herbert Spencer, "What Knowledge is of Most Worth," in *Essays on Education and Kindred Subjects* (London: J. M. Dent & Sons, Ltd., 1963). Also see: Wayne C. Booth, ed., *The Knowledge Most Worth Having* (Chicago: The University of Chicago Press, 1967).

having" into one whose main purpose is to service the largely vocational interests of those who seek to "major" in a departmentalized, specialized, morally sterilized, and philosophically ungrounded "discipline." Public relations rhetoric to the contrary, the contemporary liberal arts college has now abandoned any serious commitment to general education, and is now in the business of special education.

Criticism of Theories of Special Education

As we have seen, the liberal arts college may be subservient to a dogma if in fact it sponsors a program of general education that is based upon principles that are exempt from criticism in the college's educational program. Unfortunately, the college's abandonment of general education and its transformation into an institution for special education does not allow it to escape dogma. It merely replaces one dogma with another. This can be seen in a number of ways:

1. The contemporary departmentalized college lacks coherence. In spite of the fact that the college is usually embarrassed to be called a "college," and often imperiously claims for itself the title, "university," it makes this claim in seeming disregard for the etymology of the word. The contemporary college is more appropriately called a "diversity" or a "multiversity." In spite of some degenerate, vestigial general education devices, such as "distribution requirements," the contemporary college is in fact little more than a collection of academic departments, each of which markets a specialized, autonomous "discipline" or "body of knowledge." Each of these has its own set of principles in addition to its own set of conclusions and methods.

The trouble with this arrangement, aside from the dishonesty in the way that it is marketed, is the fact that the principles that ground these disciplines cannot justifiably be subject to criticism within the disciplines that they ground. Physics, for instance, cannot--as the discipline of physics--study its own mathematical, logical, and ontological presuppositions. Yet the contemporary college does not recognize a privileged, architectonic, or integrative discipline whose task it is to examine the principles and methods of the specialized disciplines. It thus dogmatically ignores the most important assumptions of the various disciplines which it sponsors. If general education is dogmatic because it rests on principles that are exempt from criticism in the college's academic program, then special education is equally dogmatic because the principles of its constituent disciplines are also exempt from examination in the college's educational program.

It is important to recognize that this lack of curricular integration cannot be remedied by the device of "interdisciplinary studies." Interdisciplinary studies are simply new, emergent disciplines. Like disciplinary studies, they have no warrant to examine their own principles.

2. In an earlier era the liberal arts college provided a program of liberal education that was prescribed for all students. In view of the fact that these students had elected to receive this kind of education, it was not surprising that

this program should be prescriptive. In more recent times, as the ideal of liberal education has receded from the collective consciousness of the academy, the prescriptiveness of the prescribed program has been seen as dogmatic, and the college has embraced the "elective principle" as a way to escape from this apparent dogmatism.

As we have seen, the trouble with this strategy is that it does not really eliminate prescriptiveness in the "curriculum." Since the college has replaced the general education curriculum with departmentalized curricula, and since the curricula of the various departments are mostly prescribed, all that the college has done is to eliminate prescriptiveness in the general education program and reintroduce it in the special education programs.   Strangely enough, this inconsistency is usually missed. Faculty members and students who would consider it dogmatic and coercive for the college to require a liberal arts student to study the liberal arts, do not seem to have any problem with requiring a sociology "major" to study sociological research methods.

3. Moreover, the dogmatism of the departmentalized college is intensified by the fact that the college lacks any educational principles governing the inclusion and exclusion of its various academic departments.   Departmental and interdepartmental courses and programs may be added or deleted from the curriculum because of variations in student "demand" caused by a single cover story in *Time* magazine, because of perceived public relations "needs," or because an ambitious new administrator or department chair is in need of "career visibility." One year, Greek is the mark of an educated person; in another year, it is the mark of an intellectual snob; one year, Western civilization is the center of the curriculum; in another year, it is regarded as an ethnocentric embarrassment; one year, rhetoric is the only prescribed course in the curriculum; in another year, it is not even available as an elective; one year, dialectic is recognized as the architectonic liberal art; in another year, no one seems to know what the word means; one year, history is regarded as the key integrative discipline; in another year, all history written prior to 1950 is regarded as hopelessly biased by white Western males--and so on. Today new departments and programs and disciplines and "interdisciplinary" disciplines are born and die with the tempo of the appearance and disappearance of insect mutations in a tropical rain forest. To add immorality to this insanity, this tolerance and desire for constant change is typically rationalized by the college as a virtue. Change is celebrated as if it were itself intrinsically valuable. "Innovation," "creativity," and "experimentation" are hyped as if they provide evidence of high academic purposes, while the secret truth is that they most often only provide evidence of careeristic ambition.

4. The dogmatism of the departmentalized college is intensified in another way. A major factor in the determination of the constituent departments of the college is student interest, or "course demand," as reflected in the bottom line of enrollments. But this fact makes it apparent that to a considerable extent the educational program of the college is determined by the constantly vacillating

interests of its students. And since these students seek, but do not possess, an education, the college allows its educational program to be determined by the uneducated. Strangely enough, once again, such an abdication of academic responsibility is seen as "democratic" and undogmatic, while the pandering to student interests is not seen as what it really is--an abdication by the college of its educational responsibility, and a shameful, commercially motivated sellout to the uninformed, uncriticized prejudices of those who lack and need a liberal education.

5. There is a final dogmatic consequence of the fact that the contemporary departmentalized college has no curriculum, has no principle for inclusion or exclusion of the disciplines, and refuses to recognize any integrative discipline. Since in this kind of curricular egalitarianism all disciplines are regarded as equal, no order of value can be established among them. As a consequence, no order of value can be established among their conclusions. Consequently, all disciplinary conclusions must be treated as descriptive, not prescriptive, and all of the disciplines must be regarded as "value-free" in the sense that they are without normative import. As a result, the classical "practical" or normative sciences are excluded from the college's educational program because their admission would threaten the equality of the college's constituent disciplines. This exclusion of the normative disciplines from the curriculum is in accord with the modern paradigm for the university, the German research university.[41] The consequences of this educational egalitarianism and positivism are by this time apparent. For the liberal arts college to graduate students who are morally ignorant not only violates the ideal that a liberal education is intrinsically valuable, but, because it does not provide for the unrestricted criticism of its constituent disciplines, it violates the ideal that a liberal education is undogmatic.

Educational Dogmas: Theories of Humanistic Education

During the nineteen seventies the "human potential" or "humanistic education" movement was an important influence on American education. Its appeal was magnified by the fact that it promised the development of a "new human type" to a generation disillusioned by the national trauma of Viet Nam. The leaders of this movement argued that the task of education was the development of the "person" who is "psychologically healthy or "fully functioning."[42]

---

[41]Clark Kerr, *The Uses of the University* (Cambridge, Mass.: Harvard University Press, 1963).

[42]Carl Rogers, *Freedom to Learn* (Columbus, Ohio: Charles E. Merrill Publishing Co., 1969). Also see: Abraham Maslow, "Some Educational Implications of the Humanistic Psychologies," *Harvard Educational Review* 38 (Fall 1968): 685-696. A bibliography on humanistic education is included in: H. C. Lyon, *Learning to Feel--Feeling to Learn: Humanistic Education for the Whole Man* (Columbus, Ohio: Charles E. Merrill Publishing Co., 1971).

Criticism of the Theories of Humanistic Education

While the humanistic education movement was a powerful stimulant to both the theory and practice of liberal education, it was marred by a dogmatic ideal. It took a particular psychological model of the "fully functioning adult" and imposed it on the college as the goal of liberal education. What was forgotten was that it is possible for a person to be psychologically healthy in different ways, and that a person may be psychologically healthy in any one of these ways, but still lack wisdom. The evangelically dogmatic features of the humanistic education movement are on display in such works as Harold C. Lyon's *Learning to Feel--Feeling to Learn: Humanistic Education for the Whole Man.*[43] A devastating criticism of the dogmatism of this movement can be found in Andrew Malcolm's *The Tyranny of the Group.*[44] Malcolm's suggestion is that the energy of ideological movements like the human potential movement derives from the human will to believe--that is, from what Nietzsche called, "the wish to be Elsewhere." Under the spell of this will to believe, human reality and the social world must be remade according to the official plan. And in this plan the dogmatic consequences of utopian ideology become apparent. The college becomes the primary institution for the creation of the "new man" and the new society. In this way, according to Malcolm, humanistic education becomes one more illustration of what J. L. Talmon calls the "curse" on all "salvationist creeds": "to be born of the noblest impulses of man and to degenerate into weapons of tyranny."[45] Thus, insofar as the college adopts an official conception of the ideal human being or the ideal society, it compromises the process of unrestricted criticism, and makes liberal education impossible.

Conservative Ideologies

During the seventeenth century Harvard, like the other colonial colleges, was understood to be an institution for the education of the Christian gentleman.[46] This ideal came to the colonial colleges from sixteenth century England, where it

---

[43]Lyon, *Learning to Feel--Feeling to Learn: Humanistic Education for the Whole Man,* chap. 7. This provides hints on how to manipulate people by treating them as unique individuals who should not be manipulated.

[44]Andrew Malcolm, *The Tyranny of the Group* (Totowa, N. J.: Littlefield, Adams & Co., 1975). Malcolm writes: "The breathless anticipation of the Age of Aquarius, or whatever else it may be called, is certainly an indication of the rebirth in our time of an ancient myth, but we must be aware of the fact that this myth is an expression of one of the profound needs of man: the need to give birth to *Homo transcendentia* with his rule of peace and bliss." Malcolm notes that the "magic humanists" [the members of the human potential movement] are perfectly comfortable with the dictum of Alfred Rosenberg, Hitler's ideologist: "This is the task of our century, to create a new human type out of a new life myth."

[45]Ibid., 145.

[46]Samuel Eliot Morison, *Three Centuries of Harvard: 1636-1936* (Cambridge, Mass.: Harvard University Press, 1936), 22.

evolved out of a milieu that included the medieval ideal of knighthood, the humanist ideal of scholarship, and the religious ideal of Christianity. Instrumental in the development of this ideal was Erasmus' *The Education of a Christian Prince* (*Institutio principis Christiani*) (1516), and later, Sir Thomas Elyot's *The Boke Named Governour* (1531), one of the earliest major treatises on education to appear in the English Language.[47] Elyot believed that the purpose of education was to train the hereditary aristocracy in the cardinal virtues of wisdom, courage, temperance, and justice, and in the gentlemanly virtues of majesty, nobility, affability, placability, mercy, humanity, benevolence, beneficence, liberality, and friendship. The educated aristocrat was envisaged as the Elizabethan gentleman portrayed by Spenser in the *The Faerie Queene*, personified by Sir Walter Raleigh, and confirmed in the American mind through the writings of Longfellow, Lowell, Holmes, and Emerson. The adoption of this ideal by the American liberal arts colleges justified an educational program oriented to the cultivation of the moral, as well as the intellectual virtues, through the study of language, history, art, and music. This program sought to "humanize those born to rule."[48]

Criticism of Conservative Ideologies

In our own day the liberal arts college continues to enjoy the benefits and to carry the burdens of a tradition that at least implicitly understands the college as an instrument for the perpetuation of aristocratic obligation and privilege. Sustained by high tuition and private endowment, and supplied by the best high schools and preparatory schools, the elite private liberal arts college continues today to be the college of choice for the families and children of those with aristocratic aspirations.

In the egalitarian spirit of contemporary America the elite liberal arts college's record of service to the interests of the aristocratic classes is an anomaly and an embarrassment. Today, in order to escape this reputation the college has adopted a number of programs and practices that are intended to broaden its appeal. Financial aid is employed in an effort to bring the high cost of college education within the means of all economic classes. Recruitment practices are devised to obtain greater racial, ethnic, and religious diversity. Curricula are purged of the vestiges of traditional aristocratic education--required courses in the liberal and fine arts, foreign languages, and the history of Western civilization. In particular, the study of Western or "high" culture is de-emphasized in favor of the study of "non-Western and Third World" cultures. Since many of these attempts to make the college more acceptable to an egalitarian society risk making the college less attractive to its traditional clients, they pose potentially serious threats to the continued existence of all but the most prestigious of these institutions.

---

[47]Lawrence A. Cremin, *American Education: The Colonial Experience, 1607-1783* (New York: Harper and Row, 1970), 62.
    [48]Ibid., 67.

Nevertheless, in our time any attempt to make the liberal arts college an instrument to serve the interests of the privileged classes is sure to be condemned as undemocratic. But more important is the fact that if the college is made to serve the interests of a particular class, then the interests and values of this class cannot justifiably be critically examined in the college's educational program. As a consequence, the college cannot act as an institution for unrestricted criticism. Thus, for the liberal arts college to allow itself to be used as the instrument for the propagation of aristocratic values requires that these values be excluded from institutionalized criticism, and this is tantamount to the adoption of a dogma and to the identification of the college as a species of the "political university." As a "political university" the college can no longer act as an institution of liberal education.

Liberal Ideologies

During the twentieth century, while the elite liberal arts college continued to be favored by those who aspired to aristocratic class and culture, the college struggled to serve a different clientele. It sought to propagate democratic values and to educate the citizens of a free society. This purpose was clearly announced by the "Harvard Redbook"--the 1945 Report of the Harvard Committee on the Objectives of a General Education in a Free Society.[49] In this report the university was viewed as an "instrument" to prepare students for citizenship in a liberal democracy.[50]

Criticism of Liberal Ideologies

If the liberal arts college commits itself to acting as an instrument for the propagation of "democratic values" or for the education of the "citizens of a free society," then, by virtue of this commitment, it has adopted a partisan political purpose. Once the college has committed itself to this purpose, then, unless it is to violate its commitment, it cannot treat this purpose or the values which it presupposes as problematic, but must regard them as norms that are exempt from criticism. Thus, for instance, if the college is to serve the interests of American democracy, the values of American democracy cannot justifiably be called into question within the college's educational program.

It is probably true, especially in the World War eras, that most Americans

---

[49]*General Education in a Free Society* (Cambridge, Mass.: Harvard Universiity Press, 1945), x, xv.

[50]A more recent statement of the position that the college is properly an instrument of society can be found in Charles E. Silberman, *Crisis in the Classroom: The Remaking of American Education* (New York: Random House, 1970). Silberman argues that liberal education has the task of creating a "humane" society. He does not recognize the possibility that a "humane" society (whatever that means) might be objectionable, and that by requiring the college to adopt this ideal as a dogma, criticism of this ideal will be prohibited.

found nothing objectionable in the college's service to American democracy. Even today, it is likely that most would regard "democratic values" as self-evidently good, and would agree that the American liberal arts college has a social responsibility to prepare students for citizenship in American democracy. Nevertheless, today, as in the past, there are some who are critical of democracy, or specifically, American democracy, and who favor a different form of government. More importantly, alternative forms of government are at least conceivable. This means that, for the liberal arts college to act as an instrument for the realization of "democratic values," these values must be excluded from criticism within the college's educational program. As a result, these values have the status of dogmas. Once this is done, the college becomes in effect a "political university," and as such, denies to itself the possibility of acting as an instrument for liberal education.

While some of those on the political left may argue that "democratic values" are self-evidently or undeniably good, and that they therefore constitute a political ideology that cannot be rationally questioned, this ideology as ordinarily understood can be rejected without evident inconsistency. This point has been made by both radical and conservative critics. James Burnham, for instance, has demonstrated this by contrasting the elements comprising the doctrinal dimension of what he calls "the liberal syndrome" with one possible set of consistent non-liberal elements, and by showing that the order of values of justice, freedom, peace, and liberty may differ without inconsistency for political liberals and non-liberals.[51]   Certainly many important philosophers have been critical of democratic institutions and values. This list would barely begin with the mention of Plato, Hobbes, and Nietzsche. Thus, liberal political ideology has not been demonstrated to be self-evidently or undeniably good. It follows that liberal political ideology cannot justifiably be exempted from criticism within the educational program of the liberal arts college. If such criticism is proscribed by the college, then the college ceases to be an institution of liberal education. We may well grant that, at least for our time, democracy is the best polity, and that liberalism is the best political ideology, but for liberal education the principle of unrestricted criticism cannot be waived without transforming liberal education into indoctrination.

Radical Ideologies

Frank Lentricchia, in *Criticism and Social Change*, takes a radical position on the function of education. For him, education's proper concern is not with determining the "representational truth" about reality, but with the "exercise of power for the purpose of social change."[52] If this position were to be generalized to include the liberal arts college, then the college's task is "to work against the

---

[51]James Burnham, *The Suicide of the West* (New York: The John Day Company, 1964).

[52]Frank Lentricchia, *Criticism and Social Change* (Chicago: University of Chicago Press, 1983), 11.

political horrors of one's time."[53] Paulo Freire takes a comparable position in *The Politics of Education* when he argues that "education must be an instrument of transforming action, a political praxis at the service of permanent human liberation."[54] Some deconstructionists would join Marxists in this advocacy. They would defend the position by arguing that the "fiction of an unbiased position is perhaps the most ideologically biased of all possible positions."[55] In addition, they would deny that there is "an isolable realm of 'freedom' or self-sufficient autonomy which academics can claim."

Criticism of Radical Ideologies

Radical theorists provide considerable force to their arguments on the basis of two premises: First, they claim that pedagogic and institutional neutrality is in fact disguised partisanship. Many leaders of the post-Viet Nam counter-culture, together with many Neo-Marxists, structuralists, and antifoundationalists, have made a strong case for this claim. Second, they assert that it is in fact impossible for education to be unbiased. On the basis of these premises radical theorists conclude that both teachers and colleges should be committed to some form of radical politics.

The problem with the radical position was most clearly exposed during the nineteen seventies when radical activists turned against their former allies, the "humanistic educators," for trying to be "non-directive" in their educational practice.[56] Jonathan Kozol, for instance, condemned this practice on the ground that the "open" teacher and the "open" schoolroom were frauds:

> For the teacher to . . . silence her own convictions, sit down on the floor, smile her inductive smile and await the appearance of "spontaneous desires" on the part of children, may look to us, or to a uninformed observer, to be open and unbiased, "innovative," "honest," and relaxed. It may be innovative, but it is not open. There is a deep and powerful area of self-deception working here . . . . The open-structured classroom is a means by which the teacher is enabled to imagine that he does not have to choose.[57]

---

[53]A similar proposal is made by Isaiah Berlin in *The New York Review of Books* (17 March 1988): 11-18, in arguing that "the search for [political] perfection" seems to be "a receipe for bloodshed," and that "the first public obligation is to avoid extremes of suffering."

[54]Paulo Freire, *The Politics of Education* (South Hadley, Mass.: Bergin & Garvey Publishers, Inc., 1985), 140.

[55]Michael Ryan, "Deconstruction and Radical Thinking," *Yale French Studies* 63 (1982): 45-58.

[56]For a recent criticism of the radical position, see: Roger Kimball, *Tenured Radicals: How Politics Has Corrupted Our Higher Education* (New York: Harper & Row, 1990).

[57]Jonathan Kozol, "The Open Schoolroom: New Words for Old Deceptions," *Ramparts* (July 1972): 40-41.

Thus, according to Kozol, "open education" is "just a better form of salesmanship . . . . It buys out the revolutionary instincts of our children."[58]

Kozol's contempt for what he regards as a cowardly practice is clearly shown in the following:

> 'Wow!' I hear some of these free-school people say, 'We made an Iroquois canoe out of a log!' Nobody, however, *needs* an Iroquois canoe. Even the Iroquois . . . . What [we] need are doctors, lawyers, teachers, organizers, labor leaders.

Kozol's condemnation of "humanistic educators" for their cowardice and reactionary passivity seems rooted in his conviction that "education is always political in one way or another."[59] "In the long run," he says, "there is, and can be, no such thing as an unbiased or a neutral teacher."[60]

This argument is persuasive in part because it is so often true that what is presented as being educationally neutral turns out to be bias in disguise. After raising our anger to a kind of critical mass by a recitation of the ways in which apparent teacher and institutional neutrality turn out to be bias in disguise, Kozol makes the shocking claim that it is in fact impossible for the teacher or school to be unbiased or neutral.

This is the claim that radicalizes us. It seems to tell us that the teacher who makes every reasonable effort to be objective and fair is no better than the most bigoted sophist. It makes us embarrassed by our lack of self-knowledge and by our deluded pursuit of objectivity. And, on the assumption that it is not possible for us to be unbiased or neutral, we feel compelled to join the radical cause to escape our self-deception and moral cowardice.

The problem with Kozol's argument is that it is what Gilbert Ryle would call a logical "howler."[61] It achieves its persuasive force by a grammatical deceit, which is exposed when we look closely at the word, "unbiased," in the claim that it is impossible for a teacher to be unbiased. To say that no teacher can be "unbiased" ordinarily would mean that no teacher can provide good reasons for a conclusion. This claim would be shocking, but it would be false. But "unbiased" could also be given a technical sense so that to say that no teacher can be unbiased would mean that no teacher can be without (something like) a theoretical perspective. This claim would be true, but it would be trivial. Confusion results when the ordinary and technical meanings of the word, "unbiased," are conflated in such a way that the resulting claim appears to be both true and shocking, rather than shocking but false, or true but trivial.

---

[58]Ibid.

[59]Jonathan Kozol, "Politics, Rage and Motivation in the Free School," *Harvard Educational Review* 42 (1972): 414-422.

[60]Kozol, "The Open Schoolroom: New Words for Old Deceptions," 40.

[61]Gilbert Ryle, *Dilemmas* (Cambridge: Cambridge University Press, 1965): 115.

The radical position represented by activists like Kozol and Lentricchia assumes a normative dogma--for instance, that a certain political ideal such as the elimination of "the political horrors of one's time" is in fact an obligation that takes precedence over all other obligations. But the determination of what qualifies as a just political ideal is far too important and problematic to be excluded from criticism in a form of education that is said to be undogmatic and intrinsically valuable. The determination of political and moral ideals is a project that cannot have any hope of success unless it is undertaken in an environment of intellectual freedom. If the liberal arts college acts as an advocate for partisan political ideologies, then it cannot engage in the unrestricted criticism of these ideologies, and therefore must be disbarred as an institution for liberal education.

Institutional Political Actions

During the twentieth century the liberal arts college has been used not only to propagate various ideologies, but it has also been used as an instrument for specific political actions. For instance, as we previously noted, it was used during the nineteen seventies to bring pressure on the government to end the Viet Nam war. During the nineteen eighties it was used to bring pressure on the government of South Africa to end *apartheid*. Currently, it is being used to further the political objectives of "historically oppressed" groups such as gays, lesbians, ethnic minorities, women, and the "educationally disadvantaged."

Criticism of Institutional Political Actions

There is little doubt that the United States involvement in the Viet Nam war, the practice of *apartheid* in the Republic of South Africa, and practices like racial and gender discrimination, are immoral actions in the view of the majority of the American people. Many members of the academic community, motivated by high moral purpose, believe that it is not only appropriate, but is indeed imperative for the college to engage in specific kinds of political action to remedy these and other immoral practices. There are, however, certain anomalies in these actions. Some of these were noted in Chapter 2 in the critical examination of the "Viet Nam Moratoriums," divestiture campaigns, and "Sexual Ethics Teach-ins" of the recent past.

Aside from these anomalies there is a more fundamental issue at stake whenever the liberal arts college is used as an instrument for partisan political purposes. What is at stake is certainly not the right of the individual members of an academic community to participate in political activity. Members of an academic community, like all citizens, have the legal right to pursue their political purposes in a variety of ways. They can speak, write, agitate, litigate, organize, join, demonstrate, and vote. Rather, what is at stake is the need for the liberal arts college to remain unpoliticized as an institution within a politicized community.

There are major objections to the politicalization of the college:

1. Politicalization diverts the college from its chartered purpose. The liberal arts college is incorporated by law, defined by its aims and objectives, understood by society at large, and given tax exemptions as an educational institution, not as an instrument for partisan political action.

2. Politicalization poses a threat to the college's relationship to society. This occurs because our society extends special privileges to the college to facilitate its educational mission. It permits academic freedom and provides economic support. If the college is politicized, society is certain to find that the college's political purposes are frequently in opposition to its own. Under these conditions it is only reasonable to expect that the college will be regarded as an adversary and will be required to forfeit its special privileges. In a similar way it is likely that the many other benefactors and potential benefactors of the college will be unhappy with an arrangement which permits the faculty, or any self-selected group from the college community, to use the college's prestige, power, or endowment for purposes that are contrary to their own. A college and its endowment are seldom the possession of a particular group. Normally, endowments are brought into being by people who give up their own resources with the understanding that these resources will be held in trust for strictly educational purposes. Attempts to violate such trust are not likely to go unchallenged in the court of public opinion or in the courts of law.[62]

3. Politicalization imposes obligations on the college which exceed its competence. If the college is appropriated for even one partisan political purpose, a dangerous precedent has been set. Given this precedent, it is likely that in due course the college will be subjected to endless political pressures on behalf of every conceivable cause. If the college takes a political position or action for or against *apartheid* or divestiture, then it will not be long before others will demand that it take a political position or action on other foreign or domestic policies, on abortion or pornography, or on the rights of dogs and cats, or on a million other issues where passions are inflamed by the conflict of self-evident truths and moral intuitions. Even if the college dismissed its students and held endless faculty meetings, there would not be enough time, personnel, or resources to research, evaluate, and implement proposals to responsibly resolve even a fraction of these issues. The liberal arts college is neither constituted nor qualified to conduct such political activities.

4. Politicalization guarantees the disintegration of the academic community. Once the college becomes available for partisan political purposes, then all actions within the college will become politicized. Faculty and staff recruitment, promotion, and tenure decisions, for instance, will become bitter controversies in

---

[62]For a discussion of the effect of political activities on an educational institution's tax exemption, see: Robert H. Bork, Howard G. Krane, and George D. Webster, *Political Activities of Colleges and Universities: Some Policy and Legal Implications* (Washington, D. C.: American Enterprise Institute, 1970).

which ideology and personal loyalty will replace professional integrity and objectivity. In the end, intellectual independence and tolerance of diversity will disappear from the community.

5. Most importantly, politicalization subverts academic freedom, and in doing so defeats the highest purpose of the liberal arts college. Academic freedom is much more than a matter of personal or professional courtesy. It is a necessary condition for the unrestricted criticism of ideas. If a college adopts a partisan political purpose, then the institution's pursuit of that purpose will restrict the academic freedom of those who oppose the institutional orthodoxy. In this way any attempt to use the college as the means for the realization of putative moral ends subverts the very institution which makes it possible for individuals to understand what ends are moral.

The dangers of the political university and the desirability of institutional neutrality, have been eloquently stated by a number of educators. These include Karl Jaspers in *The Idea of the University*,[63] Richard Hofstadter (in a 1968 commencement address to Columbia University),[64] Fritz Machlup and Walter P. Metzger (in a Carnegie Foundation Bulletin),[65] Winton U. Solberg (in an article for the *AAUP Bulletin*),[66] and Harvard University's former president, Derek Bok.[67] A more general critique of the modern tendency to politicize all institutions is provided by Jacques Ellul in *The Political Illusion*[68] and by Christopher Lasch in *The New Radicalism in America*.[69]

Those who oppose institutional neutrality have offered a number of arguments that deserve more detailed responses:

1. Some have argued that universities have a responsibility to society to exercise "moral leadership."

This claim is voided by the fact that the responsibility of the liberal arts college is to provide wise leaders, not wise leadership. Moreover, it is important not to misunderstand institutions as corporate persons. The university, Fritz Machlup has written, "has no brain and no heart and should have no mouth either."[70] And it is also important not to allow institutional actions to inhibit

---

[63]"The university is meant to function as the intellectual conscience of an era. It is to be a group of persons who do not have to bear responsibility for current politics, precisely because they alone bear unlimited responsibility for the development of truth . . . . Value judgments and practical action are suspended in favor of the ideal of pure truth." Karl Jaspers, *The Idea of the University* (Boston: Beacon Press, 1959), 121.

[64]Richard Hofstadter, *The American Scholar* 37 (Autumn 1968): 583-589.

[65]Fritz Machlup, "The Faculty: A Body Without Mind or Voice," and Walter P. Metzger, "Institutional Neutrality: An Appraisal," in *Neutrality or Partisanship: A Dilemma of Academic Institutions* (New York: The Carnegie Foundation for the Advancement of Teaching, 1971).

[66]Winton U. Solberg, "On Institutional Neutrality," *AAUP Bulletin* (Summer 1970): 11-13.

[67]Derek Bok, *Chronicle of Higher Education* (19 March 1979): 9.

[68]Jacques Ellul, *The Political Illusion* (New York: Vintage Books, 1972).

[69]Christopher Lasch, *The New Radicalism in America: The Intellectual as a Social Type* (New York: Knopf, 1965).

[70]Fritz Machlup, "The Faculty: A Body Without Mind or Voice," 31-37.

individual initiative. "Men of conviction," Winton Solberg has written, "need not wait to receive a moral imperative from their university in order to work for a better world."[71]

2. As was noted above in our criticism of radical ideologies, during the nineteen sixties and seventies a number of radical critics such as Paulo Freire, Neil Postman, Charles Weingartner, Theodore Roszak, Jonathon Kozol, and Ivan Illich attacked the idea of institutional neutrality on the ground that institutional neutrality is in fact an impossibility, and that all educational institutions are inevitably politicized.[72]   Contemporary post-structuralists, deconstructionists, and antifoundationalists contributed to the idea that institutional independence is an ideologically biased position.[73]

There is a grammatical error in this position that is similar to the one that was noted in the radical's use of the word "unbiased." To assert that all educational institutions are inevitably politicized is to conflate two uses of the word "politicized." In ordinary use, this word is pejoratively descriptive of the situation in which an institution is used to further a partisan political purpose. In contrast, the radical's use of the word "politicized" applies a priori to all institutions irrespective of what actions are taken. In this use the word becomes part of a tautology, and therefore, cannot be pejoratively descriptive. In this tautological use the word merely indicates that an educational institution, as an institution, necessarily takes actions that have political consequences. Once we recognize these two very different uses of the word, "politicized," we can admit that all educational institutions are inevitably "politicized" in the innocent tautological sense that they, like all institutions, take actions that have political consequences, but we can at the same time deny that every educational institution is inevitably "politicized" in the pejoratively descriptive sense that they cannot avoid being used to further partisan political purposes. If all actions taken by an institution inevitably "politicized" the institution in the pejoratively descriptive sense, then the word "politicized" would cease to have any use in our language. Thus, for instance, the fact that a college has investments in South Africa politicizes the college in the tautological sense that these investments have political consequences, but does not politicize the college in the pejoratively descriptive sense--unless these investments prejudice the college's educational program. To claim otherwise would be like claiming that the college is politicized by serving food in the dining halls, since serving food in the dining halls benefits certain vendors.   Thus, colleges are inevitably politicized in the innocent and uninteresting sense that their actions have political consequences, but they are not inevitably politicized in the important, pejoratively descriptive sense that they cannot avoid being used to further partisan political purposes.

Admittedly, institutional neutrality is an ideal, and it is one that is difficult to

---

[71]Winton U. Solberg, "On Institutional Neutrality," in *AAUP Bulletin* (Spring 1978): 13.

[72]For instance, see: Freire, *The Politics of Education*, 102.

[73]Michael Ryan, "Deconstruction and Radical Thinking."

realize. As Derek Bok pointed out in his defense of institutional neutrality, colleges "cannot escape from dealing with moral questions in establishing their normal academic policies and procedures."[74] They must make decisions on such matters as stockholder resolutions on equities in their investment portfolio, on rules for experiments on human subjects, on college and community relationships, and on admissions policies. While it may be difficult for the college to avoid such decisions, there are at least ways to minimize the prejudicing effects of these. Investments may be placed in a blind trust. Laws may be passed governing experiments on human subjects or on college admissions. And above all, criticism and ideological diversity can be encouraged. In any case, there is a clear difference between institutions that are minimally and reluctantly involved in activities that have prejudicing implications and those that are committed to institutional political activism. In every case the liberal arts college should seek to eliminate or minimize any political involvement that will prejudice its educational program.[75]

3. Radical demands that educational institutions abandon institutional neutrality are sometimes abetted by the charge that the American universities remained silent during the McCarthy era and German universities remained silent during the rise of National Socialism. This "immorality of silence," they insist, must never be allowed to happen again.

But in this regard it is instructive to remember that in fact the American universities did not remain silent during the McCarthy era. Rather, unfortunately, many of them willingly joined in the hunt for Communists, and contributed to the repressive conditions of that era.[76] It is also instructive to remember that the

---

[74]Derek Bok, *Chronicle of Higher Education*, 9.

[75]Kennith Strike, in *Liberty and Learning* (Oxford: Martin Robertson & Co., 1982), 95, argues for the "impartial neutrality" of the university on the ground that "impartial neutrality" is essential to academic freedom, and academic freedom is essential to the "process of inquiry and the growth of knowledge." Strike's argument differs from my argument in that it applies to all universities without differentiation, and therefore is not restricted to the liberal arts college. As a result of this difference in application, Strike's argument allows some departures from institutional neutrality if the university's actions are "reasonable extensions" of its functions of "research and teaching." In contrast, my argument does not justify any such departure from institutional neutrality. This is a consequence of the fact that the purpose of the liberal arts college is not "research and teaching," but liberal education, and while there are some familiar ways that a university can serve political purposes by doing "research and teaching" for the government (for example), there is no way that the liberal arts college can serve political purposes and also serve the purpose of liberal education. An even more important reason for Strike's willingness to allow some exceptions to institutional neutrality is his belief that "there is much good to be done in the world that universities can do and do best, and this good will not be done unless universities deliberately set out to do it." He thus posits some political ideals as being superior to the ideal of liberal education. My argument does not recognize any political ideal as superior to the ideal of liberal education. Consequently no ideal should pre-empt this ideal.

[76]Ellen W. Schrecker, *No Ivory Tower: McCarthyism and the Universities* (New York: Oxford University Press, 1986).

German universities did not remain silent during the Nazi era.   Rather, unfortunately, many made official pronouncements *endorsing* Hitler's doctrines. A case in point was the proclamation of support of the Nazi party in 1933 by the National Socialist Teachers Association of Saxony, a document signed by some 960 faculty members from several German universities.[77]   The "immorality of silence" can best be avoided by politicizing individuals, not by politicizing the universities.

4. Some have argued that a college's maintenance of institutional neutrality can never be fully realized, and that therefore, the pretense to neutrality should be dropped.

We have admitted that institutional neutrality is an ideal that is not easily attained.   Still, for the encouragement of academic freedom and unrestricted criticism, the college's commitment to this ideal and a continuing conscientious effort to approximate this ideal is enough to make the difference between what is for all practical purposes a liberal arts college and a college that has abandoned liberal education for political indoctrination.

5. Others have argued that, while institutional neutrality may be desirable as an ideal in ordinary circumstances, there are certain to be extraordinary circumstances when this ideal should be suspended.   One such extraordinary circumstance would be when the interests of the university itself are in jeopardy, such as when a government interferes in its internal affairs, threatens its economic security, or suppresses academic freedom.   Another extraordinary circumstance, suggested by Leszek Kolakowski, would be when "a general crisis occurs where the whole existence of society is at stake."   In this situation, Kolakowski argues, "it would be vain and silly to require that the university should keep itself aloof."[78]

The trouble with making exceptions to the ideal of institutional neutrality is in determining what cases would justify making an exception.   In England during the First World War Bertrand Russell's pacifism was viewed as a threat to the "whole existence of society."   In the United States during the McCarthy era the threat of Communist infiltration of the educational system was seen as a threat to the "whole existence of society."   More recently, the radical critics of education have charged that the very idea of institutional neutrality itself is a moral cop-out and a repressive device to preserve class interests, and is, therefore, a threat to the "whole existence of society."   In a pluralistic society with an almost limitless supply of impassioned political causes there is likely to be an almost limitless variety of perceived extraordinary threats to the "whole existence of society."

Some who advocate the suspension of institutional neutrality in times of a

---

[77]Fritz K. Ringer, *The Decline of the German Mandarins* (Cambridge: Harvard University Press, 1966).

[78]Leszek Kolakowski, "Neutrality and Academic Values," in Alan Montefiore, ed., *Neutrality and Impartiality: The University and Political Commitment* (Cambridge: Cambridge University Press, 1975), 84.

general crisis justify this suspension on the ground that in doing this the university does not really betray its highest ideals, as if it were "giving up impartial thinking, logical rules and tolerance in scholarly matters."[79]   But the suspension of unrestricted criticism in the face of political dogma is in fact the giving up of impartial thinking, and is an abandonment of the highest ideal of liberal education.

"But what should be done," radical critics ask, "if the college is found to be manufacturing biological weapons for the Department of the Army?" We might as well ask what should be done if the college is found to be making bird houses for the Garden Club? Both activities are inappropriate for a liberal arts college, not because they are necessarily immoral acts, but because, if the college is to avoid prejudicing its educational program, it must maintain, as far as possible, institutional neutrality. If an action is in violation of the law, then individuals or groups (but not the college) should seek legal remedy. If an action does not violate the law, but is deemed to be immoral, then individuals or groups (but not the college) should pursue political action that will enact the appropriate laws and permit legal remedy. In any case, the neutrality of the college must be scrupulously maintained.

Today some argue that institutional neutrality in higher education is "futile and obsolete" because education cannot, and should not, be isolated from "man's struggle to improve his culture."[80]   One writer suggests that "presidents of universities should require of their heads of departments a statement of the direct or indirect relevance of their subject to the human situation today."[81] The trouble with this position is that it assumes that there is nothing problematic about "the human condition" or about what is required "to improve (human) culture." The very opposite is true: there are fundamental disagreements about the correct analysis of "the human condition" and about what is needed "to improve (human) culture." Consequently, if the college accepts a particular analysis of the human condition and subscribes to a particular ideal of human culture, then it will be unable to provide an unprejudiced education for those who otherwise could be expected to correctly analyze "the human condition" and "to improve (human) culture."

Whenever the liberal arts college subscribes to a partisan political assumption or subordinates itself to a partisan political purpose, it violates its obligation to encourage the unrestricted criticism of all assumptions and purposes. Thus, any institution that engages in political partisanship necessarily reneges on its responsibility as an institution of liberal education. The liberal arts college simply cannot guarantee due process in the contest of ideas if it also insists on acting as a litigant in this same process.

---

[79]Ibid.

[80]Nobuo Shimahara, "The Obsolete Neutrality of Higher Education" *School and Society* 97 (1969): 18-20.

[81]Lancelot Whyte, "The End of the Age of Separation," *Saturday Review* (18 May 1968): 65.

Community Service

A contemporary commonplace is that since all educational institutions are the creations of a particular society, they are all ultimately responsible to this society. It follows that the liberal arts college is responsible for servicing various social needs. In the past these needs have included the training of military officers, the education of public school teachers, and the provision of various kinds of community support programs. Today, in addition to providing these services, a number of colleges require students to participate in some "community service" program as part of their graduation requirements. In these programs students perform various kinds of charitable services for the local community.

Criticism of Community Service

As we have previously noted, these "social service" or "community service" programs require decisions as to what properly counts as a social or community need or service. Unfortunately, as political conflicts repeatedly demonstrate, these decisions are typically thoroughly politicized, and there is no obvious way to protect such decisions from prejudice. What counts as a community service to one person will count as a disservice to another. For instance, for some, students who work as literacy volunteers are performing a community service. But for others, these students are disserving the community by spending time that would be better spent on an education that will prepare them to become teachers, doctors, or leaders who will then be able to render more valuable services to the community. (One might even argue that getting a liberal education is itself the highest form of community service!)

If the liberal arts college is held responsible for providing a service or a variety of services for a community, then the college is likely to gain a vested interest in the services that are provided, and, if it is consistent, it is likely to subscribe to the normative assumptions that justify these services. In this situation those members of the academic community who object to these normative assumptions are not likely to find a tolerant environment. A faculty member, for instance, who is critical of a college's ROTC program is not likely to be accepted as a colleague by those who are invested in the program. As a result, once again, unrestricted criticism will be impeded, and liberal education will become an impossibility.

Student Interests

By its unprecedented emphasis on science and research the University of Berlin became the first modern university in 1809. With it came the ideas of *Lernfreiheit* and *Lehrfreiheit*, the idea that students should be free to learn on the basis of their interests, and the idea that similarly teachers should be free to teach on the basis of their interests. These new ideas soon spread throughout Germany and were introduced in the United States beginning with the founding of Johns Hopkins in 1876.   Meanwhile, with the spectacular successes of scientific specialization, aided by the rise of professional societies and journals, the establishment of land grant universities made possible by the Morrill Act of 1862, together with the growth of social fraternities and the development of intercollegiate athletics, American universities came to be seen as institutions that were destined to serve a great variety of public and private interests.

The notion that the university was properly a servant of public and private interests, confirmed by the ideas of *Lernfreiheit* and *Lehrfreiheit*, had profound effects on American education and culture.[82] In 1869 Harvard's President Charles W. Eliot called for an end to the classical prescribed curriculum and for the introduction of the "elective system." By 1897 Harvard's prescribed curriculum had been reduced to a single year of freshman rhetoric.[83] Since the turn of the century American colleges have continued for the most part to replace the traditional prescribed curriculum with an elective curriculum. From time to time there have been efforts to reverse this trend. The development of "distribution requirements," first proposed in 1909 by President A. Lawrence Lowell of Harvard, was one such effort. A more comprehensive and sustained effort was the attempt to revitalize liberal education by the "general education" movement that flourished between the two World Wars.   At Columbia College this movement led to the development of a two year "lower college" built around three broad, required courses--Contemporary Civilization, the Humanities, and the Sciences.[84] At the College of the University of Chicago the movement led to the introduction in 1937 of a completely prescribed four year curriculum outlined by President Robert M. Hutchins in his 1936 Yale lectures, *The Higher Learning in America*.[85] At Harvard the movement culminated in the introduction of a general education program requiring two lower-level core courses in the humanities and the social sciences, one lower-level elective course in the natural sciences, and three upper-level elective courses.[86]   Although a few colleges continued to provide a prescribed curriculum, for the most part American colleges subsequently retreated from their earlier general education aspirations. Today, by and large, they are primarily student interest-driven educational institutions.

The idea of *Lernfreiheit* and its popular embodiment as the "elective

---

[82]Clark Kerr, *The Uses of the University* (Cambridge, Mass.: Harvard University Press, 1963).

[83]Ernest L. Boyer, *College: The Undergraduate Experience in America* (New York: Harper & Row, Publishers, 1987), 63.

[84]Daniel Bell, *The Reforming of General Education: The Columbia College Experience in Its National Setting* (New York: Columbia University Press, 1966).

[85]Robert M. Hutchins, *The Higher Learning in America* (New Haven: Yale University Press, 1936).

[86]*General Education in a Free Society: Report of the Harvard Committee* (Cambridge, Mass.: Harvard University Press, 1945).

principle" provided some kind of justification for the belief that the liberal arts college is responsible for providing various courses and programs which cater to the interests of students. A recent statement of this position is Ernest Boyer's assertion that, since the goals of "an effective college . . . flow from the needs of society and also from the needs of the persons seeking education," one of the essential goals of the college is to serve the "individual preferences of each student."[87]

The belief that the liberal arts college is responsible for satisfying the various and varying interests of students has been given additional support by the assumption that a student interest-driven education cultivates the democratic personality and benefits an open society, while its opposite, the essentially prescriptive education, cultivates the authoritarian personality and benefits a totalitarian society. Further support for this belief is provided by the fact that a student interest-driven education is popular with students and profitable for the college.

Criticism of Student Interests

The major problem with subordinating the liberal arts college to student interests is that once this is done, these interests will have the status of dogmas and will be obstacles to the conduct of unrestricted criticism. This flaw will be amplified by the fact that the actual interests of students are not always identical with what even they would reflectively admit to be their real interests. This student deficiency is assumed in all education. Without it, education would be pointless.

To be sure, by allowing students to follow their own interests or preferences, a student interest-driven education avoids the familiar institutional religious and political dogmatisms of the past. But, as we have previously argued, in the end this circumlocution only exchanges one form of dogmatism for another. It replaces the familiar religious and political dogmatisms of the past with newer dogmatic assumptions and purposes that are implicit in the interests of students who by definition are not yet able to make wise or critically examined choices.

Teacher Interests

If the idea of *Lernfreiheit* conferred some kind of legitimacy on an education that catered to student interests, the idea of *Lehrfreiheit* gave some kind of legitimacy to an education oriented to teacher interests. If it is appropriate to conceive of the college as a kind of academic farmers' market that benefits the consumers, it is also appropriate to conceive of it as a market that benefits the producers. Teachers can "offer" whatever they can farm from their disciplinary fields, and students can "take" whatever products they want and can pay for. This

---

[87]Boyer, *College: The Undergraduate Experience in America*, 58.

conception of the college as a kind of farmers' market in which student and teacher interests are both satisfied is rationalized on the ground that it provides social, political, and economic benefits for all.

Criticism of Teacher Interests

There are obvious objections to the view that education should be teacher interest-driven. Many of these objections were articulated in the criticism that was directed against the careerism of American teachers during the counter-culture movement of the nineteen sixties and seventies. Typical is that voiced by Theodore Roszak in *The Dissenting Academy*. In his opening essay Roszak charged the American college with "academic delinquency."[88] The college, he said, was no longer a place of "dangerous venture"--a place where ideas were challenged in the perilous struggle for truth and the good life. Instead, it had become laden with bureaucratic fat and immobilized by moral sloth. Once a "dangerous venture," it was now a secure and profitable business, tax-advantaged, self-absorbed, and self-aggrandizing. In place of its old, unpleasant, but honorable task it had two new pleasant and glamorous responsibilities. It had become an institution for "service" and "scholarship." The "service" that it provided in the nineteen fifties went considerably beyond the kind of university service to the community originally intended by the Morrill Act. Service to the community had come too often to mean service to the government and the powerful. Such service now included doing classified research on thermonuclear and chemical-biological weaponry and the development of cold war propaganda and counterinsurgency capabilities.[89] On the other hand, the "scholarship" responsibility had become equally perverted. Hundreds of thousands of "scholars," most of whom labored mightily over trivia in the hope that they would not perish, inundated the university presses and periodical publishers with interpretations, dissertations, monographs, essays, bibliographies, and anthologies, bloated the libraries with collections which far exceeded any reasonable expectation of use, and flushed the paper and information industries with record profits.

But beyond the detrimental effects of careerism the teacher interest-driven education has other faults. Not the least of these is the fact that it limits the options available to students to the microspecialized interests of teachers. More importantly, it provides students with teacher-held theories and norms that are not themselves subject to unrestricted criticism. This is because a college that seeks to satisfy teacher interests has no mandate to examine the legitimacy of these interests. As a consequence, students have no protection against the prejudices that are introduced by these teachers.

---

[88]Theodore Roszak, ed., *The Dissenting Academy* (New York: Random House, Inc., 1967), 4.

[89]Ibid., 11.

Other Interests

Increasingly today the liberal arts college is looked upon as an institution of a free market economy that may contract with individuals, governments, businesses, or other groups for its services. The college is regarded as a kind of public utility.

Criticism of Other Interests

The modern university's possession of very sophisticated and very salable technology together with its insatiable bureaucratic appetite for funds is a perilous combination. In the past some universities have found it both patriotic and financially rewarding to provide weapons and intelligence technology. Others have found it rewarding to enter into research ventures with medical, pharmaceutical, and agricultural firms. More recently, with the explosive growth in computer and biological technology, some universities have found it both popular with its faculty and financially rewarding to join in computer and biotechnology partnerships with government and business. Even the wealthiest institutions have been unwilling or unable to resist this temptation.[90]

In an editorial titled, "Pure Knowledge vs. Impure Profits," (19 September 1988) the *New York Times* called attention to the dangers of this tendency for universities and colleges to trade technology for profits. It pointed out that there is an inherent conflict between the university's responsibility for the pursuit of knowledge for its own sake and its interest in capturing the market value of its faculty's research. In time, the desire for profit is likely to compromise the university's independence and bias its research. When a college takes as its mission the servicing of various individual and social interests, it is not free to conduct unrestricted criticism of these interests. And thus, once again, it is unable to provide a liberal education.

Once the liberal arts college has been appropriated as an instrument to serve the varied interests of students, faculty, and other individuals and groups, it has become what Clark Kerr has called a "multiversity"--"a city of infinite variety." For many this is an achievement to be celebrated. Insofar as this maneuver allows the college to escape the theoretical and normative dogmas of the past, it deserves to be celebrated. But what is too easily missed is that this maneuver does not really escape dogmatism. It only replaces the old theoretical and normative dogmas with the new dogmas of individual interests. These individual interests covertly reintroduce the old dogmas. The untoward consequences of this remain the same: the new dogmas, like the old dogmas, are exempted from unrestricted

---

[90]For instance, about 80 percent of Harvard's medical research is supported by government grants, and in 1988 both Harvard and Stanford entered into a well-publicized commercial ventures with Apple Computer.

criticism, and thus preclude the possibility of liberal education.[91] By this act the college forfeits its right to be a liberal arts college, and relegates itself to the role of an academic public utility.[92]

THE DIFFICULTY OF INDEPENDENCE

The fact that the institutional independence of the liberal arts college is compromised so often and in so many ways provides evidence of the enormous difficulty of achieving this independence. An inquiry into the rationalizations for these compromises will contribute to an understanding of this difficulty.

1.

The liberal arts college becomes a "sectarian college" when it adopts an assumption or doctrine about reality as a truth that is exempted from criticism within its educational program. By this act the college subordinates itself to an empirical dogma, and in doing so, compromises its institutional independence.

The true believers who justify this appropriation of the college do so with the convictions that these assumptions or doctrines are self-evident truths, and that those who insist on a critical examination of these putative truths are lacking in vision or virtue. These true believers are normally not unnerved by the observation that much of the history of education is the tragic story of a series of self-evident truths that eventually become self-evident falsehoods. Every era has contributed a chapter to this lamentable story. In the wars between true believers and their opponents those who failed to see what others held to be self-evident have been pitied, persecuted, exiled, and executed.

We must wonder why the liberal arts college is so easily and repeatedly suborned by these dogmas. John Dewey's philosophy provides a compelling explanation. Dewey argues that the human desire for fixed truths and certainty leads to the cultivation of theories that are detached from practice. Such "spectator knowledge" serves the psychological and cultural interests of individuals and groups by providing them with comfort and security.

2.

The liberal arts college becomes a "political university" when it commits

---

[91]For an extended criticism of the multiversity's assimilation to the interests of the marketplace, including the interests of the state, see: Michael B. Katz, *Reconstructing American Education* (Cambridge, Mass.: Harvard University Press, 1987), especially chap. 6, "The Moral Crisis of the University." Katz seconds Robert Paul Wolff's claim in *The Ideal of the University* that the multiversity "commits exactly the same error which lies at the heart of classical laissez-faire theory"--the identification of "effective market demand with true human need."

[92]On this issue, see: Warren B. Martin, "Old Colleges and a New College," *Liberal Education* 69 (1983): 285-300.

itself to a moral or political ideal that is exempt from criticism within the college's educational program. By this act the college subordinates itself to a normative dogma, and therefore compromises its institutional independence.

Those who want the college to be subservient to some moral or political ideal do so with the conviction that this ideal should take priority over competing ideals, including the ideal of liberal education. Those who do not swear fealty to this ideal are condemned as ignorant or immoral. The faithful are not inhibited by the fact that at different times and in different situations different colleges have championed different, and even conflicting, ideals. In the past these ideals have run the gamut from the religious to the secular, and from the political left to the political right. Today these norms are more likely to be "politically correct" ideologies now identified by code words such as "multiculturalism," "social justice," and "peace." In view of the long history of ideological conflict it is troubling that the devotees of the ideology of the moment are not more cautious in their recurrent efforts to appropriate the college. Still, when caught up in the passion of a political cause, people tend to forget, as Keats once wrote, that "men praise at morning what they blame at night, but always think the last opinion right," and that, as Nietzsche once wrote, the "shop where they manufacture ideals" can "stink of lies."[93] As a result, people live and die, and the ideals offered as absolute goods by one generation are unmasked by a successor generation as absolute evils. In our own century we have dramatic illustrations of this fact in the way that the German and Soviet universities were destroyed by movements which began as efforts to create better human beings and better societies.

We must wonder why the liberal arts college is so easily suborned by normative dogmas. Aristotle provides a coherent explanation in the course of his description of the science of "Wisdom" in the *Metaphysics*. Wisdom, he writes, is the supreme science because it investigates the first principles and causes, including the highest purposes of human life. Unlike the knowledge provided by the productive or technological sciences, the knowledge provided by "Wisdom" serves no higher purpose, but is an end-in-itself. Accordingly, the kind of knowledge provided by "Wisdom" is "useless" knowledge. Aristotle summarizes this paradoxical point when he writes, "All of the sciences are more necessary than Wisdom, but none is better."[94] It is this paradox that marks the point from which the misunderstandings of "Wisdom" arise. In our ordinary, practical orientation to the world we judge things on the basis of their usefulness to various purposes. We tend to disvalue whatever is useless. Consequently, if we persist in our ordinary, practical form of reasoning, we will fail to see that "Wisdom" is indeed useless, but useless only because it is intrinsically valuable. Without "Wisdom," nothing could be genuinely useful. Thus, the pursuit of "Wisdom," in contrast to the accumulation of useful knowledge, requires us to reverse our

---

[93]Nietzsche, *The Genealogy of Morals*, First Essay, XIV.

[94]Aristotle *Metaphysics* 1.2.983a10.

ordinary habits of thinking.[95] For people who are for the most part immersed in the practical thinking required in everyday life, this reversal is a formidable task. A much easier solution to the problem is to adopt a normative dogma. Then there is no need to engage in the difficult dialectic required for the discovery of universal principles. Aristotle notes this when he writes: "The most universal are the hardest for men to know, for they are furthest from the senses."[96]

3.

The liberal arts college becomes a "multiversity" when the college refrains from adopting an empirical or normative dogma as its educational ideal, and instead licenses its students (or other customers) to elect their own educational ideals on the basis of their own interests. By adopting this procedure the college avoids institutional dogmatism. But it avoids this dogmatism only by abandoning its own mission and subordinating itself to extrinsic interests. And since these interests assume theories and norms that are not subject to critical examination within the educational program that indulges them, they are themselves dogmatic. Thus, the college escapes institutional dogmatism only by adopting a procedure which results in the reintroduction of dogmatic theories and norms.

The college's subordination of itself to the interests of its customers is commonly justified as being a "democratic procedure." Of course in an environment in which the appeal to "democratic procedures" is commonplace, as it is today, the college's adoption of this procedure seems beyond reproach. The "multiversity" has been acclaimed as the much-needed modern model of the college, the long-overdue replacement for Cardinal Newman's model of the "ivory tower" or "academic cloister." Those who find this vision of the college appealing believe that the college has a responsibility to serve the academic interests of its customers, and that "democratic procedures" properly determine the purposes and uses of the college. According to this view, the college is an agency of a democratic society responsible for the education of a free citizenry. Since a free people will have many interests, the interests of the society, as well as the interests of the college's students, faculty, administration, alumni, will all have to be served. Given this assumption, any institutional claim to independence will be regarded as undemocratic and elitist.

We must wonder why the liberal arts college can be so easily suborned by the adoption of "democratic procedures" and by serving the interests of the citizens of a democracy. While many philosophers have addressed this question, it is perhaps Plato who provides the most insightful answer. Repeatedly in the dialogues he shows us why the method of Platonic love--the method of

---

[95]Alfred Schutz and Thomas Luckmann, in *The Structures of the Life-World* (Evanston, Ill.: Northwestern University Press, 1973), follow Heidegger in arguing that ordinary, everyday practical life brackets out or suspends the critical attitude.

[96]Aristotle *Metaphysics* 1.2.982a23.

unrestricted criticism--is the way to wisdom. It is superior to the edict of the tyrant, the vote of the democrat, the economic power of the oligarch, and the military might of the timocrat. But criticism always remains "a dangerous venture." It requires that received opinion be challenged, that ignorance and immorality be exposed. It subordinates power, popularity, wealth, and honor. And in the end it holds out the possibility of exile or death. Plato suggests to us, then, that the examined life is a difficult life, and that because of this difficulty we are all too often inclined to flee from this obligation at the earliest opportunity. Like the prisoners in the cave of the *Republic*, we grow accustomed to the images that appear on the wall of our cave, and we then resist any effort to be led out of the security of our ignorance into the discomforting light of truth.

We have now surveyed the three classes of reasons that are used to rationalize compromises of the institutional independence of the liberal arts college. We have suggested that these compromises are the result of the human desire for comforting truths and ideals. This suggestion can hardly come as a surprise. In the etymologically primitive idea of education as an *e-ducere*, a "leading-out" from ignorance and immorality, there lies the assumption that some need to be led along the way to wisdom by those who are able to lead. It is further assumed that this way is not an easy way. The search for wisdom is arduous, and cannot be achieved without the help of others and without the help of institutions. Thus the difficulty of achieving the independence of the liberal arts college is, at bottom, the same difficulty that we encounter whenever we seek to realize any ideal in the face of a recalcitrant reality.

* * * *

The preceding arguments have considered the implications of the ideal of liberal education for the liberal arts college as the institution of liberal education. Two conclusions have been advanced on the basis of these arguments. The first is that it is *necessary* that the liberal arts college be institutionally independent. The second is that institutional independence is an exceedingly *difficult* requirement.

Institutional independence is *necessary* because the development of wise people requires unrestricted criticism, and because unrestricted criticism is impossible if the college has conspired to promulgate a theory, to establish a norm, or to satisfy the idiosyncratic interests of the uneducated. The mission of the liberal arts college is to develop people who are knowingly and responsibly committed to the realization of rationally justifiable ideals. But only if the college remains ideologically uncommitted can its students become knowingly and responsibly committed.

The ideal of institutional independence is *difficult* to realize because the unrestricted criticism required by liberal education is a demanding and dangerous venture. Unrestricted criticism is demanding because it requires that teachers have the courage to profess their beliefs and yet at the same time to have the humility to be open to the beliefs of others. Unrestricted criticism is dangerous because the expression of ideas and ideals that depart from the commonplaces of a community constantly threatens the insatiable human desire for security. The pursuit of wisdom must always overcome the resistance of the many whose lives are addicted to illusions, ensnared by irresistible desires, or cowed by fears that can only be sedated by temporizing distractions. When placed in an environment in which human interests are allowed to be the arbiters of value, the pursuit of wisdom is almost certain to fail. For most, the rigorous demands of this pursuit are without attraction when compared to the rewards of material comfort, pleasure, and psychic security. In the face of this hostile environment liberal education's survival is always in doubt.

The necessity and difficulty of the institutional independence of the liberal arts college can be understood graphically through Plato's image of the love of wisdom as an "exotic seed" in "alien soil." Like an exotic seed, liberal education carries within itself all of our desperate hopes for a meaningful life; and like an alien soil, the environment within which it must survive is inhospitable. By virtue of the very conditions that make it so necessary, it is forever condemned to a struggle for survival in this environment. It is for this reason that liberal education must be institutionalized as the independent liberal arts college, and must be resolutely defended from the hostile forces of its environment.

The need for this institutional defense of the liberal arts college can be summarized in what may be called *the principle of institutional independence*: the liberal arts college must be free from subservience to extrinsic purposes so that it can serve its own intrinsic purpose. This means that as an institution the college must be faithful to the ideal of liberal education and scrupulously resist the temptation to propagate any theory, to advance any norm, or to allow itself to be made the instrument of any interest.

The principle of institutional independence has important implications for the liberal arts college. Specifically, the principle puts a premium on the college's need to be insulated from the temporizing preoccupations of the surrounding communities. This insulation is aided if the college's campus is physically distanced from these communities.[97] The college is advantaged by being located away from the media of distraction, and by being understood by the community within which it is physically located as a unique institution that has the right to, and the responsibility for, maintaining its institutional independence. In spite of

---

[97]Empirical support for the view that the liberal arts college is most effective if it is in some way detached from the environment of the "real world" is cited in David G. Winter, David C. McClelland and Abigail J. Stewart, *A New Case for the Liberal Arts* (San Francisco: Jossey-Bass Publishers, 1981). On page 119 the authors report that "recent empirical research has pinpointed how successive total transitions [involving a cycle of withdrawal from the world, immersion in a new life, and finally, detachment from this new life and return to the world] build up the capacity for increased maturity of response to the environment, management of feelings and reactions to authority, and action."

its introverted image in an age unsympathetic to reflection and isolation, the academic cloister is the appropriate model for the liberal arts college. To be especially and strenuously resisted is the popular view that the college is the product and the property of some community, and is therefore responsible for serving "the public interest." The liberal arts college is not responsible for serving any public or private interest. It is not a public utility or a social service station. It is a unique institution. And the best measure of a good community is the degree to which it tolerates the independence of this unique institution.

7

THE PRINCIPLE OF THE LIBERAL ARTS CURRICULUM

You cannot run anything, including a college, unless you have some idea what you are trying to do. A purpose is a principle of limitation. When everything is just as important or unimportant as everything else, when there is nothing central and nothing peripheral, nothing fundamental and nothing superficial, any enterprise, no matter what it is, must disintegrate.

Robert Maynard Hutchins

In the previous chapter we argued that the ideal of liberal education has important implications for the liberal arts college's institutional relationship to society. In this chapter we consider the ideal's implications for the college's educational program--for its curriculum and academic environment.

Since the ideal of liberal education is the development of wise people, a program of liberal education must be designed to develop the essential competencies of the wise person. The need to develop these competencies will require a curriculum with certain essential components. These components, in turn, require a variety of teaching formats to develop the essential competencies. This chapter will open with a review of the essential competencies of the wise person. It will then describe the components and teaching formats necessary for the development of these competencies. It will close with the outline of a model liberal arts curriculum and a description of the academic environment essential to its success.

THE ESSENTIAL COMPETENCIES OF THE WISE PERSON

The wise person has been described as one who possesses the capacity and inclination for rational action. To act rationally is to act on the basis of knowledge of what is and what ought to be, and with prudence, and with the aid of the moral virtues. To act on the basis of knowledge is to act on the basis of conclusions that have been derived by rational methods and grounded in rational principles.   Rational methods and principles are methods and principles that practically are able to survive unrestricted criticism and that theoretically are self-contradictory to deny.   To act with prudence is to act with skill or "knowing how"[1] in the conduct of practical affairs.   To act with the aid of the moral virtues is to act with the aid of good character or habits.   This conception of the wise person yields the following essential generic competencies:

1. Knowledge (empirical and normative)
2. Theoretical skills
3. Principles
4. Practical skills (prudence and the moral virtues)

These competencies are defined as follows:

1. KNOWLEDGE

The wise person is engaged in the realization of ideals.   This means that this person acts not on the basis of mere opinions or conclusions that lack justification, but on the basis of knowledge or conclusions that are justified by rational methods and principles.   The most important form of knowledge is that which provides this person with a knowledge of his or her specific moral obligations.   Moreover, since this knowledge of specific moral obligations is in part dependent upon knowledge of ethical (and political) obligations, "ethical knowledge" is also essential.   In addition, because the values embodied in cultural artifacts both express and shape "ethical knowledge," a knowledge of cultural values is also essential to the individual's knowledge of his or her specific moral obligations.   Thus, the wise person requires "normative self knowledge," "ethical knowledge," and "cultural knowledge."

Since an action to realize any purpose or ideal requires knowledge of the reality that lacks this ideal, the wise person needs empirical knowledge in addition to normative knowledge.   This is to say that the wise person needs knowledge of both the ideal to be realized and the reality that needs to be remedied.   This person needs to know both reality and ideality--to have knowledge of what is, and knowledge of what ought to be.

The most important form of empirical knowledge is that which permits the individual to understand his or her factual situation or condition as an empirical object.   However, since the situation of an individual as an empirical object is in part dependent upon social reality (inasmuch as human beings, like languages, are inextricably social), the wise person also needs a knowledge of social reality.   In addition, since individual and social reality are in part dependent upon physical

---

[1]Gilbert Ryle, *The Concept of Mind* (London: Hutchinson's University Library, 1955), chap. 2. Also see: Israel Scheffler, *The Conditions of Knowledge* (Glenview, Ill.: Scott, Foresman and Company, 1965), chap. 5.

reality (inasmuch as individual and social life are constrained by physical factors), a knowledge of physical reality is also essential to the individual's knowledge of his or her situation as an empirical object. Thus, the wise person requires "empirical self knowledge," "knowledge of social reality," and "knowledge of physical reality."

2. THEORETICAL SKILLS

To have knowledge is to possess rationally justified conclusions. If the wise person is to possess these conclusions, this person must also have the skills that make these conclusions available. These theoretical skills are of two kinds: "skills of discovery" and "skills of justification."[2] The "skills of discovery" are essential for the discovery of the premises that justify conclusions, and the "skills of justification" are essential for the justification or demonstration of conclusions. Sometimes the skills of discovery are called "inductive" or "scientific" skills and the skills of justification are called "deductive" or "communications" (or "demonstration" or "proof") skills.

The "skills of discovery" enable us to find premises that justify the conclusions of arguments by rising above the change that characterizes our perceptual awareness to conceptions that give structure and meaning to this awareness. These skills have generic forms that may be generated by a matrix that yields all possible generic forms for the discovery of the premises of arguments. This four place matrix describes generic skills that move from the most abstract to the most concrete.[3] The first of these skills is the abstract mathematical ability to quantify and calculate. The second is the set of skills which enhance our powers of observation and experimentation. The third is the range of skills that enable us to construct scientific theories and explanations. And the fourth is the category of skills that enable us to understand the ways in which scientific theories are dependent upon historical circumstances. These four skills of discovery are the skills of mathematics, technology, scientific methodology, and historiography.

The "skills of justification" enable us to justify, demonstrate, or prove conclusions on the basis of premises. These skills have generic forms that may be derived from a matrix that yields all possible generic forms for the justification of

---

[2]The choice of the terms "discovery" and "justification," in preference to earlier terms that marked this distinction, is based on the preferred usage within the "critical thinking movement." For a review of this, see: Joanne G. Kurfiss, *Critical Thinking: Theory, Research, Practice, and Possibilities*. ASHE-ERIC Higher Education Report No. 2. (Washington, D.C.: Association for the Study of Higher Education, 1988). John E. McPeck, in *Critical Thinking and Education* (New York: St. Martin's Press, 1981) attributes the origin of these terms to Hans Reichenback in *Experience and Prediction* (Chicago: University of Chicago Press, 1938), 6ff. They were also used by Karl Popper in *The Logic of Scientific Discovery* (New York: Harper & Row, 1968), 31, 315.

[3]In this I adopt the matrix used by Plato in the *Republic* at 521C.

conclusions from premises.[4]   If justifications are treated as syllogistical (or logistical), then the required skill is one which permits propositional conclusions to be deduced from premises by the use of univocally signifying terms, truly predicating propositions, and valid argument forms. If justifications are treated as narrative (or poetic or dialectical), then the required skill is one which permits conclusions as insights to be induced on the basis of metaphorical terms and analogical arguments. If justifications are treated as pragmatic (or rhetorical), then the required skill is one which permits conclusions that are operationally defined to be produced on the basis of terms that are speech-acts and premises that are "forms of life" or commonplaces accepted by a language community. These three skills of justification may be referred to respectively as the skills of deduction, induction, and seduction.

The importance of the need for the full range of theoretical skills may seem too obvious to belabor, but the common neglect of these skills makes this assumption problematic. A contemporary argument that testifies to the need for the full range of these skills is that which charges that the prevailing concept of rationality is too narrow.   This case has been made by existential and phenomenological philosophers following Heidegger, among others, who echo earlier criticisms of rationality by Bergson, Husserl, Dewey, and G. E. Moore, and who contrast a narrow concept of rationality as "calculative thinking" with a broader concept as "meditative thinking."[5] A similar case has been made by analytic philosophers following Wittgenstein, among others, who acknowledge the limitations of a language that is restricted to factual and analytic propositions, and who recommend a practical concept of rationality and a language constituted by speech-acts.   In the light of these developments, Ch. Perelman and L. Olbrechts-Tyteca (and others) have characterized the prevailing concept of rationality as "Cartesian," and have charged that it has dominated the last three centuries of Western thought. According to these authors "Cartesian thinking" has

> made the self-evident the mark of reason, and considered rational only those demonstrations which, starting from clear and distinct ideas, extended, by means of apodictic proofs, the self-evidence of the axioms to the derived theorems.[6]

Perelman and Olbrechts-Tyteca have argued that this concept of rationality is an "unjustified and unwarranted limitation of the domain of action of our faculty of reasoning and proving." To correct this situation they have outlined a "new rhetoric," a theory of argumentation that allows us to "induce or to increase the

---

[4]For this purpose I use a matrix employed by Richard McKeon. See: George Kimball Plochmann, *Richard McKeon: A Study* (Chicago: University of Chicago Press, 1990).

[5]Martin Heidegger, *Discourse on Thinking* (New York: Harper and Row, 1966).

[6]Ch. Perelman and L. Olbrechts-Tyteca, *The New Rhetoric* (Notre Dame, Ind.: University of Notre Dame Press, 1969), 1.

mind's adherence to the theses presented for its assent." Their intention is to move from a narrow, theoretical, and purely scientific sense of rationality to a more inclusive and practical one. They want to extend the concept of rationality beyond the *logos* mode of proof of classical rhetoric, to include both *ethos* and *pathos* modes of proof.

These attacks on the narrow, "logocentric" or "logos-centered" rationality have had to date only a modest impact on college pedagogy. Most teaching continues to be dominated by a "logocentric" model. The methods of scientific demonstration and formal logic are still taken to be paradigmatic. College classes are most often conducted as lectures, supplemented by textbooks containing soritical arguments, and students are expected to master and reproduce information ideally embodied in an axiomatic system. Teachers are expected to present "interesting" lectures, to "motivate" students, and to be able to "explain the material." The effects of "logocentrism" can also be seen in the fact that the liberal arts themselves have been transformed from arts into sciences, or otherwise, have been ignored or forgotten. Logic, for instance, has become a theoretical science of valid argument forms; rhetoric--once the central requirement of every liberal arts college--is now largely neglected or narrowly conceived as public speaking; and dialectic--once the architectonic liberal art--is now simply a lost liberal art.

Of course a "logocentric" pedagogy is appropriate for the dissemination of information and scientific theory. But if a liberal education is conceived as an education for the development of wise people, not just knowledgeable people, and if rational action is understood as including a range of theoretical and practical actions, then an exclusively "logocentric" pedagogy is clearly an inadequate pedagogy. Wise people must be able to reason in scientific or theoretical ways; but they must also be able to reason in practical and normative ways. They must be able to employ arguments which begin from true premises and which achieve certainty in their conclusions. But they must also be able to employ arguments which begin from opinions and which achieve probability. And eventually they must be able to employ arguments which begin from opinions and which obtain certainty. They must be able to trade in *logos* appeals; but they must also be able to do commerce in *ethos* and *pathos* appeals. They need to be skilled in the liberal arts of logic, rhetoric, and dialectic.

3. PRINCIPLES

Knowledge requires not only skills for the discovery of premises and the justification of conclusions, but it also requires that the use of these skills, as well as the conclusions yielded by their use, be justified by rationally defensible principles. To count as rationally defensible, principles theoretically must be self-contradictory to deny, and, as a matter of practice, must be sustainable in the face of unrestricted criticism. Since it determines the priorities of both thought and action, the most important of these principles can only be an unconditioned moral principle.

4. PRACTICAL SKILLS AND MORAL VIRTUES

The wise person acts to transform reality into ideality. Thus, this person is more than someone who possesses knowledge that is justified by rational methods and principles; this person must act in the light of this knowledge. The ability to act rationally requires more than theory; it requires a set of skills that are born of experience in the agent's confrontation with particulars in the course of practical deliberation, decision, and action. These practical skills are the skills of prudence (or practical wisdom). They may be classified on the basis of a matrix that recognizes the irreducible difference between the self, other selves, and physical things. There are, therefore, skills required for the conduct of the individual self, for the conduct of the self in relationships with other selves, and for the conduct of the self in relationships with the physical environment. These skills may be referred to as the skills of self conduct, social conduct, and economic conduct.[7]

Philosophers have periodically warned us of the error of limiting "rational action" to the activity of knowing. The wise person cannot be a person who is adept at theory but inept in practice. Hence, the wise person needs both knowledge and prudence, or practical wisdom. But, in addition, it is evident that wisdom and prudence are themselves impossible unless human beings possess certain habits of thinking and acting. For this reason the wise person must also be a person of good character. Traditionally, some habits or traits of character have been privileged over others because of their importance to rational thought and action. These "cardinal virtues" may be classified on the basis of a matrix that recognizes that habits benefit rational action in matters of self conduct, social conduct, and economic conduct. These habits aid the wise person in maintaining rational self control, in conducting rational relationships with other people, and in making rational use of the physical environment. Without the cardinal moral virtues of courage, justice, and temperance, the pursuit of wisdom would be an impossible project.

THE NECESSARY COMPONENTS OF THE CURRICULUM

The development of the four essential competencies of the liberally educated person requires a curriculum consisting of four components:

1. THE LIBERAL SCIENCES

The liberal sciences have the responsibility for developing the knowledge

---

[7]"Economic" is used because of its generic etymological sense of *oiko(s)+nomos+ikos*, i.e., the stewardship of the house or place or environment in which life occurs.

competencies. The knowledge developed is "scientific" because it consists of theories--that is, systems of justified conclusions or truth claims. This knowledge is "liberal" in the sense that the theories included are included on the basis of their relative importance to the ideal of liberal education. Since the ideal of liberal education requires two kinds of knowledge competencies, there are two generic liberal sciences: normative science and empirical science. The former consists of those theories concerned with ideality (norms, values, imperatives), and the latter consists in those theories concerned with reality (actuality, facts, existence).

The normative sciences may be conveniently divided into three kinds on the basis of their concern for norms applicable to the self, society, or culture:

Normative self science
Political science
Cultural science

The term "self science" is introduced as a neologism to name that component of the curriculum that is responsible for the development of knowledge, both normative and empirical, about the individual student.[8] "Normative self science" is responsible for providing each student with a comprehensive knowledge about his or her being as an intentional or valuing agent. "Political science" is the generic science that is responsible for providing each student with a comprehensive knowledge of social norms, including ethical and political ideals. "Cultural science" is the generic science that is responsible for providing each student with a comprehensive knowledge of those cultural norms or ideals that are most relevant to the achievement of wisdom, especially those values or ideals embodied in the products of literature and the fine arts. Together the normative sciences are responsible for providing each student with normative scientific literacy.

Like the normative sciences, the empirical sciences may be conveniently divided into three kinds on the basis of their concern with the reality of the self, social reality, and physical reality:

Empirical self science
Social science
Physical science

"Empirical self science" is responsible for providing each student with a comprehensive knowledge about his or her being as an object of empirical investigation. The terms "social science" and "physical science" are here used with their ordinary meanings. Consequently, social science and physical science are responsible for providing each student with a comprehensive knowledge of

---

[8]For an argument for what I call "self science" see: Alfred Schutz and Thomas Luckmann, *The Structures of the Life-World* (Evanston, Ill.: Northwestern University Press, 1973), II, 57-65.

those social and physical theories that are most relevant to the achievement of wisdom.   Together the empirical sciences are responsible for providing each student with empirical scientific literacy.

The liberal sciences have several features that deserve emphasis:

1. The liberal sciences are "liberal" in the sense that they are free of servitude to purposes other than the purposes of liberal education. They are concerned with that knowledge that is most essential to the capacity for rational action. They are not concerned with knowledge that serves technological, vocational, or other purposes that are extrinsic to the ideal of wisdom.

2. The inclusion of the normative sciences within the liberal sciences points to the truth that the wise person must be a moral person, and therefore must have knowledge of the good life. This normative interest makes a program of liberal education unique among all other college and pre-college educational programs. These other programs normally do not find a place for the study of personal ideals, and they treat the study of social and cultural ideals as mere elective options. But in a program of liberal education the normative sciences are as essential as the empirical sciences.

3. The importance of the normative sciences within a program of liberal education is amplified by the fact that these sciences are not appropriately introduced in pre-college education.   As educators have often noted, the normative sciences are not in general successfully introduced in precollege curricula because the subject matter of these sciences is truly meaningful only to those who have lived long enough to appreciate the reality and range of adult normative problems. With the systematic presentation of personal, social, and cultural ideals by the normative sciences, the stage is set for the transformation and prioritization of all previous and future empirical knowledge by normative principles. In this action a program of liberal education performs an educational function of decisive importance for the moral development of students. For most students this action will constitute the dawn of critical moral awareness. Because of its performance of this function the liberal arts college is the most important of all educational institutions.

4. The inclusion of self science in a program of liberal education points to the fact that the knowledge that is most essential to the wise person is the knowledge that is required for personal decision and action, not the kind of knowledge that is "abstract," "objective," "value-free"--knowledge that is detached from practical or normative concerns. This essential knowledge is that which is needed by the person who is a rational agent--a participant in the realization of ideals--not the knowledge that is preferred by the disinterested, uninvolved "spectator."[9] The introduction of self science is made necessary by the fact that a program of liberal education is in effect an institutional campaign to enlist students in the most exalted of all endeavors, not a device to satisfy student interests or to prepare students for a vocation, and not an aesthetic or recreational stroll through a

---

[9]John Dewey, *The Quest for Certainty* (New York: Minton, Balch & Co., 1929), 23.

museum of dead ideas.

5. A measure of indeterminacy is introduced into the liberal sciences by two facts: First, the knowledge available to each of the generic sciences is, for all practical purposes, infinite, and yet in current practice a program of liberal education is limited to a very finite four year period. This means that the knowledge that is most important for liberal education will have to be selected from the much larger body of available knowledge. Second, the ideal of wisdom does not provide a decision procedure that can mechanically determine a fixed body of knowledge for all people for all time and for all places. To some extent, the knowledge that is most important for liberal education will vary with individuals, times, and places. Consequently, the specific knowledge provided by the liberal sciences will need to be determined by specific faculties for specific students for specific times and for specific places. This is why a prescribed, fixed list of conclusions, arguments, or canonical texts is inappropriate for determining the content of the liberal sciences, much less the content of a liberal education. In view of this indeterminacy, an important faculty responsibility is the need to make periodic and prudent decisions about the knowledge that is most valuable for a specific program of liberal education. The principle that must provide general guidance in these decisions is the principle of liberal education itself. As we have argued, a program of liberal education must provide each student with normative knowledge of personal, political, and cultural ideals, and empirical knowledge of personal, social, and physical reality. But the details and density of this knowledge will need to be determined by a faculty in the context of specific circumstances. The principle of liberal education will guide program design by keeping a faculty oriented to the purpose of the program, by reminding it of the range of knowledge that is required, and by reminding it of the program's need to avoid indoctrination by institutionalizing the cultivation of ideological diversity and criticality.

Principles other than the principle of liberal education are not qualified to serve as a guide for the design of a program of liberal education. As we have seen, none of the familiar principles, such as religious creeds, political ideologies, or academic consumer interests, are able to avoid dogma or to count as intrinsically valuable. Neither will it do to try to determine the specific knowledge that should be included in a program of liberal education by looking to what is presently taught in the typical liberal arts college. As has been demonstrated, the educational program of the typical contemporary liberal arts college is not coherent, but is to a large extent a hodgepodge of traditional disciplines, trendy innovations, public relations gimmicks, microspecialized faculty career interests, and thinly disguised entertainment for students. No amount of propaganda for diversity or paeans to personal freedom can be expected to justify these expensive diversions as a program for the development of people who have the capacity and inclination for rational action. To expect wise people to be spontaneously generated from a four year visit to an academic theme park is as witless as to expect truths to be revealed by ouija boards.

6. The liberal sciences are responsible for providing students with the conclusions that constitute the current commonplaces of literate society. They can thus be said to be responsible for developing what is presently called "cultural literacy."[10] But these sciences cannot be content with providing students with the conclusions that are now held by literate people. Their responsibility within a program for the development of wise people requires them to develop people who treat these conclusions critically. This is why a descriptive list of the conclusions, the possession of which currently define the culturally literate person, is inadequate to determine the content of the liberal sciences, much less the content of a liberal education.

2. THE LIBERAL ARTS

The body of knowledge that is most important to the wise person differs by time and place. Continuing criticism of the conclusions constituent of this knowledge is thus a necessity. In consequence of this need, the wise person must possess the theoretical skills that are necessary for the discovery and justification of these conclusions.

In the past, these essential theoretical skills have sometimes been identified as the *artes liberales*, or "the liberal arts."[11] Sometimes these skills have been described more specifically as the *septem artes liberales* (a term first used by Cassiodorus in the sixth century in reference to Martianus Capella's *De septem disciplinis*).[12] The *septem artes liberales* then included grammar, rhetoric, logic, arithmetic, geometry, music, and astronomy. Yet at other times these arts have been augmented by the addition of medicine and architecture, among others. They have also sometimes admitted substitutions (such as grammar for dialectic, dialectic for logic, or logic for grammar), and they have often been understood differently in different eras and by different interpreters (for example, "grammar" in the seventh century and "grammar" in the fourteenth century).[13] The liberal arts traditionally have been divided into two categories--the quadrivium, or, following Boethius, the "arts of things," and the trivium, or, following Alcuin, the "arts of words."[14]

It is clear that the liberal arts were known in classical Greece. In the

---

[10]E. D. Hirsch, Jr., *Cultural Literacy: What Every American Needs to Know* (New York: Vintage Books, 1988), xiii. Cultural literacy, Hirsch argues, is the background information that makes public discourse possible.

[11]On the origin of the *artes liberales* see: Bruce A. Kimball, *Orators and Philosophers: A History of the Idea of Liberal Education* (New York: Teachers College, Columbia University, 1986).

[12]Ibid., 23.

[13]Richard P. McKeon, "The Liberating and Humanizing Arts in Education," in Arthur A. Cohen, ed., *Humanistic Education and Western Civilization* (New York: Holt, Rinehart and Winston, 1964). Also see: Kimball, *Orators and Philosophers*, 68-73.

[14]Ibid., 47, 51.

Republic 521C-532A Plato describes four "mathematical" arts (arithmetic, geometry, solid geometry, and astronomy), and in the *Posterior Analytics* 1.1.71a1-10 Aristotle describes the three arts of "instruction" (speculative or scientific reasoning, dialectical reasoning, and rhetorical reasoning). Predictably, in the High Middle Ages those schools that were under Platonic influence, such as Oxford, emphasized quadrivial studies, while those schools that were under Aristotelian influence, such as Paris, emphasized the study of the trivium, especially logic.[15]

The history of the liberal arts becomes even more complex once we include modern interpretations, including the twentieth century's tendency to treat these arts as sciences or academic subject matters.[16] During the twentieth century, for instance, the liberal arts have often been held to include language, history, literature, abstract science, etc. Today it is not unusual for the liberal arts to be understood as including all of the "subjects" that happen to be taught by a liberal arts college!

The complex history of the use of the expression, "liberal arts" (and its cognates), is likely to obscure the fact that, in spite of its diverse uses, this expression has most often picked out a set of fundamental theoretical (or reasoning) skills. Moreover, the quaint and apparently arbitrary medieval division of these arts into the quadrivium and trivium is likely to obscure the fact that this division also picks out an important difference between these skills. It distinguishes the "arts of things"--that is, those skills by which we discover premises for our arguments, and the "arts of words"--that is, those skills by means of which we justify (demonstrate, or prove) conclusions from these premises. As was noted above, in the recent literature of the "critical thinking movement" this difference is understood as the difference between "the context of discovery" and the "context of justification."[17] Finally, the subdivision of the liberal arts into the sacred number seven is likely to obscure the fact that two ingenious rhetorical matrixes have sometimes been employed to enable us to recognize the necessary constituent skills of the arts of discovery and the arts of justification. The four-place Platonic matrix for the arts of discovery utilizes the four dimensions of space-time to pick out four levels of skills that are necessary, according to Socrates, in order to "draw the soul toward being." Beginning from arithmetic, and progressing to geometry, to solid geometry, and to astronomy, these skills enable us to obtain knowledge of reality. We can interpret these levels to include (1) "mathematics" (the skills of quantification and calculation), (2) "technology" (the skills of observation and experimentation), (3) "scientific methodology" (the skills of theory construction), and (4) "historiography" (or hermeneutics), the skills of theory interpretation).[18] The three place Aristotelian matrix previously

[15]Kimball, *Orators and Philosophers*, 68-73.

[16]McKeon, "The Liberating and Humanizing Arts in Education," 159-181.

[17]Kurfiss, *Critical Thinking: Theory, Research, Practice, and Possibilities*, 2.

[18]"History" is used here in one of its many senses--as historiography or "hermeneutics" or "historical semantics." It includes the skills required for the interpretation of theory. For this use

noted allows us to pick out three ways of justifying conclusions from premises. We may employ (1) "logic" to generate conclusions that are certain from premises that are known, (2) "rhetoric" to generate conclusions that are probable from premises that are opinions, and (3) "dialectic" to generate conclusions that are certain from premises that are opinions.

If we generalize the skills of discovery and justification in this way, we will have a contemporary version of the seven classical liberal arts:

Arts of Discovery
Mathematics
Technology
Scientific methodology
Historiography

Arts of Justification
Logic
Rhetoric
Dialectic

3. PHILOSOPHY

The liberal sciences and the liberal arts themselves ultimately require integration--that is, rational justification by the discovery of principles. The curricular component that facilitates this integration is "philosophy."

This use of the word, "philosophy," to name the component responsible for facilitating integration in a program of liberal education must be distinguished from the more familiar use of the word to name a specialized department of knowledge. The view that philosophy is a specialized department of knowledge has been encouraged by the popular view that a college is a mere collection of academic departments, and by the opinion that a faculty is a collection of disciplinary experts. These views obscure the uniqueness and importance of philosophy as the discipline for the facilitation of integration. As a component of a program of liberal education, philosophy is not an art or a science, or even a metascience. Its concern is not with methods or conclusions, but with principles-- ultimate justifications, the final premises governing the making of theoretical and normative conclusions.

This discipline is appropriately called philosophy for two reasons. First, there is ample etymological evidence that philosophy as *philosophia* signified the love or pursuit of wisdom where wisdom was understood as integrated opinions. Second, philosophy, understood as the love of wisdom, clearly indicates a process, not an achievement. It is the love or pursuit of wisdom, not a body of

---

of "history," see: Richard P. McKeon, "Truth and the History of Ideas," in *Thought Action and Passion* (Chicago: University of Chicago Press, 1954). Also see: Stephen Toulmin, "Rediscovering History," in *Encounter* 36, no. 1 (1971): 53-64.

knowledge.   Philosophy as a component of liberal education has these two characteristics.   It embodies the ideal of the integration of opinions, but this ideal in practice is a continuing demand, not an achievement.   Philosophy is not a discipline that is responsible for providing conclusions, but one that has the task of maieutically eliciting principles and promoting their critical examination.   This examination is terminated, ideally, by each student's discovery of principles that theoretically are self-contradictory to deny and that practically are able to survive unrestricted criticism.

4. THE PRAXES

The "praxes" (practical liberal arts) have the responsibility for the development of the practical skills that are necessary if an agent is to be able to realize ideals.   This development takes place by teaching and training.   The requisite skills are of two kinds: the skills of prudence (or practical wisdom), and the moral virtues.

The Greek word "*praxis*" contrasts with the word "*poiesis*" and distinguishes activities that are intrinsically valuable from activities that are only instrumentally valuable.   In the latter, a product is at issue, while in the former, conduct alone is at issue.   In remembrance of this etymology, the word "praxes" is appropriated here to name the component of the liberal arts curriculum that is responsible for the development of the most general practical skills essential for the realization of ideals.   Since these prudential skills are those that are essential for the rational conduct of the self in relation to itself, to other persons in the community, and to the physical things of the environment, the resulting praxes are:

Self praxis
Social praxis
Economic praxis

The prudential skills that are developed by these praxes are themselves dependent upon the agent's exercise of certain moral virtues.   These virtues are habits of rational self-control, rational behavior in relationships with others in a community, and rational behavior in relationships with the physical environment.   These essential, "cardinal" academic virtues are species of courage, justice, and temperance.   It is a second responsibility of the "praxes" to develop these moral virtues.

In the development of the moral virtues the "praxes" must walk the fine line between moral indoctrination and moral permissiveness.   On the one hand, the typical liberal arts college's laissez-faire, tolerant attitude toward student (and teacher) immorality not only does not serve, but rather subverts, the purposes of its own educational program.   On the other hand, the liberal arts college must never tolerate moral dogma or indoctrination.

This problem cannot be solved by ignoring it, or by a cowardly retreat in the face of student or faculty opposition to *in loco parentis*. From the standpoint of liberal education, the development of the moral virtues is one of the most crucial responsibilities of this form of education, and it should not be abandoned in the face of objections by those who find it a laborious or unpleasant task. A college must be courageous enough to commit itself to the development of those moral virtues that are essential to the success of its educational program. But it must also be temperate enough to resist the temptation to try to inculcate virtues that are not truly essential to the development of the knowledge, skills, and principles of a liberal education. As difficult as it may be, a line must be maintained between those minimal, cardinal moral virtues that are essential to the college's educational program, and all other virtues. The college should not act as an institutional sponsor for traditional virtues favored by the larger community (such as those that are "religiously orthodox"), the avant-garde virtues that are currently favored by the power elite or the intelligentsia (such as those that are "politically correct"), or the "in" virtues of the student peer culture. Because of these restrictions, the "praxes" must be guided by a set of limited, public, and carefully defined developmental purposes, and its program must be constantly monitored to guarantee that there is no violation of these purposes. Not to be vigilant in this matter is to risk the loss of academic freedom and thereby to forfeit a necessary condition for a liberal education.

Some institutional insurance against the possibility of moral indoctrination can be purchased by requiring that, even though all "praxes" programs must share a common set of purposes, they should include a variety of strategies to realize these purposes. Students must be required to participate in the "praxes" program, but not to participate in any specific constituent of the program. While courses should always be required, classes should never be required.

THE "LIBERAL ARTS" CURRICULUM

A program of liberal education is appropriately called a "liberal arts curriculum" because this program is a series of curricular devices that have as their fundamental purpose the development of the liberal arts. The theoretical skills that these arts develop make possible the knowledge of the sciences and the principles of philosophy, and the practical skills that these arts develop make possible the application of this principled knowledge to principled action. These arts--the arts of rational thought and action--are appropriately called the liberal arts because these are the instruments which make it possible for human beings to liberate themselves from ignorance and immorality.

THE IDEAL TEACHING FORMATS

From a description of the curriculum of a typical contemporary liberal arts college it is possible to infer the college's view of the essential competencies of the liberally educated person. These competencies seem to be as follows: (1) a "major" or specialized, "in depth" knowledge of one academic "field," presumably achieved by "passing" eight to fourteen mostly elective courses given by one academic department, (2) a "breadth" knowledge of "the most general areas of knowledge," presumably achieved by "passing" three elective "distribution requirement" courses, one from "the natural sciences," one from "the social sciences," and one from "the humanities," (3) some knowledge about a "non-Western or Third World topic," apparently achieved by taking one elective course from a category called "Non-Western and Third World Studies," (4) some knowledge of what is called "the classical liberal arts," presumably achieved by taking one elective course in mathematics and one in the "arts or forms of expression," or one elective course in mathematics and one in a foreign language, or one in a foreign language and one in the "arts or forms of expression," and (5) some knowledge of "the principles of fitness and wellness that will be useful throughout the adult years, presumably achieved by taking "Physical Education 100." The curriculum may also seek to develop (6) "the ability to write competent prose" and (7) "critical thinking."

Aside from the last two, which are seldom the responsibility of any one component of the curriculum, and which are often regarded as remedial, all of the competencies are theoretical (or cognitive or knowledge) competencies. The curriculum is understood to be an instrument that provides students with various kinds of knowledge (or theories or information). Since the knowledge that is provided is understood to be the possession of specialized disciplinary experts, its provision is presumed to require a curriculum with academic subject matter departments as components. And since knowledge is most efficiently provided by teacher-scholars who teach students and write monographs, the curriculum overwhelmingly employs the familiar course format. A course normally consists of a series of professional lectures (possibly supplemented by discussions), readings from textbooks, and examinations or papers designed to test student mastery of the course "content" or "subject matter." The typical contemporary liberal arts curriculum is understood to be almost entirely a collection of courses provided by academic disciplinary departments in which teachers acting as professors or disciplinary experts provide students with various specialized theories or information.

The monomorphic character of this typical curriculum stands in striking contrast to the polymorphic character of the curriculum required by the ideal of liberal education. While the typical contemporary liberal arts curriculum is almost entirely concerned with providing students with specialized knowledge, the curriculum required by the ideal of liberal education is concerned with the development of the diverse competencies essential to those who have the capacity and inclination for rational action: empirical and normative knowledge, the liberal theoretical skills, principles, and the liberal practical skills. The development of these diverse competencies requires a curriculum with dissimilar components: the liberal sciences, the theoretical liberal arts, philosophy, and the praxes (the practical liberal arts). These disparate components can best develop the required competencies by using disparate teaching formats:

1. THE LIBERAL SCIENCE COURSES

The familiar *course* format is appropriate for the *liberal sciences*. In this format lectures and class discussions are the primary devices for critically presenting to students the competing comprehensive empirical theories of the social and physical sciences and the competing normative theories of the ethical and cultural sciences. This format is by design an effective way to develop the empirical and normative scientific literacy required by a liberal education. Only in self science, where the concern is with the empirical reality and ideals of individual students, rather than with abstract scientific theories, must the course format give way to a *counseling* format.

2. THE LIBERAL ARTS LABORATORIES AND DISPUTATIONS

For the development of the skills of the *theoretical liberal arts*, theory is of secondary importance to the need for student participation and practice. This need calls for a format of *laboratories* and *disputations*--laboratories for the development of the skills of discovery and disputations for the development of the skills of justification.

The Laboratories

Many people report that the best teaching that they have experienced occurred not in a college or university but in a business or in the military service. My own experience confirms this. I remember as being particularly exemplary a four month program for infantry officers given by the United States Army at Ft. Benning, Georgia. The main purpose of this program was to develop combat leadership skills. Theory and information were certainly important to the development of these skills, but they were introduced only in response to practical, specific, and pressing leadership problems. Performance was primary, and was repeated until proficiency was attained. Instruction was largely carried out by demonstrations, dramas, physical models, and illustrations. Interestingly enough, this pedagogy was also successful in imparting theory and information. The entire program was a convincing illustration of the relevant sense in which people learn by doing.

Later on during my military service I was responsible for the training of infantrymen in a number of combat skills such as the conduct of patrols and the attack of fortified positions. The most effective way of conducting this training, I found, was by means of a "course" or "curriculum" modeled on the etymological meaning of these words: *currere*, to run, to follow a path or mode of procedure. This "course" or "curriculum" consisted in a series of practical exercises in which squads advanced through sections of terrain in which many different combat problems were encountered. These problems included attacks by snipers, booby traps, medical emergencies, enemy prisoners, natural obstacles, and other situations that called for immediate decision and action. Information and theory were provided, but for the most part, they were provided only after practical problems made the need for them apparent.

On the assumption that combat skills are most effectively developed by repeated practical exercises supplemented by clearly needed information and theory, it seems reasonable to assume that other skills of thought and action, such as the skills of the liberal arts, will be most effectively developed by a similar format that gives priority to practice. My own experience has confirmed this for the development of reasoning and communications skills.

For practical decision and action the wise person requires knowledge of concrete, particular situations. This knowledge is empirical, and consists in justified conclusions about the nature of empirical reality. These conclusions are made possible by the application of certain theoretical skills, such as the skills of discovery. It is the responsibility of the arts of discovery component of the liberal arts curriculum to develop these skills in students. Specifically, this component (consisting of mathematics, technology, scientific methodology, and historiography) has the responsibility for the development of the skills of calculation and measurement, scientific observation, scientific methodology, and theory interpretation. The development of these skills requires a format that gives priority to practice. This requirement is satisfied by the *laboratory* format--a format that allows students to use empirical theory to confront empirical reality, and thus to either confirm or to disconfirm a theoretical conclusion by repeated and repeatable experiments.

The Disputations[19]

The high quality of some of the military training that I received was seldom matched in my undergraduate education. My first course in logic, for instance, was a disappointment. If I remember correctly, I enrolled in this course with the hope of learning something about correct thinking. And I surely hoped that it would help me to think more correctly. I soon found, though, that the course followed a familiar format: there were lectures that seemed to slow the movement of clocks, a textbook that could put me to sleep in one page, and examinations that taught me more about mnemonics than logic. I remember only dimly the "content" of the course. There seemed to be endless syllogisms concluding that Socrates was mortal but invalid because of some quaint defect like "Illicit Process." There were "p's" and "q's" and formal proofs that were totally useless in resolving any of my many problems. By the end of the semester I knew little about logic except that it had created more problems than it had resolved.

---

[19]The argument of this section has been adapted from my essay, "Logic as a Liberal Art," *Liberal Education* (Winter, 1980): 377-381.

When, as a new teacher, I had to teach my first logic course, I tried hard not to forget my undergraduate disappointment. I struggled to give lively lectures, to use interesting textbooks, and to avoid nit-picking exams. Still, in the end I was forced to conclude that my course was a failure. My students did not seem to learn all that much about logic, nor did they become appreciably more logical. I had the anguished feeling that I was condemned to repeat the disappointment of the past.

Only after an inexcusably long time did it dawn on me that the typical college logic course fails not so much because it is mistaught but because it is simply inappropriate for a program of liberal education.

I found two reasons for this. In the first place, the typical logic course is at best concerned with logical theory; at worst it is concerned with assorted logical facts. In either case, though, the course has primarily a theoretical orientation. What is taught is either theory or information. The teacher's job is thus to "cover" a certain amount of "material," that is, to efficiently transfer a body of theory and information from teachers and textbooks to students. The students' job, accordingly, is to efficiently engorge themselves with this logical "material." Never mind that this process tends to become "cramming" or "fact-stuffing." And never mind that the theory and information obtained seem irrelevant to most of the practical problems of human life. After all, the typical logic course is presumably certified by the gray-haired scholarly experts who teach it, and by the printing presses of great universities and corporations. Moreover, this course appears no different from most of the other course "offerings" of our educational institutions. All of these seem legitimized as contributions to that demanding, obviously necessary, and recondite transaction in which books are read and students are credentialized.

To my mind, what had been forgotten in any rationalization for the theoretical orientation of the typical logic course was the proper purpose of a program of liberal education. As was argued in Chapter 5, a program of liberal education is not properly understood as a production line in the "knowledge business." Its purpose is not the production and reproduction of knowledge, but rather the development of people who have the capacity and inclination for rational action. Once understood, this purpose pointed to the need for a logic course that would not so much teach students *about* logic as train them to *be* logical. What was fundamentally important was the development of a set of skills, not the promulgation of theory. In the liberal arts college, logic as a liberal art should be given preference over logic as a science.

There is a second reason why the typical logic course is not appropriate for a program of liberal education. This course may well study "correct thinking," but its conception of "correct thinking" gives the course a narrow content. What is studied is what has sometimes been called "logistic" or "calculative thinking."[20] This is the kind of thinking exemplified in the deductions of axiomatic systems

---

[20]Heidegger, *Discourse on Thinking*, 46 ff.

and the mathematical sciences. Moreover, when this thinking is judged for "correctness," it is judged largely on the basis of the formal and technical sense of "correctness" known as "validity." Logic is then conceived as formal logic. Philosophers and scientists sometimes recommend this kind of thinking as the paradigm for all thinking that is clear, distinct, and certain. It seems that without it, we would not have modern science and technology. Nevertheless, it is a fact that most incorrect thinking fails for reasons other than the invalidities of formal logic. And it is true that calculative thinking is not the kind of thinking we normally do in those situations of life in which practical decisions are required.

What has been forgotten in this rationalization for the narrow content of the typical logic course is, once again, the proper purpose of a program of liberal education. If this purpose is to develop in human beings the capacity and inclination for rational action, then the required reasoning cannot be limited to that which is prescribed in formal logic and is exemplified in the theoretical sciences. This reasoning must also include that which is essential for our moral and political involvement in the world, for philosophical reflection, and even for the advancement of the theoretical sciences. As some logical theorists have pointed out, the narrow concern of formal logic is shown by the fact that the kind of reasoning that it is concerned with turns on the rules for the use of a few formal, operator-like expressions in our language, such as "all," "some," "not," "or," and "if . . . then." [21] It ignores the reasoning that turns on the rules for the use of the vast number of "informal" expressions that are the vehicles for our most fundamental human concerns.

Unfortunately, because educators have so often forgotten the purpose of liberal education, they allow the narrow professional interests of the graduate school to dominate the liberal arts college. As a consequence of this, undergraduate courses become watered-down versions of graduate school courses. The individual career and research interests of logic specialists then determine the content of the typical logic course. Because these interests have traditionally been in the area of mathematical or calculative reasoning, the content of the typical logic course tends to become narrowly theoretical. While this narrow content is appropriate for the professional training and research curriculums of the multiversity, it is inappropriate for the curriculum of the liberal arts college.

Although these criticisms of the typical logic course evolved only slowly and painfully, they eventually revealed as their assumptions the principles for the design of a logic course that would be consistent with the ideal of liberal education:

1. This course should give priority to practice. Its primary aim should not be to provide information about a subject matter, but to develop a set of reasoning skills. It should not be treated as a science, but as an art.

2. This course should develop the full range of reasoning skills. It should not

---

[21]Gilbert Ryle, *Dilemmas* (Cambridge: Cambridge University Press, 1956), Lecture VIII.

be limited to the narrow range of skills required for calculative reasoning, but should include all of the reasoning skills that are required if people are to be able to think and act in rational ways. This would require a shift from an exclusive attention to formal logic--a logic of validity--to a more inclusive concern for both formal and "informal" logic--that is, rhetoric. This points to the need for courses which treat both logic and rhetoric as liberal arts.

If logic is understood as the art of justification (or "demonstration" or "proof") in which known premises ground conclusions that are certain, and if rhetoric is understood as the art of justification in which opined premises ground conclusions that are probable, we will have, in fact, two of the arts of the medieval trivium. With the addition of dialectic, understood as the art of justification in which opined premises ground conclusions that are certain, we will no longer be limited to a narrow conception of justification, but we will have the full range of the arts envisaged in the classical trivium.

These liberal arts, being responsible for the development of the skills of justification, need a format appropriate to this purpose. The history of education provides us with a format that has been frequently found in the past to be effective for the development of the skills of the liberal arts. It was called the *disputation*. It was a prominent feature of the liberal arts curriculums in classical Greece and Rome, in the medieval schools, in the American colonial colleges, and even in the American colleges during the early years of the nineteenth century. Disputations were formal student debates that took a variety of different forms. "Syllogistic" disputations were prominent in the colonial colleges. These, following their medieval prototype, were conducted in Latin, limited to theological issues, and governed by the canons of Aristotelian logic. With the decline in the use of spoken Latin and of interest in theology, spurred by the democratic opposition to elitism in education during the later decades of the eighteenth century, the syllogistic disputation gradually gave way to the "forensic" disputation. The "forensic" disputation was practiced in English and took as its model not the medieval theological disputes, but the political debates of the Roman forum. It thus admitted a range of secular topics, and included *ethos* and *pathos* proofs as well as *logos* proofs. During the early decades of the nineteenth century, due to the growth of the elective system and the popularity of written composition, "forensic" disputation gave way to collegiate debating societies. These were in fact intellectual fraternities. Following the Civil War, with the rise of social fraternities and intercollegiate athletics, and with the continued popularity of written compositions, even the debating societies gradually lost favor. By the early decades of the twentieth century the last vestige of the disputation could be seen in intercollegiate debate--an optional, extracurricular activity for students interested in public speaking. Today, disputation, once the fundamental liberal educational format, has been replaced by the academic "course." Like the liberal arts themselves, disputation has completely disappeared from the liberal arts curriculum.

The disputation, unlike its replacement, the academic "course," is admirably suited for skill development. It gives priority to practice, and allows students to learn by doing and to learn by repetition. Theory becomes useful to practice, not something to be committed to memory for its own sake.

The disputation format is appropriate for the development of the logical, rhetorical, and dialectical skills of justification. An effective way of employing this format is to use the model of a team sports competition. For this model, most of the meetings of a class are neither lectures nor discussions, but are "games" in which two rotating two-member student teams compete in front of two two-member student jury teams and tutors in the performance of a variety of assigned reasoning tasks. The games are supplemented by lectures, which provide instructions and a minimum amount of theory and information necessary for the conduct of the games. Since the responsibility of the teacher is not to profess a theory or to provide information, but to facilitate the students' acquisition of the various reasoning skills, the teacher model for the disputation is the tutor. To provide the intensive individual attention required by this format, senior students who have successfully completed the disputation assist the teacher as tutors in the games. Because the disputation is designed to encourage practice, it is not centered on a textbook. And because it is designed to develop a set of justification skills, the grading system gives priority to skill achievement, not to the mastery of theory.

The skills of justification to be developed by the disputations are the theoretical skills essential for rational action--the skills of logic, rhetoric, and dialectic. Students learn how to analyze, criticize, and present arguments (both written and oral), and to participate in debate and dialogue. Different kinds of games are designed to develop these diverse justification skills. The arguments analyzed, criticized, presented, and debated in the various games are intended as possible solutions to concrete normative problems, not as abstract puzzles. They typically call for moral decisions which must be made on the basis of probability, not certainty.

3. THE PHILOSOPHY SEMINAR

Philosophy as a component of the liberal arts curriculum must not be misunderstood as a science or an art. Its purpose is not to provide knowledge or to develop skills. Rather, its purpose is to facilitate the student's integration of knowledge through the discovery of principles. The discovery of these principles enables the student to transform a set of conclusions into a coherent weltanschauung or philosophy of life. The method required for this discovery is dialectic. Because dialectic requires a seminar format, the appropriate format for philosophy is the *seminar*.

4. THE PRAXES PRACTICUMS

The theoretical liberal arts are responsible for developing the theoretical skills--that is, those skills by means of which students discover the premises and justify the conclusions of the liberal sciences. These skills provide the knowledge that is needed for rational thought and action. But, as has been argued, rational action requires more than knowledge of what is and what ought to be; it also requires the practical skills necessary for transforming what is into what ought to be. These skills include the practical skills of self, social, and economic conduct. These skills have sometimes been called the skills of "prudence" (or "practical wisdom"). The development of these skills is the responsibility of the *praxes*. Like the theoretical liberal arts, the practical liberal arts, or praxes, require a format that gives priority to practice. But this format must differ from the laboratory and disputation formats of the theoretical liberal arts because the skills that must be developed by the praxes are the practical skills of rational conduct rather than the theoretical skills of rational thinking. These practical skills can only be developed by individuals through involvement in concrete situations in which reality is transformed into ideality. This format may be called the *practicum*.

The practicum format is also the appropriate format for the development of the cardinal moral virtues--courage, temperance, and justice. This means that the practicum will be used for the development of the full range of the practical virtues.

Different kinds of practicums are required by the need to develop the different virtues. In addition, various practicum options are required because of the need to accommodate individual differences and to minimize the possibility of moral indoctrination. Some of these practicum kinds and options are indicated in the model curriculum now to be described.

A MODEL LIBERAL ARTS CURRICULUM

Any project to develop the essential competencies of the wise person is itself an action that is intended to realize an ideal. Like any such action, this project will differ depending on the specific circumstances of the reality that is to be transformed. Accordingly, the design of a liberal arts curriculum is a problem that may admit a variety of different solutions. The following is an outline of a possible design. Given current educational assumptions and practices, this design is certain to appear utopian and, of course, unmarketable. But that it should appear so is, hopefully, less an indication of its unrealizability or undesirability than an indication that for too long too many people have aspired for too little and compromised too much.

The proposed design is summarized in the table on the following page as a set of thirty-six curricular requirements.

THE CURRICULAR REQUIREMENTS

Component	Units/Format	Competencies

Empirical Liberal Sciences
  Self Science
  Social Science
  Physical Science
	10 courses	Empirical
		scientific
		literacy

Normative Liberal Sciences
  Self Science
  Political Science
  Cultural Science
	10 courses	Normative
		scientific
		literacy

Liberal Arts of Discovery
  Mathematics
  Technology
  Scientific Methodology
  Historiography
	4 laboratories	Theoretical
		skills of
		discovery

Liberal Arts of Justification
  Logic
  Rhetoric
  Dialectic
	4 disputations	Theoretical
		skills of
		justification

Philosophy	2 seminars	Integration

Praxes
  Self Conduct
  Social Conduct
  Economic Conduct
  Senior Tutor Program
	6 practicums	Practical
		skills of
		prudence and
		the moral
		virtues

Total	36	

The curricular requirements summarized in the preceding table can be glossed as follows:

Liberal Sciences Courses

The knowledge of the liberal sciences is provided by a twenty-unit series of required courses (but elective classes). One series is in the empirical sciences and one series is in the normative sciences. The series in the empirical sciences consists of ten courses that are intended to provide students with a knowledge of the real self, and a comprehensive, general knowledge of social and physical reality. The series in the normative sciences consists of ten courses that are intended to provide students with a knowledge of the ideal self, and a comprehensive, general knowledge of political and cultural ideals. The liberal sciences are responsible for providing students with a critical empirical and normative scientific literacy.

Liberal Arts Laboratories and Disputations

The skills of the theoretical liberal arts are developed by an eight-unit series of required laboratories and disputations. The required laboratories (but elective classes) consist of a four-unit series in the arts of discovery. The laboratories are intended to develop those skills of discovery that are essential to the liberal sciences--the skills of mathematics, scientific observation and experimentation, scientific theory construction, and historiography. The required disputations (but elective classes) consist of a four-unit series in the arts of justification. The disputations are intended to develop the skills of justification that are essential to the liberal sciences--the skills of logic, rhetoric, and dialectic.

Philosophy Seminar

The integration of knowledge and the consequent development of a rationally defensible personal philosophy is the project for each student in a two-unit required (but elective class) philosophy seminar.

Praxes Practicums

The skills of the praxes (or practical liberal arts) are developed by a six-unit series of required (but elective class) "activities" practicums. The "activities" practicums are supervised practical exercises devoted to the development of the practical skills required for the realization of ideals. The skills to be developed by these practicums are the prudential skills of self conduct (self relationships), social conduct (relationships to other people and the community), and economic conduct (relationships to the physical environment), and the cardinal moral virtues. In addition to the six-unit "activities" practicums (scheduled for special winter or summer terms), all students are required to participate in a one unit "service practicum" as a senior tutor, and a "residence practicum." The options of these three types of practicums are as follows:

"Activities Practicums"

"Athletics"

"Athletics" practicums include individual or team goal-oriented activities requiring physical skill or prowess. These practicums do not include recreational activities or "sports," i.e., "disports"--those that are directed at amusement or diversion. Neither do they include activities that are intended to benefit a won/loss record, to develop professional athletes, to advance the careers of professional coaches, to contribute to the public relations image of the college, or to entertain students, faculty, alumni, or the local community. Rather, these activities are directed to the liberal educational benefit of the participants. Their primary purpose is to develop in students the two essential practical competencies of the wise or liberally educated person--prudence and the cardinal moral virtues. As such, these practicums are integral to the curriculum, not extracurricular activities. The conduct of these practicums is the responsibility of teachers acting as coaches.

"Adventures"

"Adventure" practicums are literally "undertakings of uncertain outcomes." These include outdoor adventure activities which confront students with the factuality of the physical environment, the creativity, resilience, adaptability, and limitations of human beings, and the advantages and disadvantages of social cooperation. These activities might include wilderness exploration, mountain climbing expeditions, backpacking, canoeing, sailing explorations, survival training. These are conducted by coaches, and, when necessary, by professional guides. These practicums are available during special winter and summer terms.

"Projects"

"Project" practicums are group or individually designed activities for the realization of ideals. These are conducted under the supervision of a coach during special winter and summer terms.

"Apprenticeships"

"Apprenticeship" practicums allow individual students to apprentice themselves to alumni or other adults not in order to learn a trade, but to learn about the conduct of adult life. These would be available during special terms.

"Community Practicums"

"Fraternities and Cooperatives"

All students are required to participate in a "community practicum." This may take the form of membership in a "fraternity" or a "cooperative." A "fraternity" is understood here to be a limited self-governing association of students who share a common residence. A "cooperative" is understood to be a fraternity which is economically self-supporting. Like the original Greek letter societies, these associations have a primary commitment to the cultivation of the prudential skills and the moral virtues. Unlike conventional social fraternities, these associations are strictly accountable to the college and are staffed by resident coaches and senior tutors. Membership is determined by a rush that provides each association with a measure of diversity and that enables all parties to have a choice of their association preferences.

"Service Practicums"

"Senior Tutors"

All seniors are required to serve as tutors in the liberal arts laboratories or disputations, or in the fraternities or cooperatives.

THE ACADEMIC ENVIRONMENT

1.

Both teachers and students agree that all colleges are divided into two parts--a curriculum and an extracurriculum (sometimes called a "paracurriculum"). But agreement ends with this agreement. Most teachers think of the curriculum as a kind of faculty-led expedition in which students discover knowledge, and they think of the extracurriculum as a kind of rest stop that rehabilitates students so that they can continue on this expedition. Most students, on the other hand, see the curriculum on the order of a forced march in which they must surmount a series of faculty imposed, largely unpleasant obstacles, and they see the extracurriculum as an enjoyable opportunity to participate in some of the activities and satisfactions of adult life. For these students, the curriculum is gray with theories of doubtful practical value, while the extracurriculum is green with practices that yield generous present and future benefits. Not surprisingly, therefore, students are inclined to grudgingly cede the curriculum to the faculty as a necessary evil, but to jealously guard the extracurriculum as an inviolable private preserve. Social, fraternity, cultural, athletic, and residential activities, including, of course, parties--in short, all those activities that take place "outside the classroom"--are regarded by them as off-limits to "educators."

Research suggests that this familiar division of the college into a curriculum and an extracurriculum is unfortunate.[22]   Too often the curriculum and extracurriculum end up in competition, and in the minds of many students (and teachers) the curriculum comes off second best.   A college may unwittingly sponsor an extracurriculum that is hostile to the values promoted by the curriculum.   In fact, the extracurriculum may effectively subvert the curriculum.

A partial explanation of the college's tolerance of the extracurricular subversion of its curriculum is made possible by the realization that the college has failed to understand the degree to which the success of the curriculum is dependent upon an academic environment that is hospitable to academic values. Studies that were cited in Chapter 3 show that a curriculum is only one of many factors affecting student educational development, and that in fact, it may not even be the most important factor. The personal and professional complexion of a college's faculty, the caliber and temperament of its student body, the constitution of its athletic, recreational, and cultural programs, the quality of its students' social life, and the ambiance of its campus--these are among those extracurricular factors that significantly affect student educational development.   A faculty, however, is inclined to overestimate the educational importance of the curriculum and to underestimate the importance of the extracurricular.   It is especially likely to overestimate its own influence and to underestimate the subtle but powerful influence of the student peer group.

A more complete explanation of the typical liberal arts college's tolerance of the extracurricular subversion of its curriculum is made possible by the realization of the extent to which the college has been unfaithful to the ideal of liberal education. Only by betraying this ideal can a college sponsor a curriculum that is oriented to the production and reproduction of microspecialized information or to adolescent-sitting entertainment, rather than to the development of liberally educated people.   And only by betraying this ideal can a college tolerate an extracurriculum that is oriented to temporizing diversions, rather than to the creation of an academic environment that is intellectually stimulating, and that enhances the curriculum.

Most colleges respond to the extracurricular subversion of their curriculums in two familiar ways.   They may attempt to make their curriculum more "rigorous" by imposing heavier classroom demands on their students, and they may try to make their extracurriculum less subversive by more strictly regulating

---

[22]The Jacob study concludes that "the impetus to change [student values] does not come primarily from the formal educational process. Potency to affect student values is found in the distinctive climate of a few institutions, the individual and personal magnetism of a sensitive teacher with strong value-commitments of his own, or value-laden personal experiences of students imaginatively integrated with their intellectual development." Philip E. Jacob, *Changing Values in College: An Exploratory Study of the Impact of College Teaching* (New York: Harper & Row, Publishers, 1957), 11. Also see: David G. Winter, David C. McClelland, and Abigail J. Stewart, *A New Case for the Liberal Arts* (San Francisco: Jossey-Bass Publishers, 1981).

and policing its constituent activities. However, experience suggests that these two strategies are most likely to exacerbate the problem. Students do not respond well to demands for increased "rigor" in a curriculum which they perceive to be largely irrelevant to their present and future needs. Similarly, they do not respond well to increased administrative regulation and policing of an extracurriculum which they regard as belonging to their own jurisdiction.

A more promising strategy for countering the extracurricular subversion of the curriculum is one which begins with the implementation of a genuine liberal arts curriculum. By this action the college replaces a curriculum that is limited to the development of narrow theoretical competencies with a curriculum that gives priority to the development of a wide range of practical competencies. The development of this liberal arts curriculum will, of course, be resisted by those teachers, students, coaches, and others who have a vested interest in the continuation of the traditional theory-oriented curriculum and the familiar, permissive, helter-skelter, entertainment-oriented extracurriculum. On the other hand, the development of this curriculum will be aided by its appeal to students who will appreciate the priority that it gives to practical knowledge and skills. And since this practice-oriented curriculum will diminish the need for extracurricular activities to compensate for the narrowness of the traditional theory-oriented curriculum, it will diminish the impetus for the extracurricular subversion of the curriculum, and increase the possibility of an academic environment that will enhance the curriculum.

The development of a genuine, comprehensive liberal arts curriculum will require that the college expropriate and reform some of the major activities and institutions that are currently subversive elements of the extracurriculum. Below are two that should initiate this project:

1. THE EXPROPRIATION AND REFORM OF THE FRATERNITY SYSTEM

Almost since its inception during the mid-nineteenth century the American social fraternity system has been accused of being a major pollutant of the academic environment. On most campuses today there are annually multiple incidents of fraternity and sorority racism, sexism, alcoholism, hazing, hooliganism, and hell week atrocities. But of even greater consequence is the chronic "animal house" contempt for intellectuality. Still, the social fraternity system continues to survive periodic demands for its abolition. This anomaly suggests that the system, in spite of its serious deficiencies, serves some irrepressible human needs. Perhaps the most pressing of these is the young adult's need for peer support at a difficult stage of adolescent development. Given the apparent importance of this need, it would seem imprudent to abolish a system that serves this need unless a satisfactory surrogate is available. At the same time, given the subversive character of the present system, it would also seem foolish to continue to tolerate the social fraternity within a program of liberal education. A possible resolution of this dilemma would be for the college to expropriate the social fraternity system and reconstitute it as an instrument of liberal education. That this might be successful is suggested by the fact that liberal education, unlike most other forms of education, is concerned with the development of prudence and the cardinal moral virtues, and the fact that the original Greek letter societies were also concerned with these important practical purposes. The ideals still encoded in the secret rituals of the present day "animal houses" provide evidence of these original, but now often forgotten, high moral purposes. In any case, the development of the practical liberal arts would be facilitated by an institution that permits students to experiment with the realization of practical ideals under conditions of limited risk. A reformed, responsible, disciplined social fraternity system might provide these opportunities.

The proposed liberal arts curriculum incorporates a reformed social fraternity system as an essential instrument in its program to develop the practical liberal arts. All students would be required to participate in a social fraternity or in a cooperative. These fraternities and cooperatives would be "local" and operate under the supervision of the college. Supervision would be the responsibility of resident faculty advisers (coaches) who would be assisted by senior tutors. Members of these organizations would be enrolled in co-ordinate self, social, and economic praxes which would prepare them for the personal, interpersonal, and technical problems of community membership.

2. THE EXPROPRIATION AND REFORM OF COLLEGE ATHLETICS

Almost everyday the media publish stories about the ways that American colleges and universities are compromised by the steadily increasing professionalization of sports. The immense wealth and power generated by what might be called the sports/industrial complex affects every constituency of our educational institutions. Coaches, under relentless pressure to produce winning teams, are routinely charged with recruitment violations, mistreatment of their athletes, financial improprieties, and miscellaneous crudities. (A college coach in Mississippi recently had the members of his football team witness the castration of a bull on their practice field to "motivate" them to a victory over Texas.) When these coaches lose, they are dismissed or downgraded to be teachers; when they win, they are treated like national heroes and paid like multinational C. E. O.'s. Meanwhile, athletes are often exploited by the institutions that are supposed to be educating them. Non-athletes are charged a premium for their education so that athletes can be given a discount for theirs. Men's sports are usually subsidized at the expense of women's sports. College administrators seem ever willing to compromise academic ideals in their insatiable desire for media sports publicity. Teachers shamelessly cooperate in the scam that allows colleges to pay for the services of their athletes in course credits instead of money, and they willingly provide gut courses and narrow professional programs to accommodate "student-athletes" who can barely read when they matriculate and barely read when they graduate--if they graduate. Alumni, educated by educational institutions dominated by sports values and still infatuated by adolescent sports fantasies, use their financial support to perpetuate quasi-professional sports programs and sports values. Students are recruited on the basis of the absurdity that the educational quality of a college or university is directly proportional to the prowess of its athletic teams. Meanwhile, institutions supposedly dedicated to education spend student fees and public funds to give college campuses the look and feel of Olympic complexes.

The impact of the professionalization of sports has been devastating for the liberal arts college. The tragedy is not so much that people use sports for the pursuit of wealth, or for entertainment, or for an escape from existential anxiety and boredom. After all, they could do worse. Nor is it that there is so much dissimulation and corruption that envelops win-at-any-price coaches, abused athletes, compromising college administrators, fellow-traveling teachers, and rah-rah alumni. The real tragedy for the liberal arts college is the college's dependency on a program that in terms of its total social costs is staggeringly expensive, and that provides so little in the way of benefits for liberal education.

These quasi-professional sports programs confuse vocation with avocation. They promulgate sports values and celebrate the athlete, not the intellectual, and much less, the liberally educated person. The language and metaphors of sports saturate campus language and culture. Today every student knows that professional athletes earn more money in one season than most people earn in an entire lifetime.[23] Hundreds of thousands of American students, teachers, and administrators spend a portion of each day "keeping up with the ball scores" (or point spreads). And this obsession with sports is not all innocent recreation. Many of those who maintain this obsession live as if the very meaning of their lives depended upon the success or failure of a team or individual with which they have for some aberrant reason identified. The result of this obsession is the subversion of academic values. The campus hero becomes the athlete, the robust and lusty contrast to the grade-grubbing, geeky, pointy-headed "intellectual." The transcendent purposes of the college are obscured or delegitimized for the students and the public. A mythology of sports achievement allows students to avoid the hard task of intellectual development for the brassy but evanescent benefits of sports achievements or the vicarious satisfactions of sports achievement fantasies. Under the dominion of this mythology the need for scientific literacy is replaced by the need for technological information; the need for moral knowledge is replaced by the need for knowledge of the rules of the game, the conventions of a culture, or the law; the need for the liberal arts is replaced by the need for the skills of career advancement; the need for philosophical principles is replaced by the need for private satisfactions or public accolade; and the need for the development of the virtues of the wise person is

---

[23]It was recently reported that the average professional baseball player now earns over one million dollars a year.

replaced by the need for the virtues of the hero.

Some liberal arts colleges respond to these accusations by simply denying that their sports programs are quasi-professional. They silence criticism and take smug pride in contrasting the virtues of the small college sports programs with the vices of the big time sports programs of the multiversities. "If you want to see the corrupting effects of quasiprofessionalism in higher education," they will say, "don't look at us, look at Ohio State or Notre Dame or Alabama." These people believe that quasi-professional sports have a much more deleterious effect on the multiversity than they do on the liberal arts college. Unfortunately, in this belief they are wrong. Quasi-professional sports corrupt the liberal arts college much more than they corrupt the multiversity. This is true because the purpose of the multiversity is to prepare students for work and professional careers, and in developing athletes and providing an environment that is enthralled to sports values the multiversity does not violate this purpose. The multiversity has as much right to develop professional or quasi-professional athletes as it does to develop accountants, engineers, or English teachers. On the other hand, the liberal arts college, dedicated as it is to providing a liberal education for its students, clearly violates its institutional purpose by developing professional athletes or tolerating an academic environment dominated by sports values.

Other colleges respond to these accusations by admitting that their sports programs are in some ways quasi-professional, and may engender a sports-oriented system of values, but they attempt to rationalize this fact in a number of ways. Sometimes, for instance, they will argue that since colleges ought to design their programs to satisfy student interests, and since students are interested in "competitive"--i.e., winning--sports teams, colleges should provide "competitive" sports teams. This argument is diminished somewhat by the fact that often the number of those who are interested in sports is inflated by the college's policy of recruiting those who are interested in sports. But more relevant is the fact that, as we have argued, the responsibility of the liberal arts college is to provide a liberal education for its students, not to satisfy student interests. Unless sports are essential or valuable to a liberal education, the liberal arts college has no justification for providing them.

At other times these colleges will attempt to justify a quasi-professional sports program with the argument that such a program is necessary for the college's public relations image and its marketing "needs." This argument is based on an assumption that since most prospective students are saturated with sports values, a "high visibility" and "competitive" sports program is needed to attract them. There are two appropriate responses to this argument. First, a college truly committed to the ideal of liberal education should have the integrity not to misrepresent itself to the public and its prospective students. It should appeal to those who, however inchoately, understand that sports values have their place in human development, but that these values must in time be supplanted by higher values. A liberal arts college should appeal to those who seek a liberal education. Second, there is no reason that a liberal arts college cannot develop a sports program that is subordinate to the ideal of liberal education, and there is no reason to believe that this program would not be appealing to the great mass of prospective students who may be saturated by sports values, but who may also aspire to the values of liberal education.

At still other times these colleges will attempt to justify their sponsorship of a quasi-professional sports program on the claim that such programs provide wholesome entertainment for the campus and the local community. While this may in fact be true, it may be fairly questioned whether it is the responsibility of the liberal arts college to provide entertainment for the campus and local community, and if it is, whether the college's sponsorship of a large and expensive sports program is cost effective for this purpose. It seems conceivable that other programs might achieve this purpose in ways that would be less costly and would provide greater educational benefits.

In Chapter 3 we noted that recently some have attempted to justify quasi-professional college sports programs on the ground that they would serve as laboratories for a new social science--"sports science." We argued that this proposal is absurd. It would create a specialized social science and laboratory with a budget that would probably exceed the combined budgets of all of the other social sciences. The liberal arts college has no need for a department so expensive and so specialized.

The various attempts to justify a quasi-professional sports program within a program of liberal education on the basis of student interests, benefits to the college's marketing and public relations, entertainment for the campus and the local community, and as a laboratory for a new social science, are not convincing. There does not seem to be any reason to believe that quasi-professional sports are either directly or indirectly essential to a liberal education. The great universities of the world manage to flourish without such dependency. Paris and Oxford and Berlin and Chicago are not unexciting places to live and to learn. Perhaps it is too early, and too much of a shock to current commonplaces to suggest that it is time for American universities and colleges to "spin off" their quasi-professional sports programs.[24] But the time is rapidly approaching for this option to be considered.

Having said this, it is important not to interpret this criticism as a wholesale condemnation of sports and athletics in the liberal arts college. Certainly educators in the past have often suggested that sports and athletics have an important role in liberal education. From Plato to the two most recent serious studies of the nature of athletics, Paul Weiss' *Sport: A Philosophic Inquiry* and H. S. Slusher's *Man, Sport and Existence*, liberal educators have been almost unanimous in their belief that athletic training and sports participation are valuable in the development of character in young people. The character traits developed are not necessarily those of some partisan ideology; they can include the prudential and the cardinal moral virtues--those virtues that are essential to the development of the capacity and inclination for rational action. When athletic training and sports participation are subordinate to liberal education, they do not

---

[24]On this issue, see: *Chronicle of Higher Education* (6 March 1991), A30.

produce bellicosity and aggressiveness, but act as an effective instrument for the development of prudence and the virtues of courage, justice, and temperance. A sports program subordinate to the ideal of liberal education would be one that is devoted to the development of those prudential skills and academic moral virtues that are essential to the liberally educated person. It would not be one centered about entertainment, profit, or publicity. This program would allow all students (male and female, stars and duffers) to benefit from coached athletics. A program with this purpose is included within the proposed liberal arts curriculum as one of the options of the "activities practicums."

Once restructured by this purpose, athletics would cease to be an extracurricular activity, and would become instead integral to the curriculum. Coordinately, the coaches within this program would cease to be entertainment impresario adjuncts and would become bona fide faculty members since they would be full participants in the college's educational program. The emphasis of this program would be on those sports and athletic activities that morally and practically (and physically) benefit *all* students, not just a privileged few. This program would be freed from any obligation to win ball games, to appeal to alumni achievement fantasies, to entertain the campus or local community, or to recruit students (and more athletes). Athletics would no longer serve the purposes of quasi-professional stars, or coaches, or nostalgic alumni. A sports program would not exist for the benefit of a small recruited elite whose sport participation is involuntarily subsidized by the tuition of the non-participants. Athletics would be returned to the students so that all of them could enjoy its special benefits.

2.

We have argued that a successful program of liberal education requires a comprehensive liberal arts curriculum and a supportive academic environment. To create this environment, we have proposed that some traditional activities of the extracurriculum be expropriated, reformed, and integrated into the curriculum. But the creation and maintenance of this environment will require a number of academic policies that will depart from what is now commonplace on most campuses. The following are illustrations:

Reinstatement of In Loco Parentis

During most of the twentieth century the doctrine of *in loco parentis* has been repudiated by American colleges on the ground that education is properly concerned only with the transmission of value-free knowledge or information, and that, as a consequence, a college has no right to attempt to influence the conduct of its students in the so-called extracurriculum. This consequence found a sympathetic audience in students, who were all too willing to be given the extracurriculum for their own devices, and it found an equally enthusiastic audience in teachers, who were all too willing to be relieved of the career stultifying and enervating traumas of trying to be surrogate parents for adolescents.

By mid-century the positivist ideal of a value-free education had been exposed as dogmatic through the realization that this ideal is itself the expression of a value, not a factual claim, and it had been exposed as dangerous by the realization that an education that maintains value neutrality can educe people who are both scientifically competent and morally depraved.

Today, while most college teachers are aware that value-neutrality rests on a dogma, they are reluctant to give up its convenient consequences. They would like to continue to be excused from any responsibility for the moral development of their students.

Clearly, for the liberal arts college, this evasion of responsibility cannot be justified. As an institution dedicated to the development of the wise person, the liberal arts college cannot escape its obligation for the moral development of its students. Happily or unhappily, the college is properly a place where surrogate parenting is necessary. In view of its mission the college is obliged to act *in loco parentis*.

Abolition of the Elective Principle

A curriculum that is practice-oriented obviously must provide its students with ample opportunities to learn by making choices. At the same, this curriculum cannot allow its students to opt out of those courses of study and practical exercises that are necessary for the development of the liberal arts competencies. Therefore, students cannot be accorded the right to elect whatever courses of study and practical exercises they choose. The so-called "elective principle" must be unmasked and vacated as the marketing fraud that it is.

Some will complain that an education without elective courses will be "rigid" and "boring" to both students and teachers. This is not convincing. Traditional academic major programs, as well as medical school and law school curricula, are not thought to be rigid or boring because they do not allow students to do whatever they please. Moreover, the curriculum's need to provide its students with ample opportunities for choice can be realized without trashing the curriculum. This can be done by having required courses but elective classes. This arrangement will preserve the integrity of the curriculum, but will also encourage healthy competition among teachers and allow students freedom in the choice of classes and teachers.

A Reaffirmation of Occcham's Razor

Ideally, a liberal education should be available to all people. For this to be possible this education will have to be reasonably priced. Most current programs of liberal education are far too expensive, and are too expensive in part because they are engorged with the fat of superfluous options. A liberal arts curriculum should be lean. It should provide all that is essential for the development of liberally educated people, and nothing that is not essential. In the liberal arts college, unlike the multiversity, entities should not be multiplied beyond necessity.

Abolition of the Disciplinary Departmental Organization of the College

Many years ago Robert Hutchins warned that a "liberal education cannot flourish in a university in which liberal education is under departmental control."[25] Despite repeated attempts by colleges to superimpose a general education program on the framework of the disciplinary departmental system, these attempts routinely fail. It should be clear by now that a condition for the success of the liberal arts curriculum is an organization of the college that has been liberated from disciplinary departmentalism. A superior organization would be one that is based on the essential components of the liberal arts curriculum.

Abolition of Major and Distribution Requirements

The model liberal arts curriculum abandons the traditional departmental major. The demand that students have knowledge "in depth" of (any) one "discipline" or "academic field" does not serve the interests of liberal education because this kind of knowledge is not one of the essential competencies of the wise person. In most cases the disciplinary "major" does not even serve vocational interests.

The model curriculum also abandons "distribution requirements." The demand that students know "a little bit about a lot of things" provides no assurance that they will develop the essential competencies of the wise person. Both the undergraduate major and the distribution system are merely life support systems for disciplinary departmentalism.

The Senior Tutor Program

The development of the theoretical skills of the liberal arts is labor intensive. The resulting high cost of developing these skills is no doubt one of the reasons that the liberal arts are so neglected by liberal arts colleges. The Senior Tutor Program of the model curriculum addresses this problem. This program requires every senior to act as a tutor in one liberal arts laboratory or disputation or in one of the praxes. This program benefits both students and student tutors.

---

[25]Quoted by Theodore Roszak in *The Dissenting Academy* (New York: Pantheon Books, 1968), 26.

The Maintenance of Media for Criticism

Unlike a multiversity, a liberal arts college needs institutions which will encourage campus-wide academic dialogue. In the past, two institutions that have served this need well are a campus newspaper and a university center. These traditional institutions should be reclaimed from those who have misappropriated them, and should be revitalized to serve the purposes of liberal education.

On most college campuses today there is a costly clutter of communications media that have been appropriated by academic departments, administrative bureaus, and other special interests. Like the rides and shows of a carnival, these academic departments, administrative bureaus, and other special interests want to promote their own projects or products. This special interest media clutter should be eliminated in favor of a medium that advances the purposes of liberal education. A newspaper should still be able to serve as this medium. This paper should be college funded and published at least semiweekly. Its primary purpose should be to advance academic dialogue, not to disseminate information or advertise products or projects. Its central concern should be the criticism of ideas. It should be student operated, but under faculty supervision. Editorial participation in the publication of this newspaper should be available to students as one of the praxes options of the model curriculum.

In addition to a medium for dialogue, the college also needs places that are hospitable to dialogue. One such place would be a student center that gives priority to the exchange of ideas rather than to the exchange of goods and services. This place should be protected from intrusion by retailers, advertisers, the public media, and popular culture.

* * * *

If the ideal of liberal education is to be realized, then the liberal arts college must provide an educational program that is oriented by this ideal. This program must integrate a curriculum, or formal academic program, and an extracurriculum, or academic environment. The curriculum must provide students with empirical and normative scientific literacy, the skills of the theoretical liberal arts, insight into philosophical principles, and the skills of the practical liberal arts. It will necessarily be multiform, and will consist in a regimen of required courses but elective classes for the liberal empirical and normative sciences, laboratories and disputations for the theoretical liberal arts, seminars for philosophy, and practicums for the praxes, or practical liberal arts. It will be successful only if it is placed within a strongly supportive academic environment. The creation and maintenance of this environment will require that much of the traditional extracurriculum be expropriated, reformed, and integrated into the curriculum. We may call this requirement for a comprehensive educational program oriented to the development of liberally educated people *the principle of the liberal arts curriculum.*

8

THE PRINCIPLE OF TEACHER AUTONOMY

It is men we need, not programs!
William Arrowsmith, "The Future of Teaching"

To this point the argument has been advanced that, if the liberal arts college is to regain its institutional integrity and fulfill its role as the instrument for liberal education, then it must urgently articulate, and commit itself to, certain fundamental principles. The first and most important of these is *the principle of liberal education*. This is the proposition that the ideal of liberal education, and therefore the mission of the liberal arts college, is the development of wise people--that is, people who have the capacity and inclination for rational action. Once a college commits itself to this principle, it is ipso facto committed to three corollaries. *The principle of institutional independence* requires that the college maintain independence or neutrality in the sense that as an institution it rigorously avoids subscription to any dogma and servitude to any extrinsic purpose. If the college is itself unable to avoid dogmas and partisan purposes, then it will be unable to develop people who are themselves unprejudiced by dogmas and partisan purposes. *The principle of the liberal arts curriculum* requires that the college provide a liberal arts curriculum--that is, a comprehensive educational program that is exclusively devoted to the development of people who have the capacity and inclination for rational action. The liberal arts curriculum will facilitate the development of people who possess the knowledge, skills, principles, and virtues that are the defining competencies of the wise person.

A fourth principle remains to be specified. This principle is needed because a program of liberal education not only requires a unique kind of ideal, a unique kind of institution, and a unique kind of curriculum, but it also requires a unique kind of agent, or teacher. In fact, the teacher is the most important factor in any program of liberal education.

This fourth principle will be developed by a description of the ideal college teacher and the ideal conditions for college teaching. These ideals are the presuppositions of the criticisms of the current concept of the college teacher and the conditions of college teaching that were detailed in Chapter 4. We will look first at the professional goal, character, pedagogy, and professional resources of the ideal college teacher, and then at the ideal conditions for teaching--the faculty organization, the teacher compensation system, the personnel policies, and the teaching facilities.

THE IDEAL COLLEGE TEACHER

1. THE INTRINSICALLY VALUABLE IDEAL

All teachers in a program of liberal education share a single, supreme, unique professional goal--the goal of service to an ideal that is intrinsically valuable. This ideal is the development of the wise person, the person who has the capacity and inclination for rational action. In order to serve this ideal, and thus to develop the diverse competencies of the wise person, the ideal college teacher must have the following specific professional goals:

1. To Provide the Knowledge of the Liberal Sciences

The college teacher must provide students with an essential fund of knowledge--an empirical and normative scientific literacy. This knowledge includes a comprehensive empirical knowledge of the self, human society, and physical reality, and it includes a comprehensive normative knowledge of the ideal self, ethical norms, and cultural norms. Insofar as practicable, this knowledge is prioritized by the student's need to act rationally throughout the course of human life.

2. To Develop the Skills of the Liberal Arts

The college teacher must develop in students the reasoning skills that are required for the achievement of empirical and normative knowledge. These skills include the skills of discovery (including the skills of mathematics, technology, scientific methodology, and historiography) and the skills of justification (including the skills of logic, rhetoric, and dialectic).

3. To Catalyze Insight into Philosophical Principles

The college teacher must facilitate the students' discovery of rationally defensible principles for the integration of knowledge and rational action.

4. To Develop Prudence and the Moral Virtues

The college teacher must develop in students those practical skills that are essential for rational action. These practical skills include the prudential skills essential for self-conduct, for conduct in relationship to other people, and for conduct in relationship to the physical environment. The prudential skills are limited to those that are essential to the pursuit of the ideal of wisdom. The practical skills also include those that, unlike the prudential skills, are less the direct result of rational decision, and more the indirect result of rationally-induced habits. These moral virtues are limited to those that are essential to the development of the essential competencies of the wise person. They include the cardinal moral virtues of courage, justice, and temperance--the generic virtues of disciplined fear, ambition, and desire.

2. THE UNCOMPROMISED TEACHER

The ordinary college teacher is familiar to us as the teacher-scholar and the teacher-administrator. The character of the ideal college teacher will be developed by a detailed criticism of these two familiar concepts.

The Myth of the Teacher-Scholar

"Hired to teach, but paid to publish." This brief statement sums up the conflict that burdens the career of nearly every teacher in the liberal arts college.[1] It is a conflict that is both unfortunate and unnecessary.

Of course, all those who aspire to be teachers in an institution of liberal education understand that they must be professionally prepared. It comes, therefore, as no surprise to them if they are at midlife by the time they have completed their graduate studies and are ready to begin teaching. What often happens next, however, may come as a surprise. Once hired, these teachers may soon discover that if they are to be promoted and tenured, or even just accepted and respected, they cannot quite yet dedicate themselves to teaching. For if their college's policy is a harsh "publish or perish" or, more likely, something that sounds better but means about the same, they will have to stake out territories of professional expertise and publish in appropriate scholarly journals. Books may be expected, too. In the time that remains they will teach. And so will pass the remaining years of their professional careers. They are teachers who are never quite able to answer their calling. They are instead part-time teachers and part-time scholars. If they are able to adapt to this demanding and divided life, though, they will at least escape the shaming epithet, "deadwood," and on their retirement day they may even shed a tear of pride when they hear the familiar eulogy for a "true teacher-scholar."

---

[1]"For most members of the [teaching] profession, the real strain in the academic role arises from the fact that they are, in essence, paid to do one job, whereas the worth of their services is evaluated on the basis of how well they do another." Theodore Caplow and Reece J. McGee, *The Academic Marketplace* (New York: Basic Books, 1958), 82. "Teaching is a necessary evil and an annoying distraction from more profitable ventures." Pierre van den Berghe, *Academic Gamesmanship* (New York: Abelard-Schuman, 1970), 71.

At a time when our liberal arts colleges can promise little more, vis-a-vis the universities, than good teaching and high tuition, we may justifiably wonder why these colleges presently disdain the dedicated teacher and give exemplary status to the "teacher-scholar." It is past time for a careful look at this strange anomaly.

A profile of the "teacher-scholar" can be obtained from the typical liberal arts college faculty handbook. Here we find that for advancement in rank and appointment to tenure, faculty members, as members of the "teaching profession," must, of course, demonstrate "excellence in teaching." In addition, though, they must demonstrate that they are "not content with merely passing on received knowledge, [but are eager and able] to make important contributions to scholarship and the arts."[2] In short, they don't "just teach"; rather, they "do something": they "publish."[3]

The Rationale for the Teacher-Scholar

The exemplary status of the "teacher-scholar" in the liberal arts college is usually justified on the basis of two widely-held beliefs:

First, it is believed essential for the teacher to make contributions to scholarship or the fine arts on the ground that such contributions benefit teaching. One faculty handbook puts it in the following way:

> Believing that effective teaching requires an atmosphere of scholarship and creativity, [the college] expects each faculty member to maintain a focus of professional interest and encourages him/her to achieve professional recognition. Such recognition may be acquired through the publication of articles and books, but [the college] interprets "publication" in a broader sense, meaning "to make public." In this sense, publication would include public lectures, research reports at professional meetings, exhibits of art, dramatic and musical productions, and other means of presenting creative work to the public.[4]

Statements of this kind clearly convey to teachers that they are expected not only to teach, but also to publish (and to achieve publicity), and to do so on the ground that publication is essential to effective teaching. Surprisingly enough for a claim of such important practical consequences, and even more surprising for a statement authored by those who should be familiar with the methods of the empirical sciences, this claim is usually presented (as it is here) not as an

---

[2]*St. Lawrence University Faculty Handbook*, 50.

[3] Abraham Flexner is reported to have once asked a college dean for the name of his best teacher. When the dean named the person, the following conversation ensued: "What is his rank?" "Assistant professor." "When will his appointment expire?" "Shortly." "Will he be promoted?" "No." "Why not?" "He hasn't *done* anything!" C. C. Bowman, *The College Professor in America* (Philadelphia, Pa.: Lippincott, 1938), 122.

[4]*St. Lawrence University Faculty Handbook*, 83.

empirically grounded hypothesis, but as a self-evident truth. The doubts of occasional skeptics are allayed by appeals to one or more of the following familiar academic commonplaces:[5]

1. Publication provides the college with publicity and prestige, leading to enhanced institutional morale and economic rewards.

2. Publication provides knowledge certified by peer review as current, authoritative, and factual.

3. Publication provides students with teachers who are appropriate role models--intellectually alive, professionally able, and productive.

4. Publication provides teachers with professional recognition, career advancement, and higher self-esteem.

Second, it is believed important for the teacher in the liberal arts college to make contributions to scholarship or the fine arts on the ground that such contributions (whether or not they benefit teaching) are one of the essential responsibilities of every college teacher. This belief is a consequence of the assumption that while colleges and universities differ in various superficial ways, they share the common purpose of all institutions of "higher education": the advancement and dissemination of knowledge and the fine arts. This common purpose requires teaching and the production of scholarly and artistic works, where "scholarly works" is assumed to include any information about any topic of theoretical interest. "Scholarly works" thus range from comprehensive systems of the principles of knowledge and the metaphysics of morals, to infinitely specialized and technical data on the behavior of any of the over 900,000 known species of insects, or on the over 3,000,000 known kinds of organic molecules, or on any "interesting" event occurring in the universe during the estimated 20 billion years since the "Big Bang." "Artistic works" range similarly over masterpieces and junk in a potentially infinite variety of objects created, at least in part, for the aesthetic enjoyment of an infinite variety and number of people.

A Critique of the Rationale

Thus, the exemplary status of the "teacher-scholar" in the liberal arts college is typically justified on the basis of two beliefs that are taken as self-evident. "Teacher-scholars" don't "just teach"; they teach and publish, and their scholarly and artistic productivity is held to improve the quality of their teaching and to fulfill one of the essential responsibilities of the college teacher.

In spite of their apparent self-evidence, we need to look critically at these two beliefs:

---

[5]For a review of these commonplaces, see: Henry L. Bretton, "On the Necessity of Research in Teaching," *Journal of College Teaching* 9 (1979): 96-97; Robert J. Friedrich and Stanley J. Michalak, Jr., "Why Doesn't Research Improve Teaching?" *Journal of Higher Education* 54 (1983): 145-163; Earl J. McGrath, "Characteristics of Outstanding Teachers," *Journal of Higher Education* 33 (1962): 148-152; Hans A. Schmitt, "Teaching and Research," *Journal of Higher Education* 36 (1965): 419-427; Dennis E. Showalter, "Publication and Stagnation in the Liberal

The belief that publication benefits teaching in the liberal arts college is a belief about an empirical fact, and its legitimacy can only be decided by an appeal to empirical evidence.

As strange as it may seem to those wedded to prevailing assumptions, the available evidence does *not* support this belief! The evidence shows that scholarly research and publication contribute little if anything to teaching.[6]

The persistence of the belief that publication benefits teaching, especially in the face of evidence to the contrary, suggests that it might be rewarding to examine the commonplaces that have allowed this belief to appear so plausible to so many.[7] This may provide some insight into the "teacher-scholar's" irresistible appeal.

1. The commonplace that "publication provides the college with publicity and prestige, leading to enhanced institutional morale and economic rewards" may well be true in our present educational environment, but this is not by itself an argument that supports the belief that publication benefits teaching. Publicity about the scholarly productivity of a faculty is likely to aid institutional morale, prestige, and enrollment--at least among those who believe that the quality of an education is to be judged by the scholarly productivity of a faculty. But experience suggests that about the same results can be achieved by a successful football team. Moreover, just as it is conceivable that a successful football team can also have a detrimental impact on education, it is conceivable that the scholarly productivity of a faculty can be inversely related to the quality of education. This would be true if publication is in some way incompatible with undergraduate liberal arts teaching. Finally, even if publication does enhance institutional morale and generate economic rewards, there is still no necessity that such benefits would accrue to the advantage of teaching. Thus, at least for present circumstances, this commonplace could be true and actually count against the belief that publication benefits teaching.

2. The commonplace that "publication provides knowledge certified by peer review as current, authoritative, and factual" is surely true. Once this is granted, it might seem almost inconceivable that this commonplace would not support the belief that publication benefits teaching. But this is exactly what would occur if the knowledge provided by publication addressed to disciplinary professionals was, on the whole, either irrelevant to the purposes of a program of liberal education, or too specialized and sophisticated to be readily applicable to the

Arts College," *Educational Record* 59 (1978): 166-172.

[6]Stanley J. Michalak, Jr., and Robert J. Friedrich, "Research Productivity and Teaching Effectiveness at a Small Liberal Arts College," *Journal of Higher Education* 52 (1981): 578-597. Also see: Virginia W. Voelks, "Publications and Teaching Effectiveness," *Journal of Higher Education* 33 (1962): 212-218.

[7]For a study of the structural sources that inhibit the correct perception of the zero correlation between teaching quality and research quality, see: Phillip E. Hammond, John W. Meyer, and David Miller, "Teaching versus Research: Sources of Misperceptions," *Journal of Higher Education* 40 (1969): 682-690.

teaching of undergraduates in such a program. Under these circumstances the commonplaces, though true, would fail to support the belief that publication benefits teaching.

3. The commonplace that "publication provides students with teachers who are appropriate role-models" seems to harbor the assumption that those who "just teach" are "content with merely passing on received knowledge," and are thus not much different from parrots, while those who publish are intellectually alive, professionally able, and productive, and are therefore human, worthy of emulation, and appropriate role-models for undergraduates. But this assumption contrasts an idealized scholar and a caricatured teacher. With equal justification the teacher might be described as a caring person dedicated to helping young people realize their highest potential, while the scholar could be described as an obsessive who is isolated from the human world of decision and action, and who has retreated into a non-threatening, spectator-world of specialized theory. If the ideal teacher and the ideal scholar are compared, not to caricatures, but to each other, the results may not favor the scholar, especially from the standpoint of liberal education. It seems possible that the ideal teacher, with an essential concern for human development, comprehensive insight, and values, is a more appropriate role-model for the undergraduate liberal arts student than the ideal scholar who is partial to theory, specialization, and value-neutrality.

It is often argued that publication forces teachers to avoid "stagnation" and to remain "professionally alive," and it is assumed that those who are "professionally alive" are necessarily better teachers.[8] Both the argument and the assumption may be questioned. Certainly for the considerable mass of publishing that mechanically applies received methods to highly specialized subject matters, and that is remote from theoretical or moral principles, it is hard to see any consequence that could count as a contribution to being "professionally alive." In any case, the determination of what it is that will force teachers to be "professionally alive" is surely a matter to be decided by experience. People are motivated differently: Some may be inspired by publishing, while others may be enlivened by jogging or gin--or even teaching!

The assumption that those who are "professionally alive" are necessarily better teachers would be mistaken if those who are "professionally alive" are preoccupied with research or bored by teaching, or are unable or unwilling to translate a professional level of sophistication and interest to a level required for the teaching of undergraduate liberal arts students. It is also possible that being "professionally alive" (even in a non-pejorative sense of this ambiguous expression) could be an obstacle to effective teaching. Undergraduate students respond poorly to a teacher whom they perceive as "narrow" or not relevant to their needs.[9] In any case, the claim that publication provides students with

---

[8]Dennis E. Showalter, "Publication and Stagnation in the Liberal Arts College," *Educational Record* 59 (1978): 166-172.

[9]"Students perceive researchers as less, not more, knowledgeable than nonresearchers, [and] this seems to detract from their effectiveness as teachers." Robert J. Friedrich and Stanley J.

teachers who are appropriate role-models obviously assumes that the "teacher-scholar" is an appropriate role-model for students in a program of liberal education. If the assumption is unwarranted, the commonplace would be false and would fail to support the belief that publication benefits teaching.

4. The commonplace that "publication provides teachers with professional recognition, career advancement, and higher self-esteem may be granted. Certainly publication currently provides teachers with professional recognition and career advancement. And higher self-esteem is a predictable consequence. But this is true only because of the contingent fact that the present college and university reward system values publication over teaching. A different system would likely yield different results. Even under the present system some teachers do not allow their self-esteem to be determined by their professional reputation or academic rank. These teachers understand that to expect them to be dedicated teachers and, at the same time, to serve as officials in professional societies, to conduct research, or to present creative work to the public is as implausible and as imprudent as to expect a physician to be dedicated to his or her practice and, at the same time, to serve as an administrator in the medical society, to conduct medical research, or to present creative work (rather than well-treated patients!) to the public. Finally, not only are professional recognition, career advancement, and self-esteem contingently related to publication, but they are also contingently related to teaching effectiveness. In fact, it is conceivable that professional recognition, career advancement, and self-esteem could work to the detriment of teaching effectiveness.[10] This might occur if teachers forget that the good teacher "always gives part of himself to help develop the self of another,"[11] and, in consequence, has the responsibility for self-expenditure, not the opportunity for career self-aggrandizement. In view of this consideration, this commonplace, dependent as it is on the prevailing reward system, could easily fail to support the believe that publication benefits teaching.

Of the commonplaces that have been examined, most can be true and yet none can justify the belief that publication benefits teaching. This suggests that these commonplaces have been joined with false premises, some possibilities of which have been suggested. These false premises must be prejudices that have allowed the "teacher-scholar" to gain its honored status.

In light of the evidence it is distressing that liberal arts colleges should celebrate and reward the "teacher-scholar" on the basis of these prejudices and the consequent false belief that publication benefits teaching. We have every right to expect that institutions dedicated to the importance of research would not make policies which cannot be justified by research. It is still more distressing to realize that even if the appropriate research had been done, and even if the

Michalak, Jr., "Why Doesn't Research Improve Teaching?" *Journal of Higher Education* 54 (1983): 145-163.

[10]Steven B. Sample, "Inherent Conflict Between Research and Education," *Educational Record* 53 (1972): 17-22.

[11]Kenneth Eugene Eble, *Professors as Teachers* (San Francisco: Jossey-Bass, 1972), 51.

evidence favored the belief that publication benefits teaching, it would nonetheless be mindless for liberal arts colleges to celebrate and reward publication on the ground of an apparent causal connection between research and teaching effectiveness. These colleges might just as well reward jogging if it should turn out that jogging seemed to benefit teaching effectiveness. Surely the reasonable response to the desire to further teaching effectiveness is to reward teaching effectiveness, not to reward some other activity whose causal relationship to teaching effectiveness is less than certain. We have every right to expect that institutions dedicated to the intelligent application of knowledge would respect the practical ideals they espouse.

I now turn to the second belief used to justify the exemplary status of the "teacher-scholar" in the liberal arts college. The belief that publication is one of the essential responsibilities of a teacher in the college is a belief not about a putative fact, but about the purpose of an institution. Its legitimacy, therefore, cannot be decided by an appeal to empirical evidence, but must be decided by an appeal to the ideal of liberal education.

In previous chapters I have argued that in our time the ideal of liberal education has been allowed to fall into obscurity. In other times a liberal education was respected as the highest form of education, a requisite for intellectual achievement, leadership, and culture. But today liberal education has lost its meaning, and the liberal arts colleges have "lost their sense of special purpose."[12]

With the institutional purpose of the liberal arts college obscure, not only do extrinsic interests structure the "hidden curriculum" of the college, but the content of the official curriculum is currently abandoned to a competition largely between student vocational interests and the professional career interests of teachers and administrators. The career interests of teachers are in turn largely determined by a reward system that expresses the educational institution's proclivity for a staff of recognized authorities or experts in the various "academic fields." Because the possession of expertise is regarded as power, prestige is attached to it. A college that can boast a faculty of recognized authorities will itself attain prestige, and this institutional prestige will be highly valued by those who regard the college primarily as a means for the fulfillment of various interests.

But the achievement of expertise requires credentials, products that give public certification of authority. The preferred products are scholarly articles and (by a strange exception) works of art.[13] Consequently, the college has an interest

---

[12]Earl J. McGrath, *The Graduate School and the Decline of Liberal Education* (New York: Bureau of Publications, Teachers College, Columbia University, 1959), v.

[13]Works of art are usually counted as publications--at least for fine arts teachers. Outside of giving evidence of expertise, it is hard to explain this curious practice. Why shouldn't fine arts teachers be required to publish scholarly articles like all other teachers? Or, to be consistent, why not encourage (say) chemistry teachers to produce (and sell) chemicals? Assuming that undergraduate students should not be forced to pay for additions to the world's collection of fine art, or to subsidize the income of fine arts teachers, these works of art must somehow benefit teaching. But how are they to do this, especially when these particular works are obviously not

in maintaining conditions that will facilitate faculty "productivity." These will include a separation of the curriculum and the extracurriculum, and specifications of such things as "teaching load" and "contact hours," all of which serve to distance and protect teachers from students. Also desirable is a research environment, including subtle "faculty development" programs, a compensation plan that rewards teachers for publications, a tenure and promotion committee that tends to attract people who love to judge "credentials," and, of course, incessant administrative rhetoric about the nobility of the "teacher-scholar." In addition, there must be travel grants and research facilities, including libraries and laboratories far in excess of anything needed by undergraduate liberal arts students. But the most important device for facilitating faculty "productivity" is the departmental administrative organization of the college.[14] The organization of the college into academic departments does more than facilitate administrative authority and efficiency. It seems to presuppose corresponding independent "departments of knowledge," "disciplines," or "academic fields," and to call for teachers who are experts in each of these. Courses can then be designed so as to appeal to student interests and to serve the faculty experts' need to cultivate their professional "fields." The "major" system reinforces the departmental system, encouraging undergraduate students to identify themselves as apprentice experts in a "field" of knowledge, even though most of them are without the vaguest conception of the organization, methods, or principles of knowledge.

The achievement of expertise also requires specialization, but specialization is impossible unless various "academic fields" can be distinguished and cultivated in relative independence of each other. This requires that the moral relevance and the theoretical presuppositions of the various "academic fields" be ignored. Thus, the specialized knowledge that is the possession of the expert must be theoretical, not normative, because the inclusion of normative concerns would compromise the independence of any "field" by making its conclusions contingent on more fundamental normative principles.[15] For example, if biology is to be studied so that human and social purposes are to be germane, this parvenu "academic field" (currently part of what is called "environmental studies") encroaches on political science and ethics, and can only produce conclusions that are conditional on the resolution of the fundamental problems of these other "fields." Moreover, even

essential to the creation, appreciation, or criticism of fine arts? Are they necessary for the teaching of artistic skills--assuming that the teaching of such skills is an appropriate objective of a liberal education? If so, what's to be done with a teacher of painting who loses his right arm?

[14]For a valuable analysis of the deleterious effect of "disciplinary professionalism" on undergraduate education, see: Frederick Stirton Weaver, "Academic Disciplines and Undergraduate Liberal Arts Education, *Liberal Education* 67 (1981): 151-165. Weaver argues that with the rise of the "culture of professionalism" in the late nineteenth century "academics managed to define competence, merit, and specialization in terms appropriate for professionalizing research rather than teaching."

[15]In the chapter of *Being and Time* entitled, "The Worldhood of the World," Heidegger provides an elaborate demonstration of the practical presuppositions of theoretical awareness.

for knowledge abstracted from its normative implications, and especially from its bearing on the values and moral obligations of the individual student, it is essential to specialization that the knowledge be further restricted to theories that can be considered in abstraction from their logical and ontological foundations. For example, an expert in American colonial history is not expected to be knowledgeable about the moral significance of this history, least of all for any particular student, and is not expected to be an authority on the history of England, much less on European history or historiography, and even less on the logical and philosophical principles of historiography. Through this process of isolating theories from their moral implications and their theoretical principles, numerous specialized, independent "academic fields" can be distinguished. The "knowledge" that is "produced" by the cultivation of these "fields" is of necessity morally sterilized and theoretically compartmentalized. It is "objective," "factual," "scientific."

When "knowledge" is thus conceived as a product, it is understood as discrete, specialized theories or bodies of information, which can be stored in experts' heads, libraries, and floppy disks. It then can be reproduced in discursive argument forms, utilizing the demonstrative methods of formal logic. Education becomes a kind of manufacturing process for the production of this "knowledge."[16]

In these circumstances teachers have a double task: They must engage in scholarly research and publication in order to produce assumption-free and value-free specialized "knowledge," and thus be certified as experts, and they also must reproduce this "knowledge" in lectures and texts for tuition-paying apprentice experts. Obviously, the exemplary teacher is the familiar "teacher-scholar."

If we turn from what is popularly called liberal education to liberal education as it has been conceived in this book, we face an astonishing contrast between the real and the ideal. According to our concept, liberal education is not an instrument to be used by students to gain entrance into a social class, to prepare for a vocation, or to satisfy an "interest." Even less is it an instrument to enable teachers and administrators to advance their careers. Least of all is it an instrument to serve the interest of other individuals or institutions, whether these be those of a business or a party, a church or a state. As has been argued, the aim of liberal education is not to satisfy any interest, no matter how esteemed, but to enable students to discover and satisfy interests that are worth satisfying. Since the discovery of what interests are worth satisfying requires the development in each student of the capacity and inclination for rational action, a liberal education properly has this as its ideal.

As has also been argued, this definition of the ideal of liberal education is in accord with those classical definitions that summarize the aim of liberal education

---

[16]One author has suggested that the "business model" of the university is responsible for the insidious idea that "the university has a definite product, viz., knowledge . . . ." Robert N. McCauley, "The Business of the University," *Liberal Education* 68 (1982): 33.

in the word, "wisdom," and that stress that liberal education is not a means to any end, but an end-in-itself. It is the most important of all human enterprises because it cannot be justified by any other one, but is itself required for the justification of all other ones.

When the aim of liberal education is understood to be the development of students with the capacity and inclination for rational action, the liberal arts college has a very unique purpose, one that makes the college qualitatively different from all other educational institutions. Unlike these other institutions, the purpose of the liberal arts college is not to enable students to pursue their idiosyncratic interests, but to enable them to pursue their moral obligations. Because of this the ideal liberal arts college is a specialized institution.

However, unlike most of our current institutions of higher education, the ideal liberal arts college is not an institution for the pursuit of specialized knowledge. It does not seek deductive theories or bodies of information that are detached from their moral implications and their theoretical presuppositions. Rather it seeks universals, or "generalized" knowledge, the kind of knowledge that comprehends the principles that ground thought and action, and thus provide insight into what is and what ought to be.[17]   This means that the college's educational program should not consist of a collection of elective courses that reproduce sterilized and compartmentalized theories, but should be a coherent, comprehensive program for the development of theoretical and practical knowledge, together with the requisite skills of rational thought and action (the liberal arts) and those qualities of character that are prerequisites for the achievement of this knowledge and these skills.   Thus, the ideal liberal arts college is properly described as a specialized institution for the pursuit of generalized knowledge.[18]

---

[17]The distinction formulated here in terms of "specialized knowledge" and "generalized knowledge" is familiar in philosophy. For Plato the terms are *dianoia* and *noesis*; for Aristotle, *episteme* and *sophos*; for Kant, *verstand* and *vernunft*; for Heidegger, *rechnendes Denken* and *besinnliches Denken*. When this distinction is ignored, the inherent conflict between teaching and publishing is missed. This error is illustrated by criticism of Steven B. Sample's "Inherent Conflict Between Research and Education," *Educational Record* 53 (1972): 17-22, where the critics fail to distinguish between the love of knowledge and the love of wisdom. They write: "To teach is to educate (*e-ducere*), to lead or draw outward, to foster within the student a love of knowledge . . . . Hence, most teachers are *doctors* (teachers) of the love of knowledge (*philosophos*)."[sic] John Harold Wilson and Robin Scott Wilson, "The Teaching-Research Controversy," *Educational Record* 53 (1972): 322.

[18]"What we want is specialized institutions and unspecialized men." Robert Maynard Hutchins, *The University of Utopia* (Chicago: The University of Chicago Press, 1964), 46. Daniel Bell has made this same point: "As between the secondary school, with its emphasis upon primary skills and factual data, and the graduate or professional school, whose necessary concern is with specialization and technique, the distinctive function of the [liberal arts] college is to deal with the grounds of knowledge: not *what* one knows, but *how* one knows. The college can be the unique place where students acquire self-consciousness, historical consciousness, methodological consciousness." Daniel Bell, *The Reforming of General Education: The Columbia College Experience in Its National Setting* (New York: Columbia University Press, 1966), 8.

Unlike most of today's colleges and universities, however, the ideal liberal arts college is not an institution to produce value-free and assumption-free knowledge to establish expertise and to satisfy the interests of apprentice experts. Its purpose is not to produce, process, store, or distribute data or theories that have their own being and value independent of any student. On the contrary, its purpose is to develop generalized knowledge or insight, the kind of knowledge which cannot be isolated from individual human beings.[19] This means that liberal education is an institution to "e-duce" people from ignorance and immorality to wisdom, not a factory to "pro-duce" specialist knowledge.[20] Thus, as we have argued, the ideal liberal arts college is a specialized institution for the pursuit of generalized knowledge for the development of wise people.

Finally, unlike most of our current liberal arts colleges, the ideal liberal arts college does not require teachers who, through the agency of an impersonal objectivity, produce departmentalized knowledge for experts and expertise, and reproduce this knowledge for apprentice experts. On the contrary, the ideal liberal arts college requires teachers who use the subjective devices of dialectic and rhetoric, and the combined appeal of intellect, character, and emotion, to persuade people to avoid ignorance and immorality, and to seek wisdom.[21] Thus, the liberal arts college is a specialized institution for the pursuit of generalized knowledge for the development of wise people through the agency of human subjectivity.

Once the liberal arts college is conceived in this way it obviously follows that the exemplary teacher for this institution is not the "teacher-scholar," one whose thought and action must be divided between teaching and publishing, but rather the full-time, uncompromised, liberal education-dedicated teacher.

The Myth and Its Patrons

The assumption that the ideal teacher for the liberal arts college is the "teacher-scholar" is a myth in the sense that it is a belief that is given uncritical acceptance by the members of a group and is used to justify existing interests and institutions.

---

[19]Joseph Tussman has put this succinctly: "The university is the academic community organized for the pursuit of knowledge . . . . The liberal arts college is a different enterprise. It does not assault or extend the frontiers of knowledge. It has a different mission. It cultivates human understanding. The mind of a person, not the body of knowledge, is its central concern . . . ." Joseph Tussman, *Experiment at Berkeley* (New York: Oxford University Press, 1969), xiii-xiv.

[20]"First-rate research faculty are primarily interested in using people, including themselves, to advance the state of knowledge, while first-rate educators are primarily interested in using knowledge to further the intellectual development of people." Steven B. Sample, "Inherent Conflict Between Research and Education," 19.

[21]Edward J. Shoben, Jr., has developed this contrast between teaching for research and teaching for education as the contrast between the "ethic of objectivity" and the "ethic of concern." Edward J. Shoben, Jr., "Departments vs. Education," in Oakley Gordon, ed., *Profess or Perish: Proceedings, Pacific Northwest Conference on Higher Education* (Corvallis, Oreg.:Oregon State

As we have seen, the myth of the "teacher-scholar" is rationalized by a web of false beliefs. Chief among these are the empirically mistaken belief that publication benefits teaching and the conceptually mistaken belief that publication is one of the essential responsibilities of the college teacher. These false beliefs are in turn reinforced by various true (but irrelevant) and relevant (but false) commonplaces and prejudices.

These commonplaces and prejudices show that the myth of the "teacher-scholar" serves many influential patrons. It appeals to those who fail to understand and appreciate the unique purpose of liberal education, and who therefore think of the liberal arts college either as a prep school for graduate study, or as just another institution of higher education, and thus one that exists for the satisfaction of various academic consumer interests. It appeals to those who think of education on the model of a business for the production and reproduction of an infinite variety of specialized scholarly and artistic works. It appeals to those vocationalists who view the student as a career-identified apprentice expert. And finally, it appeals to those who prefer to understand themselves as princely authorities who hold dominion over a province in the realm of knowledge, those who covet the publicity, prestige, and material rewards of "professional recognition," those who find solace and security in abstract theory, those who are frustrated by the uncertainties and enervations of cross-generational caring relationships with adolescents, and those who are caused unbearable anxiety by the fact that the task of the teacher is not the accumulation of vita credits through the "production " of "knowledge," but the expenditure of the self in the "e-duction" of people.[22]

The Legacy of the Myth

The myth of the "teacher-scholar" causes incalculable harm to liberal education. It betrays those who understand the importance of college teaching, and who have chosen to make this their life's work, by giving currency to the doctrine that "teaching is not enough," and that what really counts is publication, publicity, and prestige. In doing so it tries to bond careers that are incompatible, careers that have conflicting goals, that must appeal to disparate audiences, and that require contrasting skills. As we have seen, the goal of the scholar is the production of specialist theory, while the goal of the teacher in a program of

University Press, 1968.)

[22]It also appeals to those who believe that publication, unlike teaching, provides an objective measure of faculty performance. See: Thomas W. Martin and K. J. Berry, "The Teaching-Research Dilemma: Its Sources in the University Setting," *Journal of Higher Education* 40 (1969): 691-703. The psychical attractions of research are candidly expressed by Hans A. Schmitt in "Teaching and Research," *Journal of Higher Education* 36 (1965): 424: "After many a lecture I rush back to my office, close the door firmly behind me (unless I have scheduled office hours), and pounce on my microfilm reader in the pursuit of escape and solace through research." The psychopathic possibilities of the research personality are mercilessly revealed by Nietzsche in *The Genealogy of Morals* and devastatingly parodied by Sartre in novels such as *Nausea*.

liberal education is the development of value-oriented people; the scholar must address an adult, professional peer group, while the teacher must appeal to adolescent, unspecialized undergraduates; and the scholar must rely primarily on the technical vocabulary and the objective devices of logic, while the teacher in a program of liberal education must rely primarily on the subjective devices of dialectic and rhetoric, and especially on the persuasive force of individual character and personality.[23] The consequences of this devaluation of teaching are predictable: Even for those of great talent and dedication, teaching is eventually compromised to provide the resources for publication.[24] That this is so is suggested by the language of the academy: "Professors speak of teaching *loads* and research *opportunities*, never the reverse."[25] The student, originally a client, eventually becomes either a mere means or an obstacle to the career aspirations of the teacher. In the end the quality of college teaching is significantly impaired.

Not only does the myth of the "teacher-scholar" harm the quality of college teaching, but it has similarly unfortunate consequences for scholarship. While there are always a few well-publicized exceptions, relatively few first-rate scholarly and artistic works are produced by the "teacher-scholars" of liberal arts colleges. Most publications coming out of these colleges consist in reworked doctoral dissertations, book reviews, and articles on provincial and pedagogical issues. While this fact is often obscured by pride, professional courtesy, and public relations hype, most college teachers are fully aware that most of what is published by their colleagues and themselves is trivial and would never see print if it were not for a policy that hires teachers but pays scholars.[26] This situation is certainly no reflection on the ability or dedication of those whose careers and lives are entrapped by the myth of the "teacher-scholar." These individuals are not only forced to try to adapt to a career with conflicting goals, disparate audiences, and contrasting requisite skills, but they are normally compelled to labor on their scholarly projects without similarly specialized colleagues or graduate assistants, and without adequate research funds, libraries, laboratories, and other facilities, while, at the same time, they must meet the exhausting demands of a form of teaching requiring close relationships with students, and involvement in an academic community.[27] In these circumstances what is

---

[23]"To discover and to teach are distinct functions; they are also distinct gifts, and are not commonly found united in the same person. . . ." John Henry Newman, *The Idea of a University Defined and Illustrated* (Notre Dame, Ind.: Notre Dame University Press, 1982), xiii.

[24]"In the main, the overwhelming majority of faculty members attend conscientiously to their assigned classroom responsibilities, but they seldom invest in their instructional efforts the intellectual boldness or the imagination that they give to their scholarly pursuits . . . ." Shoben, "Departments vs. Education," 10.

[25]*Integrity in the College Curriculum: A Report to the Academic Community* (Washington, D.C.: American Association of Colleges, 1985), 10.

[26]One recent, up-front critic has dared to say in print what everyone knows but no one says: "I took the trouble to look at some of the articles in the *Faculty Directory of Publications*, and nearly all of them are nonsense . . . ." John Madsen, "Education--A Horse on You," *Educational Leadership* 37 (1980): 513.

remarkable is not that the scholarly productivity of the college teacher should be so modest, but that there should be any at all.

The myth of the "teacher-scholar" is injurious to liberal education not only because it compromises teaching and scholarship, but also because it contributes to a misconception within and without educational institutions of the enterprise of liberal education. When the "teacher-scholar" becomes an ideal for the liberal arts college, then the development of experts takes priority over the development of wise people, the production and processing of specialist information becomes more important than the achievement of common knowledge, the liberal arts, and moral insight, and liberal education is understood as merely another institution for the satisfaction of the uneducated interests of educational consumers, rather than an institution to develop in individuals the capacity and inclination for rational action. As a result, the nature and pre-emptive need for liberal education are obscured.

Besides diverting college teachers from their teaching responsibility and diverting liberal education from its ideal, the myth of the "teacher-scholar" exacerbates the already high cost of this education. Because the "teacher-scholar" is required to publish, and because publication requires research time, research laboratories, and research libraries, the cost of education is substantially increased. This means that those students and their families whose only need is quality teaching are being charged a premium so that teachers can teach only part-time and make gratuitous and mostly trivial contributions to knowledge and the arts. Every year more of our liberal arts colleges price themselves and their students' families into financial crises because of this unconscionable policy.

Demythologization

If the case has now been made that the ideal teacher for the liberal arts college is not the "teacher-scholar" but the full-time, uncompromised, liberal education-oriented teacher, it remains to ask what can be done to free the college from the myth of the "teacher-scholar," and, in consequence, to significantly improve the quality of college teaching. At least three actions are imperative.

1. The radical difference between the liberal arts college and the university must be made clear.[28]   Students, teachers, educational administrators, and the

---

[27]"It is probably true that a practicing academic can go through life without ever experiencing serious conflict between his research and his educational duties, providing he is content with no more than mediocre attainments in either area. However, if he seeks to achieve excellence, a conflict between teaching and research is inevitable. The intense concentration necessary to research is incompatible with a three-day-a-week, four-hour-a-day teaching schedule. Yet it is precisely this sort of concentration over a period of years which is required to achieve a significant research result." Steven B. Sample, "Inherent Conflict Between Research and Education," 18.

[28]Mervyn L. Cadwallader makes this point in calling for an "academic counterrevolution" to wrest control of the liberal arts college away from its domination by the research-oriented universities. Mervyn L. Cadwallader, "A Manifesto: The Case for an Academic

general public must be made to understand that the uniqueness and priority of liberal education require that the college be freed from its current bondage to the educational consumer orientation of the university, university college, and graduate school. This task should be facilitated by the historical insight that the liberal arts college has not always been so misunderstood and so dishonored as it is today.[29] In other times the college's unique mission was recognized and respected, and in consequence, the college was understood to be radically different than the university.

2. The liberal arts college must divorce teaching and scholarship.[30] Students, teachers, educational administrators, and the general public must realize that the liberal education of undergraduate students and the advancement of the frontiers of knowledge are for the most part incompatible educational objectives. They must be made to understand that publication harms college teaching insofar as it encourages college teachers to divide their professional lives and loyalties, to become part-time teachers and part-time scholars, and, thus, to compromise their responsibility to their students. This task should be aided by the realization that the "teacher-scholar" is in truth a myth that serves the adventitious interests of various patrons, but does not serve the ideal of liberal education.

3. The liberal arts college must create an environment that will restore teaching to a position of unsurpassed importance and dignity. College teachers must be persuaded that they are not responsible for adding to society's store of knowledge or collection of fine art, but are instead responsible for the vastly more important task of developing wise people.

The Myth of the Teacher-Administrator

Most often the ideal college teacher is assumed to be the "teacher-scholar." Only slightly less often is this ideal taken to be the "teacher-administrator." The latter is a person who holds both faculty responsibilities for teaching and administrative responsibilities for the execution of administrative policy. The "teacher-administrator" may carry a full, a partial, or no teaching load, and simultaneously act as a member of an administratively appointed committee, a chair of an academic department, a program director, a dean, or even a college president. Most college teachers and most of the general public apparently find nothing untoward about this ideal. In any case, it is obvious that the contemporary liberal arts college is staffed by many "teacher-administrators." Since the concern of this chapter is to identify the ideal college teacher, it is

---

Counterrevolution," *Liberal Education* 68 (1982): 403-420.

[29]For an overview of this history, see: Shoben, "Departments vs. Education."

[30]William Arrowsmith argues eloquently that teaching and research should be divorced because they cannot be reconciled except by making teaching "the lackey of scholarship." William Arrowsmith, "The Future of Teaching," in Calvin B. T. Lee, ed., *Improving College Teaching* (Washington, D. C.: American Council on Education, 1967), 57-71.

necessary that this familiar ideal be carefully and critically examined. The first step in this project is to reconstruct the arguments that constitute the rationale for this ideal.

The Rationale for the "Teacher-Administrator"

1. The ideal of the "teacher-administrator" can be defended on the ground that college administrating is simply the mature stage of a career that begins with teaching. New teachers start as instructors or assistant professors. The best of these are promoted to associate professors; the best of these associate professors are promoted to full professors; the best of the full professors are chosen to be department chairpersons or program directors; the best of the department chairpersons or program directors are chosen to be deans; and the best of the deans are chosen to be presidents. According to this view, teachers and administrators are best understood as "educators," and the only significant difference between an instructor and a college president is that a president has more power, and thus is better able to bring about the educational results that both the instructor and the president seek. Their ends are the same; only their means are different. Thus, "teacher-administrators" are simply better able than teachers to achieve educational efficacy. Teachers are nascent administrators, and "teacher-administrators" are empowered teachers.

2. Even if teaching and administrating are not held to be simply two stages of a single career, the ideal of the "teacher-administrator" can still be defended on the ground that college teaching is a necessary prerequisite for college administrating. College administrators should be, or should have been, teachers because the knowledge, skills, and experience of teachers are essential to administrative success. These administrators need to understand the philosophy of education, the history of education, the psychology of management, the politics of educational leadership, the economics of higher education, and so on. Since such knowledge and skills are the stock in trade of teachers, those who would be effective college administrators must have these teacher resources. Coupled with this assumption is the additional assumption that, since teaching is thought to be the "primary business" of the college, any would-be administrator should have an intimate understanding of teaching. Just as it is said that business executives should have had some experience on the assembly line, and that generals should have had some experience on the front line, so it is said that college chief executive officers, at least, should have had some experience in the classroom. This experience will enable them to better understand the needs of teachers, and therefore to be more effective as educational leaders and managers.

For practical purposes college chief executive officers must not only possess important kinds of knowledge, skill, and experience, but they must also possess the credentials that attest to this possession. Thus, college presidents and deans are expected to hold doctoral degrees. Additional degrees, such as honorary degrees, will further attest to their possession of the essential resources. Further attestation will be provided by the practice of some college presidents and deans of continuing to do some research or to teach an occasional course in addition to their administrative duties. Inevitably it is said that by doing this these administrators "keep in touch" with their discipline and with teaching. This may be true, but more importantly, these actions verify these administrators' credentials as teachers and scholars, and thus enhance their status with their faculties. It is hardly surprising, then, that the chief executive officers of colleges are normally recruited from among those who possess the resources and credentials of the college teacher.

3. Even if it could be maintained that college administrative officers do not need the resources and credentials of college teachers, the necessity of the "teacher-administrator" can still be argued on purely pragmatic grounds. This argument begins with the recognition of the fact that the management of a college and a faculty is an exceedingly difficult art. Prima facie evidence of this lies in the fact that the average incumbency of a college president is now less than five years. One reason that the art of college management is so difficult is that the values of college teachers and the values of college administrators are in endemic conflict. College teachers are properly idealistic and preoccupied with questions of truth and value. As a consequence, they are likely to prize criticism and individual autonomy, and to be suspicious of authority and organizational loyalty. Administrators, in contrast, are by nature pragmatic and give priority to the achievement of practical efficacy. As a consequence, they are likely to prize authority and organizational loyalty, and to be suspicious of criticism and individual autonomy. Because of their values, college teachers are inclined to be intolerant of what they see as administrative anti-intellectualism and the arbitrary exercise of power. Administrators, on the other hand, are inclined to be intolerant of what they see as teacher intellectual arrogance and penchant for nit-picking criticism. This contrast between the values of teachers and administrators is a guarantee of endless intramural conflict. But perhaps the most important reason why college management is such a difficult art is because college administrators ordinarily do not have, or cannot exercise, the kind of power possessed by business executives. The contemporary liberal arts college has developed in such a way that a line and staff organization is not likely to be managerially successful.

Because of the difficulty of the art of college management, and in particular, because of the constraints on the exercise of power by college administrative officers, these officers have often turned to more indirect and covert managerial strategies. The strategy that has evolved as the most effective current solution to this problem is faculty co-optation. A faculty is co-opted when administrators are able to persuade a critical number of teachers to adopt administrative values and allegiances. Crucial to this process is the deputizing of teachers as administrators. This begins when a dean is installed and vested with ex officio faculty status. This is followed by the administrative selection of associate deans, academic program directors, and departmental or committee chairs. These appointees already have faculty status or are given faculty status as part of the terms of their appointment. The process continues even further through various "courtesy" or "faculty by exception" appointments. The result is a proliferation of "teacher-administrators."

The administrative bureaucracy that results from this process overtly or covertly structures teacher values and practices. This is achieved by a variety of seemingly innocuous devices: (1) The faculty recruitment and tenure system--especially through the use of explicit or implicit tenure quotas--advances administrative power by typically maintaining between 30 to 50 percent of a faculty on a probationary status, unprotected by tenure. (2) The compensation system--especially with the addition of a so-called merit pay system--advances administrative power by providing economic rewards for those who are supportive of administrative policies, and by providing economic penalties for those who are "uncooperative" or "difficult." (3) The informal reward system--including non-monetary awards, "media exposure," privileges, and perks--also reinforces administrative allegiances and values.

The co-optation of a faculty is even more effectively sustained and extended by the largely invisible power structure that is generated by an administrative bureaucracy. For instance, in an environment in which college administration may be looked upon as the mature stage of a teaching career, large numbers of teachers learn to adopt modes of behavior that are in conformity with the values of administrators, not the values of teachers. The co-optation of a faculty cannot be measured by the number of teachers who serve in full or part-time administrative positions. Rather, as if by a hidden hand, almost the entire faculty can be co-opted. This happens because even those who have no administrative authority or responsibility are subtly drawn into conformity by the rituals, myths, mores, and policies cultivated by the bureaucracy. One of the most effective of these is the administrative practice of recruiting new administrators from among the teaching faculty. This periodic "raiding" of the faculty for ambitious, popular, and talented teachers seasonally energizes the administration and seasonally enervates the faculty. In time the faculty is encumbered by a coterie of teachers who would rather be administrators. These ambitious "teacher-administrators" unconsciously, or secretly, or even openly covet positions of administrative power. The effects of the bureaucratic power structure can be observed even in those who have little interest in administrative roles but who nevertheless modify their values and behavior because they are subject to the influence of friends and others who are beholden to, or threatened by, this structure.

As we illustrated in concrete detail in Chapter 4, the effect of the administrative co-optation of a faculty is covert, but pervasive and substantial. Administrative values are reinforced, administrative influence expands, and faculty values and influence contract. The senior administrative officers, few in number, are augmented by surrogate administrative members who are nominally teachers, while the faculty, apparently large in number, is attenuated by the inclusion of those who are teachers in name but administrators in practice.

In case this account of the phenomenon of teacher co-optation may seem fanciful, it is sobering to read the kind of advice that is now commonly provided to academic administrators by professional management consultants. In an article previously noted, two consultants advise what they call "the senior management" of colleges that if they want to introduce "change" into their "industry," they will have to exercise "normative power" over their "workers."[31] This will require "persuasive, suggestive, or manipulative efforts," and will take the form of various "reward systems." By the use of these "reward systems" administrators will be able to "manage rewards and recognition" to produce "desired behaviors" in teachers. This entire process is openly, unapologetically, and patronizingly called a "faculty development program."

The ideal of the "teacher-administrator" surreptitiously licenses teachers to pass as faculty members but to act as administrators. It thus facilitates the triumph of the strategy of faculty co-optation. To be sure, this prescription for the co-optation of a faculty will seem cynical and Machiavellian to some. But to others it will appear only pragmatic and necessary if a faculty and a college are to be successfully managed.

A Critique of the Rationale

Unquestionably, many people believe that the ideal teacher for the liberal arts college is what we have called the "teacher-administrator." However, the cogency of this belief obviously depends on the soundness of the rationale that justifies it. This rationale now deserves critical scrutiny.

1. One of the arguments that appears to give plausibility to the ideal of the "teacher-administrator" rests on the assumption that administrating is simply the mature stage of a teaching career. On this assumption, both teachers and administrators are properly identified as "educators." They differ only in that they represent different stages of one career, and have different means available at each stage. Teachers are limited to what can be done in a single classroom, while administrators may have the power to create entire programs and to affect the work of many teachers. Thus, teachers and administrators are understood to have different means, but to share a common end.

This argument is prima facie suspect because some respected teachers prefer to teach and to avoid administrative activities. While this preference may be discounted as being the preference of those who are reclusive, unambitious, or administratively inept, it cannot be discounted for those who are not reclusive, unambitious, or administratively inept, and who still prefer to have only teaching responsibilities.

[31]Richard P. Chait and James Gueths, "A Framework for Faculty Development," *Change* (May/June 1981): 30-33.

The argument that teaching and administrating are simply two stages of one career founders on the assumption that teachers and administrators differ in means but share a common end. There are compelling reasons for the contrary assumption that within the liberal arts college, teaching and administrating are really diametrically opposed in both means and ends. Ideally, college teachers rely on rational means to achieve an end that is rationally grounded. They seek to provide a program of education consisting partly of courses in which they "profess"--that is, "offer" arguments which they ground in appropriate rational premises. Their collective appeal is an effort to persuade students that thought and action should be guided by reason, not by authority in any of its latent or blatant forms. In contrast, administrators rely on authority to achieve ends that are fixed by authority. Acting under the direction of their governing boards or under their own initiatives, administrators provide a college with leadership or management. They try to shape the goals and values and influence the behavior of "their" faculties; they initiate and supervise the various educational programs of "their" colleges. Thus, the difference between the teacher and the administrator is not an insignificant difference. Rather, it marks two very different careers. But these careers are such that, if they are in any way merged, teaching is likely to suffer. This is because for most people the demands of authority are more compelling than the demands of reason. If administrators and the administrative bureaucracy dominate a college, then there is little hope that teachers can make their case on behalf of reason.

2. Another of the arguments that appears to provide some justification for the ideal of the "teacher-administrator" is based on the assumption that teaching is a prerequisite to effective administrating. If administrators are to manage teachers, so the argument goes, the knowledge, skills, and experience possessed by teachers, together with the appropriate credentials, are essential to their success. Thus, it is incumbent on chief administrative officers, at least, to be, or to have been, teachers.

The problem with this argument is not with the assumption that the effective management of teachers requires administrators who have certain kinds of knowledge, skill, experience, and credentials. The problem lies with a deeper-level assumption: the assumption that teachers should be managed or led by administrators. According to this assumption, all authority in a college is properly vested in a governing board established by a corporate charter. This governing board is charged with the general control and management of the affairs of the corporation. The chief administrative officer is appointed by the board, and is responsible to the board for the execution of the policies established by the board. The president, in turn, may be given wide-ranging executive authority. In a typical set of corporate by-laws this authority includes the "management, discipline and educational direction" of the college, the "direction" of educational policy and programs, rights as the "curator of the laboratories, museums and scientific collections," and actions as the "head" of the faculty, including the right to "select, appoint, and promote" all teachers.

At issue in this assumption that teachers should be managed by administrators is the larger question of the proper role of administrators in a liberal arts college. Those who are sympathetic to the ideal of the "teacher-administrator" seem to assume that a college is like a business. According to this model, a college has a product (educated students) that is produced by workers (teachers) who must be managed by corporate officers (administrators).

The business model is not an appropriate model for the liberal arts college. The college should not be understood as a place where products are produced, where workers produce these products, or where managers manage workers. A liberal arts college does not require a lay governing board or a professional administrator to define educational goals and to "develop" workers and "manage" an assembly line that will produce certain outcomes. The goals and methods of liberal education are not properly determined by managerial authority and handed down to obedient workers. This is because the liberal arts college must institutionalize criticism of all authority. Certainly the ideal of liberal education needs to be repeatedly interpreted, and the various means for the realization of this ideal need to be developed and supervised. But these responsibilities properly belong to a special cadre of people who have been rigorously trained and carefully selected for these purposes, and who are organized and regulated by a constitution which maximizes the role of reason and minimizes the role of authority. The ideal of liberal education is properly determined, and its pursuit is properly supervised, by a constitutionally established collegium--that is, a guild of doctors of philosophy united as colleagues committed to the rule of reason. The task of the governing board and the administration is to provide constitutional oversight, financial supervision, and logistical support for the work of the collegium. Their task should not be to lead, manage, or manipulate, but to facilitate and support. The ideal of the "teacher-administrator" confuses and conflates these responsibilities, and by doing so, ignores the fact that college teaching and administrating are inevitably in conflict. The acceptance of this ideal permits administrative hegemony over teachers and teaching, and in consequence, constrains criticism and thus adulterates liberal education.

3. The third argument that might appear to provide justification for the ideal of the "teacher-administrator" turns on the assumption that the effective management of a college requires the administrative co-optation of a faculty. Co-optation is regarded as necessary because teachers are resistant to the exercise of administrative authority. Given this situation, college management can be effective only if the college is structured as a bureaucracy and a critical number of teachers are deputized as administrators.

There can be no challenge to the belief that co-optation is an effective way of managing a college faculty. But what should be challenged once again is the assumption that a college faculty should be managed by a lay board or an appointed administrator. If in fact a faculty is so managed, then educational ends and means are imposed on it by the authority of the board or the administrator. But when the college's ends and means are determined by authority, then they are no longer subject to criticism. In particular, the college's "teacher-administrators" are not able to act as genuine teachers because their responsibilities as administrators compromise their responsibilities as teachers, resulting in the college's inability to act as the instrument of liberal education.

The Myth and Its Patrons

The assumption that the ideal teacher for the liberal arts college is the "teacher-administrator" is a myth in the sense that it is a belief that is given uncritical acceptance by the members of a group and is used to justify existing interests and institutions.

As we have seen in the preceding analysis, the myth of the "teacher-administrator" is rationalized by a set of uncritically accepted assumptions. The examination of these assumptions shows that this myth is sustained because it has a strong appeal for many teachers and administrators:

1. The myth obviously appeals to many teachers' natural but often repressed desire for power. This desire may be intensified by the teachers' exceptional talents and idealism. It may be further intensified by the long period of latency imposed by a doctoral program. The median age of those who receive a doctorate in the physical sciences is now 30.2 years, and 35.7 years for those in the arts and humanities.[32] After receiving their doctoral degrees, these new, but almost middle-aged teachers begin the sometimes prolonged search for tenure-track positions. If, and when, this is successful, they then begin the long and laborious process of achieving tenure and of progressing through the academic ranks. Early on in their careers these teachers will be presented with numerous opportunities for participation in college administration. They will be expected to perform departmental chores and to serve on faculty committees. Those who satisfy their superiors in these roles are rewarded with more important administrative assignments, by promotion, and by increased pay and perks. Many teachers, after years of graduate school poverty and humility, find administrative power, social status, and economic benefits exhilarating. It is not difficult for these new teachers to furtively regard themselves as potential committee or departmental chairs. In an immodest moment they may even imagine themselves as deans or college presidents, exercising considerable power, solemnly leading the convocation processions, and ensconced in historic homes with their proud spouses and bright children, able at last to implement their own programs and to impose their own ideals on their less able "colleagues." It is at this inopportune instant that a teacher dies and is surreptitiously reborn as a "teacher-administrator."

These new "teacher-administrators" must immediately face a new challenge. They must quickly learn the skills essential to survival in the academic bureaucracy. Suitable mentors must be found, and strategic friendships must be formed. Almost inevitably these needs will induce the new "teacher-

---

[32]*Chronicle of Higher Education* (6 March 1991): A13.

administrators" to consciously or unconsciously assimilate the perspectives and values of their superiors and mentors. Each new career advancement will reinforce these adopted perspectives and values. Power, status, and salary become the symbols of the good life. Subtly the big chair at the head of the table, generous media exposure, salary differentials, a big office with credenzas and Oriental rugs will somehow begin to make a real difference. Simultaneously the old graduate school virtues will become déclassé, and political sympathies will perceptibly shift to the right--at least on issues of college government. Thus, the ideal of the "teacher-administrator" appeals to many basic, irrepressible faculty instincts.

2. The myth of the "teacher-administrator" also appeals to administrators. This appeal derives from the administrative realization that effective power can only be achieved by faculty co-optation, and that the myth of the "teacher-administrator" facilitates this co-optation by licensing the administrative infiltration and subversion of the faculty. In this way, administrative careerism, like faculty careerism, provides sustenance for the myth of the "teacher-administrator."

The Legacy of the Myth

The myth of the "teacher-administrator" has devastating consequences for liberal education. It corrupts those who alone are capable of inspiriting this institution.

1. The myth represses criticism, and helps to create a repressive academic environment. This occurs because the myth facilitates the co-optation of the faculty by admitting as faculty members a critical number of teachers whose faculty responsibilities are compromised by administrative duties. As a result of their administrative duties, these "teacher-administrators" inevitably have divided loyalties. Having such divided loyalties, they are not able to engage in the unrestricted criticism of ideas and ideals that is the essential requisite for a vigorous and effective faculty, and for the success of liberal education. Instead, Socratic criticism is repressed as something that is "negative" and "counter-productive." Teachers who practice it, following the model of Socrates in the *Apology*, are condemned as impious. Depending on the situation, they are variously discredited as meddlers, malcontents, eccentrics, pests, paranoids, manic-depressives, trouble-makers, old curmudgeons, young Turks, opponents of change, radicals, reactionaries, mad dogs, traitors, deadwood, etc.

The growth of a repressive environment is a largely invisible process. Even a "faculty development" program is seen as benign. Time and again, like fish repeatedly taking to the same lure, teachers buy into such programs without a trace of suspicion or a murmur of protest. Paradoxically enough, those who do so include teachers who have strong personal and political commitments to the elimination of repression and the empowerment of marginalized people. Teachers who are, or who aspire to be, "teacher-administrators" are not likely to experience repression themselves, and they are not likely to recognize it in any of its subtle forms. Their sensitivity is suppressed by their undisciplined ambition. Where others see manipulation, they see nothing but the ghosts of petulant or paranoiac imaginations. They come to see a teacher's opposition to the exercise of administrative power as a "personality defect" that requires therapy or punishment. Since the models of the ideal teacher, and the root assumptions that justify these models are so disparate, any effort to try to convince a "teacher-administrator" that repressive practices are taking place will be as challenging as trying to convince a Boy Scout that the Twelve Scout Laws are all synonyms for obedience.

A repressive academic environment gives legitimacy to a special academic structure of authority--a power structure. The prevailing view is that the power structure of a college devolves from its board. In some cases these boards may themselves be in the effective control of a single person or a clique. A standard Marxist variation on this view is that, since the interest of the boards and their leaders are expressions of class interests, the power structure of these institutions devolves from the interests of the ruling class.[33] Another view takes note of the fact that most college boards are largely honorary, and exert power only intermittently and indirectly through their selection of the chief administrative officer. Since the chief administrative officer is typically given considerable authority and leeway in the exercise of power, this view understands power as devolving in practice from the chief administrative officer.

It is not enough to explain the power structure of a college as devolving from governing boards or administrative officers. A power structure is not adequately explained by a table of organization or a chain of command. As Foucault has pointed out in his analysis of predatory power in human organizations, power is not adequately explained by looking at the level of conscious intention or decision. Rather a power structure must be understood by looking at the level where "power is completely invested in real and effective practices."[34] The exercise of power in a college takes place not so much through deliberate administrative actions as through subtle and diffuse forces that are in play at every level of the administrative bureaucracy. The authority exercised in these bureaucracies is not so often overt personal authority but what Erich Fromm has called "the anonymous authority of persuasion and suggestion."[35] Even more effective is the institutionalization of conduct. When this has been effective, coercion is seldom necessary. "Most of the time, conduct will occur 'spontaneously' within institutionally set channels."[36] In most contemporary

---

[33]David N. Smith, *Who Rules the Universities?* (New York: Monthly Review Press, 1974).

[34]Michel Foucault, *Power/Knowledge: Selected Interviews and Other Writings, 1972-1977* (New York: Pantheon Books, 1980).

[35]Erich Fromm, "Forward" to A. S. Neill, *Summerhill* (New York: Hart Publishing Company, 1960).

[36]Peter L. Berger and Thomas Luckman, *The Social Construction of Reality: A Treatise in the Sociology of Knowledge* (Garden City, N. Y.: Anchor Books, 1967), 557.

colleges the power structure can only be traced tenuously and indirectly to the decisions of the boards or chief administrative officers. This structure is best understood as a function of a complex and dynamic field of forces that is generated by the entire bureaucracy.

The evolution of this power structure begins when a college's board of trustees hires a chief administrative officer. This person is normally hired on the basis of a reputation for effective personnel and financial management, and identification with certain academic principles and programs. Once installed, this administrator will secure the services of a dependable senior administrative staff, including a chief academic officer, or dean. The dean, in turn, will seek to develop a group of faculty members whom he or she can count on to provide "leadership" for the faculty--that is, to carry out his or her policies. Insofar as the bureaucracy will permit, these "teacher-administrators" will be appointed as chairs of the various academic departments and key committees of the college. Many among these will be encouraged, or will find encouragement, to think of themselves as future deans or presidents. These "deans-in-waiting" will come to take the perspective, and assume the values, of the academic administrator whose chair they eventually hope to occupy. They will, for instance, carefully temper their statements and actions in view of the interests of their superiors; they will crowd the center of their "constituencies"; they will be "positive," not "negative," in their outlooks; and they will increasingly act, often unwittingly, as apologists for administrative policy. Once the chairs of the various academic departments and key committees have been selected, then these chairs in turn will seek to establish relationships within their individual departments or committees that will reinforce their positions of authority. Some faculty members will be encouraged, or will find encouragement, to think of themselves as future chairs. These "chairs-in-waiting" will themselves quickly metamorphose and take the perspective and assume the values of their mentors. In time, and once again as if by a hidden hand, the academic bureaucracy develops a full-blown repressive power structure. Manipulative behavior becomes normal, and those who are manipulated willingly, instinctively manipulate others. Philosophy is replaced by politics, cavalierly defined as "the art of the possible." The liberal arts college, by design a place where teachers enable students to gain wisdom through the criticism of ideas and ideals, is subtly and grotesquely transformed into a place for "teacher-administrators" to manipulate people and to advance their careers by promoting the programs that will advance the careers of their superiors.

2. The myth of the "teacher-administrator" also destroys faculty collegiality. This happens because "teacher-administrators" are invested with authority that allows and requires them to exercise power over their colleagues. This power is expressed in a variety of forms--in decisions on tenure, promotion, salary, courses, working conditions, perks, and privileges. Even the mere threat of the exercise of such power is enough to domesticate those who are the potential

subjects for this exercise of power. As a result, a faculty as a society of equals who are judged only at the bar of reason degenerates into a bureaucracy in which teachers stand in hierarchical relationships to each other on the basis of the possession of power. The hierarchical nature of the academic bureaucracy is reinforced by numerous contrived "traditions." In these and in other seemingly trivial and innocent ways teachers are constantly reminded that their colleagues are not quite their colleagues. When such conditions prevail, the criticism of ideas and ideals gives way to the pursuit of personal ambition.

3. Finally, the myth of the "teacher-administrator" devalues teaching. Rather than the art that makes possible the development of wise people, teaching comes to be seen as a means to administrative advancement. College teaching becomes a farm club for aspiring administrators.

In these various ways--by making it impossible for teachers to be genuine critics or colleagues, and by devaluing teaching--the myth of the "teacher-administrator" helps to subvert liberal education.

Demythologization

If we now have warrant for the belief that the ideal teacher for the liberal arts college is not the "teacher-administrator" but the teacher who is not compromised by administrative allegiancies, it is important to ask what can be done to free the college from the myth of the "teacher-administrator," and, in consequence, to significantly improve the quality of college teaching. At least three actions are mandatory.

1. The radical difference between the liberal arts college and the university must be recognized and reaffirmed.   Students, teachers, educational administrators, and the general public must be made to understand that the liberal arts college is not properly a place where students and information are processed. The college is not a business within the "education industry." It is not an assembly line where educated students are produced by faculty "employees" under the "leadership" of "senior management." A different model is essential. A liberal arts college has ends and means that are not properly determined by authority.   These ends and means are properly determined by a faculty collegium--a constitutionally established guild of doctors of philosophy who have certain knowledge, skills, principles, and character, who are committed to a very unique educational ideal, and who stand in a unique collegial relationship to each other.

2. College administrators should not be understood as academic leaders or managers. They should not have the authority to determine the ends or the means of liberal education. It is not the task of any individual to set the goals or to determine priorities in liberal education, to initiate and terminate academic programs, or to manage or "manipulate" teacher "behavior" through "faculty development" programs. College administrators should facilitate the work of the collegium.

3. College teachers should be organized on the order of a priestly caste, and should be constitutionally denied access to personal power. When it is absolutely necessary for these teachers to perform administrative functions, they should be governed by the principle of shared authority so that power cannot become a function of personality. At the same time, college teaching should be elevated to a position of unsurpassed importance and dignity.

The Ideal College Teacher

Our examination of the myths of the "teacher-scholar" and the "teacher-administrator" argues to the conclusion that a program of liberal education requires a teacher with unique characteristics. This person must not be diverted from the responsibilities of the teacher by the desire for scholarly productivity or administrative power.[37] The ideal teacher for the liberal arts college is not the distinguished authority on some microspecialized field of knowledge or the politically adept manager of people and center-stage impresario of innovative academic programs. Rather, this person must be committed to a life of demanding and self-consuming service to the noblest of all educational ideals. This person's sole professional commitment must be to nourish those students who carry the seeds of transcendent ideals, to encourage those who aspire to the highest human possibility. The best model for this person is not the scholarly Guggenheim winner or the powerful C.E.O. The best model is more modest-- perhaps the parish priest or the loving parent. The ideal college teacher is the uncompromised college teacher.

3. MULTIFORM PEDAGOGY

Most people assume that, while college teachers may differ in the kind of knowledge that they provide for their students, they are alike in the sense that they all provide their students with knowledge about some specialized "academic field" or "discipline." Consequently, they are thought to share a single, "logocentric" pedagogy--one that exemplifies the ideals of formal logic and is appropriate for the dissemination of knowledge or theory. Accordingly, they are also thought to be alike in the sense that they conform to a uniform teacher model. This is the model of the "professor." This person teaches "courses" by means of lectures, aided by textbooks, and perhaps discussions, to provide students with specialized theoretical knowledge.

In contrast to this, teachers in a genuine program of liberal education have

---

[37]These two diversions parallel the two "corruptions of the philosophic nature" described by Socrates in the *Republic* at 490-491. We might say that some teachers are diverted by "their own virtues"--that is, by their own abundance of scholarly talent, while others are diverted by their desire for "the ordinary goods of life--beauty, wealth, strength, rank, and great connections in the state."

diverse professional goals, and thus must employ a multiform pedagogy and rely on a variety of teacher models:

1. When the teacher's goal is to provide students with the theories and information of the liberal sciences (except for self science), and when the teaching format is the academic "course," the appropriate teacher model is the *professor*. The professor is the disciplinary expert for the social and physical sciences and the ethical and cultural sciences. Self science requires a different teacher model because the knowledge that is developed in this science is student-specific. Because of this, self science requires the teacher model of the *counselor*. The counselor is responsible for helping each student understand himself or herself as an empirical object and as a valuing agent.

2. When the teacher's goal is to develop the skills of the theoretical liberal arts, and when the teaching format is the laboratory or the disputation, the appropriate teacher model is the *tutor*. In acting as a tutor a teacher acts less as a source of knowledge than as a supervisor, coordinator, or mentor for the students' participation in the practical exercises that are essential for the development of the skills of discovery and justification.

3. When the teacher's goal is to facilitate the students' integration of knowledge, and when the teaching format is the seminar, the appropriate teacher model is the *maieutic*. The maieutic is the constructive critic or midwife that seeks to induce students to labor in the conception of those principles that will enable them to hold a coherent, rationally defensible philosophy.

4. When the teacher's goal is to develop the practical skills of prudence or the cardinal moral virtues, and when the proper teaching format is the practicum, the appropriate teacher model is the *coach*. Like the athletic or drama coach, or like a parent, a coach is not a participant in the activities of the practicums, but one who provides supervision, encouragement, and criticism to those who are the participants.

4. MULTIFORM RESOURCES

Normally, when the liberal arts college recruits teachers, it recruits those who have the resources or capabilities of disciplinary experts. These resources usually include specialized knowledge of a particular academic field, and more detailed knowledge about some subspecialty within this field.

This description of the professional resources of the typical college teacher is appropriate for those colleges that have as their goal the development of disciplinary authorities or experts. However, if the goal of the college is the development of people who have the capacity and inclination for rational action, then the diverse competencies of liberal education are required, and the ideal college teacher will need diverse resources. Since liberal education requires the development of four generic competencies, the ideal teacher in the liberal arts college needs four kinds of resources:

1. Empirical and Normative Knowledge

The ideal college teacher differs from the ordinary college teacher in two noteworthy respects. First, this teacher is a generalist (in the sense that he or she knows the most general conclusions about the major empirical and normative sciences), not a specialist (in the sense of knowing details about one specialized field, and little about other fields). Second, this person possesses both empirical and normative knowledge, since for liberal education, these are equipollent.

The ideal teacher is not responsible for the cultivation of a field of knowledge, but for the cultivation of a person. Consequently, the knowledge that is important to this project is not prescribed by the need to be encyclopedic, to "cover" all "academic fields" in "breadth," nor is it prescribed by the need to be an authority on any one specialized and "interesting" subfield of knowledge. The knowledge that is important is that which provides the student with the understanding of reality and ideality that is essential to rational thought and action. The ideal teacher must provide the student with empirical and normative scientific literacy.

2. Capacity to Develop Theoretical Skills

The ideal college teacher needs to have the ability to develop in students the skills of the theoretical liberal arts--that is, the various reasoning skills that are required by the liberal sciences. This teacher differs from the ordinary college teacher in the important respect that he or she has the capacity to develop these skills by training, and is not limited to the capacity to disseminate knowledge by teaching. Since the theoretical sciences require the skills of discovery and justification, the ideal teacher must have the ability to develop student competencies in these two arts.

3. Criticality

The ideal college teacher also needs to be critical. It is essential that putative truths be relentlessly tested for their warrants or justifications. Thus, unlike the stereotypical professor of popular culture--the contented, pipe-smoking, intellectual aesthete who endearingly and entertainingly transmits information to appreciative students--this person is always subversive with respect to received opinion. And being a subversive, this person must disturb student complacencies, and be prepared to suffer the predictable personal consequences. Thus, the ideal teacher for the liberal arts college is one who, above all else, understands the meaning and implications of the truths that wisdom is impossible without criticism, that criticism is impossible without subversion, that subversion is impossible without discomfort, and that those who cause discomfort will themselves be discomforted.

4. Prudence and Character

The ideal teacher also needs to have prudence and good character. In the common view an effective teacher may be intelligent but imprudent or even immoral. But since a liberal education must develop competencies that are practical, as well as those that are theoretical, and since the development of these practical competencies--the prudential skills and the cardinal moral virtues--is best accomplished through training and example, the ideal teacher must exemplify in his or her personal life the prudential skills and moral virtues that must be developed in students. Teachers in the liberal arts college must practice what they teach. The ideal teacher must be prudent as well as courageous, just, and temperate.

The ideal college teacher is the diametrical opponent of the theoretically myopic and practically inept professor of satire and comedy. This person is one who has the capacity and inclination for rational action. The ideal teacher for a program of liberal education is, in fact, the liberally educated person.

THE IDEAL TEACHING CONDITIONS

If a program of liberal education is to be successful, it must be staffed by an effective teaching faculty. Its teachers must understand the end and means of this form of education, must be uncompromisingly committed to the service of this unique ideal, and must possess the essential pedagogies and professional resources. The faculty must not be adulterated by those whose commitments and responsibilities make them part-time teachers and part-time scholars or part-time administrators. This is to say that the faculty must be constitutionally empowered to act as the agency for the conduct of a program of liberal education. This requirement calls for a dramatic break with familiar, accepted academic assumptions and practices.

The faculty cannot effectively provide a program of liberal education unless the liberal arts college provides the faculty with the conditions that are necessary for effective teaching to take place. These conditions will be described in terms of (1) the faculty organization, (2) the teacher compensation system, (3) the personnel policies, and (4) the teaching facilities.

1. THE COLLEGIUM

For many people today the liberal arts college is understood as a small business in what Clark Kerr first called "the education industry." For these people, college teachers have no need for a deliberative assembly because they are only workers employed by managers for the production and reproduction of knowledge. But if we understand the liberal arts college as an institution for the development of wise people, and if we recognize that only teachers who have been specially trained for this purpose are qualified to understand this ideal and to determine the means for its realization, then teachers must be organized in a way that will enable them to fulfill their collective professional responsibilities. These teachers should be organized in a way that maximizes the rule of reason and minimizes the rule of authority. Any organization that will satisfy these requirements will have to possess unusual characteristics. It will have to have a common, eleemosynaric, and non-profit purpose; it will have to be a self-governing corporation; and its members will have to be related to each other as peers and colleagues.

These characteristics are found in some religious orders. They were also the characteristics of the Roman collegium. The purpose of the latter was education, and it was eleemosynaric; moreover, like the later medieval *studia generalia*, it was free to govern itself as long as it did not interfere in religious or civil affairs; and all of its members were colleagues, or co-workers of equal rank. The religious, political, and economic independence of the collegium protected it from external threats to the rule of reason, and the collegial equality of its members protected it from internal threats to this rule.

Because it possesses these desired characteristics, the collegium is the proper model for the organization for the teachers of the liberal arts college. The collegium should consist of all nonprobationary teachers. While a probationary period is necessary for the selection of teachers, once teachers become nonprobationary, they should have the status of colleagues. This professional collegiality should be reinforced by equality of rank, pay, and privilege. The familiar bureaucratization of a faculty by rank, pay, and privilege differentials is destructive of collegiality and encourages administrative cooptation and manipulation. The consequence of this bureaucratization of a faculty is the suppression of dialogue and the subversion of the rule of reason. The collegium should have primary responsibility for the college's educational program. Membership in the collegium should be humbly but jealously guarded. It should never be extended as a "courtesy" to those who are not fully qualified or empowered to act as faculty members. The collegium should be unapologetically understood as a sacred guild. The rights and responsibilities of the collegium for the design and conduct of the college's program of education should be specified in a legally binding corporate charter. This document is needed to provide the college with some protection from its external and internal enemies--that is, from those who would appropriate the college for extrinsic purposes whether this be by autocratic or democratic means.

2. INTRINSIC COMPENSATION

Any description of the ideal teaching conditions must include some guidelines for the appropriate form of teacher compensation. Recently a number of educators have argued that a so-called "merit pay" system is an appropriate compensation system for a college faculty. This proposal deserves careful consideration.

The Merit Pay System

In the nineteen eighties America and much of the rest of the world became euphoric about the virtues of a market economy. Coincident with this new appreciation of the benefits of unfettered competition the administrations of many American colleges initiated teacher compensation systems modeled on the "performance-based" pay systems often used successfully in market economy business and industry. As a result, many college teachers today receive part of their compensation on the basis of what is called a "merit pay system."

In any evaluation of the desirability of a "merit pay system" it is important to note at the outset that there is a difference between compensation or pay systems that are based on performance or "merit," and those that are technically called "merit pay systems." Almost everyone agrees that everyone should receive "merit pay" in the sense that they should receive just deserts for their labor. But those who admit this are not thereby obliged to agree that all people should be paid on the basis of what is called a "merit pay system." "Merit pay" is payment that is in some way based on performance. In contrast, a "merit pay system" is a system that bases pay on performance in an objective, calculable, and efficient way. The difference between "merit pay" and a "merit pay system" may be illustrated by the fact that professional football players receive "merit pay," but are not paid by means of a "merit pay system." Players (not necessarily the best players) who are worth more to the team are paid more than others, but there is no attempt to calculate the pay of each player on the basis of some universally applicable criterion such as the number of touchdowns scored and the number of extra points kicked. Such a system obviously would be unfair to those players who are not supposed to score touchdowns or kick extra points. Similarly, ministers might well be paid on the basis of their performance in a very general sense, but surely not on the basis of some universally applicable criterion such as the number of prayers given, theology books written, and church suppers attended. Such a system would certainly be demeaning to ministers, and would surely not serve the pastoral needs of a congregation.

Given this distinction we may now consider the desirability of using a "merit pay system" for the teachers in the liberal arts college. I want to argue that the use of this system for paying the teachers in liberal arts college is unwise and does a grave disservice to both the college and its teachers.

In spite of the fact that merit pay systems perennially fail in their application to education, many educators seem to never lose faith in their desirability.[38] In part, this anomaly may be due to the widespread conflation of the expressions

---

[38]Linda R. Pratt, "Merit Pay: Reaganomics for the Faculty?" *Academe* 74 (N/D 1988):14-16; Susan M. Johnson, "Merit Pay for Teachers: A Poor Prescription for Reform," *Harvard Education Review* 54 (1984): 175-185; Richard J. Murnane and David K. Cohen, "Merit Pay and the Evaluation Problem: Why Most Merit Pay Plans Fail and a Few Survive," *Harvard Education Review* 56 (1986):1-17; and K. O. Magnusen, "Faculty Evaluation, Performance, and Pay: Application and Issues," *Journal of Higher Education* 58 (1987): 516-529.

"merit pay" and "merit pay system." Those who believe in the desirability of a "merit pay system" for the teachers in a liberal arts college claim that this system will obtain salary fairness and benefit the college. Salary fairness is obtained whenever a superior performance receives a proportionate financial reward, and an inferior performance receives a proportionate financial penalty. The liberal arts college will be benefited if it is more effective in providing a liberal education for its students. The desirability of a merit pay system can only be decided by an examination of the truth or falsity of these two factual claims.

1. Does a merit pay system obtain salary fairness?

If a merit pay system is to be used to determine the pay of people who are picking tomatoes or selling widgets, then there is no insurmountable obstacle to devising a payment formula, or algorithm, that fairly calculates the value of the work performed. Payment can be made proportional to the number of tomatoes picked or widgets sold. But if a merit pay system is to be used to determine the pay of the teachers in the liberal arts college, there are formidable problems in devising a fair payment algorithm. First, since there is no product produced, payment cannot be tied to productivity. Instead, presumably, payment must be tied to what might be called "eductivity"--to the behavioral changes or outcomes which the liberal arts college promises its students.[39] Typically these outcomes include the students' acquisition of "skills which serve intellectual ends," "moral habits of self-discipline," "an enthusiasm for learning," "attitudes of tolerance and respect for differing opinions," "aesthetic sensibilities," etc. These important outcomes are obviously difficult to identify, let alone to measure for an algorithm. Second, for the most part the outcomes of a liberal education are attributable to a confluence of interrelated factors including individual courses, teacher-student relationships, the curriculum, the academic environment, extracurricular activities, residential life, peer group influence, sports, religion, etc. The outcomes cannot normally be attributed to the agency of particular teachers. Consequently, the task of devising an algorithm that will relate the outcomes to the performances of individual teachers is impossibly complex. In the face of this difficulty these important but inefficiently measured outcomes may be replaced in the algorithm by the more easily measured, but less important, skill and information-acquisition outcomes of individual college courses. But even if this substitution were justifiable, the resulting algorithm would still be enormously complex. This would be due to the fact that course outcomes are affected not only by the performance of teachers, but also by differing course objectives and subject matters, by whether the course is required or is an elective, by the character, motivation, and capabilities of the students, and even by such seemingly trivial variables as class size, class membership, class hour, classroom

---

[39] J. W. Gustad, "Evaluation of Teaching Performance: Issues and Possibilities," in C. B. T. Lee, ed., *Improving College Teaching* (Washington: American Council on Education, 1967), 274.

location, layout, lighting, and acoustics, etc.[40]   Moreover, and most decisively, even if course outcomes could be justifiably related to the performances of individual teachers, the algorithm would still not provide what is most essential to its utility--a comparative ranking of different teachers. This is a consequence of the fact that normally different teachers teach different courses to different classes under different circumstances, and thus produce outcomes that are incommensurable. Third, even if the important outcomes promised by the liberal arts college could be efficiently measured and factored out to the agency of individual teachers, an even more insurmountable difficulty is created by the fact that the promised outcomes are normally manifested only over an extended period of time. The impact of a particular teacher, for instance, may take many years to appear.

Given the impossibility of any algorithm which can measure the important outcomes of a liberal education, relate these outcomes to the performances of individual teachers in a way that permits intrafaculty comparison, and accomplish this in a short time period, a merit pay system may resort to an algorithm which ignores educational outcomes altogether. Thus, a college may claim that its goal is to provide a liberal education for its students, but then reward its teachers not for contributing to this end, but for conducting popular courses, for writing technical monographs incomprehensible to undergraduates, and for doing "community service."[41]   In view of these seemingly insurmountable problems in the construction of a fair algorithm, it is difficult to see how a merit pay system can obtain salary fairness.

A merit pay system is also thought to improve salary fairness by providing "accountability"--a proportionate financial penalty for an inferior performance. Here the assumption is that the teachers will benefit from a highly competitive, "free-market" work environment in which the "productive" will be rewarded and will flourish, and the "unproductive" will be punished and will perish. There are three problems with this assumption. First, an algorithm for determining inferior performance will be no less impractical than an algorithm for determining superior performance. Second, a merit pay system in education, unlike in a free-market economy, punishes, but does not eliminate the unproductive. As a result, it permits the survival of the fittest *and* the unfittest. Third, a merit pay system assumes that teachers who are judged to be unproductive, and who are, consequently, demerited, will respond to this judgment in a "rational" manner. Presumably the demerited will give up their slothful ways, redouble their efforts,

---

[40]Lawrence J. Dennis, "Teacher Evaluation in Higher Education," *Liberal Education* 62 (1976): 437-443; N. L. Gage, "The Appraisal of College Teaching," *Journal of Higher Education* 32 (1961); Philip E. Jacob, *Changing Values in College: An Exploratory Study of the Impact of College Teaching* (New York: Harper, 1957); Richard S. Kurz, John J. Mueller, Judith L. Gibbons, and Frank DiCataldo, "Faculty Performance: Suggestions for the Refinement of the Concept and Its Measurement," *Journal of Higher Education* 60 (J/F 1989): 43-58; M. Neeley, "A Teacher's View of Teacher Evaluation," *Improving College and University* 16 (1968): 207.

[41]James L. Bess, "The Motivation to Teach," *Journal of Higher Education* 48 (1977): 245.

and become productive. The trouble with this assumption is that teachers do not normally respond to the punitive effects of a merit pay system in a "rational" manner. Research suggests that few of those who are demerited will respond to the penalties of a merit pay system by increased productivity.[42] And even for the few who do increase their productivity, their work is likely to be perfunctory or opportunistic.[43] Experience suggests that most of the demerited teachers will respond to the penalties of a merit pay system by moonlighting activities (to recover lost income) or diversionary activities (to recover lost self-esteem). These teachers are likely to constitute a permanent underclass, alienated by a system that does not seem to value their labor, resentful toward those who administer it, and frustrated by failings that are often caused not so much by sloth or carelessness, as by the predictable, enervating traumas of adult life. The failings of this underclass are not the kinds of failings that are ameliorated by punishment. Thus, a merit pay system provides only a limited kind of financial penalty for what is judged to be an inferior performance, and it does so in a way that is injurious to both the individual and the institution. Once again, therefore, it is difficult to see how a merit pay system can obtain salary fairness.

2. Does a merit pay system benefit the college?

At least as important as whether the faculty gets its just deserts is whether the college gets *its* just deserts. A merit pay system has a significant bearing on this problem because it has grave consequences for liberal education.

1. It is curious that in education merit pay systems have had a recurrent appeal but a short life span. One researcher has called this the "paradox" of the merit pay system.[44] Often a faculty will be receptive to a proposed merit pay system. The system will be seen as a sensible way to obtain salary fairness and to benefit the college. But eventually, and usually after only a few years, disillusionment begins. An increasing number of teachers either dislike, but tolerate, or actively oppose the system. In place of its promised benefits, disappointment, anger, and alienation appear. In the end the faculty is demoralized and the college suffers.

That this cycle of attraction and opposition should reoccur is paradoxical enough. That educational institutions should allow the cycle to reoccur and not

---

[42] E. L. Deci, "The Effects of Contingent and Non-contingent Rewards and Controls on Intrinsic Motivations," *Organizational Behavior and Human Performance* 8 (1972): 217; Richard J. Murnane and David K. Cohen, "Merit Pay and the Evaluation Problem: Why Most Merit Pay Plans Fail and a Few Survive," *Harvard Educational Review* 56 (1986); Thomas J. Peters and Robert H. Waterman, Jr., *In Search of Excellence: Lessons from America's Best Run Companies* (New York: Harper & Row, 1982).

[43] Murnane and Cohen, "Merit Pay and the Evaluation Problem: Why Most Merit Pay Plans Fail and a Few Survive."

[44] A. Mikalachki, "There Is No Merit in Merit Pay," *The Business Quarterly* 41 (Spring 1946): 49.

understand it is even more paradoxical. It seems reasonable to expect that institutions that celebrate science and history would carefully study the nature and history of merit pay systems before they adopt them. Incredibly and unfortunately, many educational institutions do not seem to practice what they teach. They adopt a system without adequate research. Even superficial research would have revealed that merit pay systems in education do not seem to deliver what they promise. Such research also would have suggested a likely explanation for a faculty's recurrent cycle of attraction and opposition to merit pay systems. The most relevant research finding suggests that people tend to rate their own merit spectacularly higher than it is rated by others. One study, for instance, showed that 86% of research engineers rated themselves as being in the top 25% in excellence of performance, while the remaining 14% rated themselves as being in the top 50%.[45] A similar study showed that 100% of adult males rated themselves as being in the top 50% in the possession of interpersonal skills, while 60% rated themselves as being in the top 10%, and a full 25% "ever so humbly thought they were in the top 1% of the population."[46] Any tendency on the part of teachers to overestimate their own professional merit has two predictable consequences for a faculty's attitude toward a merit pay system. Initially the system will be attractive because most teachers will believe that they are deserving of merit and will be justly rewarded by the system; eventually, though, the system will be angrily opposed because most teachers will continue to believe that they are deserving of merit, but will see the system as depriving them of what they justly deserve.[47] In the end a merit pay system seriously undermines the morale of a faculty.

Management studies continue to confirm the importance of morale for the success of cooperative enterprises. In a recent book on the management strategies of America's best-run companies, Thomas J. Peters and Robert H. Waterman, Jr. observed that "excellent companies have a deeply ingrained philosophy that says, in effect, 'respect the individual,' 'make people winners,' 'let them stand out.'"[48] A merit pay system seems to be insensitive to these morale needs. It does not "make [most] people winners"; it makes most people losers.

A second research finding provides another explanation as to why a merit pay system demoralizes a faculty. Research in the field of personnel management suggests that "lasting commitment to a task is engendered only by fostering conditions that build intrinsic motivation."[49] Most teachers in the liberal arts college have strong intrinsic motivation. While they have a natural interest in the economic rewards of their labor, they also have an interest in liberal education and its high moral purpose. For them, teaching is more than a means to make a living; it is a way to justify a life. It is, consequently, a profession or "calling."

---

[45]Ibid.
[46]Peters and Waterman, *In Search of Excellence.*
[47]Mikalachki, "There Is No Merit in Merit Pay," 41.
[48]Ibid.
[49]Ibid.

Most teachers believe that their teaching may actually make a difference, not only in the lives of individual students, but even for the future of humankind. In apparent ignorance of this high motive, a merit pay system seems determined to treat teachers as being without a professional calling, and as being appropriately manipulated by (often trivial) economic rewards and penalties. Those who have demonstrated their character and professional commitment by years of school, college, and graduate study, and by years of hard work and modest compensation, can be expected to resent a system that treats them as if they are motivated like dogs or pigeons. Merit pay is truly "the ultimate insult to teachers."[50]

Another research finding provides still another explanation as to why a merit pay system demoralizes a faculty. An honest merit pay system employs a kind of "zero-sum" competition: Normally there are a limited number of rewards, and therefore, if some teachers are to be meritorious, other teachers cannot be meritorious. If some people are to be winners, other people must be losers. In fact, the value of being a merit pay system winner will vary directly with the number of people who are losers. This kind of competition is required if the system's rewards are to preserve their incentive value. (It is interesting to note that one of the apparent reasons for the survival of the relatively few faculty merit pay systems that do survive is that these systems surreptitiously award merit pay to almost everyone. This trick works only as long as most people can be kept in the dark about the distribution of rewards.[51])

Research on the effects of "zero-sum" competition has demonstrated that

> competitors are seen as enemies, and thus hostility develops toward them, perceptions of . . . competitors become distorted negatively, and interaction and communication with competitors are decreased.[52]

Now for business or sport this kind of harsh competition may be great fun. It stimulates adrenaline and alleviates boredom. But liberal education is not a business or a sport. It is a unique, complex enterprise that cannot succeed without the selfless, cooperative efforts of many diversely talented people. College teachers, for instance, must have the status of colleagues: they must be willing and able to work together to achieve a common, institutional purpose. They must share mutual respect. And above all, they must be able to sustain genuine communication. Since a merit pay system employs "zero-sum" competition, and since this kind of competition is divisive and discourages cooperation, mutual respect, and communication, it is not surprising that it is demoralizing to a faculty.

2. Whenever a liberal arts college loses its sense of special purpose and confuses itself with a university or a university college (as so many now do), a

---

[50]Stephen Friedman, "Merit Pay: the Ultimate Insult to Teachers," *Chronicle of Higher Education* (16 May 1984): 32.

[51]Murnane and Cohen, "Merit Pay and the Evaluation Problem: Why Most Merit Pay Plans Fail and a Few Survive."

[52]H. H. Meyer, "The Pay-For-Performance Dilemma," *Organizational Dynamics* 4 (Winter

faculty is induced to regard itself as a collection of experts or authorities on various disciplinary "fields of knowledge." Since authority and institutional prestige are thought to be conferred only by scholarly productivity, teachers will be required to publish. This requirement, in turn, will lead teachers to press for more specialized courses, for research libraries, laboratories, and assistants, for research grants, leaves, and travel, and for a reduced "teaching load." Inevitably and not surprisingly, these pressures lead to the devaluation of teaching.

A merit pay system contributes to this devaluation. It does this because in its need to justify salary differences on the basis of performance differentials, it is under constraint to find measurable differences in teaching quality. But, as has been argued above, teaching quality in the liberal arts college is *in practice* impossible to measure. The use of institutional or course outcomes, student course evaluations, and classroom visitation by colleagues or administrators all have severe limitations. As we have seen, institutional and course outcomes are difficult to identify, measure, and attribute to individual teachers in a way that permits intrafaculty comparison. Student course evaluations have been demonstrated to be unreliable in spite of the fact that they are conveniently quantifiable and appeal to those who view education as a kind of personal service industry. Classroom visitation by colleagues or administrators has rarely been successful because it threatens academic freedom and provides little information about long-term teaching success or failure.

Faced by the apparently insurmountable difficulties in efficiently measuring teaching quality, and yet under constraint to find measurable differences in professional performance, a merit pay system can be sustained only by pursuing drastic options. The familiar option is to assume (contrary to empirical evidence) that teaching quality can be judged on the basis of scholarly productivity, and then to use scholarly productivity as the effective measure of professional performance.[53] The predictable result of this option is that teaching is devalued in favor of scholarly productivity. Numerous studies support this conclusion.[54]

3. Unlike primary and secondary schools, whose purpose is the development of general skills and information, and also unlike vocational and graduate schools, whose purpose is the development of special skills and information, the purpose of the liberal arts college is to provide a liberal education. As we have argued, a liberal education requires that students gain more than an understanding of the world; it requires that they gain an understanding of their moral obligations in the world. And it requires that they develop more than understanding; it requires that they develop the capacity and the commitment to fulfill these obligations.

As we have also argued, to meet these requirements, teachers in the liberal

---

1975): 42.

[53]Alexander W. Astin and C. B. T. Lee, "Current Practices in the Evaluation and Training of College Teachers," in C. B. T. Lee, ed., *Improving College Teaching* (Washington: American Council on Education, 1967).

[54]James L. Bess, "The Motivation to Teach," *Journal of Higher Education* 48 (1977): 245; Henry H. Crimmel, "The Myth of the Teacher-Scholar," *Liberal Education* 70 (184): 183-198.

arts college cannot give priority to the task of pursuing and disseminating knowledge, but must give priority to the very different task of persuading people to pursue wisdom--to live the examined life. Unfortunately, at least since the time of Socrates, this task has been hazardous. Unlike scholars and researchers, whose labor adds to their expertise, and thus augments their resources and increases their value to the institution that employs them, teachers in the liberal arts college can only expend their resources in the service they render to their students. Moreover, those who are responsible for enjoining others to live the examined life, and who therefore must steadfastly challenge authority, cowardice, conformity, and complacency, are seldom treated with tolerance, understanding, or appreciation.

These hazards of college teaching can be mitigated by enlightened administrative policies and by practices that encourage the criticism of ideas. The most important of these practices is a tenure system. A tenure system provides a measure of economic security that can be used to persuade teachers to assume the risks of a career that will inevitably consume their professional resources and subject them to endemic misunderstanding and abuse.[55]

A merit pay system defeats this all-important benefit of a tenure system. While a tenure system nourishes a sense of trust and common enterprise and transcending purpose, a merit pay system promotes a sense of distrust and divisiveness and mundane purpose. While a tenure system encourages teachers to commit themselves to the liberal education of their students in a selfless and caring way, a merit pay system encourages teachers to distance themselves from students and their human concerns so that they can advance their own careers by extending the frontiers of specialist knowledge. While a tenure system helps to create the environment of academic freedom that is necessary for the unprejudiced criticism of ideas and ideals, a merit pay system helps to create an environment in which administrative and bureaucratic authority represses criticism. The essential academic freedom that a tenure system provides for liberal education by contract, a merit pay system deviously subverts by compensation policy.[56]

Many of those teachers who are attracted by a merit pay system seem to be entranced by its promised economic rewards. As a result they fail to realize that merit pay systems are normally part of what some educational administrators patronizingly call a "faculty development" program. As we have seen, a merit pay system is a low cost "faculty development" program that enables administrators to manage rewards and recognition for a faculty, and thus to

---

[55]"The great barriers to the total victory of the market place and the state [over the university] are academic freedom and tenure." Michael B. Katz, *Reconstructing American Education* (Cambridge: Harvard University Press, 1987), 179.

[56]This is the position taken by the American Association of University Professors in its "Statement on Evaluation of Tenured Faculty," *Academe* (N/D 1983): "The Association believes that periodic formal institutional evaluation of each postprobationary faculty member would bring scant benefit, would incur unacceptable costs, not only in money and time but also in the dampening of creativity and of collegial relationships, and would threaten academic freedom."

produce the behaviors that they desire. This kind of manipulation of a faculty is clearly repressive, and is antithetical to the interests of liberal education.[57]

Why is it unwise to use a merit pay system to pay college teachers? It is unwise because this system of compensation does a disservice to both the college and its teachers. It aggravates salary unfairness and gravely impairs liberal education by demoralizing the faculty, devaluing teaching, and subverting academic freedom.

This conclusion does not mean that it is impossible to prudently compensate teachers in the liberal arts college. It does not mean that both the college and its teachers cannot be given their just deserts. But it does mean that college teachers should be given compensation by a system that comprehends the unique and very complex personnel requirements of liberal education.

The Ideal Compensation System

The preceding critique of the merit pay system provides the principles for an ideal compensation system. Teachers in the liberal arts college should be given compensation so that they can do what needs to be done in the service of liberal education.   As long as teachers are nonprobationary full professors and in conformity with their contractual obligations, compensation should not be used as a device to reward or punish--to control or manipulate. If the compensation system is used for this purpose, then teachers cannot act in unprejudiced ways, and students cannot be freed from prejudice.

Given this principle, the ideal faculty compensation system cannot be far from an honest rank-based system. The rank-based system permits the most qualified teachers to be carefully and professionally selected over a period of time by a series of constitutionally-regulated peer review processes. Using this system, teachers can be given compensation on the basis of their rank.   In order to minimize manipulation it is desirable for all those within a given rank be given equal compensation. A longevity increment might be an option. This system does not treat teachers as salesmen or professional athletes or entertainers, but as members of a priestly caste with transcendent obligations. Compensation should not be used to punish those who displease administrators, or those who are "difficult" or "uncooperative"; nor should it be used to reward friends or "superstars."[58]   A good teacher compensation system is not one that is manipulative and repressive, but one that is liberating and empowering. Thus, the ideal system is one that pays teachers not so much for *being* good as pays them so that they *can* be good.

---

[57]For an unapologetic statement of the manipulative intent of a faculty development program, including a merit pay system, see: Richard P. Chait and James Gueths, "A Framework for Faculty Development," *Change* (M/J 1981): 30-33.

[58]See Mary A. Burgan, "The Faculty and the Superstar Syndrome," *Academe* 74:3 (1988): 10-14.

3. LIBERATING POLICIES

If a program of liberal education is to be successful, college teachers must be constitutionally empowered as a collegium, and they must be provided with a compensation system that reinforces their commitment to the intrinsic value of liberal education.   In addition, they must have a teaching environment with personnel policies that liberate them to act autonomously, on the basis of conscience.   The most important of these policies are those that encourage collegiality and criticality:

Collegiality

Our argument points to the need for a definition of the relationship of the college's faculty to the administration.   The responsibility of the faculty, constitutionally empowered as a collegium, and under the legal oversight of a board of trustees, is to design and conduct a program of liberal education. The responsibility of the administration is facilitate the work of the collegium. Consequently, personnel policies should not be designed by the administration, and they certainly should not be used to divide, dominate, or "manage" a faculty. Such policies should unite, liberate, and empower it.   Teachers should be encouraged to cooperate with their colleagues in the liberal education of their students, not to compete with them for power, prestige, and professional status.

We have suggested that one of the ways of encouraging collegiality in a faculty is to maintain equality of rank among all nonprobationary teachers. Since these teachers should be dedicated to maximizing the rule of reason and minimizing the rule of authority, they should not tolerate a teaching environment in which colleagues are treated as bureaucratic inferiors or superiors. Rather, all members of the collegium--that is, all nonprobationary teachers--should stand to each other as peers. They should be treated as equal members of a professional guild dedicated to the development of people who, like themselves, seek to live by the rule of reason.

We have also suggested that collegiality can be enhanced by equality of compensation for nonprobationary teachers. A common objection to this proposal is that it does not take into consideration the fact that the salary for teachers is inevitably set by the dynamics of the academic marketplace. Exotic disciplinary microspecialists and "superstars" are scarce, and can command above average salaries.   This objection, however, is not telling against a genuine liberal arts college because this college has no need for exotic disciplinary microspecialists or "superstars." It needs only capable and dedicated teachers. The contemporary liberal arts college's quest for exotic microspecialists and "superstars" is a form of public relations pandering to the parochialisms of the ignorant.

Collegiality can also be encouraged by a college constitution that provides the collegium with an independent deliberative assembly that promotes decision by consensus over decision by a parliamentary majority. When decision by consensus is not practicable, parliamentary procedures should be scrupulously followed, but should always be understood as imperfect devices to maximize the rule of reason, not as elixirs for the discovery of the truth and the good.

While it may be necessary that teachers perform certain administrative functions, it is desirable that these be performed only out of duty. When these functions are not so performed, there is the danger that those who by profession are committed to the rule of reason will develop an addiction to the rule of authority. This contagious academic degenerative disease is life-threatening to collegiality. The most promising remedy is to minimize the number of these administrative functions, and to require that they be shared by all teachers on a short-term and rotating basis. These positions should be made so that they are unattractive to teachers who covet power. Thus, the college should be administered

> not by permanently stationed bureaucrats but by [temporary administrators] who serve for short periods and with appropriate reluctance, longing, like Cincinnatus for his farm, for the day when they [can] return to teaching.[59]

As we have also argued, one of the devices most destructive of collegiality is the "publish or perish" policy. This policy devalues teaching and disenfranchises teachers. As long as colleges continue to tolerate this policy, studies suggest that most teachers will be unable to give their best efforts to teaching. A liberal arts college should require only that its teachers teach well. It is irrational for it to require that its teachers engage in activities that have no essential relationship to the teaching mission of the college. The usual objection to the elimination of a "publish or perish" policy is that it will deprive the college of a prestigious reputation. But this will be true only so long as the prestige of the college is judged by standards that are appropriate for a university or graduate school, but inappropriate for an undergraduate liberal arts college.[60]

Collegiality is also undermined by tenure quotas. Every effort should be made to maximize, not minimize, the number of nonprobationary teachers in a faculty. Any attempt to "cap" tenure or to attach to the faculty numerous "nontenure-track adjuncts" is a device that divides and debilitates a faculty. It limits the efficacy of the faculty by limiting the number of those who can act on the basis of conscience, critically.

Especially damaging to collegiality is the common practice of evaluating teachers by criteria that encourage subjectivity, favoritism, and politics to come

---

[59]Stephen Friedman, "Merit Pay: the Ultimate Insult to Teachers," *Chronicle of Higher Education* (16 May 1984): 32.

[60]See, for instance: Earl J. McGrath, *The Graduate School and the Decline of Liberal Education* (New York: Columbia University, 1959).

into play. Too often, for instance, teaching is evaluated on the basis of criteria that include "professional productivity," peer opinions, and student evaluations. These criteria may measure "professional productivity," personal loyalty, and popularity, but they do not measure learning. The only appropriate method for measuring teaching effectiveness is outcomes assessment.[61]

Criticality

The criticism of ideas needs to be understood by all as essential to liberal education; ideological conflict needs to be seen as healthy, not neurotic; the critical examination of dominant paradigms and other commonplaces needs to be seen as the prerequisite to insight and moral development. Criticality is unlikely to develop spontaneously. It requires encouragement and a vigorous intellectual environment in which teachers and students profess their beliefs and criticize the beliefs of others, but yet remain open to criticism and to the profession of contrary beliefs.

One way of encouraging criticality is by valuing ideological diversity. College teachers should not be selected on the basis of their conformity to a particular ideology, but on the basis of their ability to think and act in rational and critical ways. The attainment of this goal will be facilitated by personnel policies that encourage ideological diversity.

Experience shows that criticality cannot be maintained without a tenure system. Certainly it is important that teachers be tested through a rigorous and unhurried probationary process before they are admitted to faculty membership. It is also important that the granting of nonprobationary membership not be understood as a reward for loyal service, but as a covenant to safeguard academic freedom and to encourage criticism. In this covenant job security is promised to those who, through their probationary period, have demonstrated that they can be trusted to rise above the temptations of personal ambition and personal loyalty to act autonomously on the basis of reason.

Many of those who oppose a tenure system do so on the ground that tenure protects academic "goof-offs" or "incompetents." They then argue that a tenure system needs to be supplemented by a "post tenure review" system, or otherwise replaced by a contract system without tenure. In a "post tenure review" system nonprobationary teachers are periodically reviewed to determine if their nonprobationary status should be revoked. This dishonest and devious procedure violates the promise of nonprobationary faculty membership, and it defeats the purpose of the tenure system. If teachers who have survived a long and rigorous probationary process cannot be trusted to effectively serve the ideal of liberal education, then the probationary process itself should be reviewed, not the teachers. After carefully selecting the members of a faculty on the basis of

---

[61]See: Winter, David G., David C. McClelland, and Abigail J. Stewart, *A New Case for the Liberal Arts* (San Francisco: Jossey-Bass Publishers, 1981.)

demonstrated competence and commitment, a college should entrust them to act competently and conscientiously. The practice of reviewing tenured professors until they retire or die is patently repressive.

To be sure, it is desirable for a faculty to be free of incompetents. But the law provides means for the termination of those who meet the statutory definition of incompetence. The trouble is, once "incompetence" is defined in a loose, nonstatutory way, human nature being what it is, there is a high probability that many of those who charge others with "incompetence" will be motivated by personal or political, not professional reasons. For too many, unfortunately, the set of incompetents is identical with the set of those who disagree with them. In view of this reality, it is important to acknowledge the imperfections of a tenure system, and to admit that a system may indeed protect a few who are incompetent. But it is also true that the vast majority of tenured teachers will repay the trust that they have received many times over. And it is most important to remember that without tenure, academic freedom and criticism are impossible, and without these, liberal education itself is impossible. Thus, in spite of its imperfections, tenure remains essential to the success of liberal education.

Criticality can be enhanced by constructive competition. Since the liberal arts college's need to develop the necessary competencies of the wise person mandates that all courses be required, constructive teacher competition can be maintained by having all classes be elective.

Constructive competition requires an honest and fair grading system. Currently colleges use a common set of grading symbols but allow teachers to define these symbols in different ways and to use them in different ways. For example, grades may be used to assess student achievement, to measure mastery of material, to judge skill development, to reward effort or attitude, to evaluate potential, to appraise improvement, to reward attendance, to punish, to compensate for social or cultural disadvantages, and so on. In addition, grades are used in a variety of different courses which vary in demands and difficulty. In spite of the resulting incommensurability of these grades, they are routinely averaged together to calculate a "GPA," or grade point average, that is widely assumed to be a measure of student achievement. This practice is patently flawed and unfair to students, and should be eliminated.

A second flaw of the typical grading system is that it does not define the grading symbols in an operational way. For instance, it is common to define numerical grading symbols in terms of adjectival definientia that are as opaque as the definienda. For instance, a "3.0" is defined as "good." A grading system without operationally defined symbols is powerless to prevent chronic grade inflation and undermines student confidence in teacher objectivity.[62] While the

---

[62] In the letter grade system used at St. Lawrence University prior to 1980, a "C" grade translated into 2.0 "quality points," and was generally understood to be an "average" grade, or "gentleman's C". Today a 2.0 grade is below average. In a typical semester (fall, 1987) 77.8% of all course grades given were better than 2.0, and only 7.4% of grades were below 2.0. On the problem of grade inflation see: Louis Goldman, "The Betrayal of the Gatekeepers: Grade

multiformity of the model curriculum makes any uniform criteria for all grading impossible, it is still possible to operationally define the grading symbols, to prevent grade inflation, and to maintain teacher objectivity. This could be done, for instance, by a quartile grading system, a system in which satisfactory student performance in each course is ranked by quartile.

4. INSPIRITING FACILITIES

American visitors to Europe are inevitably awed by the Gothic church. These great structures, such as the cathedral of Chartres, reach towards the heavens and dwarf their earthly surroundings. Standing within them, overwhelmed by their proportions and the sublimity of their architecture and art, these visitors may gain some sense of the profound role that religion has often played in human life.

Visitors to America are often awed in a somewhat similar way when they visit the capitols and courthouses of this country. These massive, paneled, limestone and marble structures dominate their surroundings in much the same way that the Gothic cathedral dominated the medieval city. Visitors to these buildings, like visitors to the Roman forum, may gain some sense of the vital role that law has often played in human life.

Clearly churches as well as capitols and courthouses not only reflect a society's values, but they also sanctify them. Great churches, capitols, and courthouses are both functional and edifying. They help people to understand what is sacred and inviolable.

Occasionally the architecture and art of educational institutions have been edifying in this way. Visitors to universities like Oxford and Harvard, colleges like Amherst and Bowdoin, and boarding schools like Exeter and St. Paul's, have expressed the opinion that the buildings and campuses of these institutions convey the sense that education, like religion and law, is a sacred and inviolable enterprise. Allan Bloom, for example, describes his own experience:

> When I was fifteen years old I saw the University of Chicago for the first time and somehow sensed that I had discovered my life. I had never before seen, or at least had not noticed, buildings that were evidently dedicated to a higher purpose, not to necessity or utility, not merely to shelter or manufacture or trade, but to something that might be an end in itself.[63]

Today visitors to most of our liberal arts colleges do not have this experience. On a typical campus tour, visitors will see an obviously important administration buildings (perhaps vaguely suggestive of the Parthenon), elaborate sports and

---

Inflation," *Journal of General Education* 37 (1985): 97-121.

[63]Allan Bloom, *The Closing of the American Mind* (New York: Simon and Schuster, 1987), 243.

recreational facilities, historic old homes that have been rudely converted into fraternity and sorority houses, libraries that are marvels of electronic gadgetry, and pastoral landscapes. But classrooms--the places where *sine qua non*s should happen--are seldom on these campus tours. No wonder. These rooms are usually grim. They unmistakably convey to anyone who sees them that whatever it is that goes on within their walls, it is at best a necessary evil, and in any case, certainly not anything that might be enjoyable, much less anything that might affect the course of a human life.

The task of the teacher in the liberal arts college would be served if the facilities for teaching were to be made physically functional and educationally inspirational.   There is no reason why classrooms, for instance, cannot be functional and also designed and decorated so that they signify that they are the places where profound things may happen. There is no reason why these rooms cannot be designed in ways that invite dialogue and signal its central importance. There is no reason why classrooms, libraries, and even residences cannot be designed and decorated in ways that celebrate the life of the mind.   Similarly, there is no reason why campus media cannot be dedicated to the exchange of ideas, and protected from commercial exploitation and endless bureaucratic babble.   There is no reason why the art and architecture of a campus cannot be selected less on the basis of their appeal to pop or avant-garde aestheticism and more on the basis of their contribution to the enterprise of liberal education. There is no reason why the House of Intellect cannot be built like a sacred place.

* * * *

Drawing upon the assumptions implicit in our earlier criticism of the contemporary college teacher and the conditions for teaching, we have now described the ideal college teacher and the ideal conditions for teaching. The goal of the teacher in the liberal arts college is the goal of the doctor of philosophy-- that is, the development of the competencies of the wise person.   This teacher must provide students with an empirical and normative scientific literacy, must develop the skills of the liberal arts, must facilitate the discovery of principles, and must cultivate the prudential and cardinal moral virtues. This teacher must not be compromised by scholarly or administrative or other responsibilities, and thus must be able to participate without compromise as a rational agent in a program for the development of rational agents. The pedagogy of this teacher is multiform, and includes the full range of the skills of the liberal arts.   This multiform pedagogy requires diverse teaching formats (courses, counseling sessions, laboratories, disputations, seminars, and practicums) and diverse teacher models (the professor, the counselor, the tutor, the maieutic, and the coach). The professional resources of this teacher includes the full range of liberal education competencies (the knowledge of the liberal theoretical and normative sciences, the skills of the liberal arts, philosophy, and the prudential and moral virtues).

If the ideal teaching conditions are to be realized, teachers in the liberal arts college must be organized and empowered as a collegium, a constitutional, self-governing guild of colleagues. Their system of compensation should be such that it encourages them to maintain their commitment to teaching within a program of liberal education on the basis of its intrinsic rewards. They should be assisted by personnel policies that are liberating, not repressive. And they should be provided with spiritually edifying facilities.

The ideal teacher for the liberal arts college is best summarized as the autonomous teacher--the teacher who is able to serve the ideal of liberal education without compromise. We may call this principle *the principle of teacher autonomy*.

9

CONFIRMATION OF THE PRINCIPLES

Until . . . political greatness and wisdom meet in one, and those commoner natures who pursue either to the exclusion of the other are compelled to stand aside, [neither cities nor the human race] will rest from their evils . . . .

Plato, *Republic*

As the man is free who exists for his own sake and not for another's, so we pursue wisdom as the only free science, for it alone exists for its own sake.

Aristotle, *Metaphysics*

Whenever philosophy has been taken seriously, it has always been assumed that it signified achieving a wisdom which would influence the conduct of life.

Dewey, *Democracy and Education*

The project of this chapter is to provide historical confirmation for the four principles of liberal education that we have proposed. We will pursue this project by examining three theories of liberal education. We hope to show that, although these theories are usually interpreted as being in competition, they are in fact in agreement with each other and with the principles that we have proposed.

The theories of Plato and Aristotle have been included because of their historical influence and theoretical contrast. This contrast is graphically represented in Raphael's Vatican fresco, "The School of Athens." In this work Plato is depicted as pointing to the heavens, and thus as indicating the importance of the universal, while Aristotle is shown as pointing to the earth, and thus as indicating the importance of the particular. This opposition between monism and pluralism runs throughout the history of educational theory.

The theory of John Dewey has been included because of its historical influence, and because it represents a skeptical contrast to the foundationalism of Plato and Aristotle. This opposition, sometimes described as the conflict between the philosophers and the orators, also runs throughout the history of educational theory.[1]

PLATO'S IDEA OF LIBERAL EDUCATION

In the *Republic* Plato presents a vision of liberal education that is unmatched in terms of its historical influence, its poetic power, and its philosophical profundity. Here, in a dialogue frequently misinterpreted as a description of a quaint political utopia, is a subtle and magnificent demonstration of the nature and intrinsic value of justice. Integral to this demonstration is an equally subtle and magnificent demonstration of the nature and intrinsic value of liberal education. The *Republic* enables us to understand the ideal of this unique form of education, its ideal institution, its ideal curriculum, and its ideal teacher.

THE IDEAL OF LIBERAL EDUCATION

Plato presents his vision of liberal education in the guise of a vision of the form of education required for the realization of justice. This vision is presented within the metaphor of the "three waves." This metaphor is first announced by Socrates in Book V.[2] The metaphor occupies a strategic place in the text. It comes after Socrates has completed his demonstration that justice is an intrinsic good, and has thus fulfilled the promise that he had earlier made to his audience.[3] This denouement is signaled by Glaucon's admission that his original question about the comparative advantages of justice and injustice is now "ridiculous."[4] With this matter settled, Socrates proposes to turn to an entirely new subject, a description of the degenerate forms of the state. But at this moment--at the very beginning of Book V--Glaucon and Adeimantus interrupt him. They chide him for omitting what they regard as an important part of his story--a description of the family life of the guardians of the ideal state. Socrates readily agrees to remedy this omission, and in doing so he begins the section that is organized by the metaphor of the "three waves." This section takes up three central books of the *Republic*, and does not come to a close until the beginning of Book VIII.[5] At that point Socrates casually refers to this long section as a "digression." In view of Plato's organizational genius, Socrates' reference to this section as a "digression" is clearly ironic. There can be little doubt that this section contains the most esoteric and difficult, and yet the most essential and exalted part of the entire dialogue. Now that justice has been shown to be an intrinsic good, and thus

---

[1]On this, see Bruce A. Kimball, *Orators and Philosophers: A History of the Idea of Liberal Education* (New York: Teachers College, 1986).

[2] Plato *Republic* 453. Later references occur at 457, 472, and 473. All references to the works of Plato are to the standard Stephanus pagination and the Jowett translation.

[3]*Republic* 368.

[4]*Republic* 445.

[5]*Republic* 543.

a universal human obligation, Plato is evidently turning his attention from the ideal of justice to the conditions for the realization of this ideal.

Obviously justice cannot be realized without human agency. At the very beginning of the "third wave," Socrates identifies the "philosopher-king" as the agent necessary for the realization of justice.[6] This person is then described in considerable detail. By virtue of being a philosopher this individual possesses a certain kind of knowledge. But by virtue of also being the political authority, this individual also possesses a certain capacity for action. Moreover, such action must take place under moral constraint. The philosopher-king is forbidden to retreat to a world of theory that is detached from the world of practice. In the text this is made clear by Socrates' insistence that the guardians will not be allowed to be "star-gazers," or to be "overeducated," but will be required to subordinate their own happiness to the happiness of "the whole state."[7] They will be required to come to the aid of the unenlightened--to "descend among the prisoners of the cave, and to partake of their labors and honors, whether they are worth having or not." Moreover, when it comes time for Socrates to describe the educational program required for the development of the philosopher-king, he divides it equally between theoretical and practical pursuits. Once the prescribed fifteen year curriculum in the mathematical and dialectical arts and the sciences has been completed, the future guardians will be required to perform fifteen years of supervised public service to the state in order, in part, to gain practical experience.

From this description of the philosopher-king it is apparent that the educational program required for the realization of justice is a form that will develop in the individual the capacity and inclination for a certain kind of action. But this conclusion needs amplification.

1.

Obviously, the mere capacity and inclination for action is not sufficient for the realization of justice. Not all actions are just. Actions that are just are in some special way grounded or justified. The metaphor of the "three waves" makes it possible for us to understand the nature of this justification. The just person is not identified by physical attributes, such as sex [the "first wave"], and not by social appurtenances, such as power, inheritance, wealth, or popularity [the "second wave"], but rather by the possession of a special kind of knowledge [the "third wave"]. In the argument of the *Republic* this is a decisive move. After the "three waves" we are clearly to understand that justice is possible only when actions are guided by a special kind of knowledge.

Unfortunately, the English word, "knowledge," has diverse uses, and does not carry with it the precision of the Greek words *gnosis, episteme, sophia, synesis,* and *historia*. In English, "knowledge" may refer to quiz show trivia, profound insight, or even sexual intercourse; it may indicate uninterpreted data or

---

[6]*Republic* 473.
[7]*Republic* 489-520.

information, inductive generalizations or analytic truths, conclusions from theoretical or practical arguments, and principles or transcendentals. Certainly a person's possession of knowledge in most uses of this word is not sufficient for individual justice, and is not sufficient to qualify a person to be a guardian of the ideal state. Encyclopedic minds and world-renowned authorities in specialized fields of knowledge may be morally depraved or incapable of practical decision and action. Clearly the just person is in need of a different kind of knowledge.

The "third wave" explains this different kind of knowledge. At the very beginning of this section Socrates lays down the thesis that the knowledge that is required for the realization of justice is possessed only by the philosopher.[8] And "Who are the true philosophers?" Glaucon asks.[9] "They are those who pursue knowledge of being," Socrates replies. But this knowledge is not merely knowledge of reality. In the ensuing parable of the pilot and the mutinous sailors Socrates explains how the true pilot's study of the sky and the stars and the winds is interpreted by the ignorant sailors to be stargazing and useless. Similarly, while the philosopher's pursuit of knowledge appears to most people as useless, it is in fact essential to just decision and action. In fact, philosophers are like painters, so Socrates suggests, who will create the image of man by looking frequently "in both directions, toward the just, fair, and moderate . . . , and, again, toward what is in human beings."[10] Thus, they will make "the ways of men, as far as possible, agreeable to the ways of God." These metaphors leave little doubt that the kind of knowledge sought by the philosopher must include the kind of knowledge that is required to guide individual action as well as the ship of state. The philosopher-king must have knowledge of what ought to be, in addition to knowledge of what is. The ruler's knowledge must encompass both reality and ideality.

These textual considerations provide evidence that the kind of education that is required for the realization of justice is a kind that will develop in the individual the capacity and inclination for action that is guided by knowledge that is both theoretical and practical, i. e., empirical and normative.

2.

In the *Meno* Plato has Socrates try to explain the difference between knowledge and opinion. Knowledge, Socrates explains, is an opinion that is "fastened" like a chain by "causal reasoning."[11] Thus, knowledge itself is dependent upon a theoretical art, method, or skill.

Socrates asks Glaucon to identify the art which would "draw the soul from becoming to being," and thus provide genuine knowledge.[12] "Music" and

---

[8]*Republic* 473.
[9]*Republic* 475.
[10]*Republic* 501.
[11]*Meno* 98.
[12]*Republic* 521.

"gymnastic" are briefly considered but rejected because they aim at the development of character, not knowledge. All of the "useful arts" are also rejected, evidently because they are conditioned by various extrinsic purposes. What is needed, Socrates urges, is a universal art, one which is necessary to every man "if he is to be a man at all."[13] Socrates argues that this art is "mathematics," which he divides into a quadrivium according to the four dimensions of space-time: arithmetic, geometry, solid geometry, and astronomy. When experience seems to force on us contradictory beliefs, reason is aroused by the demand for consistency. Mathematics allows us to escape plurality and inconsistency and to achieve unity and consistency. It shows us the way in which an antithesis is the precondition for the discovery of a principle--a presupposition that stands as the ground or synthesis for the antithesis. In this way mathematics is a prerequisite to the supreme art of dialectic in that it helps us to recognize that the visible presupposes the intelligible, that becoming presupposes being, that appearance presupposes reality.

Thus, for Plato, the kind of education that is required for the realization of justice is a form that will develop in the individual the capacity and inclination for action that is guided by knowledge that is both empirical and normative, and that is obtained by means of certain theoretical skills.

3.

In Book VI Socrates indicates that he is ready to begin a final stage in his description of the kind of knowledge essential for justice.[14] For the first time, he makes an almost casual reference to "the highest of all knowledge" [*mathemata megista*].[15] Adeimantus seems to sense the profound importance of this reference, and without hesitation, he asks for an explanation. Socrates then repeats the warning that he issued earlier.[16] He cautions his audience that he may not be able to provide an adequate answer. He admits that an adequate answer really requires "a longer and more circuitous way," and that the best he may be able to do is to provide a kind of popular explanation. Adeimantus, doubtlessly puzzled by this maneuver, but nonetheless unwilling to jeopardize his chance for being a witness to what promises to be an extraordinary revelation, is only too willing to accept whatever explanation Socrates is willing to provide. There follows in rapid succession a series of celebrated metaphors in which Socrates tries to explain "the highest of all knowledge."

At this point Socrates makes the striking claim that the object of "the highest of all knowledge" is "the idea of the good."[17] Once more, though, he is cautious, warning that any definitive explanation of "the idea of the good" is beyond his

---

[13]*Republic* 522.
[14]*Republic* 502.
[15]*Republic* 504.
[16]*Republic* 435.
[17]*Republic* 505.

powers, and that he can speak only of "a child of the good." Glaucon, as unwilling as Adeimantus to risk diverting the person who is reputed to be the wisest of men, raises no objection to Socrates' evident preference for poetic language. The idea of the good, Socrates explains, is like the sun in being "seen by sight," and yet being "the cause of sight."[18] It is that "which imparts truth to the known and the power of knowing to the knower." Later it is said to be "the cause of knowledge and truth" and to have a place of "still greater honor" and beauty.[19]   Socrates points out that "all other things become useful and advantageous only by their use of this [idea]."[20]

Socrates then appeals to a more complex metaphor to aid in the explanation of this "highest of all knowledge."[21] "Now take a line cut into two unequal segments," he says, "and cut each segment in the same proportion." The two main divisions are to stand for visible things and intelligible things. The lower part of the line that represents visible things is to stand for "images" while the higher part is to stand for ordinary "things" of nature and art. The lower part of the line that represents intelligible things is to stand for "hypotheses" and the higher part represents "a principle that is free from hypotheses." This distinction between two visible objects and two intelligible objects is given greater explanatory power by a parallel distinction between two faculties of sight and two faculties of intellect. Thus Socrates speaks of the lower part of the main line as representing the "perception [*eikasia*] of images" and the "belief [*pistis*] in ordinary things," while he speaks of the higher part as representing the "understanding [*dianoia*] of hypotheses" and "reasoning [*noesis*] about a principle that is free from hypotheses." The analogy of the "divided line" now presents us with a proportion. This proportion helps us to understand something that we do not know by its analogy with something that we do know. It shows us that the unfamiliar "highest of all knowledge"--"reasoning about a principle that is free from hypotheses"--is related to the familiar "understanding of hypotheses" in a way that is like the relationship of "belief in ordinary things" to the "perception of images." The divided line thus promises a form of knowledge that is radically different from, and radically superior to, ordinary knowledge.

Plato next moves to develop this idea by adopting a temporal scheme in place of the spatial scheme of the divided line. The allegory of the cave asks us to imagine prisoners who are somehow compelled to live in the darkness of a cave and to see only images on the cave's wall. These prisoners are unwilling to consider the possibility that they are imprisoned by an illusion, and are resistant to any attempt to allow them to escape. Only after much effort would they be able to see the ordinary things that are made visible by the light of the sun, and last of all, and with the greatest effort, would they be able to see the sun itself. The "idea of the good" is now said to be like the sun in that it is itself difficult to see, but

---

[18]*Republic* 508.
[19]*Republic* 509.
[20]*Republic* 505.
[21]*Republic* 509.

without it no one would be able to see. It is in fact, according to Socrates, "the universal author of all things beautiful and right, parent of light and of the lord of light in this visible world, and the immediate source of reason and truth in the theoretical world."[22]

The analogy of the divided line suggests that the familiar form of knowledge that we value highly in ordinary life may be humble when compared to an unfamiliar form that we may at best only darkly understand. "Knowledge" is often used to refer to conclusions that are validly demonstrated to follow from premises that are accepted as true. This knowledge may be said to be "hypothetical" in the sense that the truth of the conclusions is conditional on the truth of the premises. For instance, conclusions about the nature of a physical phenomenon are conditional on observations, and observations are dependent upon a physical theory, and a physical theory will itself be dependent upon a scientific paradigm, as well as on mathematical, logical, and philosophical assumptions. In the analogy of the divided line Plato asks us to consider the possibility that not all knowledge is "hypothetical," i.e., conditional, in this familiar way. His suggestion is that there is an unfamiliar, "highest of all knowledge" that consists in a first principle [pantos archen] that is "free from hypotheses," and thus, unconditionally true. Socrates' claim is that this knowledge that is "free of hypotheses" is "clearer" than that which is contemplated by the so-called "arts" [technais]--those ways of knowing that are not "free of hypotheses."[23] The analogy of the divided line thus makes the dramatic claim that there is a highest form of knowledge, and that the object of this highest form of knowledge is a principle that is unconditionally true.

The allegory of the cave carries this claim a decisive step further by proposing that the principle that is the object of the highest form of knowledge is not only unconditionally true, but is also unconditionally good. In the allegory of the cave the highest of all knowledge is identified as "the idea of the good," which is said to be like the sun in that while the sun gives us the light to see and do things, the idea of the good makes it possible for us to know what is true and to do what is good. The irresistible implication is that the highest of all knowledge is knowledge of an unconditioned principle of morality. This knowledge would take priority over all other forms of knowledge because unless we understand our highest moral obligation, not even truth itself will justifiably matter to us. Socrates tells his audience that the idea of the good is not only the author of sight, but also the author of right. It is, he says, "the power upon which he who would act rationally either in public or private life must have his eye fixed."[24]

The analogy of the divided line and the allegory of the cave bring together the need for a principle of reality and a principle of ideality. The assent from the cave into the light is not merely the search for the unconditionally true, but also

---

[22]*Republic* 517.
[23]*Republic* 511.
[24]*Republic* 516.

the search for the unconditionally good. Our knowledge of our moral obligations is incomplete without a knowledge of the reality that is to be transformed by the fulfillment of these obligations. This interpretation is confirmed in the text by the fact that the allegory of the cave is a myth of conversion and salvation, as well as by Socrates' insistence that once the future guardians have ascended into the upper world, and have seen reality and have understood the way that the sun permits sight, then they have an obligation to return to the darkness of the cave, and to dedicate themselves to the "care and providence of others."[25]

The analogy of the divided line and the allegory of the cave have profound implications for the kind of education required for the achievement of justice. These two metaphors give primacy to a form of knowledge that is radically unlike what we ordinarily regard as knowledge. It is what Socrates usually refers to as "wisdom" [sophia]. This is the highest goal of the highest form of education. It is certainly a special form of knowledge, but it is not specialized knowledge. Wisdom is a special form of knowledge in the sense that it is knowledge of an unconditioned principle, but it is not specialized knowledge because it is not conditioned on the principles of a specialized science. In addition, wisdom has the unique feature that it is not useful for any purpose, even though, without it, nothing else is more than conditionally useful. This paradoxical point is the import of the insight that the idea of the good, like the sun, is the most difficult thing to see, and yet is that which makes it possible for us to see. Thus, the form of education that will enable us to obtain the highest of all knowledge will necessarily have two requirements: it must be comprehensive--that is, not specialized, i.e., not conditional on any assumption, and it must be pure--that is, not "applied" or technological, i.e., not conditional on any purpose. This knowledge is thus free of both theoretical and practical assumptions.

It is important to note that the *Republic* makes no effort to specify the content of the unconditional principle of morality. Plato's evident interest in *The Republic* is limited to the demonstration that knowledge of this principle is in fact possible and necessary. Socrates repeatedly insists that any attempt to specify the content of this principle will require a "longer and more circuitous way."

Many contemporary readers of the *Republic* will be willing to grant that in the ideal world Plato would be right to argue that justice depends upon knowledge of the unconditional principle of morality. The trouble is, they will say, our world is not the ideal world. In our imperfect world, they will argue, knowledge--in contrast to opinion--is simply beyond human possession. To justify this conclusion they will argue that every claim to theoretical knowledge is relative to a set of assumptions, a frame of reference, or a scientific paradigm. And they will similarly argue that every claim to practical knowledge is essentially a value preference, a power differential, or a cultural difference. On the basis of these arguments the skeptical critics of the *Republic* will regard Plato's program of education as dogmatic or naive. For them, an educational program cannot aspire

---

[25]*Republic* 520.

to any knowledge of the ultimate nature of reality or unconditioned human obligation. For them, these matters are, as it were, infinitely pending, and in the interim they can only be left to something like "personal preferences."

This skeptical treatment of Plato's argument is paradoxical in view of the fact that the *Republic* itself is a sustained argument against skepticism, as represented by the archetypal skeptic, Thrasymachus. If we are to treat the *Republic* respectfully, and not to discount it as a mere exercise of poetic license or as a quaint example of prescientific thought, then we should look more closely at Plato's explanation of the possibility of philosophical knowledge.

For Plato, the only way to philosophical knowledge is the "longer and more circuitous way" made possible by the art of dialectic, the philosophic method *par excellence*.

Socrates prepares the way for the description of the art of dialectic at the end of the allegory of the cave. There he first recognizes the need for some art which will enable a person to obtain the unconditional knowledge that he has just described as being essential to justice.[26] This art will move from hypotheses about "becoming" to knowledge about "being," not by teaching but by an act of "conversion." This act of conversion, like the act of "recollection" in the *Meno*, does not require us to learn something new, but rather, in an important sense, to remember something that we already knew but have forgotten.

Socrates next describes the "nature, divisions, and paths" of dialectic.[27] Even though he warns us that any firm understanding of the nature of dialectic can only be achieved by means of dialectic itself, he does claim that dialectic alone goes "directly to the first principle," and must be "the only science which does away with hypotheses in order to make her ground secure." What we ordinarily call "science" actually provides only an "understanding of hypotheses," while dialectic belongs to the division of the mind in which we have "reasoning about a principle that is free from hypotheses." Socrates describes the path of education necessary for the development of the dialectician. It begins with the selection of those twenty-year-olds who are sound in mind and body and character. These twenty-year-olds then undertake a ten year curriculum in general education (which includes study of the mathematical arts), a five year curriculum in dialectic, and a fifteen year period of supervised public service, after which the fifty-year-old graduates are at last ready to assume the full responsibilities of guardianship.

Socrates repeatedly cautions his audience that the highest of all knowledge cannot be obtained by instruction, but must be obtained by dialectic.[28] Consequently, it seems reasonable to expect that when dialectic itself becomes central to the argument of the *Republic*, illustration will be favored over even the most cautious description. This appears to be the case. Immediately following the section in which Socrates describes the "nature, divisions, and paths" of dialectic, he to returns to the completion of the project from which he digressed

---

[26]*Republic* 518.
[27]*Republic* 533.
[28]*Republic* 435, 504, 506, 533.

when he presented the allegory of the "three waves."[29]   That he is being ironic, and that he is not returning from a "digression" is suggested by the fact that the long section that immediately follows the "digression" contains a detailed illustration of the method that he has just cautiously described in the "digression."[30]   On this interpretation this section illustrates the employment of the dialectical method to demonstrate once again that justice is an intrinsic good. Beginning with the nature and origin of timocracy and the timocrat, the degenerate forms of the state and the individual that most approximate the aristocratic ideal, Socrates describes in succession the nature and origin of oligarchy and the oligarch, democracy and the democrat, and tyranny and the tyrant.   Timocracy and the timocrat depart from the ideal in allowing the guardians and reason [*logismos*], as well as the artisans and desire [*epithymia*], to be subordinated to the auxiliaries and "spirit" [*thymos*].   Oligarchy and the oligarch depart even further by allowing both reason and "spirit" to be subordinated to the desires that are necessary for life. Still inferior to oligarchy and the oligarch are democracy and the democrat. These subordinate both the guardians and reason, and the auxiliaries and "spirit," to the artisans and the gratification of sundry desires. Finally, tyranny and the tyrant appear as the diametrical contrast to aristocracy and the aristocrat. They subordinate the guardians and reason, as well as the auxiliaries and "spirit," to a tyrant and a single, irrepressible desire.

At this point the antithesis of justice and injustice are clearly visible: justice is the integration of the parts at the service of the whole, while injustice is the disintegration of the whole at the service of a single malignant part.   The superiority of integration--and, consequently, justice--is demonstrated by our recollection that we must engage in the act of integration in order to arrive at any justifiable interpretation of this section.

After the detailed illustration of the employment of dialectic in the description of the degenerate forms of the state, Plato provides three simplified illustrations of dialectic.[31] In this section Socrates offers "three proofs" that the just person (represented by the philosopher) is "happy" and the unjust person (represented by the tyrant) is "unhappy." In the first of these proofs Socrates asks his audience to consider the question of whether the just or the unjust person is most free.[32] The moral subjectivist believes that the unjust person is the most free because this person does what he or she pleases, and that the just person is the least free because this person does what he or she ought. Socrates demonstrates that this belief is false by providing us the opportunity to recall an assumption that we tacitly make when we consider his question. This is the assumption that, in answering his question, we can and should act freely--that is, that we can and

---

[29]*Republic* 543.
[30]*Republic* 543-576.
[31]*Republic* 576-588.
[32]*Republic* 577.

should follow the dictates of reason, not desire. Consequently, when we must decide whether the just person--the person who does what he or she ought--or the unjust person--the person who does what he or she pleases--is the most free, we only need to remember that we already know that the just person is the most free. We need to realize that freedom cannot be license, and that because of this, a free act will differ from an unfree act in terms of the purpose it serves. Since the purpose of the unjust act is to satisfy desires and the purpose of the just act is to satisfy reason, the unjust person is not free because this person is enslaved by his or her desires, while the just person is free because this person acts autonomously under the rule of reason.

In the second proof Socrates asks his audience to imagine three classes of men who are identified by their having three different kinds of love: the just, or the lovers of wisdom; the lovers of honor; and the unjust, or the lovers of gain.[33] He then asks his audience to imagine that each of these three classes is called upon to provide reasons why its particular love is the most pleasurable. The question that he then raises is the question of which class we should trust to make a wise judgment. Socrates demonstrates that we should trust the just person. He does this by getting us to recall an assumption that we tacitly make when we consider the question that he has raised. This assumption is that in answering his question we necessarily give priority to the faculty of wise judgment, and since the just, or the lovers of wisdom, are by definition those who possess the faculty of wise judgment, we should trust them to make wise judgments, rather than to trust those who by definition do not have the capacity to make wise judgments.

Socrates regards the third proof as the most decisive of the three proofs.[34] The question that concerns him is whether the pleasures of the just or the pleasures of the unjust are the best. The proof demonstrates that the pleasures of the just are the best. This is accomplished when Socrates goads us once again into realizing an assumption that we tacitly make when we consider the question that he has raised. This assumption is that since we are seeking knowledge about the relative pleasures of the just and unjust person, we already assume that knowledge will allow us to decide between genuine and spurious pleasures. But this is to admit that pleasure is to this extent dependent upon knowledge. Hence, the just person--the person who by definition has knowledge--is also the person who has the best pleasure because he or she alone is able to know the difference between genuine and spurious pleasure.

There are other, more elaborate illustrations of dialectical proofs in the *Republic*. The dialogue in the opening book between Cephalus, Polemarchus, Thrasymachus, and Socrates is an example. There Plato not only illustrates dialectic, but at the same time provides his readers with a set of instructions for the interpretation of his text. Cephalus' flawed definition of justice as "to speak the truth and to pay your debts" and Polemarchus' equally flawed definition of justice as "the repayment of a debt" warn us that we will fail in our effort to

---

[33]*Republic* 580.
[34]*Republic* 583.

properly interpret the text if we settle for an interpretation that lacks either unity or plurality. At the same time, the theses advanced by the old man dependent upon institutional ritual and the young man equally dependent upon a human authority constitute an antithesis that hopefully will enable us to become aware of the fact that the inquiry into the nature of justice need not be blind but can be guided by a process that we already take for granted when we undertake the inquiry itself. This process, later identified by Socrates as dialectic, is illustrated in the dialogue between Socrates and his arch antagonist, Thrasymachus.

Even the *Republic* is itself an illustration of a dialectical proof. The inquiry into the nature of justice already presupposes our obligation to be just, and demonstrates that justice, understood as integration, is a categorical obligation for every human being.

The method of dialectic may be summarily explained by contrasting it with the method of demonstration. The method of demonstration is familiar as the paradigm of hypothetico-deductive reasoning used by the sciences, whereas the method of dialectic is unfamiliar, except, perhaps, in philosophy.   In demonstration, Socrates explains, the understanding "descends" from hypotheses treated as premises to conclusions that validly follow from these premises, whereas in dialectic reason "ascends" from hypotheses "into a world that is above hypotheses, in order that she may soar beyond them to the first principle of the whole."[35] These principles can be none other than those assumptions that must be made if the hypotheses are even to be considered. Dialectic thus begins in the antithesis of opinions, and culminates in a synthesis of knowledge. Plato tries to help us appreciate the nature and importance of dialectic through Socrates' defense of the so-called "doctrine of recollection." This is done when Socrates criticizes "certain professors of education" for believing that they "can put knowledge into the soul which was not there before, like sight in blind eyes."[36] He then repeats the claim he makes in the *Meno* that "all inquiry and all learning is but recollection." If we indefensibly assume that Socrates speaks for Plato, and if we inadvertently think that Socrates is speaking to us literally, we may be inclined to interpret this passage as evidence of Plato's belief in metempsychosis. We are then tempted to discredit his argument on the basis of his dependence on a fanciful and unscientific theory. If, on the other hand, we remember Plato's irony, his depreciation of the written word as the dead word in the Seventh Epistle, and his penchant for the poetic, we can interpret this passage as an analogical device to help us understand the method of dialectic. Dialectic is like memory, because the principles that we discover from it are already tacitly assumed in the assumptions from which we begin.

The analogy of the "divided line" provides insight into the modality of the knowledge that is obtained by the application of the dialectical method. In treating the lower form of knowledge as familiar, and in describing it as the

[35]*Republic* 511.
[36]*Republic* 518.

"understanding of hypotheses," Socrates seems to be suggesting that this form of knowledge is the kind that we get from the empirically verified hypotheses or theories of ordinary science. Such knowledge is "hypothetical," and therefore, without certainty, because the empirically verified hypotheses or theories of empirical science are conditional on theoretical assumptions and practical purposes that are not themselves empirically verified. In contrast, in describing the higher form of knowledge as "reasoning about a principle that is above hypotheses," Socrates seems to be suggesting that this highest form of knowledge is not hypothetical, but apodictical. The miracle of dialectic is that it begins in ordinary, transient opinions, but ends in extraordinary, transcendental truths. Socrates puts this very point poignantly when he tells us that the many things that are seen but not known require other things that are known but not seen.[37]

For Plato, these considerations support the conclusion that the kind of education that is required for the realization of justice is a form that will develop in individuals the capacity and inclination for action that is guided by knowledge of what is and knowledge of what ought to be, and that is obtained by means of certain theoretical arts, and that is dialectically justified in the unconditioned principle of morality.

4.

For Plato the ideals of justice established in the *Republic* are ideals for imperfect beings in an imperfect world. Those responsible for the realization of the ideals of justice are human agents, and they are impelled by ordinary human fears, ambitions, and desires. Unless these fears, ambitions, and desires are disciplined by the cultivation of the moral virtues, these agents will be unable to understand, much less to pursue, the ideal of justice. This emphasis on the moral virtues is evident at every stage of the *Republic*. The early education of the future guardians is centered about "music" [*mousike*] and "gymnastics" [*gumnastike*]. But the main purpose of "music" and "gymnastics" is not, as is commonly thought, to develop sound minds and sound bodies, but rather to develop people who have a courageous and temperate disposition. The education of the future guardians requires a rigorous curriculum, and only those with exemplary character have any chance of survival. Later, Socrates will insist that the future guardians be chosen from among the elders, not because the elders are always wise or experienced, but because it takes time to test the future guardians for their commitment to truth in the face of "theft" (persuasion, forgetfulness), "force" (pain, grief), and "enchantment" (pleasure, fear).[38] Finally, Socrates argues that even after the future guardians have completed their fifteen year study of the mathematical arts and dialectic, they will be required to give an equally long period of public service to the state so that, in part, they can once more be tested

---

[37]*Republic* 507.
[38]*Republic* 413

for their moral virtues.[39]

These considerations make it clear that for Plato the education of the just person, like the education of the guardians in the just state, cannot be a purely theoretical process. Like the guardians, the just person must possess capacities that cannot be attained by those who lack good character. Dialectical insight, for instance, will not be available to those who lack courage and temperance. Thus, the kind of education that is required by Plato for the realization of justice is a form that will develop in individuals the capacity and inclination for action that is guided by knowledge that is both empirical and normative, a knowledge that is obtained by means of certain theoretical skills, that is grounded dialectically in the unconditioned principle of morality, and that is obtained with the aid of certain practical skills such as prudence and the moral virtues.

THE IDEAL INSTITUTION FOR LIBERAL EDUCATION

In the section of the *Republic* that immediately follows the allegory of the cave Socrates turns his attention to the higher education of the future guardians.[40] His first prescription is an educational program consisting of a quadrivium of mathematical studies--arithmetic, geometry, solid geometry, and astronomy.

Glaucon fully understands that the mathematical arts have important practical applications, as, for instance, in military operations. But he has difficulty with Socrates' suggestion that these arts also have a higher purpose. When he continues to speak of the mathematical studies only in terms of their practical utility, Socrates chides him. "I am amused," Socrates says, "at your fear of the world, which makes you guard against the appearance of insisting upon useless studies."[41]

This is not the first time in the *Republic* that Socrates has belittled the "useful" arts or praised the "useless" arts. Earlier he had referred to the "useful" arts as "mean" [*technai banausoi*].[42]

Some of Plato's modern critics see in Socrates' disparagement of "useful" studies a leisure class contempt for manual labor. But this interpretation seems unjustified by the text. At this point in the argument of the *Republic* Plato's principal concern is with the problem of education. In this context a gratuitous put-down of manual labor would seem to be pointless. A more likely interpretation is that Plato is trying, through paradox, to force his readers to understand the uniqueness of the educational program that is required for the guardians.

The analogy of the divided line has demonstrated that the kind of knowledge essential for the guardians is radically different from ordinary knowledge. Socrates explains that the leaders in the ideal state must have the highest kind of

---

[39]*Republic* 539.
[40]*Republic* 521-532.
[41]*Republic* 527.
[42]*Republic* 522.

knowledge, "science" ("reason" about "principles"), and more specifically, "wisdom," (knowledge grounded by the unconditional principle of morality), and this must not be confused with "art" ("understanding" of "hypotheses").[43] What Socrates now tells us is that the mathematical studies that are essential to the highest kind of knowledge are "useless," while the kinds of studies required for ordinary knowledge are "useful." The most plausible interpretation of this claim is that ordinary knowledge is "useful" because it is a means to some end. For instance, the kind of knowledge required to practice medicine, law, business, or other vocations is a means to the achievement of various individual or social ends. In contrast, the kind of knowledge that is provided by the quadrivium of mathematical studies is constitutive of wisdom, and this knowledge of moral obligation is "useless" in the sense that it is not a means to any end, but is itself the highest end of human life. Thus, in disparaging the "useful" arts, Plato is pointing to the priceless truth that utility cannot be the universal measure of value, and to the correlative truth that the highest art must be one which provides knowledge of the highest end of human life.

The educational program that will provide this kind of knowledge will be "useless," but nonetheless, it will be the most important form of education. Unless ends are understood, means go without justification. This same insight is captured in the allegory of the cave by the metaphor of the sun. Socrates tells us that without the sun--the source of light--nothing can be seen. Interpreted, this must mean that without the idea of the good--that is, without knowledge of our moral obligations--nothing can be genuinely "useful." This is born out by Socrates' statement that "the idea of good is the highest knowledge, and that all other things become useful and advantageous only by their use of this."[44] At issue here is the profound insight that Plato has dialectically demonstrated in the *Republic*: that the just life is intrinsically good.

Not only is the knowledge provided by the quadrivium of mathematical studies important, but, Socrates explains at 498, it is also immensely "difficult." Socrates has insisted all along in the *Republic* that the guardians' life is a rigorous one. Their educational program is fifty years long and requires endless examinations. Since their thought is directed so much to ends, and since ordinary practical thought is directed to means, they will often be misunderstood and mistreated. This point is clearly made by Socrates' parable of the ship's pilot and the mutinous sailors.[45] The sailors mutiny against the pilot because they are unable to understand his art, and they misinterpret his preoccupation with the sky, the stars, and the winds as useless stargazing. In addition, the guardians' thought is difficult because the truth that they discover is not always comforting. This point is made by Socrates' report that the prisoners in the cave will be "pained and irritated" if they are forced to give up their illusions and to be led out into the

---

[43]*Republic* 511.
[44]*Republic* 504.
[45]*Republic* 488-489.

light.[46] Above all, the sun itself will be blinding. The guardians, Socrates tells us, are like an exotic plant "in alien soil."[47] They, and the wisdom they represent, will require nurture and protection from a hostile environment.

Once we understand that wisdom is, in the ordinary sense, "useless," and that Socrates' attention to this point is a way of indicating its importance and difficulty, then we are in a better position to understand why an institution dedicated to the pursuit of wisdom must have a unique and privileged status with respect to all other institutions and individuals in a society. To the extent that this institution, either voluntarily or involuntarily, serves extrinsic purposes, and thus becomes "useful," then to that extent it fails its own special purpose. An institution dedicated to the ideal of wisdom must be the most independent of all institutions. It is responsible only for ends, not means. Its task is to facilitate the dialectical discovery of intrinsically good human purposes, not to serve as a means for the realization of the putatively good purposes of others. Socrates seeks to protect the independence of the education of the guardians by his resolute insistence on unrestricted criticism, by constantly requiring that all ideas "run the gauntlet of all objections," and by his requirement that the guardians have a proven commitment to the pursuit of wisdom uncompromised by the distractions of ordinary practical life.[48]

THE IDEAL CURRICULUM FOR LIBERAL EDUCATION

In the *Republic* Socrates outlines an educational program for the development of the guardians of the ideal state that requires fifty years for its completion. As we have noted above, this program first emphasizes the development of the moral virtues by training in "gymnastic" and "music." At the age of twenty the qualified students begin a ten year formal study of the comprehensive empirical and normative sciences, together with a program for the development of the universal theoretical skills.   These theoretical skills are developed by means of the mathematical arts (arithmetic, geometry, solid geometry, and astronomy). At the age of thirty the students qualified to continue begin an intensive five year study of principles through the philosophical art of dialectic.   Following this, the survivors begin a fifteen year apprenticeship in service to the state, during which they acquire practical experience and are once again tested for high moral virtue. Finally, at the age of fifty the graduates are ready to commence their tour of duty as guardians of the state. The competencies to be possessed by these graduates can be summarized as follows:

1. knowledge of reality and ideality
2. the theoretical ("mathematical") skills necessary to obtain this knowledge
3. dialectical insight into the principles that ground this knowledge

---

[46]*Republic* 516.
[47]*Republic* 492.
[48]*Republic* 534.

4. the practical skills of prudence and the moral virtues (especially justice, courage, and temperance) necessary to act on the basis of this knowledge

The need to develop these competencies requires a curriculum that is centered about the liberal arts and consists of the following four components:

1. the liberal empirical and normative sciences
2. the theoretical liberal arts
3. philosophy (dialectic)
4. the practical liberal arts

THE IDEAL TEACHER FOR LIBERAL EDUCATION

Inasmuch as Socrates' curriculum for the development of the guardians for the ideal state consists in a variety of components, it is not surprising that there is no single model of the ideal teacher.   Rather, if we assume the need for specialization, a variety of models is required.   Some are needed for the systematic study of the comprehensive empirical and normative sciences. Others are needed for the development of the universal theoretical skills. Still others are necessary for the study of principles. And finally, still others are necessary for the training that is required for the development of prudence and the moral virtues.

For the systematic study of the comprehensive empirical and normative sciences the ideal teacher is the scientist, or disciplinary authority. Since a just person must have a comprehensive knowledge of both reality and ideality, scientists must include authorities in two generic disciplines: the empirical liberal sciences, which seek to understand the way things are, and the normative liberal sciences, which seek to understand the way things ought to be.

For the development of the universal theoretical skills the ideal teacher is the "mathematician."   In this context the mathematician is not an authority on a subfield of the science of abstract structures; nor is this person the practitioner of a useful practical skill; rather, this person is the teacher of a universal and "useless" theoretical skill.   The "mathematician" [*mathematikos*, literally, "disposed to learn"] develops the ability to reason so that, as Socrates says, people can "rise out of the sea of change and lay hold of true being."[49]

For the discovery of principles the ideal teacher is the dialectician or philosopher. Plato emphasizes that the philosopher should not be confused with the scientist. The difference between these two is displayed in the analogy of the divided line in Socrates' contrast between "understanding [*dianoia*] of hypotheses" and "reasoning [*noesis*] about a principle that is free from hypotheses." While the scientist is concerned with the conclusions of arguments, the philosopher is concerned with the principles that ground arguments. Above all, this person is not an authority about some field of knowledge called

---

[49]*Republic* 525.

"philosophy." Socrates makes this clear in the *Republic* when he says, "But then, if I am right, certain professors of education must be wrong when they say that they can put knowledge into the soul which was not there before, like sight into blind eyes."[50] The philosopher does not labor on the frontier of knowledge or send back reports from the frontier. Rather, the philosopher is the dialectician, the person who makes it possible for others to gain insight into principles. Plato's model for the dialectician is obviously Socrates, and Socrates is repeatedly described, as in the *Apology*, as someone who is not a teacher and whose only knowledge is the knowledge that he is without knowledge.[51] The dialectician is not constructive, but critical.   This role is made clear from the various descriptions that are given to Socrates in the course of the Platonic dialogues. Here and there he is variously referred to as a maieutic or midwife, a lover in the *Republic*,[52] a stingray in the *Meno*,[53] a gadfly in the *Apology*,[54] and a satyr in the *Symposium*.[55]

For the development of prudence (practical wisdom) and the moral virtues the ideal teacher is the person who has lived a full and good life, and who is able to teach an apprentice by means of example. The teacher will be assisted by the hero and the poet. The hero provides, and the poet creates, the images that the students will imitate, given good institutions. By imitating these images the students will develop the habits that will enable them to act courageously and temperately in spite of the ever-present intrusions of fear and desire.

****

The *Republic* provides us with one of the great classical ideals of liberal education. In the course of a dramatic demonstration of the nature and intrinsic value of justice, Plato enables us to understand the nature and intrinsic value of this unique form of education. The ideal of this education is the development of individuals who have the capacity and inclination for rational action. This action is guided by knowledge that is both empirical and normative, obtained by means of certain theoretical methods, dialectically grounded in principles, and achieved by means of certain practical methods, including prudence and the moral virtues. Any institution that seeks to realize this ideal must be independent of all extrinsic purposes.   It must provide a curriculum that consists in the empirical and normative liberal sciences, the theoretical liberal arts, philosophy, and the practical liberal arts. And finally, it must have teachers who are uncompromised in their commitment to teaching in a program of liberal education.

---

[50]*Republic* 518.
[51]*Apology* 33.
[52]*Republic* 525.
[53]*Meno* 80.
[54]*Apology* 30.
[55]*Symposium* 215.

ARISTOTLE'S CONCEPT OF LIBERAL EDUCATION

In the *Nicomachean Ethics* and the *Metaphysics* Aristotle presents a description of the good human life and its highest achievements.[56] From this description, together with Aristotle's frequent comments about the educational implications of his description, it is possible to detail the Aristotelian concept of liberal education. This includes the ideal of this unique form of education, its ideal institution, its ideal curriculum, and its ideal teacher.

THE IDEAL OF LIBERAL EDUCATION

The description of the good life that is presented in the *Nicomachean Ethics* belongs to the science that we call ethics, which is itself part of a generic science that Aristotle calls politics [*politike*]. In the first four chapters of the *Nicomachean Ethics* Aristotle characterizes this science on the basis of his four causes or modes of explanation. In terms of its material cause, or subject matter, politics is concerned with human action. Since it seeks knowledge for the sake of action, or practice, not knowledge for its own sake, politics is a practical science, not a theoretical science. But it is a special kind of practical science, not to be confused with the productive sciences, those that are directed toward the creation of some product. In terms of its formal cause, or essence, politics is characterized as the architectonic practical science. It alone has the authority to determine the good for man and the state. These two projects are pursued by Aristotle in the *Nicomachean Ethics* and the *Politics*. In terms of its efficient cause, or method, politics, like all practical sciences, is limited to conclusions that aspire to probability, in contrast to the theoretical sciences, where conclusions aspire to certainty. Finally, in terms of its final cause, or aim, politics seeks to discover the highest of all goods achievable by action. This, all people verbally agree, is "happiness" [*eudaimonia*], even though they disagree on the meaning of this ambiguous word.

Aristotle's characterization of politics as a practical science which seeks to discover the highest of all goods achievable by action prefigures his eventual conclusion that the highest good for man is a kind of activity. In the text of the *Nicomachean Ethics* the insight that the highest human good is an activity is brought about in a decisive way early in Book I.[57] After having formulated the question of politics as the question of what is the highest of all goods achievable by action, Aristotle urges his readers to reflect upon the assumptions implicit in this question, and thus to see that the question raised can only be answered if we can first ascertain the human function.[58] This function, he then argues, cannot be

---

[56] All references to the works of Aristotle are to *The Basic Works of Aristotle*, Richard McKeon, ed. (New York: Random House, 1941). The pagination is that of the Bekker edition of the Greek text.

[57] *Nicomachean Ethics* 1.7.1097b23.

[58] *Nicomachean Ethics* 1.7.1095a15.

"nutrition or growth" or "perception" because these functions are not specifically human functions. The only specifically human function, he says, is "an active life of the element that has a rational principle."[59] He insists that this must be an activity, not a disposition or a state. This is brought out by his objections to the vulgar view that happiness is a sensation, and later in his summary description of happiness.[60] Happiness cannot be a sensation, such as pleasure, for if this were true, a person could be happy and be asleep or in a drug induced trance. The good human life, he insists, is a life in which things are done, not just felt. Similarly, as he argues later, the good life is not one in which things are just thought; rather we must act.[61]

On the basis of this text it is apparent that, since the good human life is a life of action, not merely thought, the educational program required for the development of this person is one that will enable this person to participate in a certain kind of activity. The meaning of this conclusion needs to be explained in detail:

1.

Being an animal, a human being will necessarily act in some ways that are involuntary. But a human being also has the capacity to act voluntarily, and often, on the basis of choice. The admission that a human being has the capacity to act on the basis of choice is at once the admission that mere action is not a sufficient condition for the good life. This is true because, as Aristotle says, "choice involves a rational principle and thought."[62] This means that the good or happy human life must necessarily include actions that are chosen on the basis of their being justified in some appropriate way. Such actions Aristotle calls virtuous actions. This important insight is indicated when he announces that the human good "turns out to be activity of soul in accordance with virtue."[63]

For Aristotle there are different kinds of virtues because there are different ways that actions are rational. Not all actions, of course, are justified on the basis of reasons. Actions involved in nutrition and growth, for instance, and involuntary actions in general, are not undertaken on the basis of reasons. Other actions are justified in a familiar and straightforward way, as when these actions are undertaken on the basis of conclusions of arguments that are justified on the basis of premises. These are the paradigmatic examples of "rational" actions. Still other actions are justified only indirectly. These actions Aristotle calls "appetitive," and they are habitual ways of behaving that are justified on the ground that they allow us to control our desires in a rational way. It is on the basis of this division of the kinds of actions for which human beings are capable

---

[59]*Nicomachean Ethics* 1.7.1098a4.

[60]*Nicomachean Ethics* 1.5.1095b14; 10.6.1176a33.

[61]*Nicomachean Ethics* 10.9.1179a35.

[62]*Nicomachean Ethics* 3.2.1112a16.

[63]*Nicomachean Ethics* 1.7.1098a17.

that Aristotle divides the virtues into two kinds: the moral and the intellectual. The *Ethics* outlines the moral virtues beginning with Book II, Chapter 7, and the intellectual virtues beginning with Book VI, Chapter 1.[64]

The moral virtues are disciplined "appetites." They are rational and habitual ways of choosing a mean between two extremes relative to the individual making the choice. Aristotle lists thirteen examples of the moral virtues. Three of the most important--and three of the four Greek cardinal virtues--are courage, justice, and temperance. Courage is disciplined fear, justice (in one of its senses) is a kind of disciplined desire for external goods such as wealth and honor, and temperance is the disciplined desire for pleasure. The moral virtues, being habitual ways of choosing, are developed primarily by training, not teaching. They are developed by repetition that is accompanied by rewards and punishments, and this development is traditionally the responsibility of institutions like the family, the school, customs, and laws.

The intellectual virtues, on the other hand, are rational ways of thinking. They are acquired primarily by teaching. Aristotle divides the intellectual virtues into two types, the "scientific" and the "calculative" (or "deliberative"), according to whether thinking has as its object necessary or contingent explanations. The "scientific" intellectual virtues include "intuitive reason" [*nous*], "scientific knowledge" [*episteme*], and "philosophic wisdom" [*sophia*]. "Intuitive reason" is the capacity to grasp the premises of arguments, "scientific knowledge" is the capacity to demonstrate conclusions from these premises, and "philosophic wisdom"[65] is the union of "intuitive reason" and "scientific knowledge" about "the highest objects." Aside from indicating that "philosophic wisdom" is not to be misunderstood as "political wisdom" or "practical wisdom," Aristotle postpones any further explanation of it until Book X.[66] His assumption in describing these "scientific" intellectual virtues is that the good human being must be able to reason in the sense of grasping truths and drawing valid inferences from them.

The "calculative" intellectual virtues include "practical wisdom" (or prudence) [*phronesis*] and "art" [*techne*]. "Practical wisdom" is the reasoned capacity to act with regard to the things that are in general good or bad for human beings, while "art" is the reasoned capacity to make things, to bring things into being. Aristotle's assumption in describing these "calculative" virtues is that the good human being must engage in reasoned actions, some of which are means to ends, and others of which are ends in themselves.

Throughout the *Nicomachean Ethic* Aristotle assumes that good human action is action "which follows a rational principle."[67] While Aristotle does not yet explain what is meant by "a rational principle," it is clear that he intends some form of knowledge, not some form of external authority or an internal feeling

---

[64]*Nicomachean Ethics* 2.7.1107a27; 6.1.1138b17.

[65]*Nicomachean Ethics* 6.7.1141a18.

[66]*Nicomachean Ethics* 10.7.1177a24.

[67]*Nicomachean Ethics* 1.7.1098a4.

such as pleasure, love, compassion, or ambition. This knowledge will necessarily be of two kinds: theoretical or empirical, that is, the knowledge that is required for us to understand the way things are, and practical or normative, that is, the knowledge that is required for us to understand the way things should be.

Given Aristotle's description of the good life as one consisting in the exercise of the moral and intellectual virtues, we can infer that the kind of education that is required to develop the good person is one that will enable this person to act on the basis of empirical and normative knowledge.

2.

For Aristotle knowledge consists in the justified, or grounded, conclusions of arguments.   Ultimately these arguments are analyzable into syllogisms that demonstrate the truth or probability of conclusions on the basis of premises. In the *Organon* Aristotle describes in detail the methods that are available for the induction of premises and for the deduction of conclusions from these premises. In the first three books of the *Organon* he develops the rules governing the signification of terms, the predication of propositions, and the inference of the syllogism.   The *Categories* considers the rules governing the univocal signification of terms. *On Interpretation* considers the rules governing the true predication of propositions.   And the *Prior Analytics* considers the rules governing valid inference in the syllogism. In the last three books of the *Organon* Aristotle considers the kinds of premises available for syllogisms. The *Posterior Analytics* considers premises that are true, and that therefore yield arguments that are scientific and certain. The *Topics* considers premises that are opinions, and that therefore yield arguments that are probable. And *On Sophistical Refutations* considers premises that are opinions that are insubstantial, and that therefore yield arguments that are fallacious.   Thus the *Organon*, together with the *Rhetoric*, provide detailed studies of the various methods or arts of reasoning that are required for the achievement of knowledge. Since no knowledge is possible without these methods or arts, we may conclude that for Aristotle the kind of education that is required for the realization of the good life is a form that will develop in individuals the capacity and inclination for action that is guided by knowledge that is both empirical and normative, and that is obtained by certain theoretical skills.

3.

As we have seen, the concept of the good life presented in the *Nicomachean Ethics* is incomplete because it does not include an explanation of the kind of knowledge that is provided by the highest intellectual virtue, "philosophic wisdom." When Aristotle describes "wisdom,"[68] he does little more than indicate

---

[68]*Nicomachean Ethics* 6.7.1141a9.

that it is the highest intellectual virtue, and that it is the highest intellectual virtue because it provides knowledge of the "highest objects." Although Aristotle tells us that these "highest objects" are "first principles," he provides us with no further clue as to their identity. The only other help that he provides for our understanding is in Book X.[69] There he characterizes this virtue as "contemplation." "Contemplation" is described as an activity that is concerned with "the best of knowable objects," that is "most continuous," "pleasantest," "self-sufficient," and "leisured," and that is "loved for its own sake." But while this description reinforces his claim that "wisdom" is the most important of the virtues, and while he does explicitly identify it as "reason,"[70] he provides no further explanation, and thus leaves us unenlightened about the kind of knowledge that is the object of this virtue.

He remedies this deficiency in the *Metaphysics*. This work describes a science which today is most often called "metaphysics," following the name given to Aristotle's work by Andronicus of Rhodes, but which Aristotle himself alternately refers to as "wisdom,"[71] "first philosophy,"[72] and "theology."[73] Since this new science, like all sciences, is a body of knowledge, Aristotle's first project is to explain the nature of knowledge, to distinguish between its different forms, and to judge the relative importance of these different forms. The most primitive form he takes to be "sensation" [*aisthesis*]. This form, such as sight, allows us to distinguish between things, and is shared by human beings with most other animals. Superior to sensation is "memory" [*myeme*]. Memory allows us to recapture the past in the present, and this kind of knowledge is shared by human beings with some, but not all, of the other animals. Superior to memory is "experience" [*empeiria*]. This capacity is exceptionally developed in human beings and allows them to anticipate particular events on the basis of memories of past events. A significantly higher form of knowledge is "art" [*techne*]. "Art" is superior to "experience" because only at the level of "art" do human beings intuit the universal implicit in the particular, and thereby grasp the cause or the reason why things are as they are. Still higher than "art" is "science" [*episteme*]. Eventually Aristotle refers his readers to the *Nicomachean Ethics* in order to explain the difference between "art" and "science."[74] There he explains this difference as the difference between a true course of reasoning required to achieve some good, and a true course of reasoning required for the demonstration of a truth.[75] Finally, Aristotle describes the highest form of science, and therefore, the highest form of knowledge, as "wisdom"--that is, "philosophic wisdom" [*sophia*].[76] "Wisdom" is a form of knowledge that is concerned with the truth about "the first principles and causes."

[69]*Nicomachean Ethics* 10.7.1177a12-10.8.1179a33.

[70]*Nicomachean Ethics* 10.7.1177b18.

[71]*Metaphysics* 1.1.981b26.

[72]*Metaphysics* 4.2.1004a3.

[73]*Metaphysics* 11.7.1064b2.

[74]*Nicomachean Ethics* 1.1.981b25.

In the *Metaphysics* Aristotle explains the terms "principle" [*arche*] and "cause" [*aitia*].[77] A principle is a beginning, and in one of its senses it is a beginning for an argument--that is, a premise or a reason. Causes are beginnings, or reasons, that account for the being and becoming of things. Since in both the *Metaphysics*[78] and the *Posterior Analytics*[79] Aristotle rejects the possibility of an infinite regress in a causal series as being self-contradictory, a first principle or cause is a beginning or a reason which accounts for conclusions which cannot themselves be demonstrated on the basis of superior principles or causes.

Aristotle provides several examples of first principles and causes. One example is the "unmoved mover" of *Metaphysics* XII, a cause which is a presupposition of the existence of natural change. Other examples are the "axioms" of mathematics and the "common axioms" of Book IV of the *Metaphysics* and Book I of the *Posterior Analytics*. The latter include the principle of non-contradiction (the law governing the signification of terms), the principle of the excluded middle (the law governing the predication of propositions), and the principle of the syllogism (the law governing the inference of arguments). A further example is the moral ideal of the rational life of politics and ethics, a presupposition of all action that is voluntary and intentional.

Once "wisdom" has been characterized as the science of first principles and causes, and once the expression, "first principles and causes," has been defined and illustrated, Aristotle is ready to explain why "wisdom" is the highest theoretical science. This is done in a succinct and elegant way in *Metaphysics* I.[80] There, in what is surely one of the greatest of the *loci classici* of the ideal of liberal education, he argues that "wisdom" is the highest theoretical science because the knowledge that it provides (1) is the most comprehensive (because its objects are universals--laws, principles, causes, truths--and universals in a sense include all of the particulars that fall under them), (2) is the most difficult (because its objects are farthest from the senses), (3) is the most exact (because its objects are first principles, and first principles are more exact or certain than the particulars that fall under them), (4) is the most instructive (because its objects are the causes of things, and a knowledge of the causes of things is the essence of instruction), (5) is the most independent (because its objects are the first principles and causes, which, by virtue of being first, are presupposed by all other forms of knowledge, and because it is desired for its own sake and not as a means to some other end, as is productive knowledge [*techne*]), and finally, (6) is the most authoritative (because its objects are the highest ends of human life, and therefore are presupposed by any practical science [*phronesis*]).

---

[75]*Nicomachean Ethics* 6.3.1139b14.
[76]*Nicomachean Ethics* 6.7.1141a16.
[77]*Metaphysics* 5.1.1012b34ff.
[78]*Metaphysics* 2.2.994a1.
[79]*Posterior Analytics* 1.19.81b38ff.
[80]*Metaphysics* 1.2.982a5-983a23.

Aristotle summarizes his explanation and encomium of "wisdom" by the statement that it is "the only free science," and, as a consequence of this, it is "the least necessary," but "the best" science.[81]

Aristotle's assessment of the absolute importance of "wisdom," just as his assessment of the relative importance of the other forms of knowledge and virtue, is clearly based on the same functionalist principle that he uses to determine the character of the good life. If a person is to achieve the human good, and thus, to be "happy," then this person must act in accordance with the moral virtues. But, since the exercise of the moral virtues requires knowledge and choice, action in accordance with the moral virtues requires the intellectual virtues. This is to say that one cannot, for example, be courageous unless one has the reasoned capacity to act with regard to the things that are in general good or bad for man ["prudence" or "practical wisdom"] and the reasoned capacity to bring particular things into being ["art"]. And "prudence," in turn, is impossible unless one has the capacity to grasp truths about the situation that calls for the courageous act ["intuitive reason"], as well as the capacity to validly reason to conclusions that follow from these truths ["scientific knowledge"]. Thus, the good or "happy" human life requires action, and action requires the moral virtues, and the moral virtues require the intellectual virtues, and the intellectual virtues must include "wisdom." "Wisdom" is required because it alone provides us with knowledge of those theoretical and practical principles that enable human thought and action to be rational. And unless human thought and action are rational, no human life can be good.

Since for Aristotle the good life requires action guided by theoretical and practical knowledge, and since such knowledge cannot be grounded in an infinite regress of principles, but must be grounded in first principles, the legitimacy of these first principles must be established. This poses a problem. Obviously these first principles cannot be treated as arbitrary assumptions. If they were so treated, then they could not be considered as grounds for the knowledge of the various special sciences. Nor can they be treated as mere beliefs or personal preferences. If they were so treated, then the knowledge that is required for the guidance of human action would be grounded only in beliefs or preferences which themselves would be ungrounded, and which could just as well be replaced by their own contradictories. Nor can these first principles be treated as hypotheses or as the dicta of some authority. If they were, they would not be first principles, but would be dependent on principles required for the verification of hypotheses, or on the principles legitimizing the dicta of the authority. Aristotle's general problem, therefore, is the need to justify principles that justify the conclusions of the various sciences, but which cannot themselves be justified by the conclusions which they justify.

Aristotle illustrates this problem in the *Metaphysics* in his attempt to justify one of the "common axioms," the principle of non-contradiction. The principle that "the same attribute cannot at the same time belong and not belong to the same

---

[81]*Metaphysics* 1.2.983a10.

subject and in the same respect" makes scientific proof or demonstration possible. If we were to demand that this principle itself be demonstrated, we would, in Aristotle's view, show a "want of education" due to our inability to see that such a demand would require an infinite regress or a *petitio principii*. At the same time, if this principle cannot be justified, then all scientific knowledge is problematic.

It is at this point that Aristotle makes a decisive move. He recognizes that, although the first principles cannot be demonstrated to follow from more fundamental truths, they can be "defended" as necessary presuppositions of there being any truths whatsoever. Aristotle's strategy in the "defense" of the principle of non-contradiction is to show that anyone who might want to demonstrate that the principle is false would have to assume its truth. This means that this principle is "the most certain of all principles."[82] A similar strategy is followed in the defense of other theoretical first principles.

This same strategy is also appropriate for the defense of practical first principles, such as the first principle of morality. In the *Nicomachean Ethics*, after arguing in Book I that the good or happy life is determined on the basis of the human function, he reveals in Book X that his entire argument is grounded in the principle that the human good is the life of reason. "Reason more than anything else *is* man," he declares.[83] While this principle cannot be deduced from any more fundamental principle, and therefore, cannot be "demonstrated" to be true, it can be "defended" as a necessary presupposition of any action required to determine an alternative proposal. Those who doubt that the highest human obligation is the life of reason tacitly acknowledge this obligation. It is the possession of this knowledge that entitles "wisdom" to be called the "most authoritative" science,[84] and the "least necessary, but the best" of the sciences.[85] The wise person, above all else, has knowledge of the principles of morality.

Aristotle's "defense" of first principles is an application of a method that he calls "dialectic." While Plato holds dialectic to be a method of reasoning that has universal application, Aristotle holds it to be a method of reasoning which has limited but nonetheless necessary applications. While scientific demonstration reasons from premises that are true and establishes conclusions that are certain, and while rhetoric is a sort of demonstration which reasons from premises that are opinions and seeks conclusions that are probable, dialectic reasons from premises that are opinions and establishes conclusions that are certain. This is discussed in *Posterior Analytics* I, 1-2, *Rhetoric* I, 1, and *Topics* I, 1. In the *Topics* Aristotle points out that dialectic alone is essential for the criticism of the principles of the special sciences since these principles cannot be criticized on the basis of the conclusions that the principles themselves justify.[86]

---

[82]*Metaphysics* 4.3.1005b18.
[83]*Nicomachean Ethics* 10.7.1178a7.
[84]*Metaphysics* 1.2.982b5.
[85]*Metaphysics* 1.2.983a10.
[86]*Topics* 1.2.101a37.

To a skeptical age the Aristotelian method of dialectic has the appearance of an imposture. But Aristotle insists that even though it begins from mere opinions, it can establish truths that are certain and essential to the justification of all of the special sciences. Without it, human beings are left with mere opinion.

These considerations support the conclusion that for Aristotle the kind of education that is required for the realization of the good life is a form that will develop in individuals the capacity and inclination for action that is guided by knowledge that is both empirical and normative, that is obtained by certain intellectual skills, and that is justified dialectically in the unconditioned principle of morality.

4.

For Aristotle the good life is godlike. In describing it in the *Nicomachean Ethics*, a philosopher who ordinarily personifies the ideals of cool analysis and scientific objectivity becomes impassioned and poetic:

> If reason is divine, then, in comparison with man, the life according to it is divine in comparison with human life. But we must not follow those who advise us, being men, to think of human things, and being mortal, of mortal things, but must, so far as we can, make ourselves immortal, and strain every nerve to live in accordance with the best thing in us; for even if it be small in bulk, much more does it in power and worth surpass everything.[87]

Obviously the good life is an ideal that challenges the refractoriness of human reality. In its pursuit human beings will be aided by the generosity of nature and by good fortune. But good will alone will not suffice. "External goods," such as food and good health, cannot be disregarded, so he argues in the *Nicomachean Ethics*.[88] Still, he says, we must not overestimate these needs. "We can do noble acts without ruling earth and sea; for even with moderate advantages one can act virtuously . . . ."[89] But the good life cannot be lived without the intellectual virtues. And these require study, discipline, care, and effort. This is particularly true for "philosophic wisdom," which seeks knowledge that is farthest removed from the senses, and therefore is the most difficult to obtain.

The intellectual virtues, in turn, cannot be obtained without the moral virtues. Study, discipline, care, and effort require the good habits that constitute good character. "Philosophic wisdom," above all else, cannot be obtained without the moral virtues of courage, justice, and temperance. Courage is essential because the news is not always good news, and our tasks are sometimes formidable.

---

[87]*Nicomachean Ethics* 10.7.1177b30.

[88]*Nicomachean Ethics* 1.8.1099a31 and 10.8.1178b33.

[89]*Nicomachean Ethics* 10.8.1179a4.

Justice is essential because our ambitions must be restrained. And temperance is essential because rational action cannot be obtained unless our desires are disciplined.

The importance of prudence and the moral virtues for the good life is also clearly shown by Aristotle's insistence that ethics is not a proper study for a young person. He justifies this by reminding his readers in the *Nicomachean Ethics* that a young person is inexperienced in the actions of life that constitute the subject matter of ethics and "tends to follow his passions," and by arguing that because of this, and because the aim of ethics is not knowledge but action, "his study will be vain and unprofitable."[90]

The importance of the moral virtues to the good life is also apparent from Aristotle's claim that good individuals require good upbringing, good friends, good laws, good customs, and good constitutions. This is true, he says, because "the good man must be trained and habituated" by these institutions.[91]

These considerations make it clear that for Aristotle the education of the good person cannot be a purely intellectual matter. The good person must possess capacities that are difficult to obtain, and these capacities cannot be obtained by those who lack good character. Consequently, we can conclude that the kind of education that is required by Aristotle for the development of the good or happy person is a form that will provide people with the capacity and inclination to act on the basis of knowledge that is both empirical and normative, that is obtained by means of certain theoretical skills, that is dialectically grounded in an unconditional principle of morality, and that is acquired with the aid of certain practical skills such as prudence and the moral virtues.

THE IDEAL INSTITUTION FOR LIBERAL EDUCATION

In his treatment of the intellectual virtues in Book VI of the *Nicomachean Ethics* Aristotle remarks that philosophers like Thales and Anaxagoras lacked prudence or "practical wisdom" but possessed "philosophic wisdom." He describes "philosophic wisdom" as knowledge that is "remarkable, admirable, difficult, and divine, but useless."[92] Similarly, in the *Metaphysics*, as we have previously noted, he states that all of the other sciences are "more necessary" than "philosophic wisdom," but that "none is better."[93] Since it is common practice to judge the value of something on the basis of its use or necessity for some purpose, Aristotle's description of "philosophic wisdom" as being a science that is "useless," but nonetheless the best, is paradoxical, and calls for explanation.

In the *Metaphysics* Aristotle uses both "art" and "science" to refer to knowledge of universals. As we previously noted, "art" [*techne*] is distinguished

---

[90]*Nicomachean Ethics* 1.3.1095a2-12.
[91]*Nicomachean Ethics* 10.9.1180a14.
[92]*Nicomachean Ethics* 6.7.1141b7.
[93]*Metaphysics* 1.2.983a10.

from "science" [*episteme*] in that art is applied knowledge, while "science" is pure knowledge. Knowledge that is applied is used as a means to some end. For instance, the knowledge of a craftsman could be a means to the end of wealth. But wealth in turn could be a means to a higher end, such as happiness. A corollary to this is that from the standpoint of the agent, whatever is an end relative to a means is thereby more desired or better than the means. For instance, for Aristotle knowledge about the nature of happiness is better than knowledge of how to obtain wealth. Moreover, if there should be an end which is not in turn a means to some higher end, then this end would be the "best" end. From these considerations it follows that some knowledge could be "useless" and still be the "best" if in fact this knowledge is intrinsically valuable--that is, if it is an end which is not itself a means to some higher end. Aristotle argues that what he calls "philosophic wisdom" (or "wisdom") meets this rigorous requirement, and therefore deserves to be called "useless," but still "the best" science, or form of knowledge.

"Wisdom" is described in the *Nicomachean Ethics* as the union of "intuitive reason" and "scientific knowledge" about "the highest objects."[94] It has two essential characteristics: (1) It is a "science," not an "art," because it is knowledge of universals that is pure, not applied. It is thus knowledge that is desired for its own sake, not, as in the case of "art" (e.g., technology), knowledge that is desired for the sake of a productive purpose. Because of this, "wisdom" is a "useless" science. (2) In addition, "wisdom" differs from all other species of "science" in being the highest science. It is the highest science because it has the highest objects--the most comprehensive universals, specifically, the "first principles and causes."[95] Because of this, "wisdom" is "the best" science.

The claim that "wisdom" is "useless" but also "the best" science is Aristotle's way of recognizing that it is the most paradigmatic form of knowledge; it is knowledge of universals that are comprehensive because they are not limited by practical purposes or by theoretical assumptions.

Anyone who has the most comprehensive knowledge, and who therefore knows "the first principles and causes," including the unconditioned principle of morality, and who therefore knows "to what end each thing must be done" should be in a position to lead others, and not to be led. "Wisdom," therefore, is the "most authoritative" science. Its importance is also shown in the *Nicomachean Ethics* by the fact that Aristotle refers to the lover of "wisdom"--the person who lives the life of reason--as supremely happy, and "the dearest to the gods."[96]

Not only is "wisdom" the most important of the sciences, but, as we noted earlier, it is also exceedingly difficult. It is difficult because it studies the first principles and causes; and since these universals are farthest from the senses, they

---

[94]*Nicomachean Ethics* 6.7.1141a18.
[95]*Metaphysics* 1.1.981b27.
[96]*Nicomachean Ethics* 10.8.1179a30.

are the hardest to know.[97] It is also difficult because "wisdom" cannot be obtained without the moral virtues, such as courage and temperance, and the acquisition of the moral virtues is a long and arduous task.

Once we understand why "wisdom" is both difficult and supremely important, we are in a position to describe the kind of institution that would be required for an educational program having "wisdom" as its goal. Clearly this institution would have a unique and privileged status with respect to all other institutions and individuals in a society. It would differ from all other educational institutions in having a purpose that is intrinsically good. To the extent that this institution, either voluntarily or involuntarily, would serve extrinsic purposes, and thus become "useful," then to that extent it would fail to serve its own special purpose. An institution dedicated to the ideal of "wisdom" cannot at the same time be used to serve individual or institutional interests since the interests of individuals and institutions do not always coincide with the ideal of "wisdom." Therefore, an institution dedicated to "wisdom" must be the most independent of all institutions. It is a caretaker only for an intrinsic good. Its ultimate task is to facilitate the development of wise people, not to serve as an instrument for the realization of individual purposes.   Just as Aristotle has summarizes his description of "wisdom" by the claim that it is "the only free science, for it alone exists for its own sake,"[98] we might, with equal justification, say that any institution dedicated to the development of wise people must be the only free institution, for it alone exists for its own sake.

THE IDEAL CURRICULUM FOR LIBERAL EDUCATION

For Aristotle, the good (i.e., the "happy") person possesses the following competencies:

1. empirical ("theoretical") and normative ("practical") knowledge
2. the theoretical skills (the "intellectual virtues") necessary to obtain this knowledge
3. dialectical insight into principles to ground this knowledge
4. the practical skills ("prudence" and the moral virtues) necessary to act on the basis of this knowledge.

The required components of a liberal education are those that are necessary to develop the essential competencies of the good person:

1. the liberal ("free") empirical and normative sciences
2. the theoretical liberal arts (the "arts" of the "organon")
3. philosophy ("metaphysics" or "dialectic")

---

[97]*Metaphysics* 1.2.982a11.
[98]*Metaphysics* 1.2.982b26.

4. the practical liberal arts ("practical wisdom," i.e., "prudence," and the "moral virtues")

THE IDEAL TEACHER FOR LIBERAL EDUCATION

Inasmuch as the wise person must possess a variety of competencies that can only be developed by different curricular components, and, assuming the need for specialization, Aristotle has no single model of the ideal teacher. Liberal education requires a variety of teaching competencies. Some are needed to provide the knowledge of the liberal sciences. Others are needed for the development of the theoretical skills required to obtain this knowledge. Others are needed to catalyze the integration of this knowledge by the discovery and defense of principles. And finally, still other are needed to conduct the training that is required for the development of prudence and the moral virtues.

For the systematic study of the liberal sciences, the ideal teachers are scientists, disciplinary authorities. These scientists must include authorities who have an understanding of the way things are, and authorities who have an understanding of the way things ought to be. For the development of the universal theoretical skills, the ideal teachers are scientists, logicians, rhetoricians, and dialecticians. To catalyze the discovery and defense of principles, the appropriate teachers are the dialecticians. For the development of the prudential skills, the ideal teachers are those who are prudent, and who can teach by personal example. For the development of the cardinal moral virtues, the ideal teachers are those who have good character, and who can best train others in the formation of habits.

****

Aristotle's *Ethics* and *Metaphysics* provide us with another of the *loci classici* of liberal education. In describing the educational program required for the development of the wise or "happy" person, Aristotle presents us with an ideal that coincides with the Platonic ideal. Both require an institution that will develop people who possess the capacity and inclination for action that is guided by knowledge of what is and what ought to be, that is obtained by means of the theoretical liberal arts, that is dialectically grounded in the unconditioned principle of morality, and that takes place with the aid of prudence and the cardinal moral virtues. Any educational institution that is committed to this intrinsically valuable purpose must be independent of all extrinsic purposes. The curriculum of this institution must include the theoretical and practical liberal sciences, the theoretical liberal arts, philosophy, and the practical liberal arts. And finally, this institution must be staffed by teachers who are uncompromised in their commitment to teaching in a program of liberal education, and who are able to develop the requisite knowledge, skills, principles, and virtues.

DEWEY'S THEORY OF LIBERAL EDUCATION

Dewey's Criticism of Liberal Education

John Dewey has the reputation for being a resolute and life-long opponent of liberal education. In *Democracy and Education*, his major work devoted to educational theory, he deplored the "illiberality" of this form of education.[99] Many years later, at the age of 85, he restated his criticism in an interview in the *New York Times*, attacking Robert M. Hutchins' theory of liberal education, charging that it was "reactionary" and "fatal to the whole democratic outlook."[100]

Dewey's opposition to liberal education can be summarized in three familiar charges:

1. Liberal education is undemocratic.

Dewey identifies liberal education as "cultural education." He means by this that the effective purpose of this form of education is to provide the members of the aristocratic class with the cultural credentials that certify their privileged status. Since it serves this purpose, and thus is "for the few economically able to enjoy it,"[101] it disserves a democratic society. It perpetuates a division between those who live lives of "idle conspicuous display,"[102] and those whose labor as a servile class makes an effete, leisured class possible.[103]

2. Liberal education is exclusively theoretical.

Dewey criticizes liberal education for its devotion to disinterested contemplation or knowledge for its own sake, for making "an individual more at home in the life of other days than in his own,"[104] and for subordinating "civic relations to the purely cognitive life."[105]

3. Liberal education is nonvocational.

Dewey also criticizes liberal education for its condescension toward what is useful or practical, and for being opposed to the "recognition of the vocational

---

[99]M10:200. Whenever possible, notes to the works of Dewey are to *John Dewey: The Collected Works, 1882-1953*, Jo Ann Boydston, ed. (Carbondale, Ill.: Southern Illinois University Press, 1991). Notes will identify the series ("E" for "The Early Works," "M" for "The Middle Works," and "L" for "The Later Works"), the volume number, and the page number.

[100]*New York Times*, 20 October 1944, 32.

[101]M9:329.

[102]M9:323.

[103]M9:143, 200, 259, 265, 269.

[104]M9:369.

[105]M9:287.

phases of life . . . ."[106] This attitude is seen by Dewey as a consequence of liberal education's preoccupation with abstract theory, and ultimately, as a consequence of its subservience to the interests of the aristocratic class.

An Evaluation of Dewey's Criticism

Even a cursory review of Dewey's works on educational theory provides reasons for the suspicion that his reputation as a resolute opponent of liberal education may be undeserved. For example, Dewey uses the word "education" in many different ways, and this diversity may occasion misunderstandings. In its broadest sense "education" is understood by him to be "the means of social continuity of life."[107] Through education a society transmits and conserves its achievements, and thus perpetuates itself in spite of the finite lives of its individual members. But Dewey also uses "education" in a number of more restricted and technical senses. He variously speaks of "general education," "traditional education," "vocational education," "trade education," "professional and industrial education," "moral education," "cultural education," "progressive education," "the democratic conception of education," and "liberal education."

A more careful review of Dewey's charges against "liberal education" suggests that his opposition is not at all directed to what in this book has been defined as "liberal education." Evidence for this can be found in each of his major charges:

1.

As we have noted, Dewey holds that since "liberal education" is "for the few economically able to enjoy it," it does not serve the interests of a democracy. Instead of aiding in the formation of an egalitarian society, it perpetuates a division between those who live lives of "idle conspicuous display," and those who live lives of involuntary and demeaning servitude to support this leisure class.[108]

Dewey seems to be at least partially correct in this charge if what he means by "liberal education" is the educational institution that in his day was called by this name. But he is arguably incorrect if he is speaking of the Platonic or Aristotelian ideal of liberal education, and he is patently incorrect if he is speaking of the ideal of liberal education as it has been defined here.

Some might challenge this interpretation by pointing out that Dewey does in fact regard the most valued form of education--what he calls "progressive education"--as subservient to the needs of democracy. He frequently identifies progressive education as "the democratic conception of education."[109] His

---

[106]M9:329.
[107]M9:5.
[108]M9:143, 200, 259, 261, 266, 269.
[109]M9:87-106.

extended defense of this concept and his even more extended defense of the politics of democracy may easily lead to the conclusion that "the democratic conception of education" is responsible for developing democratic citizens and constitutions. However, Dewey explicitly disowns this interpretation. He rejects the view that "progressive education" should be an instrument for the realization of particular political purposes.[110] He contends that the most valued form of education is a process of "growth" which aims only at an added capacity for "growth" or further education. "Education for growth," he writes, only "adds to the meaning of experience, and increases ability to direct the course of subsequent experience."[111]

Those who read Dewey as subordinating education to political purposes are likely mislead by his occasional failure to remind his readers of the difference between democracy as a special political end and democracy as a political means. Nevertheless, Dewey does make this distinction:

> In the first place, democracy is much broader that a special political form, a method of conducting government or of making laws and carrying on governmental administration by means of popular suffrage and elected officials. It is that, of course. But it is something broader and deeper than that.   The political and governmental phase of democracy is a means, the best means so far found, for realizing ends that lie in the wide domain of human relationships and the development of human personality. It is . . . a way of life, social and individual. The keynote of democracy as a way of life may be expressed . . . as the necessity of the participation of every mature human being in the formation of the values that regulate the living of men together.[112]

"Liberal education" as it has been defined here is democratic in Dewey's "broader and deeper" sense. It not only does not reject, but in fact explicitly assumes, the need of every mature human being to live a life that is free--that is, ultimately, rational. At the same time, this form of education, like Dewey's, is not democratic in the sense that it is subordinate to any particular polity, policy, or party.   Consequently, any charge that the ideal of liberal education is undemocratic in the "broader and deeper" sense must be rejected as groundless.

It might be helpful to note that for Dewey education in its "broader and deeper" sense "stands in principle for free interchange, for social continuity."[113] Thus, when speaking of "progressive education" or the "democratic conception of education," Dewey might better have said "an education based upon open,

---

[110]In *Experience and Nature* (L1:411) Dewey allows philosophy to be "an instrument for social reforms" only if "social reform" is conceived as "the liberation and expansion of the meanings of which experience is capable."

[111]M9:82.

[112]L11:217.

[113]M9:354.

unbiased communication." This usage might have prevented the common misunderstanding that Dewey views education in its most valued sense as subordinate to a specific political dogma or purpose.

2.

As we observed earlier, Dewey criticizes "liberal education" for its exclusively theoretical orientation. But as "liberal education" has been defined here, its preference for "pure" knowledge over "applied" knowledge is simply a consequence of its quest for knowledge in its most valued sense--that is, knowledge that is not subordinate to uncriticized assumptions or purposes. This "knowledge most worth having" is wisdom, and it necessarily includes knowledge of what is and knowledge of what ought to be. Clearly, "liberal education" so defined is not exclusively or even primarily theoretical.

Dewey supports his criticism of the theoretical orientation of what he understands by "liberal education" by frequent criticism of the Platonic and the Aristotelian theories of liberal education. He faults Plato's educational philosophy for being "in bondage to static ideals,"[114] but in doing so he ignores the fact that Platonic ideals are static only in the sense that they are the ideals of a completed dialectic. He criticizes Aristotle for "subordinating civic relations to the purely cognitive life" and for justifying this on the ground that "the highest end of man is not human but divine,"[115] but in making this criticism he neglects the fact that Aristotle does not hold that the highest end of man is divine, but only divine-like.[116] "Contemplation" [*theoria*] is divine-like for Aristotle not because it is a state of detachment from the world, but because it is the only form of knowledge that "exists for its own sake."[117] As such, it is "the only free science," and alone qualifies as wisdom.[118]

These considerations suggest that when Dewey criticizes "liberal education," he is most often thinking of an existing educational institution, and not an educational ideal. This appears to be the case in his assertion that "the chief content" of the term "liberal" is "uselessness for practical ends."[119] This way of defining "liberal" would not do justice to classical concepts of "liberal education," nor would it do justice to what we have defined as the ideal of liberal education. The import of the word "liberal" in our use of the expression, "liberal education," is "free or independent" in the sense of being an end-in-itself, or being intrinsically valuable. The contrast to this expression is "being dependent" in the sense of being a means to an end, or being extrinsically valuable. Since Dewey

---

[114]M9:97.

[115]M9:287.

[116]"If reason is divine, then, in comparison with man, the life according to it is divine in comparison with human life." Aristotle *Nicomachean Ethics* 10.7.1177b30.

[117]Aristotle *Metaphysics* 1.2.982b24.

[118]Ibid.

[119]M9:266.

insists that the ideal of education that he advocates and calls "progressive education" must be intrinsically valuable, he cannot object to liberal education for possessing this quality. This provides us with some reason to believe that the criticism and hostility that he directs towards "liberal education" is largely directed to what in his own day was known as "liberal education," and not to the ideal that we have defined. This view is given additional confirmation by Dewey's identification of "progressive education" as a form of education that gives priority to the development of wise people.[120]

3.

As we also previously noted, Dewey understands "liberal education" to be "opposed to the requirements of an education which shall count in the vocations of life."[121] "Liberal education" is thus thought to exclude all instruction that is useful or practical. This exclusion of "vocational education" is further assumed to be evidence of liberal education's preference for disinterested theory, of its commitment to "the conservation of the aristocratic ideals of the past," and finally, of its subordination to the interests of the privileged classes.[122]

Like the other charges that we have reviewed, this charge may well be justified if it is meant to apply generally to the institution known in Dewey's day as "liberal education." But it is probably not justified if it is meant to apply to the Platonic or Aristotelian ideals of education, and it is certainly not justified if it is meant to apply to the ideal of education that has been defined here.

The grounds for this assessment are as follows: The expression, "vocational education," is commonly used today to refer to an education designed to prepare students for a career or trade. If Dewey's charge is that what in his own day was called "liberal education" generally excluded career or trade preparation, then his charge is probably justified. But it seems unlikely that he would make this charge because he conceives of "progressive education" as being similarly opposed to career or trade education.[123] When "vocational education" becomes "trade education," he writes, it becomes "an instrument of perpetuating unchanged the existing industrial order of society, instead of operating as a means of transformation."[124] In contrast to the common use of the expression, "vocational education," to mean career or trade education, Dewey uses this expression to refer to an education that prepares students for a "calling"--that is, for the discovery of their "true business in life."[125] It is obviously this use that Dewey employs when

---

[120]M9:328, 334.

[121]M9:329.

[122]M9:329.

[123]M9:329. Note also M9:320: "To predetermine some future occupation for which education is to be a strict preparation is to injure the possibilities of present development and thereby to reduce the adequacy of preparation for a future right employment."

[124]M9:326.

[125]M9:318.

he states that the purpose of a "vocational education" is "to develop a courageous intelligence, and to make intelligence practical and executive."[126]   This is similarly the case when he writes that "the dominant vocation of all human beings at all times is living--intellectual and moral growth."[127]   In view of these statements it seems fair to say that Dewey's criticism of liberal education for excluding "vocational education" is justified only if it applies to what in his own day was popularly known as "liberal education." It would not be justified if it applies to what we have defined as liberal education because this form of education alone enables students to discover their "true business in life."

It should be noted that, along with an undeserved reputation for being opposed to "liberal education" because it excludes practical and useful interests, Dewey also has an undeserved reputation for subordinating education to student interests. Clearly Dewey insists on the pedagogical importance of interests. He writes that "the problem of instruction" is to find "material which will engage a person in specific activities having an aim or purpose of moment or interest to him, and dealing with things not as gymnastic appliances but as conditions for the attainment of ends."[128]   But this emphasis on the pedagogical importance of satisfying the interests of students should not be read as an argument in favor of the thesis that students can become liberally educated by studying whatever they are interested in. It is only an argument against allowing educational material to become "scholastic, academic, and professionally technical," and not "count in the vocations of life."[129]   "Satisfaction," Dewey emphasizes, "is not sufficient; the quality of satisfaction is essential."[130]   Moreover, when the issue of the subordination of education to student interests is recast as an issue of student rights to freedom of choice, Dewey is also opposed to a position that is often attributed to him. "The democratic idea of freedom," he writes, "is not the right of each individual to do as he pleases, even if it be qualified by adding 'provided he does not interfere with the same freedom on the part of others.'"[131] The "basic freedom," he argues, "is that of a freedom of mind and of whatever degree of freedom of action and experience is necessary to produce freedom of intelligence."[132]

The Ideal of Progressive Education

Our review of Dewey's criticisms of liberal education suggests that, while these criticisms may be justified if they are understood to be directed at an institution that was known in Dewey's day as liberal education, they are not

[126]M9:329.
[127]M9:320.
[128]M9:139.
[129]M9:143.
[130]M9:231.
[131]L11:220.
[132]L11:220.

justified if they are understood to be directed at what we have defined as the ideal of liberal education. This result suggests a possibility that heretofore would have seemed absurd: that Dewey may in fact be in agreement with the ideal that we have defined.

Early in *Democracy and Education* Dewey broaches the subject of the most valuable form of education. "As a society becomes more enlightened," he writes, "it realizes that it is responsible *not* to transmit and conserve the whole of its existing achievements, but only such as make for a better future society."[133] He then argues that this most valuable form of education cannot be one that has "an aim which is imposed upon [it] from without."[134] Otherwise it will be subordinate to "some authority external to intelligence"--that is, one which will stand independent of the process which must provide its justification.[135] "There is nothing to which education is subordinate save more education," Dewey writes.[136] Since it does not have an end, but rather *is* an end, it is intrinsically valuable.[137] This kind of education Dewey calls "progressive education."

Dewey describes this kind of education as a social or personal "reconstruction or reorganization of experience" which adds to "the meaning of experience," and which increases our "ability to direct the course of subsequent experience."[138] We add to "the meaning of experience" whenever we increase our "perception of the connections and continuities of the activities in which we are engaged."[139] We increase our ability to direct the course of subsequent experience whenever we become aware of the "significance" of these connections and continuities--that is, whenever we understand the consequences that will result when natural and human "connections" are acted upon.[140] Dewey also calls "progressive education" education for "growth." What he means by "growth" is not chaotic change; rather, he means our overcoming a difficulty "by the exercise of intelligence."[141] Intelligence, moreover, is not an amoral efficiency. This is clear from his contrast of the "training of animals" and the "education of man."[142] The former develops mere "efficiency," while the latter develops "significance." Human choice gains "significance," Dewey writes in *Experience and Nature*, when "reason for the choice is found to be weighty and its consequences momentous."[143] The development of intelligence is inseparable from the "forming of a socialized disposition."[144] The "forming of a socialized disposition"

---

[133]M9:24.
[134]M9:117.
[135]M9:111.
[136]M9:56.
[137]M9:51-53.
[138]M9:82.
[139]Ibid.
[140]L13:68.
[141]L13:79.
[142]M9:215.
[143]L1:35.
[144]M9:204.

is not to be confused with a process of indoctrinating people into a particular ideology or domesticating them into the mores of a particular society. When education is indoctrination or domestication, intelligence is limited by an external authority. Since for Dewey there is no authority external to intelligence, the "forming of socialized dispositions" must be identical with the forming of moral dispositions.[145] "The social interest," he insists, "is identical in its deepest meaning with a moral interest, and this interest is necessarily supreme with man."[146] "The dominant vocation of all human beings at all times is living-- intellectual and moral growth . . . ."[147] From this it follows that the ideal of "progressive education" is to enable individuals to conduct their lives in an intelligent, socially responsible, and moral manner.[148]

The Identity of the Ideals of Progressive and Liberal Education

These results show that the aim of "progressive education" cannot lie outside the educative process. If it did, as we have noted, it would be "imposed by some authority external to intelligence," and it would then "limit intelligence."[149] Consequently, this aim is "both means and end,"[150] and can only be formulated paradoxically. The aim of "progressive education," Dewey repeatedly says, is to enable people "to continue their education."[151] This means that "progressive education" cannot be justified by an end for which it is a means; it is rather what has been called "an end in itself." In this important respect "progressive education" is in agreement with liberal education. Both are intrinsically valuable enterprises.

By "growth" Dewey means "intellectual and moral growth."[152] Such "growth," he insists, is the "dominant vocation" of all human beings at all times.[153] In making this claim Dewey is clearly announcing that "progressive education" is from beginning to end inseparable from human action or conduct. "Our constant and unescapable concern," he writes in *Experience and Nature*, "is with prosperity and adversity, success and failure, achievement and frustration, good and bad."[154] Dewey's insistence on this point shows that in a second important respect "progressive education" is in agreement with liberal education: It gives priority to practice, not theory.

The agreement of "progressive education" with liberal education is confirmed

---

[145]M9:368.
[146]M9:297.
[147]M9:320.
[148]M9:368-370.
[149]M9:111.
[150]M9:113.
[151]M9:107.
[152]M9:320.
[153]M9:320.
[154]L1:33.

in a third and more obvious way by Dewey's thesis that "progressive education" is in fact an education in philosophy, where philosophy is assumed to be "the love of wisdom,"[155] and where wisdom is assumed to be that which "would influence the conduct of life."[156] In *Experience and Nature* Dewey makes it clear that there is nothing novel in his conception of philosophy. "It is a version of the old saying that philosophy is the love of wisdom, of wisdom which is not knowledge and which nevertheless cannot be without knowledge."[157] "Education," he writes, "offers a vantage ground from which to penetrate to the human, as distinct from the technical, significance of philosophic discussions."[158]   In fact, Dewey concludes, "philosophy may even be defined as the general theory of education."[159]

Thus, "progressive education" is like liberal education in being intrinsically valuable, in being primarily concerned with human conduct, and in being essentially philosophical. It seeks to develop in individuals the capacity and inclination for intelligent or rational action.[160]

THE IDEAL OF LIBERAL EDUCATION

Now that we have seen that Dewey's criticism of liberal education is directed to the institution as he knew it, and not to the ideal that we have defined, and since we have seen that his ideal of "progressive education" is essentially identical with our ideal of liberal education, we can detail what we can now call his theory of liberal education. We will first give specificity to the ideal of this unique form of education.   Subsequently we will describe its ideal institution, its ideal curriculum, and its ideal teacher.

1.

We have noted that one of Dewey's most persistent themes is the claim that all genuine education must give priority to the practical--in the sense of the normative. The "supreme issues," he writes in *Experience and Nature*, are "life and death."[161] It is not that thought is unimportant; rather it is that all thought is properly oriented to intelligent choice or moral action. Even thought itself is best understood as a mode of action. "All knowledge," Dewey writes, is "an outcome of activity bringing about certain changes in the environment."[162]   To act

---

[155]M9:334.

[156]M9:334.

[157]L1:305.

[158]M9:338.

[159]M9:338.

[160]"The knowledge which comes first to persons, and that remains most deeply ingrained, is knowledge of *how to do* . . . ." M9:192.

[161]L1:309.

[162]M9:227.

"intelligently" is "precisely intentional purposeful activity controlled by perception of facts and their relationship to one another."[163] Such action requires the "capacity to refer present conditions to future results, and future consequences to present conditions."[164] The priority of the practical also comes out clearly when Dewey turns his attention to the problems of the liberal arts college. "The present function of the liberal arts college," he writes, "is to use the resources put at our disposal alike by humane literature, by science, by subjects that have a vocational bearing, so as to appraise the needs and issues of the world in which we live."[165]

For Dewey, intelligent action requires two kinds of knowledge: knowledge of present conditions and knowledge of "legitimate aims."[166] The former consists of "grounded knowledge" and is the province of "scientific thinking," while the latter consists of "philosophic thinking" and is the province of "philosophy."[167] The purport of both of these kinds of thinking "is to [render choice] less arbitrary and more significant."[168] Thinking "loses its arbitrary character when its quality and consequences are such as to commend themselves to the reflection of others after they have betaken themselves to the situations indicated."[169] In these two ways knowledge "influences the conduct of life."[170]

These considerations show that for Dewey liberal education has a "double task": that of "interpreting the results of specialized science" and "criticizing existing aims."[171] Science provides us with "the best tools which humanity has so far devised for effectively directed reflection."[172] It provides us with empirical knowledge. Philosophy, on the other hand, is "thinking what the known demands of us--what responsive attitude it exacts."[173] These claims justify the conclusion that the ideal of liberal education is to develop in individuals the capacity and inclination for action that is guided by knowledge that is both scientific, i.e., empirical, and practical, i.e., normative.

2.

Dewey notes that for Herbert Spencer, scientific knowledge, or knowledge in its perfected form, is the "knowledge of most worth."[174] Dewey takes issue with Spencer's view. He criticizes those who teach scientific conclusions but ignore

---

[163]M9:110.
[164]M9:110.
[165]L15:280.
[166]M9:111.
[167]M9:336.
[168]L1:35.
[169]L1:35.
[170]M9:334.
[171]M9:339.
[172]M9:197.
[173]M9:336.
[174]M9:229.

the methods by means of which these conclusions are obtained. In this kind of teaching "pupils learn a science" instead of "learning the scientific way of treating the familiar material of ordinary experience."[175]   As a result, knowledge is identified with a body of propositions stating "inert information," and education becomes a matter of "cramming" of "facts" to acquire merely "verbal" learning.[176] Dewey wants to de-emphasize the role of this kind of knowledge in liberal education, and to give greater emphasis to the methods, skills, or arts required for the achievement of knowledge.[177] In doing so, he is giving priority to the liberal arts as the arts of "reflective thinking."

Whenever Dewey makes suggestions for the development of the arts of "reflective thinking," he is careful to insist that such thinking is not a "single, unalterable faculty," and that it cannot be developed by means of a catechism or "formal-discipline."   Neither should it be treated in abstraction from subject matter.   "Reflective thought," he writes, is an "active, persistent, and careful consideration of any belief or supposed form of knowledge in the light of the grounds that support it and the further conclusions to which it tends."[178]

This definition brings out the two distinguishable but inseparable movements in reflective thinking.   One is a movement from observed or recollected particulars or facts to a general hypothesis that provides meanings, and the other is a movement that subjects this general hypothesis to development, application, and testing in particulars. In *Logic: The Theory of Inquiry* Dewey describes the first of these movements as comprising the methods of "induction" or "discovery," and the second comprising the methods of "deduction" or "demonstration"--or what might be called "justification."[179]   The inductive methods apply to "existential data," while deductive methods apply to "conceptual data."   While the complexity and interdependency of these methods leads Dewey to resist the temptation to isolate and canonize specific inductive and deductive arts or disciplines, he does provide a variety of strategies for the discovery and justification of the conclusions of the sciences.   Collectively these inductive and deductive methods constitute the methods of "inquiry" or the "organon of criticism."[180]

In view of these claims, liberal education, for Dewey, is a form of education that will develop in individuals the capacity and inclination for action that is

---

[175]M9:228.

[176]M9:195.

[177]At L9:98 Dewey writes: "The obligations incumbent upon science cannot be met until its representatives cease to be contented with having a multiplicity of courses in various sciences represented in the schools, and devote . . . more energy . . . to seeing to it that the sciences which are taught are themselves more concerned about creating a certain mental attitude than they are about purveying a fixed body of information, or about preparing a small number of persons for the further specialized pursuit of some particular science."

[178]L8:118.

[179]L12:415-436.

[180]L1:305.

guided by knowledge that is both empirical and normative, and that is obtained by means of certain theoretical methods.

3.

Intelligent action requires more than knowledge and the theoretical methods that make knowledge possible. It requires that the requisite knowledge and methods be grounded in rationally defensible principles. This is the burden of Dewey's thesis that the general theory of education is philosophy, where philosophy is conceived in its traditional sense as the "love of wisdom," and where this love of wisdom is understood as "an attempt to comprehend" that yields "ultimate principles" which "influence the conduct of life."[181]

In *Experience and Nature* Dewey restates this need for philosophic principles in education when he defines philosophy as "inherently criticism"--a "criticism of criticisms."[182] This makes it clear that philosophy must not be understood as a science which is in competition with the empirical sciences. Philosophy is limited to criticism, and criticism is "intelligent inquiry into the conditions and consequences of a value-object."[183] We engage in criticism, Dewey writes, "not for its own sake, but for the sake of instituting and perpetuating more enduring and extensive values."[184] The purpose of philosophy "is criticism of beliefs, institutions, customs, policies with respect to their bearing upon good."[185] This shows that for Dewey philosophy has a necessary and normatively critical function in liberal education. It also shows that this critical function presupposes certain standards or values which must themselves be intrinsically valuable.[186] Since, according to Dewey, objects do not have their values stamped upon their faces, philosophy must appraise values "by taking cognizance of their causes and consequences."[187] Philosophical reflection "is the instrumentality of securing freer and more enduring goods."[188] It subjects values, criticisms, and critical methods to further criticism in order to make them as "comprehensive and consistent as possible."[189] It is itself, therefore, a "unique intrinsic good."[190] This makes it clear that philosophy's ultimate concern is with "the moral end," and that this moral end is "the unifying and culminating end of education."[191]

This interpretation is given confirmation in Dewey's ethical theory. In

---

[181]M9:334.
[182]L1:298.
[183]L1:298.
[184]L1:302.
[185]L1:305.
[186]L1:305.
[187]L1:305.
[188]L1:303.
[189]L1:302.
[190]L1:304.
[191]M9:370.

contrast to "customary morality," Dewey argues, "reflective morality" "notes the inconsistency and arbitrary variations in popular expressions of esteem and disapproval."[192] It then "seeks to discover a rational principle by which they will be justified and rendered coherent."[193] Once natural human desires become subject to the criticism of "reflective morality," "needs cease to be blind; thought looks ahead and foresees results. It forms purposes, plans, aims, ends-in-view."[194] As a consequence, out of the facts of human nature we develop a conception of the good, and we develop "the intellectual phase of character, which amid all the conflict of desires and aims strives for insight into the inclusive and enduring satisfaction: wisdom, prudence."[195] Thus, for Dewey, liberal education is essentially the development of criticism, and criticism is the search for moral principles. These principles, of course, cannot be arbitrary or artificial; they are not "imposed upon human nature from without."[196] Rather, they are generated through the operation of philosophical criticism. This criticism is dialectically self-correcting and self-confirming.

These considerations support the conclusion that for Dewey liberal education--what he often calls "education for growth"--is a form of education that will develop in individuals the capacity and inclination for action that is guided by knowledge that is both empirical and normative, that is obtained by means of certain theoretical methods, and that is dialectically justified in an unconditional practical or moral principle.

4.

In *Democracy and Education* Dewey states that it is futile to conceive of the moral end as "the unifying and culminating end of education" unless "the learning which accrues in the regular course of study affects character."[197] He thus insists on the distinction between education's responsibility for "intellectual results" and its responsibility for "the forming of socialized disposition."[198] Liberal education--the most valued form of education--is simply "the process of forming fundamental dispositions, intellectual and emotional, toward nature and fellow men."[199] "All education forms character, mental and moral."[200]

In a chapter of *Democracy and Education* devoted to the discussion of educational values Dewey lists the kinds of character traits that are essential to

---

[192]L7:236.
[193]L7:236.
[194]L7:308.
[195]L7:308.
[196]L7:309.
[197]M9:370.
[198]M9:204.
[199]M9:338.
[200]M9:77.

liberal education: "trained intellectual method, or interest in some mode of scientific achievement," "sensitiveness to the rights and claims of others-- conscientiousness," "sociability, or interest in the companionship of others," and "executive competency in the management of resources and obstacles encountered (efficiency)."[201]   The first of these includes the need for the conclusions, methods, and principles of the empirical and normative sciences, while the last three include the need for practical skills and moral virtues. Using different words we could list these essential competencies as follows: (1) empirical and normative knowledge, (2) theoretical skills, (3) principles, and (4) practical skills and the moral virtues.

Dewey's concept of the ideal of liberal education clearly requires that liberal education be more than a purely intellectual or theoretical matter. Wisdom cannot be attained by those who lack prudence and good character. Scientific knowledge and philosophical insight will not be available to those who lack courage and temperance and the other cardinal virtues.   In summary, for Dewey, liberal education is a form of education that will develop in individuals the capacity and inclination for action that is guided by knowledge that is both empirical and normative, that is obtained by means of certain theoretical methods, that is grounded dialectically in an unconditioned practical or moral principle, and that is obtained with the aid of certain practical skills such as prudence and the moral virtues.

THE IDEAL INSTITUTION FOR LIBERAL EDUCATION

Dewey recognizes that liberal education requires "a special social environment."[202]   This is because "the development within the young of the attitudes and dispositions necessary to the continuous and progressive life of a society cannot take place by direct conveyance of beliefs, emotions, and knowledge."[203] But the institutionalization of liberal education is constrained by two important and often conflicting requirements: First, the institution must provide a locus for unprejudiced criticism.   This is necessary because liberal education must render "ordinary life experiences . . . more significant, more luminous to us, and make our dealings with them more fruitful,"[204] and because this cannot be accomplished through any "private store of knowledge or of methods for obtaining truth."[205]   Consequently, progress in this enterprise can only be made through a process of unencumbered criticism of the "conditions and consequences of a value-object."[206]   Second, this institution must not be allowed

---

[201]M9:252.
[202]M9:27.
[203]M9:26.
[204]L1:18.
[205]L1:305.
[206]L1:298.

to serve the special interests of any class or group. This is necessary not because it is undemocratic, but because any such service prejudices the realization of unprejudiced criticism.

The first of these requirements would seem to argue for an institution that is independent of all social and personal interests. The second of these, by contrast, would seem to argue against this institutional independence because such independence could be expected to limit the accessibility of this form of education, and thus to encourage undemocratic practices.

The resolution of this conflict depends on the realization that, while institutions that provide a locus for unprejudiced criticism often have been less than accessible and often have been used by undemocratic interests, there is no necessity that this be the case. In fact, to the extent that these institutions have wittingly or unwittingly served special interests, they have failed to realize unprejudiced criticism.

These considerations show that Dewey's perennial concern about the elitist, undemocratic character of what in his day was called liberal education is really an additional argument for the need for the institutional independence of the liberal arts college.

Dewey's theory recognizes three ways that the liberal arts college can compromise its institutional independence:

1. It can compromise its independence by the adoption of an institutionally approved theory. Philosophy, like science, can become dogmatic. "Even while professing catholicity," Dewey writes, philosophy "has often been suborned."[207]

2. It can compromise its independence by subordinating itself to special interests or to a particular political ideology or party or society. On this issue Dewey is often misunderstood because of his strongly-held conviction that education is a means for the realization of social ideals. Many readers assume that Dewey regards education as a means to social ends. Israel Scheffler gives us reason to reject this assumption:[208]

> The notion that education is an instrument for the realization of social goals . . . is a conception that one would expect from an instrumentalism inspired by Dewey's notion of the continuity between means and ends, and it is ironic that the main stress in certain passages of his work is on the school as means. When one considers, however, that Dewey takes the end to be not society as it happens to be, but a reformed society, illuminated by an ideal imagination and a critical intelligence that it is the school's office to foster, it becomes clear that any simple minded doctrine of the school as social instrument is inadequate . . . . For the fact that the larger society that the school is said to serve at any given time cannot be taken for granted as providing an ultimate end. It must

---

[207]L1:306.
[208]Israel Scheffler, *Reason and Teaching* (Indianapolis, Ind.: Bobbs-Merrill, 1973), 134-135.

itself be judged worthwhile by reference to the rational standards and the heritage of critical values to which the school bears witness.

Here Scheffler highlights the fact that for Dewey the school is not subordinate to any particular society, but is subordinate only to the good social life. Moreover, the content of "the good social life" is not fixed, even by the use of the word "democracy." This can only mean that the institution of liberal education must be independent of any particular society or social ideal. This interpretation is confirmed by Dewey's charges that even among those who champion the ideal of service, "there is a deplorable absence of any statement as to *what* the colleges should serve, and just how it should serve," and that, "as long as these matters are left vague, service is near to subservience, and loyalty to blind conformity."[209]

3. The liberal arts college can compromise its independence in a third way by subordinating itself to the interests of individuals.

For Dewey, the ideal institution for liberal education is the independent liberal arts college. This is an institution that stands aloof from the particular and immediate concerns of the society within which it is physically located, and by doing so is protected from those individuals and institutions that may be disposed to appropriate its resources or to divert it from its educational mission. The liberal arts college's "remoteness from common affairs," Dewey writes, "has a protective value for a certain kind of free intellectual life and has rendered possible the growth of independent standards of intellectual excellence."[210]

THE IDEAL CURRICULUM FOR LIBERAL EDUCATION

In spite of his view that all classifications can have only a provisional validity, Dewey provides at least some suggestions on the proper organization of a curriculum for liberal education. His suggestions include the following:

First, a curriculum for liberal education must engage the interests of students, but must not pander to these interests. As we previously noted, Dewey insists that no program of education can be successful unless it engages the interests of its students.[211] But from this it does not follow that students in a program of liberal education should be allowed to study whatever they please. It only argues that a liberal arts curriculum may not be of interest to all students, and that students who do choose a liberal education should have at least a nascent interest in a liberal education. A liberal arts curriculum is not responsible for satisfying or reinforcing subjective, uncriticised interests. Its responsibility is to facilitate the examination and redirection of these interests.

---

[209]M15:206.
[210]M15:205.
[211]M9:139.

Second, a curriculum for liberal education must include the so-called "extracurriculum." This is necessary because, as we have noted, Dewey holds a liberal education responsible for the development of certain "attitudes and dispositions," and these cannot be developed by ordinary classroom instruction, but must be developed by activities within "a special social environment."[212] To limit a curriculum to classroom instruction is to forget that a liberal education seeks both "intellectual results" and "the forming of a socialized disposition."[213] Hence, the "so-called extra-curricular activities are really a part of the educational offerings of the college and should be subjected to the same critical analysis, selection and guidance desirable in other phases of the curriculum."[214]

Third, a curriculum for liberal education should include practical knowledge in the sense of normative knowledge, but should exclude practical knowledge in the sense of technological knowledge. "Aristotle was permanently right," Dewey writes in *Democracy and Education*, "in assuming the inferiority and subordination of mere skill in performance and mere accumulation of external products to understanding, sympathy or appreciation, and the free play of ideas."[215] The ground for Dewey's agreement with Aristotle is that "the moral end" is "the unifying and culminating end"[216] of liberal education, while "trade education" develops only "efficiency," not "significance."[217]

Fourth, a curriculum for liberal education cannot be grafted onto the present departmental organization of colleges. Dewey condemns the departmental organization because it intellectually isolates members of faculties and branches of knowledge from each other in sterile compartments.[218] It also contributes to "a narrow specialization" that is "fatal to the very idea of education."[219]

A curriculum for liberal education should develop certain competencies:

1. There should be "intellectual results."[220] These are the conclusions of "scientific thinking" in the special sciences. "Spatial, natural connections" are the concern of the generic natural science Dewey calls "geography" and "human connections" are the concern of the generic social science he calls "history."[221] For Dewey the proper educational aim of these natural and social sciences is not disinterested theoretical contemplation, but "knowledge of the conditions of human action."[222] In addition to the intellectual results of the natural and social

---

[212]M9:26.
[213]M9:204.
[214]*The Curriculum for the Liberal Arts College: Being the Report of the Curriculum Conference Held at Rollins College, January 19-24, 1931, John Dewey, Chairman* (Winter Park, Fla.: Rollins College, 1931), 12.
[215]M9:264.
[216]M9:370.
[217]M9:215.
[218]*The Curriculum for the Liberal Arts College*, 13.
[219]M9:255.
[220]M9:204.
[221]M9:218.

sciences, there are the results of the normative or value sciences. Dewey includes the development of aesthetic taste within the responsibility of these normative sciences.[223]

2. There should be "trained intellectual method."[224] As we have noted, Dewey believes that it is a mistake to accumulate scientific conclusions while ignoring the method by which these conclusions are obtained.[225] Consequently, he develops a "theory of inquiry." Inquiry requires methods of discovery and methods of proof or justification. Dewey includes formal logic not as an independent, *a priori* discipline, but as a science of implication within inquiry conceived as a process of inference.[226]

3. There should be philosophic as well as scientific thinking. Philosophic thinking is "inherently criticism."[227] Its object is "clarification and emancipation"--the escape from prejudice.[228] Thus, philosophic criticism is undertaken "not for its own sake, but for the sake of instituting and perpetuating more enduring and extensive values."[229] It "enriches prior purposes and forms new ones."[230] Through it we gain "insight into principles."[231]

4. There should be "socialized dispositions" as well as "intellectual results."[232] This conclusion is a consequence of Dewey's definition of education as "that reconstruction or reorganization of experience which adds to the meaning of experience, and which increases ability to direct the course of subsequent experience."[233] As examples of the requisite "socialized dispositions" Dewey lists "executive competency in the management of resources and obstacles encountered," "sociability," and "conscientiousness," i.e., "sensitiveness to the rights and claims of others."[234]

Since Dewey's theory of liberal education requires a comprehensive curriculum that will develop a set of competencies that are centered about the theoretical and practical liberal arts, it seems appropriate to describe this curriculum as a liberal arts curriculum. This curriculum will require the following components:

1. the liberal empirical and normative sciences

---

[222]M9:236.
[223]M9:252.
[224]M9:252.
[225]M9:228.
[226]L12:309.
[227]L1:298.
[228]L1:40.
[229]L1:302.
[230]M9:231.
[231]M9:233.
[232]M9:204.
[233]M9:82.
[234]M9:252.

2. the theoretical liberal arts (the arts of "inquiry")
3. philosophy ("criticism")
4. the practical liberal arts

THE IDEAL TEACHER FOR LIBERAL EDUCATION

Inasmuch as the liberally educated person must possess a variety of competencies that can only be developed by a variety of curricular strategies, it is not surprising that Dewey has no single model of the ideal teacher. He requires instead a variety of teacher models. Some teachers are needed to provide the knowledge of the empirical and normative sciences. Others are needed for the development of the universal theoretical skills required to obtain this knowledge. Others are needed to catalyze the integration of this knowledge by the discovery and defense of principles. And finally, still other are needed to conduct the training that is required for the development of prudence and the moral virtues.

For the systematic study of the comprehensive empirical and normative sciences, the ideal teachers are scientists, disciplinary authorities. Since liberal education requires a comprehensive knowledge of both reality and ideality, scientists must be authorities in two generic disciplines: the empirical sciences, which seek to understand the way things are, and the practical (or normative) sciences, which seek to understand the way things ought to be.

Dewey cautions that even this relatively narrow teaching responsibility cannot be best accomplished by scholarly experts. "The teacher," Dewey writes, "should be occupied not with subject matter in itself but in its interaction with the pupils' present needs and capacities."[235] Consequently, "simple scholarship is not enough."[236] Too often, he observes, scholarship gets in the way of effective teaching.[237]

Dewey also observes that administrative responsibilities too often get in the way of effective teaching. In "The Liberal College and Its Enemies" he writes: "Among the intrinsic causes which restrict intellectual liberty is the undue importance given to administrative activities, which then encroach upon the time and energy which should go to study and teaching."[238]

For the development of the universal theoretical skills, the ideal teachers are those who are versed in the scientific, logical, rhetorical, and dialectical methods.

To catalyze the discovery and defense of principles, the best teachers are philosophers.

For the development of the prudential skills, the ideal teachers are those who have lived a full and just life, and who are able to teach an apprentice by various means, including that of personal example. For the development of the required

---

[235]M9:191.
[236]M9:191.
[237]M9:191.
[238]M15:208.

moral virtues, the ideal teachers are those who can best train others in the formation of habits.

Dewey emphasizes that the ideal teacher is one who keeps "a degree of distance and detachment" from the world. This is essential if teachers are to avoid the distractions of careeristic competition and material gain. "Thinkers often withdraw too far," Dewey cautions, "but a withdrawal is necessary, unless they are to be deafened by the immediate clamor and blinded by the immediate glare of the scene."[239] The ideal teacher must always be an uncompromised critic, an autonomous teacher.

****

By reputation, John Dewey's philosophy of education is a pragmatic, skeptical contraposition relative to the great classical ideals of liberal education. But a more careful review of his work shows that his philosophy is not really opposed to the classical ideals. In describing education or "growth" as an intrinsic good, Dewey provides an educational ideal that requires the development of individuals who possess the capacity and inclination for action that is guided by knowledge that is both empirical and normative, that is obtained by the universal theoretical methods, that is dialectically grounded in the unconditional principle of morality, and that takes place with the aid of prudence and the moral virtues. In order to achieve this ideal an educational institution must be independent of all extrinsic purposes. The curriculum of this institution must include the empirical and normative sciences, the theoretical liberal arts, philosophy, and the practical liberal arts. And finally, this institution must be staffed by teachers who are uncompromised in their commitment to teaching in a program of liberal education, and who are able to develop the requisite knowledge, theoretical skills, principles, and practical skills. In these essential features Dewey's ideal coincides with the ideals of Plato and Aristotle, and with the ideal that we have proposed and defended here.

---

[239]L1:306.

10

CONCLUSION

Book X of Plato's *Republic* is seen by some commentators as a kind of afterthought or appendix.[1] Unlike the preceding nine books of the *Republic*, this final book is apparently not concerned with justice, but with two seemingly unrelated topics: poetry and the afterlife. This prima facie lack of coherence in the *Republic* can be removed, however, if we recall that in Book II Socrates had proclaimed that justice is both an intrinsic and an extrinsic good, and that up to Book X he had considered it only as an intrinsic good. This leaves open the possibility that Book X is concerned with justice as an extrinsic good. Plato's strategy here may be to give us a final defense of justice, one that is less philosophic and more poetic than its predecessors. If we adopt this interpretation, Plato is presenting us with a work of the poetic imagination, prefaced by an appropriate warning about the dangers of misinterpreting poetic truth as literal truth. In the "Myth of Er" he has Socrates suggest that those who lead a just life can hope for the rewards of eternal life.

In concluding my argument I would like to imitate what I take to be Plato's poetic strategy. Up to this point I have offered a dialectical demonstration of the ideal of liberal education, and, in addition to developing some of its consequences, I have provided a rhetorical defense of this ideal by showing that it is superior to all alternative ideals (including the claims of vulgar skepticism), and that it is confirmed by classical arguments for liberal education. My final defense of this ideal will be by a flight of the imagination which will contrast the rewards of a life that is informed by this ideal with the tragedy of a life that fails to be informed by it. This defense will be in the guise of an "Orientation Speech" which is addressed to a newly arrived class of college freshmen.[2]

* * * *

---

[1]See, for instance, Paul Shorey, *What Plato Said* (Chicago: University of Chicago Press, 1933), 248-258.

[2]In an earlier draft this speech was given during Freshman Orientation Week for the St. Lawrence class of 1985.

At the west end of the Midway in Chicago there is an immense hollow cast concrete sculpture by Lorado Taft entitled "The Fountain of Time." It depicts a silent procession of humanity rising and then falling like waves from right to left, ascending from youth to adulthood and then descending from adulthood to old age. This procession takes place behind a reflective pool which is dominated in the foreground by a tall, shrouded, immobile figure of Time. The inscription on the sculpture reads in austere simplicity: "Time goes, you say? Ah, no;/ Alas, time stays, we go."

Even though this sculpture stands mutely in the midst of the noisy flow of city traffic and hurried people, it invites reflection. It reminds us of a profound truth that most people--and especially, most young people--are not likely to take seriously. It reminds us that it is not time, but we who are in motion. We are, in fact, not long for this world. But the irony that we unconsciously impute motion to time rather than to ourselves reminds us of an even more profound truth--that we humans unknowingly try to conceal from ourselves the fact that life is short, and that death is imminent. We live all too often without knowledge and moral courage. For me, this mysterious sculpture is a silent call to all people to knowingly and courageously orient themselves to a life that is here today but gone tomorrow.

Certainly, as you begin a liberal education it is important that each of you carefully orient yourself to an opportunity that will never reoccur and that will end four years from now almost before you can catch your breath.

The trouble is, many of you have already oriented yourselves to this education on the basis of your *interests*. For example:

You have an interest in preparing for a *career*. So you're planning to use the curriculum to develop a "major" which you hope will lead to a rewarding career.

You have an interest in making *friends*. So you view the extracurriculum as an opportunity for meeting people, for developing friendships, and perhaps to find a mate (a "#10" or a "#9"). You look forward to some good fellowship and some good parties.

You have an interest in being a *success*. So you view college as an important step to a successful life. You believe that there are no insurmountable limitations on the success you can achieve. Your spirits are high because "the sky's the limit"!

I want to advise you that this orientation is a *mistake*! Liberal education is not an institution for indulging your interests. (I don't blame you entirely if you have this orientation. For several generations we have been told that we should "do what we are interested in," "do our own thing," and "feel comfortable." And education is often sold to us as a means for satisfying our interests. We are told that if we come to this or that college we will be free of requirements, and able to "satisfy our interests" and "actualize our own potentials.")

An orientation based on interests is a mistake because people may be interested in things they shouldn't be interested in. (Hitler, for instance, was interested in genocide. Rev. Jim Jones was interested in "white nights" with

Kool-Aid and potassium cyanide.) Today's interests may lead to tomorrow's tragedies.

How could an orientation based on today's interests lead to tomorrow's tragedies for your class?

Let's assume that the future will be like the past, and imagine how you will be at the time of your 25th class reunion:

Twenty-nine years from now seems distant, but it isn't. By that time you will have less hair, more fat, and appear at least slightly debauched. (No amount of jogging, yogurt, or oat bran will help for long.) You will have married a "#5" (or a "#4"). You will have 2.2 children.

By your 25th reunion most of you will have a *career* unrelated to your college "major." You will have changed your job several times. Not only will your job be unrelated to your college "major," but also, for 80% of you, your college grades will have had no relationship to your job success. (That may be consolation to a few!) Most of you will not be able to remember the name of a single professor or the content of a single course. That isn't shocking when you realize that much of what you learn in the classroom is out of date within five years anyway. More shocking is the fact that most of you will have chosen the wrong career both from the standpoint of your midlife interests and from the standpoint of what is in demand when you are pressing fifty. Three out of every four of you will hate your jobs. The occupations that are popular, stylish, and economically rewarding when you are around twenty are likely to be stodgy, unfashionable, and low paying when you are around fifty. By that time occupations like environmental law, computer programming, and oceanography may be hopelessly overcrowded, poorly paid, and undesirable. Today's glamorous occupations often are tomorrow's pits; and tomorrow's glamorous occupations are almost unpredictable today. Technology and fashion change too rapidly in an age of future shock. It's futile to try to pick a college "major" to match a career. Some of you will realize this when you are at midlife and will regret that you wasted so much of your college time playing career make-believe instead of getting a liberal education. Some of you will also realize that if you want to get rich, a college education is (in the words of Caroline Bird) "about the dumbest investment you can make." (If you don't believe this, consider the current cost of four years at a good liberal arts college. It is rapidly approaching $100,000. If, instead of purchasing a college degree you invested your money at 10%, at retirement you would have almost nine million dollars, far more than the average lifetime earnings of a college graduate!) By midlife many of you will feel imprisoned by your careers. You will suspect that while you work, life is passing you by. You may also suspect that your preoccupation with your career is a way of escaping life, that your business is a kind of busyness, a way of putting blinders on yourself so that you can avoid thinking about serious things. A writer recently confessed this:

I have always used my work as a substitute for solving problems in my life . . . . I packed my life with activity in order to avoid major personal decisions. What I do is give up autonomy by creating a high-demand situation, so that I must always jump from project to project, never really allowing time to think about what I'm doing it all for. Since I turned 40, it's become clearer to me that the reason I do this is that I really haven't wanted to scrutinize what my life is all about.

Gail Sheehy, in her book, *Passages*, agrees that many in their forties wake up to the fact that their career has demanded too much and has stunted their development as human beings. She writes:

Whatever rung of achievement he has reached, the man of 40 usually feels stale, restless, burdened, and unappreciated. He worries about his health. He wonders, 'Is this all there is?' He may make a series of departures from well-established lifelong base lines, including marriage. More and more men are seeking second careers in midlife. Some become self-destructive. And many men in their forties experience a major shift of emphasis away from pouring all their energies into their own advancement.

Sheehy is here speaking of men, but the same could be said of women who have allowed their careers to steal away their lives.

At the time of your 25th reunion your *friends* will have changed. Your college friends will have scattered, and most of your close personal relationships will be with members of your family. At the same time, your midlife will be a difficult time for your family. Your parents will be old and sick. Your children will be rebelling. Your 22-year old son will be wondering whether to join a religious cult or to "hang out" as a surf bum in Australia. Your eighteen-year old daughter will be having trouble deciding whether she wants to join a commune or to go out for power lifting. Five percent of your teenage daughters will get pregnant out of wedlock, and twelve percent of your teenage children will be arrested for a serious crime. Your children will be harshly critical of your life-style. Over half of you will be sorry you even had children! Meanwhile for most of you, your closest relationship will fail. At least one out of every four wives will have committed adultery, and fully half of your husbands will have been unfaithful. Forty-five percent of you will suffer through the tragedy of divorce and about one-half of your children will be living in broken homes. With this breakdown in our social institutions many of you will find yourselves seriously dependent on physicians, shrinks, and quacks. At least one out of every ten will be hopelessly dependent on alcohol or drugs. (In fact, on the average you will spend more on alcohol and drugs than you will spend on automobiles!) Some of you will be strong enough to survive the midlife disintegration of your personal life. Some of you will realize that your youthful obsession with making friends and conforming to their expectations was not innocent and innocuous, but in reality an expression of insecurity. You were eager to win your independence from parental authority, but at college you were just as eager to surrender your new independence to the authority of a mindless peer group. This act diminished your development of moral courage, and the ability to stand alone when you must. Only some of you will be as fortunate as a middle-aged woman who discovered her self-deception in time, and who wrote:

> I find I'm telling the truth more often. I didn't realize I was lying. I just thought I had good, ladylike manners. The one thing in the world I always wanted was to have everybody like me. Now I don't give a damn. I want *some* people to like me, and I'll settle.

For all too many of you, though, midlife will be too late to gain moral courage and true independence. The habits developed by years of conformity will be too difficult to break. Those who are afraid to wear clothing without a brand name logo are not likely to be courageous when the crowd demands that principles be compromised to expediency.

By your twenty-fifth reunion you will have had serious doubts about your ability to realize the level of *success* that you thought possible when you were in college. In spite of a few modest achievements a sense of failure, vulnerability, and panic will oppress you. Some of you will already be dead. For almost everyone serious health problems and moral defects will have surfaced. Your hormone levels will be falling. Stress will be incessant. Missed opportunities and mistakes will haunt you. Like so many in a midlife crisis you will be tempted to cut a few corners--to lie or to cheat just a little--feeling that if you don't, you won't have another opportunity to "make it." (These acts of desperation will be easier for those who learned to lie and cheat in college.) In the end, of course, these acts will be pitiful and pathetic. For all of you this year will be a year in which "the sky's the limit," but in twenty-nine years for many of you "the sky will be falling."

Just in case it is not yet clear how, for this class, the pursuit of today's interests can lead to tomorrow's tragedies, let's take one more brief leap through time, and imagine how you will be at the time of your 50th class reunion: You will be in your seventies and frail. Your mouth and your shoulders will slump; your belly and breasts will sag grotesquely; you will wear bifocals to see, a hearing aid to hear, and dentures to eat. You will be covered by varicose veins, liver spots, and precancerous lesions. You will have sold your family home and moved into the Sunbelt Estates Trailer Park. You will have a big TV.

Your *career* will have ended ten years earlier with a patronizing retirement party and a gift rocking chair presented by your smiling, obnoxious boss. Most of you will now have a useless, obsolete feeling. The younger, busy people around you will constantly urge you to occupy yourself with silly hobbies. The people in your senior citizens group will talk your head off without the slightest provocation. You'll learn how to play shuffleboard, and you'll shuffle without having to learn. You'll take half a day to read the large print newspaper. You'll spend most of your day napping and watching TV commercials, soap operas, and "The Wheel of Fortune." You may regret that in sacrificing so much of your vital energies to your career, you were ill equipped to handle the larger, human problems of life. You may regret that at college you did not learn how to reflect on life, to understand your moral and political obligations, and to appreciate science and art and literature. While of course there will be some among you who will remain relatively alert and vigorous, most of you will already have started your irreversible slide into senility.

Your *friends* you will count on the fingers of one hand. In a couple of years 50% of the men and 25% of the women of your class will be dead. One third of the women will bury their husbands and live alone or with a cat or a poodle for an average of eight more years. While most of you will understand the triviality of "social success," and while you will look back with regret on the youthful years you wasted in courting the approval of others, at the same time you will still feel a sense of dread when you are forced to assume responsibility, to make decisions, and above all, to face your own mortality. In the end, ready or not, you will have to suffer the cruelest fate: you will have to die alone. No mate, friend, or support group can accompany you.

Your *success* will now seem, at best, modest in comparison to your failures. You will complain a lot. But of course many of you in your seventies will not feel well. Growing old hurts. Eventually 40% of you will have to suffer from heart attacks, 20% from cancer, and 5% from strokes. Thirty six of the people now in this room will die in automobile or other accidents, and thirteen of you will commit suicide. Moreover, many of you will not think well. Thirty percent will have significant psychiatric symptoms, especially depression. The loss of neurons in the central nervous system will take place so rapidly that if you have the misfortune to live to be 90, your brain will weigh less than the brain of a three year old infant. Some of you will be completely senile, in nursing homes, incontinent. Your highest hope--at least in you lucid moments--will not be to set any new records, or to make any new contacts or conquests, or to achieve any kind of success, but simply to live out the few months left to you free of pain. Some of you will be like the old man who, angry at losing control of his bodily functions, and unwilling to continue being a burden on his family, one day simply took out his false teeth and refused to eat again. Many of you, though, disoriented and disappointed at your failure to realize your college dreams, will go down whimpering in bitterness and despair.

Enough! Let's quickly escape the oppressive darkness of this possible future, and return to the lightness of the hopeful present! But I trust I've given you some reason to think that it might be a mistake to orient yourselves on the basis of your current interests.

Ordinary education indulges our interests, and encourages us to identify ourselves with a career. It induces us to find security in the conformity of the herd. It fuels the illusion that we can achieve what is called "success." In contrast, liberal education helps us to confront the reality of life and to seek genuine ideals. It prepares us to act independently on the basis of reason, and with courage, temperance, and justice. It provides us with principles.

Let me summarize my advice in specific terms:

Don't waste your college years preoccupied with a "major," preparing for some narrow vocational role that you probably will never assume. Instead, give priority during these few years to gaining an understanding of reality and ideality--of what is and what ought to be.

Don't waste your time seeking friends and conforming to the styles in the hope of "feeling comfortable." Instead, seek to develop the liberal arts and the moral virtues so that you will have true independence, and have the will and the way to realize your ideals.

Don't waste your few years here preparing to live a successful life. Instead, think about how it is possible to live a good life. Think about how it is possible to justify your life in philosophic principles.

Why is a liberal education so important? Our reflection on "The Fountain of Time" suggests an answer. We humans live lives that are brief and too frequently undone by ignorance and immorality. We are all too likely to blindly follow today's interests, and in due course, like dumb animals, we will be overtaken by tomorrow's tragedies. A liberal education offers us a wiser option.

* * * *

INDEX